THE WAR DIARIES
NOVEMBER 1939—MARCH 1940

JEAN-PAUL SARTRE

THE WAR DIARIES
NOVEMBER 1939 – MARCH 1940

TRANSLATED FROM THE FRENCH
BY QUINTIN HOARE

PANTHEON BOOKS, NEW YORK

Library of Congress Cataloging in Publication Data
Sartre, Jean–Paul, 1905–
The War Diaries,
Translation of: Les Carnets de la drôle de guerre.
Includes index.
1. Sartre, Jean–Paul, 1905– —Diaries.
2. Authors, French—20th century—Biography. 3. World
War, 1939–1945—Personal narratives, French.
4. World War, 1939–1945—France. I. Title.
PQ2637.A82Z46313 1985   848'.91403 [B] 84-18947
ISBN 0-394-74422-5

CONTENTS

TRANSLATOR'S INTRODUCTION

On 1 September 1939 German forces attacked Poland, inaugurating World War Two. On the same day, the French and British governments issued orders for general mobilization. Throughout the ensuing eight months — apart from a minor border skirmish or two in the first few days — German and French troops entrenched in their respective fortified lines faced each other along several hundred kilometres of common frontier with little more than an occasional perfunctory exchange of shelling, in what became known as the 'phoney war'. Poland was crushed in the course of September; the Soviet Union invaded and at great cost defeated Finland between November and March; the Germans invaded Denmark and Norway in April 1940: but during these momentous events, all indeed remained quiet on the Western front. In France itself, large areas of Alsace and other frontier regions were evacuated, and troops billeted among what remained of the civilian population. These were rotated between frontline and reserve positions, just as if actual fighting were taking place. But the only gunfire most of them heard was loosed off by their own officers, to give them a taste of the real thing; and the only destruction they witnessed was caused by French soldiers looting evacuated homes. This was the context in which the journal published here was composed: a seemingly incongruous one to have given birth to a masterpiece.

Among the hundreds of thousands of reservists mobilized on 1 September was Jean-Paul Sartre. Born in 1905, Sartre had done his military service in 1929 in the meteorological corps, where he was instructed by his then friend and subsequent political antagonist Raymond Aron. Upon his call-up, he was accordingly assigned to the meteorological section attached to an Artillery HQ, in Sector 108, just behind the front in Alsace. The HQ was stationed successively in a series of small towns a few kilometres to the east or north of Strasbourg: Brumath, Morsbronn, Bouxwiller, then back to Brumath. Sartre's section consisted of a corporal (still living, here called 'Paul'), and three others: Pieterkovsky ('Pieter'), 'Keller' and Sartre himself.[1] Its duties were not onerous: ' . . . my work here consists of sending

---

1. Pieter's real name was Pieterkovsky; he shortened it to disguise his Jewish origins in case he was captured by the Nazis. 'Paul', on the other hand, was really called Jean Pierre, 'Keller' was in fact Muller: as with so many of the women with whom Sartre had relationships, the names have been disguised by the editor of the notebooks.

up balloons and then watching them through a pair of field glasses: this is called "making a meteorological observation". Afterwards I phone the battery artillery officers and tell them the wind direction: what they do with this information is their affair. The young ones make some use of the intelligence reports; the old school just shove them straight in the wastepaper basket. Since there isn't any shooting, either course is equally effective.'[2]

At Brumath, where the first of Sartre's surviving notebooks was written, the meteorologists shared a former schoolroom, still equipped with its desks and blackboards, with Warrant-officer Courteaux, Staff-sergeant Naudin and Private Hang, of the Artillery Intelligence Service (when, that is, the latter were not out on their motorcycles carrying dispatches or locating gun emplacements). In the room next door worked three staff secretaries (all Alsatians): Courcy, Mistler and Hantziger. These were the essential dramatis personae of Sartre's wartime existence, supplemented by a floating cast of drivers, chasseurs from the regular regiments at the front, or (very occasionally) officers. The schoolroom, and the inns in the town – the Cerf, the Écrevisse, the Rose — provided the settings: banal and not after all so very different from the classrooms where Sartre taught and the cafés where he wrote and met friends in civilian life. Yet the transition to this new situation — 'I am no longer the same: my character hasn't changed, but my being-in-the-world has. It's a being-for-war.'[3] — represented a basic existential metamorphosis.

'I was quite comfortably ensconced in my situation as an indi-vidualist, anti-bourgeois writer . . . What exploded all that was the fact that one fine day in September 1939 I received a call-up paper, and was obliged to go off to the barracks at Nancy to meet fellows I didn't know who'd been called up like me. That's what introduced the social into my life . . . Up till then I believed myself sovereign; I had to encounter the negation of my own freedom — through being mobilized — in order to become aware of the weight of the world and my links with all those other fellows and their links with me. The war really divided my life in two. It began when I was thirty-four and ended when I was forty and that really was the passage from youth to maturity. At the same time, the war revealed to me certain aspects of myself and the world . . . You might say that in it I passed from the individualism, the pure individual, of before the war to the social and

2. See Simone de Beauvoir, *The Prime of Life*, Harmondsworth 1981, p. 427.

3. Jean-Paul Sartre, *Lettres au Castor*, two vols, Paris 1983, p. 321 (references to this work henceforth are given in the form LC I or II). An English translation is forth-coming from Hamish Henderson (London) and Macmillan (New York).

to socialism. That was the real turning-point of my life.'[4]

Characteristically, Sartre's way of living that turning-point in his life was to write about it. To write about it prodigiously. In the few months which intervened between his call-up in September 1939 and his capture by the advancing German forces in late June 1940, his output rivalled even the notorious paroxysm of 1958, when he almost killed himself racing to complete his *Critique of Dialectical Reason* under the stimulus of constantly increasing doses of amphetamines.[5] In contrast to that later bout of creation, however, there was nothing frenetic about Sartre's wartime productivity. On the contrary, he seems never to have been more serene — apart from a couple of 'pseudopods' from the affective universe he had left behind in Paris, and some anxieties regarding his eyesight.[6] Emphasizing repeatedly with a kind of amazement, in his letters to De Beauvoir, how much more time he has for writing than in civilian life, Sartre produced in that short space of time: notebooks, of which the present volume contains about one third; letters, of which the 550 printed pages published in 1983 by De Beauvoir represent only a small part (he was writing *daily* to his mother and to Wanda Kosakiewicz — his current innamorata, figuring here as 'Tania' — as well as to De Beauvoir herself, quite apart from a host of minor correspondents); and his novel *The Age of Reason*, plus a few lesser literary experiments when the first draft of this was completed. In all, perhaps one million words!

The thirty-four-year-old Sartre who received his call-up papers was, of course, not an unknown. On the contrary, since the publication in 1938 of *Nausea*, he had won a certain renown as an up-and-coming novelist, in the running for one or other of the big literary prizes, despite the 'controversial' nature of his work (he was already being denounced by bienpensant critics – a destiny that has pursued him beyond the grave). In the world of philosophy, too, he had begun to make something of a mark in academic circles. In the year preceding the war, moreover, critical texts by Sartre – on Faulkner, Dos

---

4. See 'Self-portrait at Seventy', in *Life/Situations*, New York 1977, p.

5. Simone de Beauvoir, *Force of Circumstance*, Harmondsworth 1981, p. 397.

6. At the end of November, Sartre was seized by a fit of passionate jealousy regarding 'Tania', who was (perhaps) being pursued by a member of the Atelier theatre company, Roger Blin (for the episode, see below pp. 47–48; also LC I 433, 441, 446 and 495–96). Then in February 1940 a new crisis arose in his relations with 'Tania', when she in turn became jealous of Sartre's past relations with 'Martine Bourdin', after the latter showed a common friend letters written to her by Sartre during their affair (see below, pp. 242 and 248; also LC II 88–111 *passim*). This latter crisis set off a series of reflections in the notebooks on Sartre's relations with others.

Passos, Nizan, Nabokov, etc—had been appearing regularly in the prestigious *Nouvelle Revue Française*. Yet, despite all this, the prewar years seem in retrospect to have been but an apprenticeship (even if *La Nausée* remains probably Sartre's most artistically achieved novel), giving small hint of the vast expansion of his abilities—and fame— that was to follow. The excitement of the notebooks published here, even in their present incomplete state, comes from the fact that they represent the essential transition from that apprenticeship to the full flowering of Sartre's talents: 1. as an original philosopher, in *Being and Nothingness* (1943), drafts for many of whose key passages will be found here, but in a more immediately accessible form; 2. as a playwright, whose first piece was to be written in captivity in the autumn of 1940; 3. as the 'engaged' or committed social thinker who was to found the monthly review *Les Temps Modernes* as soon as the war ended, inaugurating a political and cultural interventionism that he was to maintain till his death; 4. as the biographer whose work on Flaubert, which occupied the last fifteen years and more of his active life, has been described as the most sustained and ambitious attempt ever made by one individual to understand another; and 5. as the autobiographer whose dazzling *Words* was to win him the award (refused) of a Nobel Prize for literature. In the notebooks presented here, Sartre can be seen already exploring in all these directions.

A mere ten days after his call-up, Sartre wrote to De Beauvoir: 'Reflecting upon the world of war and its nature, I hatched the project of writing a journal. Please include in your parcel a stout black notebook—thick but not too tall or wide, cross-ruled of course.' (LC I 292) And two days later he seized the opportunity of a visit to the local town to buy one himself, leatherbound and not too large to slip into his pocket. 'War Journal I, September–October 1939' he was later to put on the fly-leaf. What did this project of a journal in fact represent for Sartre? He gives a number of different replies, in the notebooks themselves and in his correspondence. Testimony of an 'average' soldier in an average situation in the phoney war; search for authenticity, by an individualist suddenly plunged into the social; calling into question of a human personality and search for childhood determinations of an adult character; process of liberation from past models and influences; freewheeling intellectual and literary experiment; direct preparation for future work; private alternative dimension to an enforced communal existence; sui generis literary form—Sartre at different times saw his notebooks as all of these things. But what at all events cannot fail to impress the reader now at last able to read them is that, multi-faceted and diverse as they are, they are unmistakably unified by a profound sense of a total human project in process of formation. Certainly not simply drafts or jottings—though they do indeed contain the embryo of *Being and Nothingness*, and they do indeed record vividly Sartre's immediate ambience—they both prefigure and map out the virtual entirety of the writer's subsequent oeuvre, and also stand without question as a marvellously successful work in their own right, with their own virtues of pungency, directness, freedom, spirit of inquiry, humour (ranging from the wry to the knockabout), self-knowledge and a breathtaking universalist confidence in the potentialities of human reason.

From the outset, it should be stressed, Sartre saw his journal as a work written for future publication. Only four days after he started the first notebook he was telling De Beauvoir: 'I am giving myself short shrift in my little black notebook. Whoever reads it after my death—for you will publish it only posthumously—will think that I was a dreadful character, unless you accompany it with explanatory annotations of a kindly sort.' (LC I 300) On 26 October, it is true, he was stressing the subjective advantages of his journal: 'I have heaps of ideas at present and I'm very glad to be keeping up this little diary, since it's what brings them into being . . . It gives me a whole little secret life over and above the other, with joys, anxieties, regrets, half of which I shouldn't have known without this little object of black leather.' (LC I 377) But the very next day he was once more relating the enterprise to the Other: 'Even my notebook or my novel, which will be destined for others, are first of all destined for you, and only through you for others. You are like the objectivity of this world surrounding me, which otherwise would be mine alone—but which is ours.' (LC I 380) Perhaps, indeed, it was precisely the fact that the journal was simultaneously *private*, destined for a future *public*, and written first and foremost for *De Beauvoir*, which gives it that combination of the spontaneous and the composed which is the secret of its achievement.

Sartre was certainly aware of the journal as literary form: 'Since I shook off my inferiority complex vis-à-vis the far left, I have felt a freedom of thought I'd never had before; vis-à-vis the phenomenologists too. It seems to me that I'm on my way, as biographers say around page 150 of their books, to "discovering myself". By this I simply mean that I am thinking now without looking over my shoulder at certain injunctions (the left, Husserl), but with total freedom and gratuitousness, out of purely disinterested curiosity . . . I think that, apart from the war and everything being called into question, the notebook *form* is very important here; this free, broken form does not enslave one to former ideas, one writes everything on the spur of the moment and sums up only when one feels like it.'(LC II 21) He was even conscious that a second stage of composition—through selection—might be needed before publication. When the philosopher Alexandre Koyré invited him to send any text he liked for publication in the journal *Recherches Philosophiques*, Sartre commented to De Beauvoir: 'I'm in two minds about writing him something on Nothingness. To tell the truth, it depends on you. The fact is I've nasty little feelings of greed where anything concerning my journal is involved, I shouldn't like to take the bloom off it by speaking elsewhere with style and composition of what it treats in casual garb. If, when you read it, you judge that on publication one could—or rather *should*—suppress the too technically philosophical passages, then Koyré will have Nothingness. If, however, you think that the *history* of my thinking about Nothingness, which is registered day by day, is as interesting as the ideas themselves, then he'll get something else, any old thing. It's up to you to decide, little judge.' (LC II 58–59)

But if the notebooks were intended for eventual publication (with the possible exception of the philosophical passages, which constituted a genuine first version of a future work: *Being and Nothingness*), what of the autobiographical dimension which, increasingly as the journal progresses, comes to constitute perhaps its richest lode? Here, there is no question of an Ur-text of *Words*, that most consciously composed and synthesized of all Sartre's books. There is no prior thesis to be demonstrated here—on the contrary, autobiographical exploration is a means to understanding a present self which Sartre knows to be in a state of rapid transformation. As he says himself, in an extraordinary passage of the notebooks: 'I went more than fifteen years without looking at myself living. I didn't interest myself at all. I was curious about ideas and the world and other people's hearts. Introspective psychology seemed to me to have yielded its optimum with Proust; I'd tried my hand at it rapturously between the ages of 17 and 20, but it had seemed to me that one could very quickly become a dab hand at that exercise, and in any case the results were pretty tedious . . . It has taken the war, and also the assistance of several new disciplines (phenomenology, psychoanalysis, sociology) . . . to prompt me to draw up a full-length portrait of myself. Once launched upon this undertaking, I go at it with a will . . . I want to make as complete a portrait as possible . . . I used to have a horror of private diaries and think that man isn't made to see himself, but must always keep his eyes fixed before him. I haven't changed. It simply seems to me that on the occasion of some great event, when one is in the process of changing one's life like a snake sloughing its skin, one can look at that dead skin—that brittle snake-image one is leaving behind—and take one's bearings. After the war I shall no longer keep this diary, or if I do I shall no longer speak about myself in it. I don't want to be haunted by myself till the end of my days.'[7]

The fact is that Sartre was quite prepared to scrutinize himself with remarkable lack of inhibition, perhaps precisely because he was tempted to see what he was doing not as a simple review of his past life, but as an active process of self-transformation in the present: 'You have precipitated me into abysses of perplexity and floods of notes in my journal: am I simply taking stock of myself, or do I not hope to shed that hardened, somewhat dead personality along with peacetime?' Such barriers as he did impose came, in the main, neither from any reticence on his own part, nor from any thought of a future public, but rather from the fear of what reactions excessive candour might provoke in the little milieu he had left behind in Paris: above all on the part of 'Tania'.[8] This is not the place to enter on a discussion of the complex relations Sartre maintained with women, and in particular the Kosakiewicz sisters who were to play so central a role in his life from the mid thirties up to the mid forties and beyond: Olga, to whom he dedicated *The Wall* and De Beauvoir *She Came to Stay*, and who married Jacques Bost; Wanda, to whom he dedicated *The Age of Reason*, who provided a basis for the character of Ivich in that book, who acted in most of his early plays, and who remained a close friend for the rest of his life. Much of the story is already there in De Beauvoir's autobiographical volumes and the published wartime correspondence. Suffice it to say that whereas Sartre was quite willing to be candid in letters to De Beauvoir that would be for her eyes alone, he

7. See p. 138 below.
8. Sartre's milieu in Paris contained an inner circle of close friends, many of whom appear in the notebooks: De Beauvoir and her sister Poupette, Bost and Olga, 'Tania' and her friend Mouloudji, Mme Morel and her family, De Beauvoir's old friend Gégé, Marc Zuorro, Nizan and his wife Rirette, Simone Jollivet and Charles Dullin, 'Marie Girard' and her husband, Sartre's former Le Havre colleague Bonnafé. This circle had been recently supplemented by former students of De Beauvoir (Bianca Bienenfeld, Nathalie Sorokine) or of Sartre himself (Jean Kanapa, R.J. Chauffard). There were also old friends now no longer so close, like Pierre Guille and René Maheu, or at a greater distance Raymond Aron; and newer acquaintances such as the philosophers Bernhard Groethuysen and Alexandre Koyré, or *NRF* contributors and editors like Jean Paulhan and Brice Parrain. Finally, there were the members of Dullin's Atelier Theatre company (Blin, 'Martine Bourdin', 'Lucile', etc).

was well aware that his notebooks would be read also by 'Tania', as indeed by other friends. And 'Tania' certainly did react with violence, on more than one occasion, to what he had written in them. So it is no surprise to find him writing to De Beauvoir, on 2 March 1940: 'I was fully absorbed in drafting an account of my relations with others. Just imagine, since the day before yesterday I've written a *hundred* pages about this, without exhausting the subject. It's a pity, moreover, but I'd need to talk about Olga, about Bost, about you, about Tania, and then I'd have to doctor it all shamefully. So I stopped *before* the Olga affair with a few sibylline sentences destined for Tania announcing a total transformation occurring shortly afterwards. It was highly entertaining. I clearly perceived the sources of my imperialism and all that, but now I'm a bit sickened, as always when one has spoken of oneself for too long.' (LC II 112–13) The pages to which Sartre is referring here are lost, but what remains testifies to the honesty and persistence with which he carried out his project of self-examination.

* * *

It is necessary to say something about the fate of the notebooks, and the putative contents—in so far as they can be reconstructed—of those that have not survived (or at least not resurfaced). A careful reading of the *Lettres au Castor* shows that Notebook I was handed to the latter when she visited Sartre at Brumath in early November 1939, and was subsequently lent by her to 'the boxer', a former teaching colleague of Sartre's called Bonnafé (LC I 378, 492). Notebooks II and III were transmitted to De Beauvoir on 10 December by Mistler during his leave, and were read a few days later by her friends Fernand and Stépha Gerassi (LC I 497). Notebooks IV-X, plus the partly completed XI, were taken to Paris by Sartre when he himself first went on leave in early February; after they had been read by De Beauvoir, they were passed on to 'Tania'—with the exception of XI, which Sartre took back to Alsace with him to complete (LC II 68, 77, 89, etc.). Notebooks XI-XIV were then taken to Paris on the occasion of Sartre's second leave at the end of March (LC II 151, 158). By this time, in fact, Sartre had virtually ceased writing in his journal, although he did begin XV, writing briefly in it on Malraux and the categories of being/having/doing (27 April) and on Nothingness (9 June); he seems to have intended to fill it gradually with such occasional jottings during the three months he reckoned he would need to complete his novel, whereupon he would start keep the journal again in earnest, in a fresh set of notebooks (LC II 192).

Thus by the time the German invasion first of Belgium, then of northern France, put an end to the phoney war in May/June 1940, the fourteen completed notebooks had all been transmitted to Paris. However, 'three or four' had subsequently been lent to Bost when he came there on leave, and been taken back by him to the Belgian front where they were apparently lost when he was wounded at the end of May (LC II 262 n., 268). Nevertheless, Sartre was clearly under the impression that most of the notebooks were still in De Beauvoir's possession: inquiring about the fate of those sent to Bost, he wrote on 1 June: 'If they're lost, well it's just too bad. All one can say is that they weren't meant to see the light of day—I shan't be too unhappy about it. But if by any chance they were safe, I'd like to know. What I'd be most unhappy about would be my last philosophical stuff, more than my elucubrations on myself. But there must, in fact, be quite a lot left in the notebooks which you've still got and I'll be able to make do. Don't worry too much about it.' (LC II 262) A few days after this, the German thrust south from Belgium and Luxemburg had cut off the French armies of Alsace behind the 'impregnable' Rhine frontier, and Sartre was himself captured near Épinal during their precipitous retreat. He recorded an account of his unit's experience in the final days before the débâcle in Notebook XV, but even though he later wrote from prison camp inside Germany (undated, winter 1940) that his 'notes' had been restored to him, this apparently did not survive (LC II 302).

Such, then, is the sum total of our knowledge concerning the fate of Sartre's war journal. Clearly much remains to be explained. Quite apart from the brute fact of the loss of nine of the fourteen completed notebooks—surely one of the great intellectual losses of the kind in our century—the circumstances in which they went astray and the reasons why the particular ones translated here happened to survive are entirely mysterious. The editor, Arlette Elkaïm-Sartre the philosopher's adopted daughter and heir, writes in her Foreword below of the missing notebooks being 'mislaid in a train forty years ago by a recently wounded fellow-draftee' (presumably referring to Bost). But Bost supposedly only had three or four notebooks. Furthermore, in an undated letter of 1941 written after his release from captivity (LC II 307), Sartre writes that 'Cavaillès[9] is with me, and there was indeed a manuscript of mine in the form of a journal (a notebook?) found on a railway-track, which he is keeping for me': this seems likely to refer to

9. Cavaillès was a philosophy teacher who joined the Resistance and was subsequently captured and shot.

one of the notebooks lost by Bost. As for the other missing notebooks—in the absence of more detailed information from either De Beauvoir, Wanda or Bost, or from some quite other source—one can only conjecture. As Elkaïm writes: 'perhaps they have been destroyed, or else the people in whose hands they lie are not prepared to let the fact be known'.

As things stand, what precisely has been lost? Each reader will have his or her special regret. At all events, based upon the copious references in Sartre's own letters, there follows a partially reconstructed contents list of the fourteen completed notebooks (those surviving indicated by bold type).

Notebook	Dates	Topics identified
I	14/9–24/10	Sartre's character (stoicism, sense of superiority); death and the way in which his life between the wars now belonged to a bygone epoch; relations with De Beauvoir; being-for-war/being-in-war/fighting the war; Gide (?); transcendental consciousness; irritation at an officer's remark; motives and reasons
II	24/10–12/11	Historicity; war as *chosen* destiny of his epoch; unexpurgated reflections on his loves (?); attempt (failed) to reconcile Heidegger and Husserl, including with respect to volition; his adolescence (and the social)
III	12/11–7/12	**Future; morality in war; characters of himself and his 'confederates'; humanism; Alsace and evacuation; will; Koestler, Exupéry, Gide; youth and moral development; peace-war; Flaubert; ethics**
IV	8/12–16/12	Ethics; life/essence; Paul Morand;

XII	20/2–29/2	authenticity; modern warfare; the future; lack; Pieter's reminiscences; crisis with 'Tania'; possession/property; poem; seduction/love; his 'imperialism' and relations with others (childhood, adolescence, women)
XIII	1/3–5/3	Relations with others (slightly doctored) up to Olga
XIV	6/3–28/3	Heroism; self-definition; individual and history; William II; poetry, pride, frivolity; Germany; memories (Rouen); Populist Prize; relation to his fictional characters; relation to words; Renard; Malraux

*　　*　　*

It remains only to say a brief word about the translation. While I have endeavoured where possible to adopt a 'mid-Atlantic' style, when it comes to colloquialisms this is clearly precluded, so the slang tends to be British—though I trust not too much so for US readers. Where Sartre's characteristic philosophical vocabulary has become familiar in a particular rendering through earlier translations (particularly that of *Being and Nothingness* by Hazel Barnes), I have usually preferred to stick with the familiar usage. I have also usually followed precedents set by existing translations of Heidegger into English, though I have kept 'human reality' for *réalité humaine*—the French rendering of *Dasein* ('being-there'). The noun *morale* has in most places been translated as 'morality' rather than the more customary 'ethics', since I felt it was important to preserve a semantic unity with adjectival uses where only 'moral' would do. Finally, I would like to express my gratitude to Patrick Camiller, Michel Contat and Marie-Thérèse Weal for help of various kinds with this translation—though the responsibility for any shortcomings is, of course, mine alone. Thanks are also due to Arlette Elkaïm-Sartre for a number of editorial notes translated here, though the overwhelming majority of footnotes have been prepared specially for the present edition. In the text itself, square brackets indicate interpolations by the translator.

BRIEF CHRONOLOGY OF SARTRE'S LIFE UP TO THE WAR

1905   born; his father Jean-Baptiste dies

1905–11   lives at Meudon, near Versailles, with his mother Anne-Marie and his maternal grandparents Charles and Louise Schweitzer

1911   the ménage moves to Rue Le Goff in Paris, near the Panthéon

1913   attends Lycée Montaigne

1915   transfers to Lycée Henri-IV, meets Nizan

1917–20   his mother remarries and follows her new husband (Mancy) to La Rochelle, where he has been appointed director of the naval shipyard; Jean-Paul attends the fourth, third and second lycée classes

1920   the Mancys and Jean-Paul return to Paris, where the latter attends werthe Lycée Henri IV once more, meets Nizan again and they become friends

1922–24   transfers to Lycée Louis-le-Grand, as does Nizan

1924–29   École Normale Supérieure; meets Maheu, De Beauvoir and Guille

1925   meets and falls in love with Simone Jollivet

1929–31   military service in meteorological corps, first at Fort de St Cyr, then at Saint-Symphorien

1931–33   philosophy teacher at lycée in Le Havre

1932   holidays with De Beauvoir in Spanish Morocco

1933–34   philosophical studies in Berlin; affair with 'Marie Girard'

1934–36   back in Le Havre post

1935   holidays with mother and stepfather in Norway, with De Beauvoir in central France

1936   holiday in Italy; meets Olga Kosakiewicz

1936–37   teaching post at Laon

1937   moves to Lycée Pasteur in Paris; holiday in Greece; begins *La Psyché; Nausea* accepted for publication

1938   *Nausea*, 'Intimacy', 'The Room' published; holiday in Morocco; brief affair with 'Martine Bourdin' (July); flirtation with 'Lucile' (July); beginning of affair with 'Tania' (kisses: end July); begins writing *Roads to Freedom*

1939   *The Wall* published; critical essays in *NRF*; affair with 'Louise Védrine' (July); affair with 'Tania' consummated (end July) at Aigues-Mortes; call-up (1 September)

EDITOR'S FOREWORD

Of the notebooks written by Sartre during his time as a mobilized reservist in Alsace, between September 1939 and June 1940, only those we are publishing here have come to light. The others, mislaid in a train forty years ago by a recently wounded fellow-draftee, have apparently not been seen since. Perhaps they have been destroyed, or else the people in whose hands they lie are not prepared to let the fact be known. However this may be, Sartre wrote first and foremost for his contemporaries: we can see no reason for waiting any longer to release the surviving notebooks to the public.

Sartre wanted this journal to be a typical soldier's testimony on the war and the bizarre turn it was taking: on that state of inactive service into which, along with millions of others, he had been plunged. He wanted it also to be a self-interrogation, facilitated by that enforced interlude far away from the normal course of his life: an interrogation marking the end of his youth. There will also be found here, in embryo, many of the interests that his works were to elaborate subsequently: the outline of *L'Être et le Néant* and *Les Mots*; his first ideas about constructing a Moral Philosophy; and even the question 'How can a man be grasped in his entirety?', which was to receive a full reply only in his very last work, *L'Idiot de la Famille*.

Arlette Elkaïm-Sartre

NOTEBOOK 3
NOVEMBER-DECEMBER 1939
BRUMATH/MORSBRONN

12 November (cont.)

' . . . as though he had been completely transported from one state of being to another. All his senses were equally affected, eyes, lungs, mind, and limbs. Nothing, within him or without, but was different from what it had been a moment before.'[1]

But his geography, his Unanimism and his statistical naturalism at once lead him to spoil the effect: ' "Trench fear" is a purely local product. Like the "trench louse" it thrives only in the front line.' [p. 56][2] But that's stupid: what need is there for him to represent this fear as an autonomous organism, like some kind of pest, requiring favourable climatic conditions to develop? Just when he has almost understood – has fully understood, for an instant – that this fear was the organ or sense through which the man perceived the world of the trenches.

Page 12 [9] (ibid.): 'Another truth that was borne in on the military mind was that, whereas for an attack to stand any chance of success it must avail itself of every novelty of equipment, that it could never have too much, could never have enough, of technical resources, a defence could be conducted to perfection by employing the simplest materials, the trivialities of daily use, tricks as old as the human race, odds and ends of the most humiliating ordinariness: earth just thrown up with the spade; bags and boxes filled with soil or stones; wattle of

1. Jules Romains, *Men of Good Will*, vols 15/16, *Verdun: The Prelude* and *The Battle*, London 1940, p. 53. The passage quoted begins: 'Jerphanion was conscious of a sudden change of mood, a special kind of shock which he had no difficulty in recognizing since it had happened to him before. It was as though . . . '
2. Unanimism was a poetic movement of the years before 1914, to which Romains belonged. Its central theme was transcendence of the individual spirit by more global collective 'souls'—such as church, family, city, nation-at-war.

twigs and clay; the kind of barbed wire that is commonly employed by gardeners.' In short, it's as I observed in my last notebook: destruction destroys itself. If one seeks to destroy the destroyer (counter-battering fire), one relapses into that profusion of means bearing their own death within them. But if one seeks to do one's job as a man, that's to say *ward off* destruction, a minimum of means will suffice as the most humble shelter does against the mightiest wind. Artificial destruction inherently tends to become like a natural force (shells scattering, etc.), and like nature tends to compensate for the chance and uncertainty of each individual case by the profusion of means and the number of cases. Destruction, being blind, is statistical.

Every present has its future that illuminates and disappears with it, that becomes past-future:

But where are the futures of yesteryear?

This is the meaning of the celebrated catchphrase: 'How fair was the Republic, under the Empire!'[3] After 1870, the dead Empire's erstwhile future was the Republic. Not at all that of Jules Ferry and Gambetta, but another that was solely future and, as it slipped into the past, retained its future character. One day last spring, I was at St-Cloud walking along the railway-track. I could see that station with its platforms and rails and the fever-white and grey roofs of the suburban trains. For a moment, I relived a time gone by: two years earlier, the Beaver had been taken to a clinic at St-Cloud suffering from pneumonia, and I used to visit her every day.[4] But it was the last stage of my passion for O.: I was nervy and restless, each day I used to wait for the moment of seeing her again—and beyond that moment for some kind of impossible reconciliation.[5] The future of all those moments spent waiting for the train in the station at St-Cloud was that impossible love. Well, on that day last spring, the earlier time lived anew with a sweet and poignant poetry. But what above all lived anew was its then future. What I saw once more was a St-Cloud oriented towards Paris, towards Montparnasse where I was on my way home to

3. Saying of the historian Alphonse Aulard, which has become a catchphrase.

4. The Beaver (*le Castor*): pet name coined by René Maheu for Simone de Beauvoir during their days at the École Normale Supérieure, in allusion to her beaver-like capacity for work (and also, perhaps, with a play on the similarity of the English translation of the word to her surname). The nickname stuck, and has been used by her intimates to this day.

5. O. = Olga 'Zazoulich' or Kosakiewicz, with whom Sartre had a love affair in 1935–37. Her relations with Sartre and De Beauvoir are discussed at length in the latter's *Prime of Life*, Harmondsworth 1965, pp. 225 ff. (where she is referred to as Olga D.). She later acted under the name Olga Dominique, and married Jacques Bost.

be reunited with O. Yet now I had another future, other hopes, other loves. But nothing was more moving that this moment when I turned away from my living future, from the Paris and the people awaiting me beyond the horizon of St-Cloud, in order to contemplate for a moment that dead future. And it was also a dead future, rather than a series of defunct presents, that we went off to seek in Rouen last year, the Beaver and I.

When I left, in September, every instant had a vague, faraway future: the end of the war. And that distant, indefinable future rendered the present overpowering: the lighter the future is, the heavier the present. And then, gradually, that future vanished and I have nothing but an everyday future, plus a few landmarks: visits, my next leave. That's enough to make life very tolerable.

Monday, 13 November

Excellent phrase that J. Romains puts in the mouth of Maykosen (who doesn't like the French but loves Paris): 'Men are like bees. They are worth a great deal less than their products.' [p. 186]

From time to time one of us, warrant-officer, sergeant or private, fired by bashful emotion after reading some letter or being struck by some memory, will start to talk about his friends, his past, his civilian life. This is greeted by a sepulchral silence. The others write, stare out of the window, couldn't give a damn. The fellow's voice seems thin and feeble. Eventually it fades away altogether, and the fellow is left disconcerted and silent, a vague, embarrassed smile on his lips. Then he'll turn away and resume his work.

The Warrant-officer, Staff-sergeant Naudin and Private Hang are all three discussing our departure for the front. Heroically. With a heroism that really does end up having an effect on them.

Warrant-officer (soldierly and derisive): 'You can always go and make your confession, Hang old chap.'

Hang: 'Why should I make my confession?'

Naudin: 'Don't you know what your wife told you?'

Warrant-officer: 'I'm not going to confession, I have no sins.'

Naudin: 'Oh, I'll go, if the shit's flying up there.'

Hang: 'Where'll you go?'

Naudin: 'To confession, for Chrissake!'

Warrant-officer: 'No need.' (Sententiously, and stumbling somewhat over the words): 'In the event of war, there's a general dispensation for us. There's no need for confession; whatever your faith or political party, you go straight to heaven.'

Hang: 'Oh, it's a Mohammedan paradise, then!'

They laugh, and then enjoy the idea that fat Staff-sergeant Thibaud will be frightened.

'If there are any fireworks, he'll shit in his pants.' Cheering up, each of them repeats: 'He'll shit in his pants, he'll shit in his pants!'

Hang: 'He'll want to come with us on watch.'

Naudin: 'You'll see! You'll see!'

Hang: 'Oh, if he does come, I hope there'll be a bit of shelling.'

I: 'Yes, so long as it doesn't hit you – or him, because you don't want him killed – or anybody.'

Hang: 'Right. A hundred metres away.'

Naudin (seriously): 'One shouldn't hope for anyone's death.'

Warrant-officer: 'A nice big shell exploding twenty metres away, then you'd see old fatso! And I'd offer him a chair and say to him: "Sit down, Thibaud, my poor old fellow, you look sick." '

They talk about the fat sergeant's latest misdeeds, and each of them explains what a splendid trick he'll be playing on him one of these fine days.

Naudin: 'Oh, there are two or three chaps here, I'd rather not even mention their names. who've really got him by the short and curly! It's all down in writing. They're not talking, because it'd be too serious; but if he messes us around, then you'll soon see! The documents'll be brought out and he'll just have to rip off his stripes and shave his head.'

Hang: 'The nasty ones always get paid back in the end.'

Naudin: 'That's for sure: if you play it nasty, you always get paid back.'

Tuesday, 14 November

Yesterday evening my eyes are aching, so I break off work; at that moment, Pieter tells me one of his friends has just written him the following: 'Some people's jealousy and lack of understanding is surprising and hurtful.' This irritates me, because the same fellow wrote him the same sentence, word for word, a month earlier. The fellow's a tradesman, in an anti-aircraft battery fifty kilometres from Paris, in some backwater. His mates are sleeping in the mud. Five hundred metres away from their position, there are six houses and a grocery store. This fellow and one of his mates, who's a cafe-waiter at the Coupole, have found some good woman who gives them board and lodging for 100 francs a month. So they don't eat lunch or supper with their comrades. they don't even sleep with them. In addition to that, the proximity of Paris enables the fellow's brother to get out by car two or three times a week with a chicken and a few good bottles of wine. His girl-friend has been to see him and spend the night with him. He also receives sumptuous parcels. After all this, he's surprised and hurt that he arouses envy among his comrades. I tell Pieter what I think, but dare not add that if this fellow has one tenth of Pieter's self-satisfied, jovial generosity, if he shares his parcels with hearty enthusiasm, shows pictures of his girl-friend and offers to be of service, speaking all the while of his affairs with a certain air of critical impartiality, then he undoubtedly must have made himself hated.

'What it comes down to,' says Pieter indignantly, 'is that you'd like the lad to go without a bed, a woman and food just to please the dolts who are with him?' I reply: 'Yes, I would.' And I can see that what shocks him, though he is unable to formulate it clearly, is that the fact of being with dolts should create additional duties. He says: 'That's all very fine in theory, but in practice . . . You live in theory, but I'm a tradesman, a practical man.' I say: 'You can drop all that theory and practice nonsense, once and for all. You're neither more nor less practical than I am: you need me in certain practical cases, just as in other cases I need you.' At once, another argument from Pieter, as predictable as its predecessor: 'Anyway, you don't do that yourself.' I should have answered: 'Granted I don't do it, and I'm a swine; but I'm not talking about myself, I'm saying it's what one ought to do.' (To which he would no doubt have replied: 'It's all very well to say one *ought* to do something, but that's easy when you don't do it yourself', etc.)

But I was tired and let myself be drawn onto the terrain of accusation and apology – the terrain where I always feel most ill at ease, because I'm not used to talking about myself and because my pride rebels as soon as I'm placed in the dock. So I reply: 'If it were the will of fate that I should find myself with a bunch of footsloggers, I would certainly do it. But here things are not the same.' 'I'm beginning to know you,' says Pieter, 'you don't like anyone messing you around; you write all day, and when you feel like going off on your own for lunch in a restaurant, you just tell us so to our faces.' I tell him: 'That's because you're all bourgeois; I wouldn't put myself out for bourgeois people, and besides I have nothing you haven't got or couldn't get yourselves.'

Here the conversation switches suddenly. Pieter asks me somewhat tartly: 'But if it disgusts you as much as all that to be surrounded by bourgeois, why do you stay here?' Why indeed? That's the whole question, it's still the same social problem I was talking about the other day, all my deep uncertainty. I answer in the easiest and most disastrous way: 'Because in 1929 I made the mistake of wangling myself a safe spot in the Met. corps. It was a rotten thing to do, I admit.' Pieter: 'Ha! Ha! So you're a slob!' Sincerely indignant at being reproached for so ancient a mistake and at being forced to assume responsibility for the person I was in 1929, I retort clumsily: 'You're not really going to condemn me *now*, are you, for something rotten I did in 1929!' It's my pride which makes me speak, my sense of progress and that way I have of refusing responsibility for what I was the day before. Whenever anybody seems struck by the permanance of my ego, I am overcome by anxiety.

Of course, I bring the predictable riposte down on my head: 'Do you know who you're like? The fellow who's stolen a bar of chocolate, and who eats it with relish a week later, saying as he does so: "I'm a thief, I'm a slob, I feel so guilty." I'm more honest than you are: I got a few strings pulled, I'm satisfied with the result, and I say so.'

I: 'I don't know why you call that being honest: you're hiding from yourself the fact that you're a slob.'

Pieter: 'I'm not a slob. Oh, in a society where justice reigned, if I committed some injustice for my own benefit I might feel guilty. But in this world of ours, I tell myself I'm no exception: there are five hundred thousand individuals who've pulled strings just like me, and if I wasn't where I am, somebody else would be. As for you, you say you're a slob: that's more cunning, but you enjoy the advantages of the Met. just like me. A fellow who said 'I'm a slob' and then refused all these advantages and went off to serve as a footslogger, I'd call him sincere. But what proof do I have that you're sincere?'

Paul: 'And there's something else that bothers me about what Sartre says: if you take that line, you should always put yourself on the level of the most disadvantaged.'

I: 'No, on the level of the masses.'

Pieter: 'And then another thing: I, honest as ever, am delighted to learn that my wife has reopened the shop and it's doing well. Here again, I'm one of the lucky ones. But you're even luckier than I am: you're still getting your salary.[6] Meanwhile, there are other fellows who have nothing to live on but their ten *sous* a day, and their wives have nothing but their separation allowances. Why don't you give up your salary to them?'

6. Teachers, like all French civil servants, continued to draw their salaries after being called up.

Paul: 'I quite agree.'

I: 'That's different. There are peacetime privileges and a society built upon those privileges. In peacetime, the point is not for an individual to give up these privileges, which would be a drop in the ocean, but for him to struggle for the suppression of *all* privileges.' (In saying this, prompted by the presence of Paul, a socialist, I am thinking of Blum and Zyromski, and have some vague notion of drawing him onto my side.[7]) 'What I want is to avoid adding new, wartime privileges.'

What nobody realizes is that the conversation has deviated, and deviated dangerously for me, thanks to my clumsiness: all I was saying was that, in every particular military situation, a person should adapt his standard of living to the average level. But the idea has become modified in the course of our conversation: it's now a question of sharing the fate of the least fortunate in military society *as a whole*: to have no sleeping-bag if others, invisible and far away, have no sleeping-bag; not to receive visits if others, at the front, cannot have their wives up, etc. And this is probably because the initial idea was slippery and inconsistent – basically a pretence. So it's because I have thought *badly* that I have ended up suddenly defending this unprincipled exaggeration: the notion of sharing the fate of the most wretched. Or rather, the principle of this new idea – whose presence I obscurely sense – is Guille's humanism, which is entirely defensible but which I do not share.[8]

This distinction between peacetime and wartime privileges does not convince Paul: he shakes his head and falls silent. But Pieter endeavours to convince me that I enjoy numerous privileges: I have a bed – which he has procured for me – I eat in a restaurant, etc., etc. I know it all only too well. I resume the offensive, but from this moment on I'm already groggy. I shall get the better of Pieter, because wounded vanity makes me want to get the better of him; but in my heart of hearts I know he has got the better of me. I tell him: 'You have still evaded the question. You've shrugged off what I was saying to you about my being quite aware of my culpability, by pretending it was mere words, just an attitude.' 'Yes, of course. What proof do I have that you're telling the truth? It could be just your taste for the theatrical.' He is leaning back against the stove, flushed and

7. Jean Zyromski (1890–   ) led the *Bataille socialiste* (left) tendency within the Socialist Party (SFIO: Section française de l'Internationale Ouvrière), and edited the economic and social page of *Le Populaire*, the party newspaper.

8. Pierre Guille, a friend of Sartre since their days together at the École Normale Supérieure (1924–29). He appears in De Beauvoir's autobiography as Pagniez.

oratorical. I tell him (I'm sitting at my place): 'Take a look at yourself and tell me which of us two is the more theatrical.' (Bad faith, since this is not the issue, but I score a point by making Keller and Paul laugh.) 'You could have mentioned that nothing proves my sincerity, but not stopped there, since the conversation then just comes to an end. I can't prove it to you, any more than you can prove to me that your good conscience is sincere. But if you really wanted to discuss, you should instead have accepted the hypothesis of my sincerity and fought me on that terrain. You had no shortage of arguments.' I mention a few, feeling sure he won't dish these ones back up to me, since I'm supplying them myself: he'll think I have the answers pat. In fact, I have no answers.

I add: 'The truth is, you're incapable of understanding what it means to think about oneself. If I tell you that in such and such a situation I acted like a bastard, you reduce this to *words*; you don't see what the effort to judge oneself can be. And you don't see it because you're incapable of making that effort. The way you reason is: "I'm not a bastard, because five hundred thousand other fellows are bastards just like me." You run away from yourself and, instead of looking at yourself as a single, unique individual, you seek reassurance by dissolving yourself into a social category, You evade any examination of your own conscience, Isn't that true? Aren't you silenced?'

He: 'Oh, you've silenced me all right, you're so clever.'

I: 'It's not a matter of cleverness. The other day, on the topic of marriage, it was just the same: I situate myself on the plane of values and thought, whereas you remain indefinitely at the level of words and deeds.'

Pieter: 'All right, then, from now on whenever I argue with you I'll begin by playing on words.'

This completes his downfall: with a weary gesture to Paul, and to Mistler who has just come in, I point to him and say: 'Just look at him! Incurable!' Laughter. 'Oh,' says he, 'you'll always be in the right.' Whereupon it's nine o'clock and we all go home. We talk about other things. I am irritable and have a bad conscience, because my victory is only apparent; the truth is that Pieter caught me on the raw. As we take our leave at his landlady's front door, he says with a sly dig at me: 'Ah, now we can go back to our comfortable beds. Privileges like that are a real pleasure.' I tell him: 'As you very well know, I can sleep on straw, I don't give a damn. How many times have I stood in for you, when you had guard duty? And at Marmoutier I slept on the bare ground.'

But all the same, as I return with Paul to the room we share I feel ridiculous, and just like one of Don Passos's characters (Richard).[9] So I recite the story to myself in Don Passos style: 'And Sartre lost his temper and said they ought to be living in privation because it was wartime. And he condemned Pieter, because Pieter had got people to pull strings for him. And he declared that they were all bastards, himself included, and that they ought to sleep on straw or in mud like the soldiers at the front. It struck nine and everyone went home. Sartre greeted his landlady, then retired to a comfortable bed with an eiderdown over his feet.' It would be a bit thick, even as something out of Dos Passos. I prowl irritably round the room for a while, wanting to reopen the subject with Paul, since he has a greater familiarity with ideas and I will thus be able to dupe him more easily, and by duping him reassure myself. He listens to me, hesitant, polite, not very convinced. The truth is the subject affects him personally, inasmuch as he is an anti-militarist socialist and yet highly privileged by the war (civil servant, Met. corps, etc.). We turn off the lights, and it's a while before I can fall asleep.

There are a number of things to be learnt from this comic episode: about Pieter, about Paul, and about myself.

About Pieter. In the light of this conversation he appears as a fine specimen of inauthentic rationalism, or, to be precise, of the impersonal Heideggerian 'one'.[10] A specimen all the more perfect in that he is not stupid and has a taste for discussion and argument. He is loquacious, but like a Greek he establishes principles, draws out their implications, examines secondary hypotheses as he proceeds, raises objections to his thesis and refutes them, makes concessions to a supposed adversary the better to confound him, and finally reaches his conclusion. Never is it the case that what he's out to establish is not clear *before* he even begins to speak. It sometimes even happens that what he's about to expatiate on for a full fifteen minutes has, in fact, already been expressed in a few well-chosen words. He doesn't care, because for him the important thing is not to convince or teach, but to enjoy for as long as possible his mind's agreement with itself.

He starts all his pronouncements with the word 'No'. But this 'No' is not genuinely negative – with respect to some sentence, previously enunciated by an adversary, that is in contradiction with his thought.

9. The reference is to the novel *1919*, second volume of the *USA* trilogy: in the August 1938 issue of the *Nouvelle Revue Française,* Sartre had published an essay 'À propos de John Dos Passos et de "1919" '.

10. *das Man*: rendered as 'the "they" ' in the standard English translation of *Being and Time,* Oxford 1962.

It is a nihilating 'No', designed to make *tabula rasa* of all that has been said on the subject, true or false, so as to be able to begin everything afresh and recast it from scratch. It even happens that he repeats and expands on what one has just said to him, while prefacing this with a categorical 'No'. As in the following example, which I have remembered because it's the most typical. I: 'Paul is a funk.' He : 'No. The thing about Paul is, he's the kind who's frightened, a funk . . . etc., etc.'

He particularly relishes exercising his practical reason: principles of action, planning, projects, details, etc. Explaining his projects, he regularly concludes with the words: 'D'you get it? D'you get – the idea?', with a short pause between 'D'you get' and 'the idea'. The word 'idea' here has the double meaning of scheme or undertaking, and of topic under discussion or intelligible matter, as in the expression 'to swop ideas'.[11] For this disputatious, Jewish reason is social: it needs an audience. The audience is indispensable, because it alone can transform the pure and simple exercise of logic into an 'idea'. Playfulness, self-satisfaction and courtesy are features of his logical expositions. His reason is social also by virtue of the matter to which it is applied: habits and customs, advertising psychology, courtesy. It is a bourgeois reason that thinks men and not things (though it's neither maladroit nor stupid when faced with a tool to be repaired or used).

But it is a reason never directed back upon itself: not simply because it knows nothing of abstraction, but also because anything resembling a thought or judgement is outside his ken. Not that he does not think or judge; but as soon as he judges his judgements – or judgements in general – he destroys their universality and their absolute character on principle. This is what emerged naively from what he was saying yesterday. First of all, *thought* is reduced for him to words. I *say* that I feel guilty. I *say* it, but what proves it? I quite understand that here – and this is what bothered me – he reckons that *actions* would prove it: if I applied to enrol in the infantry, my thought would be solid and juridically valid. But these actions in turn, when they occur, he explains by temperament. If a person acts in such and such a way, it's because it's *natural* for him to act like that. I'd been struck right at the outset by the way in which he'd tried to demonstrate that heroism was a fairy-tale: that those who are dubbed heroes are, in fact, driven by their temperament – or else it's the

11. Not an entirely satisfactory translation of the original 'discuter le coup', but it was necessary to find some equivalent for *coup* that could bear approximately the same duality of meaning in English as that multivalent word carries here in the French.

occasion that creates them. The argument wasn't worth much; but what interested me was his tendency to reduce every obligation or constraint to something unfolding naturally.

Of course, he has no trouble proceeding from this to the morality of interest: since everyone follows his temperament, everyone is pursuing his own interest. But, in addition, he is unwilling even to acknowledge the individual temperament – another absolute and one that would be too complex for him: there exist only types. These types, moreover, are formed by the intersection of their inherited nature and their professional activity. He'll never say 'Paul's scared', but 'Paul's the scared type.' Not just out of a basic vulgarity that makes him choose instinctively the most vulgar turns of phrase, but out of a need to refer to clearcut categories. This is why, to him, I'm 'the bohemian', 'Montparnasse', etc. And he'll explain my every reaction by my bohemian character and intellectual calling.

This morning, reverting to our discussion of yesterday, he explained most charmingly how well he understood my position: 'You see, we're not the same, you and I. I'm a tradesman, so are you. But in my case, at half-past seven I shut up shop and don't have to account to anybody for my private life. Whereas you never shut up shop, day or night, and you have to account for everything you do. I can wangle myself a safe niche in the Met. and say I'm glad – it's nobody's business but mine. But if you say that in your books, no one will buy you. So you're obliged to sacrifice certain thoughts, just as I sacrifice certain items in my stock.'

So, what with thought and actions being an emanation of one's temperament, and the latter in its turn deriving from one's heredity, profession and environment, everything is drowned in a universal relativism. The conclusive argument itself is reduced for him to a technical success. The workman is congratulated for it, but the very congratulations make his success a chance, individual one. If he's silenced by some argument, he'll never say that the argument's valid, but rather that I'm *clever*. He deliberately loses himself in this relativism; dissolves himself in the social. Like Heidegger's inauthentic being, which says 'One dies' in order to avoid saying '*I* die'. He relates to himself only through society; speaks of himself in the same tone he uses for others, simply with greater affection. He says 'I'm the type who . . .', in the same way he speaks of Paul, again implying that he comes to himself via categories. If he's defending himself against some accusation (for it's beyond his comprehension that one might accuse oneself), he appeals for help to the category of which he's a member – which varies from one situation to another – saying, for example:

'There are five hundred thousand shirkers like me, and if I wasn't here, somebody else would be here instead', and in his own eyes this very interchangeability of the 'shirker' mitigates not just his fault, but also his irreplaceability as an individual.

On the other hand, he does consider himself, with a certain fierceness, as having rights. But they are social rights: it's in a given society, and statute-book in hand, that he intends to exercise his rights – and only those the statute-book accords him. It would never occur to him to dream of others; if he doesn't find any where he thought he would, he doesn't press the matter but squeezes every last drop out of those that do exist, always half exploiter of the law and half citizen with a strong sense of what's due to him.

All this is accompanied by a total blindness to values: he is incapable of distinguishing what should-be from what is. If you speak to him of the *value* of a free union, he replies with the words: 'All the ones I know have ended up in marriage or turned into cohabitation.' Or else I tell him his friend *should* assume the average living-standard of his comrades, and he replies: 'You wouldn't act like that yourself.' And that in itself would be nothing: after all, everyone comes out with this kind of reply spontaneously, because it's easiest. But what I cannot convey here is that, despite my efforts to make clear to him the distinction between values and facts, and though he understands with his reason the distinction I'm making, he does not thereafter manage to adapt his discourse to it, but reverts two minutes later to the same old arguments.

Individuality lost in the impersonal 'one'; social relativism and universal tolerance; polite rationalism; blindness to values: these comprise the basis of his inauthenticity. Combined with his Jewish self-importance; his need to clasp hands and do good turns, both from true generosity and from long-term calculation; his busybody's curiosity; his need to rub shoulders with everybody, especially those in high places: these features constitute what I would be inclined to call his 'radical-socialism'. What strikes me is that his inauthenticity, unlike most people's, has no gaps at all. It's a coherent and seamless world system. This is where the Beaver's question is most pertinent: 'If inauthenticity is consistent, though, what proves it is any less valid than authenticity?' His La Rochefoucauld-style psychology does indeed end up being disturbing – not in itself, because it's too crude, but because it suggests to you another of the same kind. After all, is it not because I'm a professional thinker, etc. that I'm writing this notebook? The dizziness of causal explanation. And, precisely, I receive a letter from L. telling me that some arts lecturer called

Ullmann, whom I don't know from Adam, says that '*La Nausée* reeks of the philosophy teacher'.[12]

On Paul. It was nothing really, but it charmed me. Following on from yesterday's discussion. He was worming his way with a series of wriggles into his sleeping-bag, I was already lying on the couch. We chat and I say: 'When you're an officer, even if you're a socialist, even if you're "kind to your men to the point of weakness", you're complicit.' He agrees with me, saying thoughtfully: 'Even if you're a corporal!' 'Oh, Corporal . . .', I say politely. 'Yes, yes! Even if you're a corporal. I didn't want to be one, you know. But there was no other way of getting to Nancy, and my wife was there. So I let myself be promoted, but I hid it from her. Only, when the gendarmes came last year to change my call-up papers, I wasn't at home. It's my wife who took them. What a time she gave me when I got home!'

All of which says a great deal about his sly nature and his relations with his wife. He has just asked me for the *NRF*'s address, so that his wife can order *Le Mur* and *La Nausée*;[13] but this embarrasses me horribly, because I detect in it a colleague's courtesy. I say awkwardly: 'You know, you shouldn't feel obliged . . .', and he says, very much at his ease: 'Oh, yes, I insist, I shall be delighted for my wife to read you, and I myself as well, next time I'm on leave . . .' He tells me in the conversation that he's had socialist sympathies since the age of 15, and been a SFIO party member since 1930. This amuses me, because he told me a month and a half ago: 'Hm . . . I'm a sympathizer, but I'm not in the party.'

I'm stopping for today, I can no longer manage to think of anything because my eyes are hurting too much. I've never felt so clearly that I *think with my eyes.* Today I have a restricted horizon; an inability to focus my thoughts, because I'm incapable of focusing on an object; the impression that I have two dark walls to my right and my left, and between these walls a kaleidoscopic dazzle. The impression that my thoughts display their surface alone to me, only to slip away and vanish before I've been able to grasp them. In excellent spirits, though.

12. *La Nausée*, Paris 1938, now in *Oeuvres romanesques*, Paris 1981; English translation *Nausea*, New York and London 1949. For L., see note 4 on p.119 and note 1 on p.220.

13. *NRF* = *Nouvelle Revue Française*, major French cultural journal founded in 1908, associated in its early days particularly with Gide, and sponsor of a publishing house which became the present firm Gallimard. The *NRF* published Sartre's prewar stories and essays, Gallimard became the publisher of all his later books. 'Le Mur' was published in the June 1937 issue of *NRF*, now in *Oeuvres romanesques;* see *The Wall and Other Stories*, New York and London 1948.

Thursday 16

I didn't write in this notebook yesterday, because my eyes are hurting too badly. Luckily, because I can see more clearly what I have to say about myself. I shall say it as soon as I am able. Today, I shall just note down Paul's adventure. He had a message to take by bicycle. He fusses and frets. We tell him: 'You'll have to take helmet and rifle.' That's orders. At the idea of taking his rifle, he has one of those outbursts of nervous, violent rage that are habitual with him, and that come not from nastiness but from fear. He says: 'Oh, no, not a rifle! I'm not going, I absolutely refuse to go.' And he explains that he has semicircular-canal trouble, and will never be able to keep his balance on the bicycle with a rifle over his shoulder. In the end, the colonel lends him an old revolver. I note here, incidentally, that this revolver, though unloaded and obsolete, inspires Pieter with respectful terror: 'Hey, watch out there!' he says, 'Don't play around with that!' Paul sets off, helmeted, looking like some old maid. An hour goes by. He returns. When he comes in, I first see his helmet and goggles, then his dirty, grey face wearing an ominous expression. He has the whole of one side of his jacket and trousers all smeared with mud. His left hand is bleeding, his right swollen. He swerved to avoid a car, the bicycle-chain snapped, and he flew forwards landing on his head and hands. I begin to understand the element of self-fear involved in his hatred of war and in his perturbation. In order to preserve one's equanimity, it is obviously quite something to have a docile body that keeps quiet. But as he set off, he must have had the impression of being abandoned to his body, which he can master only in peacetime under the most favourable circumstances, but which, if let loose among rough men in wartime, will cut capers, play nasty tricks on him and avenge its servitude.

J. Romains: 'In wartime, there are no innocent victims.' [p.443]

Yesterday I received a card from Nizan, which made me happy.

Friday 17

My eyes are still hurting. I give way somewhat to anxiety and nervousness, because there's no justification for this trouble. It's no longer a question of taking up a firm stance with respect to a social upheaval, but merely of bearing a minor everyday trouble without anxiety. That's more difficult. And then, since I dare not *harden* my eyes, my thoughts retain a certain fuzziness, they lack precision. Just the precision I'd need in order to think my ailment bluntly and clearly, as I should with a pain in my hand or liver. I have the impression that my visual field is restricted by disturbing metal shutters. All the same, I've worked at my novel – well, I think – writing rough drafts for it with my eyes closed. But I have a certain reluctance either to write in small characters in this notebook, or (a collector's foible) to alter the size of the characters or the spacing of the lines.

The result is a kind of laziness about thinking, and an eager readiness to welcome daily chores – shoe-cleaning, sweeping out the schoolroom, etc. – that will exempt me from having to think and write. I talk more. Yet I know I'm behindhand with a lot of things in this notebook, particularly the observations I want to make about myself in connection with my conversation on the 13th, and also the definition of being-in-one's-class and the conclusion of my reflections on politics. But the military indolence in which all my confederates are steeped is there to induce me to idleness, to belime me. It's so easy living here to do nothing without getting bored, because thanks to the war expectation is suppressed. Expectation and worry. This eyetrouble, moreover, is much more bearable than a mere headache. What there is, is anxiety. Precisely the anxiety I'd thought one would be rid of in war. And in point of fact I think one usually is rid of it – but *with respect to* the ills that come from war. This trouble of mine is attended by all the civilian worries: fear of losing my sight, not being able to write any longer, etc. All of it, of course, in the imaginarybelief category. I'm not 'panicking', but I am in somewhat less of a good mood than usual,

What I was wanting to say, and what I saw clearly on the occasion of my conversation on the 13th, is that since I have been at Brumath I have been adopting the stance of a moral clown. Something like *Ridendo castigat mores*.[14] The other day, I was caught up in it. I went home to my landlady's very much affected and was taking myself seriously. I said to myself: 'It's true, I ought to enrol in the infantry.' And then suddenly: 'Oh, no, that's not what I should be reproaching myself for! The fact is, I act the fool and that's what I'm guilty of.' The root of it all was my moral pedantry. In the beginning, I used to make unpleasant remarks to my confederates out of moralizing spleen and because I couldn't restrain myself. Besides, as I have recorded here, I sometimes reproached myself for it. I had no real intention of *reforming* them, I was not so crazy. There were simply two 'natures'

14. In fact, 'castigat ridendo mores' ('She chides men's ways with laughter'): motto invented for Comedy by the French author of Latin works Jean Santeul (1630–97).

which irritated me profoundly: Paul's fearful, meticulous self-dispersal; and Pieter's easy-going, soft self-abandon, his greedy, corpulent way of seeming in all he does to be 'indulging' some endearing whim. If he stands up to go and fetch some bread, one has the impression he is complacently indulging some urge. Besides, it's true, that great fellow licks himself like a cat. From this point of view, the sticky smackings of his lips when he eats are signs to me of that abandon, just as much as any studied action.

But enough of Pieter. What I wanted to signal was that it was above all their moral atmospheres that I found disagreeable. When I made an unpleasant comment upon some aspect or other of their behaviour, it was because I could criticize them in the name of a simple moral principle. But fundamentally, the criticism was not so much directed at a particular venial fault as at their very existence itself; it was the symbol of a more radical criticism which, after all, I could not inflict upon them, and which, by virtue of its very exaggeration, would have left them more unmoved than a thousand little specific criticisms. So at first these criticisms were little shameful pleasures that I would allow myself, and I used to consider them more as weaknesses than as merits. Thereupon Mistler arives, who is amused by these criticisms, generally delivered in a clownish manner, laughs at them and also approves their content. This discreet, amused admiration then gives me the impression that my grotesque speeches contain a 'substantific marrow'.[15] And what do I do but spice up their grotesquerie and cram them fuller every day of that 'substantific marrow'. Not only when Mistler is there, but all day long.

I amuse myself by teaching them freedom. So that my speeches, at first purely negative and referring to a shared morality, become positive indoctrinations. But in proportion they become cruder, through an aesthetic balancing. This time, the stance is adopted: I become a moralizing fool. Of course, I need hardly say I don't care a fig about freeing Paul from his bonds. It's the stance which pleased me: it allowed me to discharge my bile, to expose my ideas, to make truculent speeches, to play a part. For I am social and an actor – here, no doubt, out of boredom and the need to expend an overflow of boisterousness; elsewhere to win hearts; on other occasions simply to reflect a clearcut image in the eyes of other people.

15. See Rabelais, *The Most Horrific Life of the Great Gargantua*, 'Author's Prologue': 'Following the dog's example, you will have to be wise in sniffing, smelling, and estimating these fine and meaty books . . . after which, by careful reading and frequent meditation, you should break the bone and suck the substantific marrow . . . ' In *The Portable Rabelais*, Harmondsworth 1977, pp. 49–50.

And also, I think it was a way of having sustained relations with my confederates: since they do not amuse me, I had to amuse myself at their expense, in other words 'sport with them', as Montaigne says;[16] I drew them into a play I was staging for myself, under the pretext of staging it for Mistler. I see in it also a kind of bashful withdrawal, a way of not wanting to be with them unceremoniously, precisely because we are living unceremoniously. These are not excuses I'm giving, but explanations. The fact remains I shouldn't have been caught up in it; it was tolerable only in the form of disinterested buffoonery. And then, on that day of 13 November, I let myself be caught up. Happily, my prompt discomfiture brought me back to my senses. I have since returned to a disordered, planless distribution of criticisms. I think they can put up with me better like this: they prefer to explain those criticisms by my aggressiveness than by my pros-elytizing.

Today at the Écrevisse I have lunch with a chasseur who's just back from the front. He says: 'The Germans are two hundred and fifty metres away, we can see them quite clearly. During the first days, they used to play in the grass and they had accordions and harmonicas. But a week ago, a Moroccan from our side brought down one of their lads with his rifle, and since then there's no way of leaving cover any more without their firing at us.' He concludes gloomily: 'There's always somebody who'll be a bloody idiot, and it's the others who have to pay for it' – a stock phrase here, but one that I usually hear pronounced when some drunken soldier has caused a rumpus and the cafés have been put out of bounds.

I should like to know the average age of those called up for the present war. Their number, a lot higher I think than the number drafted at the start of the last war, and the fact that there are 'lean years', encourages me to believe that the average age is higher than in the '14 war. In any case, in our division the '23 enrolment is the most numerous, and represents two-thirds of the total, with the remaining third being made up of all the other yearly enrolments on reserve going right back to 1912. And Paul, '29 enrolment, is the youngest in any unit. So it seems the average age of the division is thirty-six, the two extremes thirty and forty-seven. True, it is regarded as being a division of veterans. It isn't at all uncommon to meet people from it who have 'been through the other one'. The mail clerk with big black eyebrows, for example.

16. The reference is probably to the famous passage in Book II, Essay 12: 'Quand je me joue à ma chatte, qui sait si elle passe son temps de moi, plus que je ne fais d'elle.'

It must be admitted that, if I consider only myself, strictly myself alone, I should be a bit disappointed to see this war end abruptly in a month. Now that I have been projected into it, I should like to see it give its all (its full complement of swindling and fiddles) before disappearing.

Saturday 18

In the morning, medical examination known as 'posting inspection'. In the saloon of a tavern, they made us piss into beer-mugs. My confederates stripped to the buff. Me too. I shall say nothing of myself except that, as I sought a relaxed pose in front of six soldiers who sat at a table checking documents, I felt *I had a back*. But my confederates surprised me: in the buff, they were no more naked than usual. Paul's bottom and the slight curvature of his spinal column did not embarrass me. I felt I had always known them. Nor did the vast belly mischievous as a smile that Keller displayed, with an air of saying 'That's a fact!' as the M.O. dictated to his aides: 'Obesity o-b-e-s-i-t-y.' I feel I have always seen them naked. I think that, despite these tunics and coarse blue breeches, we live in a state of total nakedness. Our sexes gave that respectable gathering a tinge of melancholy. Wrinkled, wilting, ashamed, they strove vainly to conceal themselves in their hair. The M.O. inspected them with an elegant finger, saying: 'Cough'. And I understood and approved whole-heartedly that phrase of André Breton's: 'I should be ashamed to appear naked before a woman without having an erection.' No two ways about that, it's a question of good taste. After the inspection, walk in the countryside. I don't know why, it made me think of Doctor Faust's walk when he meets the spaniel.[17] I was walking in front, my confederates were following. Mild disgust, from seeing all those pricks. But what's disgusting about that? It was sexual, I suppose: a way of asserting my heterosexuality. Perhaps, though, I'm accusing myself wrongly; at any rate it was mild and spontaneous. The odour of urine perhaps had something to do with it too. Paul's has a sourish smell, as I had already noticed. He himself is colourless and grey, but his bodily humours have a certain pungency.

Monday 20

The whole morning Hang and Sergeant Naudin have been reproach-

---

17. The dog was in fact a poodle (*Pudel*): see Goethe, *Faust*, Part One, Harmondsworth 1983, p. 68. Sartre was relying on Nerval's famous early translation.

ing each other for not being at the front, and calling each other shirkers.

Cassou, *48*: speaking of the atmosphere before '48: 'What must be taken into consideration here, at the movement's outset, is belief or the religious act. It is by means of a religious act that man separates himself from his beliefs and his religions, in order to satisfy himself with that Religion through which he reveals himself to himself as species: "cosmic man" as the Lyonnais mystic Ballanche used to say, or "collective being" as St-Simon used to say. "Man," the St-Simonians would add, "is a religious being who is developing. Humanity has a religious future." . . . "The interest of the human race," proclaims Lamartine, "is directed at the human race itself".'[18] This is precisely the basis of humanism: man viewing himself as *species*. It is this abasement of human nature that I condemn. Species whose destiny is to conquer and order the world: cosmic man, as Ballanche says. On the opposite side, those who define man by taking the customs that suit their own book as features of his nature: man will always make war; inequality is a natural law, etc. Maurras and his experimental pseudo-positivism. The end-result is that this crops up in a jumbled, hybrid form in every political consciousness: man as a biological species, with his destiny as a species; man as a positive reality to be determined through experiments. Nothing shows better the urgency of an undertaking such as Heidegger's, and its *political* importance: to determine human nature as a synthetic structure, a totality endowed with essence. It was certainly urgent in Descartes' day to define mind with methods pertaining to mind itself. But this was precisely to isolate it. And all subsequent attempts to constitute the complete man by adding something to mind were condemned to failure, because they were only additions.

The method of Heidegger and such as may come after him is basically the same as that of Descartes: interrogating human nature with methods appertaining to human nature itself; knowing that human nature already defines itself by the interrogation it formulates upon itself. All of a sudden, however, we posit as the object of our interrogation not the mind, not the body, not the psychic, not historicity, not the social or the cultural, but the human condition in its indivisible unity. Idealism's error is to posit the mind first. The error of materialism and all kinds of naturalism is to make man into a natural being. The religion of man conceived as a natural species: the error of

18. Jean Cassou, *Quarante-huit*, Paris 1939, p. 43.
Pierre-Simon Ballanche (1776–1847) developed mystical conceptions of universal religion, of 'harmonies', and of poetry as the expression of the universal mind.

'48, the worst error, the humanitarian error. Against this, to establish human reality, the human condition, the being-in-the-world of man and his being-in-situation. The notion of human species has made incredible ravages; even the Beaver noticed in conversation one day that she has two fixed reference-points in the infinite series of time: the appearance of the human species, in the past; and the disappearance of the human species, in the future. My unease at great scientific and fictional predictions: extinction of the sun, collision of the earth with a comet, etc. To me, this means nothing and is *boring*.

Pieter has the gripes. He stares miserably back when I look at him. He is eager to inspire pity. I deny him that pleasure.

Letter from Paulhan: 'Captain Marchat interrogates Alain, very courteously, at his home. "When I saw the word *peace* in the manifesto," says Alain, "I signed without reading the rest".'[19]

The war has never been more elusive than in these last few days. I feel the lack of it, for after all, if it doesn't exist, what the hell am I doing here?

A decree published in the *Journal Officiel*[20] discreetly establishes concentration camps in France. Civil servants will be subject to summary dismissal. About time too. But what in the world am I supposed to defend, if it's no longer even freedom?

Wrote a stupid letter to Paulhan, that I don't send. I transcribe it here to mortify myself (and also because I find it witty):

'For the moment I am quartered in a little village where I am working on my novel: I am entirely free and completely alone: it is a retreat. If the Germans were shelling, perhaps that would disturb me; but if the Germans were shelling, it would be another war (and Sartre another Sartre, as Vandal would say[21]). This one is like the Oustric

19. Alain: pen-name of Émile-Auguste Chartier (1868–1951), influential essayist and, with Brunschvicg, the dominant figure in French philosophy between the wars. He was prosecuted with others in 1939 for having signed a tract by the pacifist Louis Lecoin, entitled *Paix immédiate!*
Jean Paulhan (1884–1968), critic and essayist, was editor of the NRF from 1925 to 1940, later on editorial board of *Les Temps Modernes*.
20. *Le Journal Officiel*: founded in 1789 as the *Moniteur Universel* to report parliamentary debates, in 1799 it became the official newspaper publishing government laws and decrees; renamed in 1848 *Journal Officiel de la République Française*, taken over fully by the government in 1869. Cf. the *London Gazette*.
21. Albert Vandal (1853–1910), historian of the Napoleonic period famous for his classic studies of Bonaparte's rise to power and relations with Tsar Alexander.

affair and Brunschvicg's philosophy.[22] That's hardly to its honour – every epoch has the war it deserves. So much the better. I was keenly interested to learn that Petitjean had been wounded.[23] I could not have supposed it would be otherwise. Or else, once again, Petitjean would have been another Petitjean. Besides, if one considers the daily tally of casualties, one can say it is pure chance and this confirms my belief in fate. I was very touched by the *NRF* which you so kindly sent me. But how astonished I was when I read the column by "Caerdal". Is there no one who can give M. Suarès's sleeve a tug?[24] This war is pretty minor and technical for such imprecations – and such naive ones. Like him I passed through Rothenbourg, but I did not feel the little children were laughing at me: that must vary from one person to another.'

Absurd, distasteful letter. In the first place, it isn't simple. As soon as I settle into position for a reply to Paulhan, I lose all simplicity, influenced undoubtedly by the reputation for malice that he credits me with – and that I do not deserve. I try to be brief and incisive, but polite. Then I play the very *NRF* game of 'false confidence in the reader'. Here's what I mean by this: I'm sure that Paulhan can't understand right off why I compare the war to Brunschvicg's philosophy. A few words of explanation are needed. But, precisely, I do not write them. I honour him with a false confidence, convinced that he will understand something, no matter what – for it goes without saying that *NRF* people always understand – and even that he will simultaneously adopt a multiplicity of incompatible explanations. And these interpretations, which I anticipate without knowing them, give my phrase, at the very moment I am penning it, a delightful profundity and a touch of strangeness in my own eyes. Generalize the system of false confidence, extend it to all possible readers, and you have the manufacturing technique for the critical glosses one reads in the *NRF*. Then I was annoyed because in each of his letters Paulhan speaks to me about Petitjean: in the first, he told me that Petitjean's regiment had been having a hard time of it; and here now, in the second, he informs me that Petitjean has been wounded. The fellow's

22. The Oustric affair was a financial scandal which caused the fall of the Tardieu cabinet in 1929.
Léon Brunschvicg (1869–1944): the dominant figure in French philosophy between the wars.
23. Armand Petitjean: a bookseller friend of Paulhan's.
24. André Suarès (1868–1948): essayist, critic and Christian mystic poet utilizing themes from Celtic mythology; he adopted the pseudonym Caërdal, and published a 'Chronique de Caërdal' in most issues of the *NRF* for 1939.

the hero of the *NRF*. Not that I envy him, or begrudge him his glory. But I suspect Paulhan of establishing a discreet parallel, in each of his letters, to keep me on tenterhooks. And then I'm not sure that his 'Do you suffer much from the mud and cold?' isn't ironical. So I insist upon the innocuous nature of the war, in order to display a cynicism that is my only defence.

But there's something more. Within myself I feel the birth of rights I want to stifle. These are new rights. The rights of the combatant. Let us say more modestly, the rights of the serviceman [*mobilisé*]. There are two kinds of servicemen's rights – and they're contradictory. The first, with which I shall never be infected, are crude: to claim the admiration and gratitude of civilians, to feel oneself important and heroic. That soldier who, recalled from leave on 15 August, *before* the war, was putting his feet up on the railway-carriage seat with the words: 'We what's gonna get arselves killed.' To feel essentially different from civilians, and deny them any right to talk about the war – whether to speak ill of it or to speak well of it – because only those who are fighting it can talk about it. But the other kind, those that are a threat to me, are more insidious: since it's *my* war, I have the right to belittle it. Let others find it terrible – those who aren't fighting – but I have the right to say, very modestly : 'Oh, no, it's really nothing.' And I once again find the tactic I've mentioned in connection with my political stance – or at least I can see it peeping through – that ruse of my pride that I called placing myself with the weak against the strong among whom I'd naturally belong: with the wife against the husband, with the child against the parents, with the pupils against the teachers. Horrified to find myself part of a new elite equipped with its own rights – the elite of 'servicemen' – I can already feel stirring within me a tendency to range myself with the civilians against the combatants, by the way I tell them: 'Oh no, don't get any wrong ideas. It's not hard, out there. You haven't got any duty to us, etc.' This wouldn't be so distasteful if I were really a combatant. But the fact is I'm not: just in uniform. And I know very well that if I were actually in combat, the result would be to exaggerate this tendency in me. But since I'm not in combat, I should just hold my peace on the subject.

Tuesday 21

Thanks to Cassou, I understand the specific logic, and the dialectical developments, of that idea of humanity whose emergence he places around the middle of the July Monarchy. The analytical spirit of the 18th century dissolves communities into individuals. The French

Revolution is an analytical and critical revolution, in the sense that it envisages a society as a contract among *individuals*. The spirit of synthesis reappears with Maistre and Bonald.[25] It opposes the critical spirit, asserting that analysis destroys that which it dismembers. For example, the spirit of analysis will see a king as a man on a throne. The conservative spirit will retort that an analysis of this kind destroys precisely what makes the king: his royalty. The theoretical triumph of the spirit of synthesis over the spirit of analysis is expressed in politics by a triumph of conservative thought over revolutionary thought. Society becomes a hierarchy of irresolvable forms. If revolutionary force proved able to overturn monarchical institutions, this was because the analytical spirit had dissolved them first, by destroying their meaning. For to reduce an institution to its elements is to miss its meaning, which lies in its irresolvable totality.

Under the influence of these official doctrines, there occurs among reformers and revolutionaries a dissociation between the spirit of analysis and the spirit of revolution. The *motives* [*mobiles*] for changing the social structure remain and increase, but the reasons [*motifs*] have to be altered. The spirit of analysis is crushed; what remains of it is cornered by old Voltairian liberals. It's the spirit of synthesis that will be called upon by the new opposition to supply it with reasons. Conservatives employ the spirit of synthesis when they declare that a whole is not reducible to its elements – hence that society cannot be reduced to individuals. So the revolutionary will no longer think of demanding individual rights as in 1789. He abandons that outworn conception of the world, the analytical *Weltanschauung*, whose edge has grown blunt. He will no longer pit the elements against the whole, individuals against society. Instead he will seek a vaster synthesis incorporating the disparate societies within it, so that he may reproach each of these for rebelling against that totality, just as conservatives reproach individuals for rebelling against the collective totality.

The synthetic object is soon found: it is humanity. But this expression 'humanity' may have many meanings. The modern meaning – the human condition of every individual – has not yet been unveiled. Consequently, humanity must perforce be the historical totality of the men who have lived, are living and will live. This allows revolutionaries and reformists to pit a human tradition against the mon-

25. Joseph de Maistre (1753–1821): moralist, Christian philosopher, nationalist and monarchist opponent of enlightenment ideas and the progress of physical science.

Louis de Bonald (1754–1840): conservative politician and political philosopher, supporter of church and crown.

archical or national tradition. But this humanity, as soon as it is named and thought as a totality, at once transcends its history. There is no history other than *in* humanity. Here again, a door might have been opened towards the human condition. But the synthetic spirit of '48 passed it by. The only concept transcending history which it found was that of *species*. But this notion of species was furnished by biology. It is necessarily accompanied by the complementary idea of planet Earth, since a species undergoes the conditioning of its milieu. So there is a double degradation here: that of human condition into human species, and that of the world into planet Earth.

But the paradoxical thing (albeit fairly common, in fact) is that these degraded concepts have not yet been glimpsed. The degradation is historically anterior to the notions it degrades. The inauthentic presents itself before authenticity. Through the idea of species, man is thrown out of himself not *into* the world, in the Heideggerian sense, but amid the world or, more accurately, upon the earth. The intimacy of his connection with the world is indeed sensed, but in the degraded form of a symbiosis with the earth and the physical universe. In this sense, Ballanche may well speak of 'cosmic man', but what this means is clear: the idea of a cosmic *fauna*, that's the idea of being-in-the-world. Whence phrases like: 'man's earthly destiny'. Whence the appearance – at this watershed – of the idea of *work* or man's action upon the earth. Idea of the St-Simonians: the exploitation of planet Earth by humanity. Corbon writes: 'The most significant of life's phenomena . . . is the progressive constitution of the instrument of work, and the progressive increase of human action upon the world.'[26] We can see here that work and the creation of tools are given as phenomena of life. But not of individual life: of the life of the species. And Renan : 'The great reign of the spirit will begin only when the material world has been entirely subdued by man.'[27] Whence the dignity of *work*, by means of which the human species each day takes more effective and complete possession of the universe. Whence the sanctity of work: 'O work, sacred law of the world', Lamartine (*Jocelyn*).[28]

26. Anthime Corbon (1808–91): artisan-journalist, vice-president of the constituent assembly in 1848, later abandoned socialism and wrote *Le Secret du peuple de Paris* (1863) as an exposé of the 'real' nature of the working class, before becoming a senator for life in 1875.

27. Ernest Renan (1823–92): historian, philologist and critic, author of numerous biblical studies, notably *Vie de Jésus*, first volume of *Origines du Christianisme* (1863–83). Opposed to fundamentalist doctrines, he argued that it should be recognized that the future of the world lay in the progress of science.

28. *Jocelyn*: narrative poem by Alphonse-Marie-Louis de Prat de Lamartine (1790–

Why sanctity? Because the idea of human species has two sides: a biological and a religious aspect. For man it is a religion, because every individual is a 'collective being' (St-Simon) and always lives in a 'corner of the human species' (Blanqui). Humanity for him is a fleshly and spiritual environment. He is never on earth except *through* that humanity. It's the privileged species, which is absolute and an end in itself. Cassou rightly insists upon this aspect of humanitarianism: 'It is by a religious act that man separates himself from his beliefs and his religions, to find his satisfaction in that Religion through which he reveals himself to himself as species . . .' (Cassou, p.43). St-Simonianism and positivism are religions: 'Humanity has a religious future' (St-Simon). But these religions are degraded like the rest, since their object is a species. There is a sort of racism of humanity here.

It is to guard against this *thingism* that the second aspect of the notion of species is useful: its biological aspect. The discovery of the century is that species *evolve*. Ballanche is the first to use this expression. Human progress will stem from the most silent and organic forces of the species; it now relies upon transformism. The human species, rather than being poor and static as it had been in Linnaeus's day, thus bears within itself a future still undifferentiated and unknowable, but of immense richness. Thereby we recover the adorably undifferentiated character of the mystics' God, that we were losing through the degradation and inauthenticity of the former notions. At the same time, thingism and idolatry are avoided: humanity is adored, but it *is* not, it becomes. Thereby, moreover, it contrasts all the better with present societies and their political systems. which simply *are*. As Cassou says: 'Henceforth the future is the substance in which we are, we live and we move.' [p. 66]

Whence – final dialectical avatar of the idea of human species – the cult of woman, as universal womb and symbol of fecundity. It is through woman that the Future of humanity is secured for us.

Thus the synthetic idea of a totality of men is transformed by its own dialectic into the idea of biological species transcending its history. This summons up the complementary idea of 'terrestrial environment', which is transformed into a 'universe to conquer'. This idea of the conquest of the globe as humanity's specific mission will

1869), recounting the story of a young seminarist who falls in love with a girl dressed as a boy: he becomes a priest notwithstanding, she burns out her life in dissipation, he absolves her before she dies and himself dies shortly afterwards. The poem contains careful descriptions of peasant life: see especially its ninth section 'Les Laboureurs' from which this passage is taken.

recur in the antiphysis of Comte and Marx: it endows *work* with a dignity that will recur in the Marxist definition of value. Yet the idea of transformism, which is attached to that of species, combats the inherent tendency of the concept of 'mankind' to become impoverished and set. And the individual lost amid the human substance, like Spinozan man in his infinite God, does not find it hard to adore this synthetic whole of which he forms part.

The doctrine does not hold together. And yet it has marked us. Humanitarianism gave birth to our humanism. Gide himself is marked by it. One of these days I shall copy in this very notebook some curious humanitarian passages from his journal, where he says that God is in the future. When all is said and done, if we are looking for political principles today, we have really only four conceptions of man to choose between. The narrow conservative synthetic conception (*AF*, for example);[29] the updated narrow synthetic conception (racism, Marxism); the broad synthetic conception (humanitarianism); the analytical conception (anarchic individualism). But nowhere do we find any reference to the human condition, determined on the basis of individual 'human reality'.

We get through an enormous quantity of newspapers here (to black out the windows, for the toilets, etc.), but we never use today's copy. Keller forbids it. Although by noon it has been read, reread and commented on by everyone – and everyone, moreover, has agreed there was nothing in it – if we make as if to take it, he indignantly seizes it from our hands: 'Not that un, it's today's.' He requires every newspaper to do its stint, of mysterious and also variable duration, in the schoolroom. This stint once over, the newspaper is classed as over-ripe, demoted from its status as a newspaper and reduced to the rank of mere paper. Degrading action of pure duration and ageing.

Keller is neither fearful nor a poet. Yet when he is on guard-duty at the school, instead of sleeping on the straw mattress like all the rest of us, he stays awake all night. We have never been able to discover why. If you ask him next day: 'What did you do?' he says: 'Oh, I read the paper till midnight. At three I had a snack. At four I had a shit.' – 'But why do you stay awake?' He grows flustered and tongue-tied, or else he says: 'I dunno, we've still got light . . .' All next day he's in a daze

29. *AF—Action Française*: extreme right-wing political group founded in 1899, associated with the names of Charles Maurras and Léon Daudet; it was monarchist, Catholic, anti-Semitic and ended in support of the Vichy régime of 1940–44.

and periodically nods off in his seat, breaking the silence with plaintive little snores.

AUTUMN

The leaves fall, we shall fall like them
The leaves die because God wills it so
But we, we shall die because the English will it so
By next spring no one will remember either dead leaves
    or slain *poilus*, life will pass over our graves.

This text is printed on a ragged-edged, leaf-shaped piece of paper, with veins and a beautiful russet tint. It's a leaflet that German planes dropped two hundred metres away and that a peasant picked up. He brought it to us, we pass it from hand to hand. Beneath the text, a skull wearing a helmet.

Pieter complains that his wife is starting to call him a shirker. She writes to him, in connection with an urgent business letter: 'Write it yourself, since you've got nothing else to do. I don't have time myself.'

Wednesday 22

Read in Cassou's *48* the following sentence: 'Flora Tristan's exotic blood and adventurous destiny were to be reborn in that sublime hero of art and anarchy, her grandson Paul Gauguin.'[30] [p 98] Unpleasant shock. In relation to Gauguin, Van Gogh and Rimbaud, I have a distinct inferiority complex because they managed to destroy themselves. Gauguin through his exile, Van Gogh through his madness, and Rimbaud most of all, because he managed to give up even writing. I am more and more convinced that, in order to achieve authenticity, something has to snap. This is really the lesson Gide drew from Dostoevsky, and it's what I shall show in the second book of my novel.[31] But I have protected myself against anything snapping. I have bound myself hand and foot to my desire to write. Even in war I fall on my feet, because I think at once of writing what I feel and what I see. If I question myself, it's in order to write down the results of this examination; and it's clear to me I only *dream* of questioning my desire to write, because if I really tried even for an hour to hold it in

30. Flora Tristan (1803–44): feminist and revolutionary socialist writer, associate of Fourier and some of the Saint-Simonians, founder of the Union Ouvrière.

31. i.e. in *Le Sursis* (*The Reprieve*, Harmondsworth 1963), second volume of *Les Chemins de la liberté*, now in *Oeuvres romanesques*, Paris 1981.

abeyance, place it in parenthesis, all reason for questioning anything whatsoever would collapse. It's clear to me there's a self-confidence here that's most annoying to others (to T., for example, or the Moon Woman[32]), since it derives after all from the fact that I'm bastard enough to leave something of myself *intact*.

One of Naudin's stories. A German officer can be seen across the Rhine, looking over at France through binoculars. A French lieutenant orders a man to shoot him. The man refuses. 'Why?' – 'He's a man. He hasn't done me any harm. I don't want to take a man's life.' The officer orders a second soldier (he had only two with him), who refuses likewise. Then he tells them: 'All right, both of you fire; that way you won't know which of you has brought him down.' They fire, and the officer falls.

To make me doubt the truth of this story, it's enough that it's Naudin who's recounting it. Still, the fact is he does recount it, and without the least indignation: as a quite natural event. The fact is *people* are recounting it – for he has certainly got it ᶠrom somebody, who has got it from somebody else, etc. The Warrant-officer's re-action is quite different (old war-horse): 'Well, there's two men who've had it lucky. If it had been me, I'd have pumped a dozen rounds into 'em and serve 'em right.' Annoyed, I explain to him that such isolated exchanges of fire are useless and cost us purely wasted lives. He pipes down at once, since he has great respect for education, continuing on a quite different track: 'Batteries mustn't fire without orders, because they can be located by sound.' And in order to recapture his self-assurance, upon that selfsame educational terrain where he has just lost it, he explains the principles of location by sound on the board, chalk in hand.

Naudin, moreover, has an odd kind of detailed pessimism, that comes from puerility; from an unconscious sulking at the war; from a wish somehow to get a taste of this elusive war and to redeem his inactivity through myths; that comes, lastly, from a peasant's whining self-importance. It is not enough for him that the German planes dropped

---

32. T. = 'Tania Zazoulich', or Wanda Kosakiewicz, younger sister to Olga, with whom Sartre had a love affair for several years after 1937 (see *Lettres au Castor*, Paris 1983, passim), and who remained close to him for the rest of his life. She acted in several of his plays, under the name Marie-Olivier.

The Moon Woman was 'Marie Girard', with whom Sartre had a love affair in Berlin in 1933–34; for a description of her other-worldly character, see Simone de Beauvoir, *The Prime of Life*, Harmondsworth 1965, pp. 183–84.

leaflets yesterday; he wants them also to have showered the area with fountain-pens that explode if you touch them. We vainly explain to him that they cannot *simultaneously* carry out propaganda in favour of peace, and compromise this by 'atrocities'. He falls silent at last, overcome by our voices but not by our reasons. He chews over his pessimism in silence. In the end, he goes out slamming the door and the Warrant-officer, self-important and sorrowful, points to the door that has just closed: 'A fellow like that would be disastrous for the morale of a battery. A leader, a real leader . . . ' The door reopens, Naudin comes back in and now the Warrant-officer will never tell us what a real leader should do; he fidgets about, that suppressed speech visibly burning his tongue.

These latent rebellions of Naudin's are most interesting. He is a *stunted* rebel. He is shot through and embittered by envy: a mobilized peasant, he envies the workers who stayed in the factories or are going back there; a staff-sergeant on reserve, he envies the regular NCOs who are getting army pay; he also envies public employees, who are still receiving their peacetime salaries. But this discontent will never reach the point of revolt, because too many factors brake and disperse it: Catholicism, righteous conformism, stupidity, empty-headedness, inability to tot up his grievances and make a nice big bunch of them, inferiority complex with respect to education. And then he 'has property'. But let a smooth-talking fascist come along to muster his local resentments under the banner of righteousness, and Naudin will march. All the way? I don't know, because he's a coward. But he'll march.

At the start of the war Naudin used to say: 'I've been called up three times: in September '38, and in March and August '39. I'm fed up with it, things can't go on like this and I want to have it out once and for all: I'd rather have a few fireworks and then some peace and quiet when it's all over.' Three months have gone by. He had a big disappointment when the NCOs got their pay. At present, in between his fitful bouts of heroism, he says resentfully: 'All I ask is to get back safe and as soon as possible.' That apart, he's a big, strapping fellow, whose body is happy to be alive. He's twenty-nine, good-looking, red-cheeked, a light, pleasing voice. Pieter says he must be the cock of the walk in his village. Good muscles, but already a bit of a stomach. Dimpled chin. His beard grows so thickly that his cheeks, wherever they're not red, are iron-blue. Comical, questing look of a puppy; something of an adventurer too, a heart-breaker.

In civilian life, every evening Keller places a ladder against the front of his house, connects two loop-wires to the electricity supply line, and is thus able to light his premises without going via the meter. Each morning, as dawn breaks, he fetches his ladder again and disconnects the wires. Later, after the war, his ambition is to buy a plot of land and build on it. But he'll have no gas in his house because with gas, savings of this kind are impossible. He'll have an electric cooker, that he'll supply by the same method. 'It's a big advantage of the suburbs over Paris,' he says to Paul. 'In Paris, you see, all the mains are in steel pipes.'

Thursday 23

In the evacuated districts over towards Sarreguemines, the soldiers billeted there have smashed everything, crapped in the beds, broken into the cupboards with axes. I take this opportunity of noting that the French 'from the interior' – though received with open arms by the Alsatian population, lodged free of charge by the townspeople, cosseted by the girls, applauded by the children – condemn the Alsatians severely. Sometimes, as they drink their Alsace wine and eat their sauerkraut, they commiserate with each other: 'What do you expect?' said a well-read sergeant gravely the other day, 'those people will never be like us.' 'Yes,' he said sadly. 'we were too soft, much too soft in 1918. Respecting beliefs is all very fine, but we should have made Frenchmen of them first.' Many of the soldiers are upset by hearing the children speak Alsatian: 'Just imagine. One hour of French a week, in their schools!' They slap their thighs in indignation. They have all met some Alsatian who has told them: 'I'm neither French nor German, but Alsatian.' Once, when the Beaver fended off the advances of a drunken soldier in a Brumath inn, he said to her with displeasure: 'So you're Alsatian, then!' And as he returned to the attack: 'Are you for us or against us?' While gorging themselves on the local sausages, they'll sometimes shake their heads gravely: 'Savages! You can't find a hunk of *saucisson sec* anywhere in Brumath!' And the other day a corporal lamented: 'I tell you, I'm a *charcutier*, I got the Brumath butcher talking and, d'you know, they take the cows with foot-and-mouth or TB, scrape the meat a bit, and that does them as sausage-meat. That's how it's made, their famous Strasbourg sausage.' And a warrant-officer: 'You'll see: the real joy of leave won't be to see the old lady or the kids again, it'll be to hear French spoken by Frenchmen from France.' Obviously, this righteous indignation can quite easily lead to crapping in the evacuees' beds. Moreover, the mothers and wives of these good Frenchmen, for their part, make it very clear to the Alsatian women that they really mustn't get the idea they are French. In the Limousin or the Dordogne, they're treated like dirt. Poupette writes that when the town-crier of St-Germain-les-Belles walks round the village to announce the evacuees' arrival, he finishes his harangue with these words: 'And don't forget they really are French.'[33]

This morning we discuss politics. Hang, Pieter, Paul, myself, on the organization of Europe after the war. We say a whole number of silly things. Naudin, at the other end of the room is trying to write a letter. The noise of our conversation prevents him from doing so, and he fumes: 'You give me a pain in the ass, you really do.' Hang tries to interest him in our discussion, but to no avail. So I say to him out of the blue, as he clutches his head in his hands and tries to shut himself off from the world: 'You know, Naudin, near Wissembourg the Germans flayed a French prisoner alive.' He gets up and comes over to me with a questing look: 'Who told you that?' I reply, purposely vague: 'A fellow . . .' I give a few details: 'There were two prisoners. One of them wouldn't talk, so they flayed him alive. They threatened to pour petrol on the other one's clothes and put a match to him. Then he got scared and blurted everything out.' Naudin is outraged and forgets all about his letter: 'Oh, the bastards! Just let them come! Man to man, I'd like to see them try; we'd soon see if they can flay me.' He goes off to sit with folded arms in a corner, shaking his head over and over again, terrified, furious, serious and happy: he has got his ration of horror for this morning.

Isolated by his rank, the Warrant-officer lends himself to our discussions without giving himself fully.

Last night, woken abruptly around one in the morning, I started to think about will. I haven't understood everything by a long chalk, but I think I've unravelled the question a bit.

I can see, in the first place, that the classical conception of volition, as a specific act arising within consciousness, comes to grief on two shoals.

In the first place, a voluntary act – just like consciousness, which must be consciousness of itself – should itself be willed. I want to go to Paris. All right. But if my will is motivated by a desire, it is no longer a

33. Poupette: sister of Simone de Beauvoir.

will, a privileged act arising from within consciousness; it is a motivated structure similar to others. Will must be willed. Otherwise my will to go to Paris would be involuntary. This is what Kant clearly saw, with his autonomy of will: a will that aspires to be right for the occasion of the act it wills. It would be of no avail, as he also saw, to derive will from the Ego, for it would still emanate from a given (it makes little different if this given, rather than *being*, *lasts* like Bergson's deep Ego: will, in any case, will be a *natural* emanation of it). Will can derive from the Ego only if the Ego derives from will. So will, like consciousness, reflects back upon itself. And, as with consciousness, unless we are to fall into a whole reflexive series of willing and willed wills, we must grant that this reflection back upon itself corresponds to the infrastructure of will. So what is involved seems to be a kind of ontological argument for will: will willing itself as a willing of X.[34] We thus have a non-thetic infrastructure (as with consciousness): will (to) will; and a transcendent voluntary intentionality: the willed willing is a willing *of* X.

However, the analogy with the typical structure of consciousness should not deceive us here. That a consciousness should be consciousness (of) self, nothing better; for in the non-thetic consciousness, consciousness is not an object for consciousness. What is involved here is not *knowledge*, which supposes object-subject duality, but the translucidity intrinsic to consciousness as its existential condition. On the other hand, it seems that this willed willing is of a piece with knowledge – in other words, it inherently involves a duality. If we are not to be satisfied by mere words, it is impossible to conceive of the immanent unity of will and its object, be it even an act of willing. And this for the obvious reason that the object of will is future. It is a certain type of possibility whose ontic substance is the future. There is thus by definition a temporal interval between will and its object, however small this interval may be. The idea of an act of willing willed in the infrastructure of a single consciousness is contradictory. Yet this is where the idea of voluntary act logically ends up – unless we make of it a strictly determined process (but then the voluntary act has lost its specificity, and it becomes impossible to distinguish it from desire, passion, mechanisms, etc.).

The second difficulty is that the object of my will is distant from me by virtue of its position in time. Now freedom itself, which you posit in the volitional act, forbids you to will *against* time. You want to take

34. Throughout this passage, *le vouloir* has been translated as 'willing' or 'act of willing', as distinct from *volonté* = 'will' or *volition* = volition.

such and such a step tomorrow. But who guarantees you against yourself? Tomorrow, your will of today will have fallen into the past, outside consciousness; it will have become ossified, and you will be entirely free with respect to it: free to adopt it once again as your own or to commit yourself against it. One cannot swear an oath either against oneself or against time. The pledge to oneself, prototype of all pledges, is a vain incantation by means of which man strives to charm his future freedom. Moreover, he swears only when he is quite aware there is a risk he may break his pledge. The pledge is an avowal of distress. Well, every volitional act of the above-mentioned kind – and we often make them – is ultimately nothing other than a disguised pledge. What I will is my tomorrow's willing. And we indeed find again the duality willed willing, but I precisely cannot will my subsequent willing. If I roll my eyes, if I clench my fists and grit my teeth saying: 'I *will* be faithful to her', I will emptily, I will a host of particular willings that threaten to escape me one by one.

I would term volitions of this kind – very common, by the way – empty volitions, by analogy with Husserl's empty intentions. I fear they may have served as models for the classical conception of will. They emerge in the course of consciousness and are accompanied by a strong tension, which is no doubt what gives the impression they are full. But they precisely lack the flesh that could fill them, the very act of willing that seems the original phenomenon and to which we find ourselves returned. More than one person, noting the ineffectiveness of these empty volitions, has been induced by disappointment and scepticism to consider as will only consciousness that extends through the execution of the act. There is no longer any difference between volition and act. Not only is my act evidence for me of my willing, but at the same time my willing is given precise definition by the act, in the sense in which Alain says that the execution of the statue rough-hews the sculptor's governing idea until, eventually, the concrete idea at its last point of development and richness is the statue itself. It is the everlasting circle: acts must be judged by intentions. But the intentions themselves, by what shall we judge them except by the acts themselves? The act is the material support of volition and that which makes it explicit, just as speech is support and the making explicit of thought. The act is the external aspect of will, and will the internal unificatory theme of the act; no will without act, any more than thought without speech.

I shall not condemn this severe, moralistic decision that is tantamount to judging the intention by the result. It is an excellent precaution. And precisely, it is the existence of empty volitions that enforces this precaution in order to uncover and eliminate them. However, if I examine myself at this moment, I know and have proof that there exist in me a certain number of full, effective willings which are nonetheless not conjoined with realization. The will to remain steadfast and firm, regret nothing, and not succumb to the blues; to question myself; tomorrow or the day after, to leave Brumath for Morsbronn without regret; to finish my novel before starting something else; to keep up this notebook every day; to write to the Beaver every third day and my mother every second. Decisions closer at hand: to reply to Paulhan tomorrow – or even this evening after finishing with the notebook – to the Beaver, to T., etc., etc. More faraway decisions still, affecting my return to civilian life, when peace has returned. Yet for the time being I do nothing to realize them – and I have nothing to do.

And yet these are not empty volitions, nor are they full volitional acts which once existed and are now lying dormant until such time as they can manifest themselves anew by acts. These are not memories of wishes, but real wishes, actually existing and constituting my very being. Everybody can find in themselves similar deep-seated, avid wishes that are nevertheless not *realized*. Does the error, perhaps, not come from the fact that will is usually considered as an *act* of consciousness, brief and localized in time? In other words, precisely as an empty volition? Which comes down to the same thing as saying that consciousness – usually not voluntary – may in certain conditions take on a voluntary structure. But I have already signalled in my 2nd notebook that it's impossible to tack will onto consciousness if it's not already there. So we must return to Spinoza's doctrine and identify will and consciousness. I shall explain what this means tomorrow.

This evening, all of a sudden, I feel a bit wretched. But then it passes.

Friday 24

Fresh bout of sleepwalking by Paul last night. He suddenly begins shouting: 'Hey Hey Hey Hey Hey! O-oh!' The last 'oh' slow-drawn, vibrant and shocked. 'Paul!' I say.

Paul (in a sleepy voice): 'Whassit?'

I: 'Paul!'

He (with an embarrassed, polite little laugh, and in the tone in which you tell a person who has come up claiming to know you: 'I really have no idea who you are.') : 'I have no idea where I am.' And then, in amusement at his own plight, and with a kind of psychological gluttony: 'No! really no idea!' He sniggers.

I: 'You're at Brumath.'

Paul (very much annoyed): 'Oh, I know that.'

I: 'Why did you cry out?'

Paul (in bad faith): 'I? Cry out?' Silence, then I hear a great stir, the rustle of silk, heavy objects being dragged along, panting.

I: 'What are you doing?'

Paul (dignified and offended): 'Nothing. Only I'm awake.' And *immediately afterwards* an even, strong breathing that soon changes into little snores. We agree this morning that he remained fast asleep throughout this conversation. He answered me – almost properly – without having woken up.

Let us go back to will. I note that its essential structure is transcendence, since it aims at a beyond that can be only in the future. But this transcendence presupposes a given to be transcended. Will needs the world and the resistance of things. It needs them, not simply as a purchase to help it reach its goal, but essentially, in itself, in order to be will. For only the resistance of something real enables one to distinguish what is possible from what is, and to envisage the possible beyond what is. Here, as everywhere, the real is anterior to the possible. The world of dream, which is imaginary, does not allow this distinction, because in dream what is conceived receives from conception itself a kind of dreamed existence. In a dream, there is no distinction between wanting to drink and dreaming that one is drinking. So the mind, victim of its omnipotence, *cannot* wish. It cannot even wish to wake up. It will only dream that it does wake up. For it to be itself again, the real must invade its dream in some way. Thus the dreamer is bound hand and foot by his absolute power.

The same would be the case, if we take it to the limit, with a divine mind that proceeded by creative intuitions. If, for this mind, simple conception is enough to produce the object intuitively, if it meets no inertial resistance, if there is no temporal gap between conception and realization, God is dreaming. His creations cannot be distinguished from his affections. He is imprisoned in himself and cannot will anything. Divine omnipotence is tantamount to a total subjective servitude. God is precipitated from creation to creation without being able to 'distance himself' either from himself or from the object.

There is no will that is not finite or does not belong to a finite being, and the finitude of will derives not from any external limitations but from its very essence. A world's resistance is contained within will, as the principle of its nature. And since we cannot conceive either that

will is posterior to the world – which would take us back to materialism – or that the world is produced by will – which would cast us back
into the domain of creative intuitions and suppress will forthwith – it
is clearly necessary to conceive world and will as being given simultaneously. There is no will except that of a being thrown into the
world. It is the world which frees consciousness vested by its own
dreams – by its total freedom. Will characterizes the human condition, as the necessity for a being abandoned in the world to discover its
own goals beyond a real that makes their immediate realization impossible. It is defined by the necessary gap between the goal and the
conception of the goal. There can be will only if the whole world is
interpolated between my consciousness and its ends. Let a genie give
me power to realize my desires there and then, and at once I fall asleep
– being unable to hold them off, to *prevent* them from being realized.
This is what has been dimly perceived by all those story-tellers who
spin us tales of wishes being granted but then taking a tragic turn.

Will thus appears as a 'being-in'-the-world that is a 'being-for'
changing the world. Any willed possible is always only a change in a
given situation: a change that can be *willed* only if it appears on the
horizon of the given situation as the outcome of a development of that
situation's specific potentialities. In this sense, we perceive in order to
change, and we will the change on the basis of the perceived. All
perception emerges against a background of possible change – but
regulated change – which it simultaneously defers, by virtue of its
very materiality. To perceive a window as closed is possible only in an
act that projects through it the regulated possibility of opening it.
Without this act, the window would be neither closed nor open: it
would be nothing at all. But conversely, without the present closed
state of the window, there could be only a nihilating image of an open
window, or – in the case of the magically realized wish – the magical
appearance of an open window that is not *thing*, because it cannot
resist (it will be annihilated or closed as I wish), and that will not be
able to rid consciousness of its immanence. So the primary structure
of will is to be a transcendence that posits a possibility in the future,
beyond any currently given state of the world. This makes clear the
deeper meaning of will, which can be itself only by escaping from
itself, only by leaping out of itself towards the future. It is pro-ject
(*Vorwurf*).[35] The obvious consequence of this is that the world is

35. In Heidegger, from whom this concept is taken, the standard term rendered by
French and English translators as 'project/*projet*' is, in fact, *Entwurf*. *Vorwurf*, much
rarer, usually carries the meaning of 'reproach' or something 'thrown in a person's
teeth'.

known in its present state only on the basis of the future. Thus will and perception are inseparable. Which further means that will is not an individual act arising at a given instant of the temporal chain, but the relationship between consciousness and its own possibles.

It remains to be determined what this relationship between consciousness and its possibles is. So far we have basically followed Heidegger. But now we can follow him no longer. Effectively, for him, the *Dasein* [being-there] *is* quite simply its own possibilities. But it would then be useless to posit transcendence like him, if we fall back into another kind of immanence. Will, in effect, is the power that consciousness has to escape itself. All immanence is a dream state. Even the Heideggerian immanence, since being *rediscovers* itself as possibilities beyond the world. And I am well aware that *there is time* between the projecting being and the projected possibilities. But as this time is read backwards, it loses its separating virtue and ceases to be anything but the substance of the *Dasein*'s union with itself. The possibilities of consciousness, in fact, are transcendent. It sustains them, it wills them, it is willing consciousness *of* these possibilities, but, precisely, they are outside it. They draw their transcendent objectivity from the matter through which they are grasped, which is precisely the present object to be modified. So they are external existences of a very particular kind. Let us name them exigencies.

By this must be understood objects that demand [*exigent*] to be realized. They are options upon us. But if they only demanded they would not be *willed*, for we can conceive of exigencies that would remain unsatisfied: 'meliora video proboque deteriora sequor'.[36] They inspire confidence as well: I *foresee* their realization. And I have the impression of being privileged in this foresight. It seems so obvious as to be virtually certain. Other future objects – those that are not willed – I may indeed *foresee*, but their possibility is itself a probability. Whereas the possibility of the willed object is certainty. For example, it may happen that I do not in fact write the word 'certainty' which comes to my pen: I may be disturbed in a thousand and one ways. But I know that *if* I am not disturbed, it will be born: I know that what will be disturbed is *its* birth. I shall not be prevented from forming any other word than that; and it will have this existence at least, of being the one whose birth has been prevented. Whereas if I entrust all my fortune to the waves in the form of merchandise

---

36. The quotation, which should run 'Video meliora proboque, deteriora sequor' ('I see the Good and approve it, I follow Evil'), is given to Medea by Ovid in *Metamorphoses*, VII, 20.

intended to be sold abroad, it is possible that a shipwreck may ruin me by destroying the cargo, but I shall never know if what the shipwreck prevented was really a *successful venture*: it might equally well have been my ruin, due to unfair competition, miscalculation, etc. The successful venture has only been *probably* prevented. With these possibles/options, on the other hand, I do not know them in a contemplative sense, I realize them. This means that they appear on the horizon of my actions, as their meaning. Heidegger put it well when he said that we do not thematize them. In point of fact, to thematize them would be to nihilate them, to make concepts or images of them. It is by acting that we cause them, albeit unnamed, to emerge most clearly.

Thus the meaning of our situation is given at every instant by these possibles/options, noematic correlatives of our will awaiting us in the future. And it is they that motivate and shape our perceptions. Let us note that they are *my* possibles in two senses: first, because they are my own options, as we have seen; then, because they are the objective and transcendent image of my being-in-the-world. In effect, these options have a lien on our own future. Heidegger rightly signalled that the world is 'that whereby human reality discloses to itself what it is'.[37] It's for us that these options exist. For us or for others. That is to say, ultimately, for a human reality. But the error would be to believe that this possible human reality, projected beyond the world by *our* human reality, *is* our human reality. It can only be transcendent, precisely because it is on the other side of the world, beyond options. Options are the noematic correlative of projects that are realized through acts, and projected human reality is the synthetic unity of options. Granted this is not thematized either, but we only have to think of it as unity of transcendent options to understand that it is transcendent itself. Consciousness cannot escape its immanence, cannot be an object of its own will, unless it projects its passivized image to the other side of the world. Thus the options waiting in the future are coloured by humanity. They are human possibilities and possibilities of mine. They exist 'for man's own end'. On the other hand, however, let them disappear and transcendent human reality will no longer be anything but an empty form, for it is merely the unity of these options. This is what we shall call the ipseity or shadow of consciousness beyond the world – which has nothing to do with the

---

37. Note that 'human reality' translates Sartre's *réalité humaine*, which is simply the rendering adopted by the French translator of Heidegger, Henri Corbin, for the latter's central concept of *Dasein*.

Ego, unity of reflexive consciousnesses.

It follows from this that at every instant a certain number of possibilities exist for consciousness, which are its own: which, in other words, appear to it in the form we have just described. These possibilities are the noematic correlative of what we shall call the will of consciousness, and in point of fact this will is nothing other than the particular-being of consciousness. Consciousness itself determines itself at every instant as the consciousness that has certain possibles. This must be understood existentially: it is the being of consciousness to be consciousness surrounded by certain possibles, and that is why its existence is qualitatively different from the existence of such and such another consciousness, that is why it has its own way of throwing itself into the world. And, of course, although this throw is single, the options that manifest it noematically may be legion, since this throw is refracted through the diversity of the world. All such options are simultaneously present to us, though not thematically. Thus, at every moment, to be consciousness is to will one's possibles and those alone. And the bond between consciousness and its possibles is as real and concrete a bond as that between consciousness and things perceived. Consciousness at every moment itself determines itself when it non-thematically grasps a concrete plurality of possibles/options, through a *situation*. The situation is the inert resistance of things, ordered in a hierarchy of motivations and a hierarchy of tools. Finally the situation is the world ordering itself as a whole in terms of the inherent possibles of consciousness.

In these conditions it will be understood that what I will, at every moment, is precisely my situation in the world. I *am* what I *will*. And that is inevitably limited. I am a finite being, deeply and totally responsible for myself. It will also be understood that what is usually called a singular voluntary act: *either* is an empty volition towards possibles that are not *my* possibles, but that I should like to be such for various reasons (the case with the pledge); *or else*, in the case of full volitions, are only the abrupt thematization of possibles as yet not thematized. In this latter case, far from there being a reinforcement of options, what is called volition is merely nihilation of the wish of consciousness. A provisional nihilation which, besides, no more suppresses the nihilated option than imaging nihilation suppresses the imagined presence. It abolishes it for as long as nihilation lasts, neither more nor less. Thus I am all will, since I will what I am. No particular volition can arise on this basis. To change one of my possibles is to change all my possibles at the same time; it is to change my situation; it is to will myself other. Something that happens constantly, moreover; but any modification, however frequent, is always existential and total.

In short, over against consciousness there is the totality of the real, at every moment, as group in situation. And this real comprises: things perceived – presences; options – values; options that are not *my* options – possibles that are not one's possibles. Certain of these realities are given thematically (things perceived, for example) and others non-thematically. There is consciousness *of* all this.

Options represent the real future, meaning of my present. But this future – future of the world, future of ipseity – *transcends* consciousness.

I would condemn someone definitively for a linguistic mannerism, but not because I'd seen him murder his mother.

Saturday 25

How injunctions operate in dreams: Paul wakes me up last night with his little stereotyped 'Hey Hey Hey Hey'. But he suddenly breaks off and stammers 'Sorry!', turns over and goes back to sleep. The striking thing is that in all the three months I have known him, he has never expressed his terror other than by these 'Hey Hey Hey Hey Hey! Oh!' This seems to be a set ritual. There is something indefinable in those 'Hey Hey Hey Hey': the irritable, fussy reprimand of a superior (teacher) – a bit of a pedant; the disconsolate impotence of an old man (my grandfather, when he was senile, used to utter similar cries if he lost his balance while walking in his room on my arm: 'Hey Hey Hey Hey! Hold me tight, my dear, hold me tight!'); something dry and sobbing, quavering. The final 'Oh!', on the other hand, spreads out with a kind of obviousness – as if the first cries signalled the prophetic reprimand for an imminent catastrophe, and the final 'Oh!' a lament for the catastrophe come to pass. At first, the fellow is in a hurry and his little prophetic cries attempt to warn, to check by a reprimand, as when one chides a child who is playing with some precious knick-knack. But the catastrophe overtakes him, there on the ground lies the knick-knack in fragments, and the last 'Oh!' is extended at leisure, prolonged into the shocked and bitter satisfaction of the prophet who sees his prophecy realized: 'It's just as I told you.' In general, if he's not woken, Paul bursts out immediately afterwards into inhuman cries. And then the movements begin: he sits up, gets onto his hands and knees and crawls round the room.

One of the oddest phenomena of this technical war will turn out to have been the methodical transplantation of the Alsatians. There had been refugees in '14, but they'd been uprooted from their native soil by the pressure of circumstances. The exodus of the Alsatians by contrast is organized; and instead of scattering them throughout France, the government has thought it wise to transport them by whole communes and villages, very carefully so as not to break them, together with their municipal councils and civil servants. 'Inspired' newspapers emphasize the fact with satisfaction: 'Strasbourg (Dordogne)' writes *L'Oeuvre*. But the result is obviously paradoxical: had they been isolated, they would have been disarmed, immersed in a social milieu that would have impregnated them. But as it was, entire little collectivities were transplanted along with their collective representatives, their customs and their ceremonies, but stripped of the environment to which those customs and those ceremonies are adapted: climate; geography; civilization materialized in architecture, style of houses, and farming. Not surprisingly, the more that social ritualism comes to lack real foundations, the more exacerbated and frenetic it becomes. It is now a kind of landless society, dreaming its spirituality instead of apprehending it through the thousand and one tasks of everyday life. This spurs pride as a defensive reaction, and an unhealthy tightening of social bonds. The result is a frenetic, upside-down society.

In such circumstances, it would not have been a bad idea to put these people into contact with centres of high culture: with the industrial civilization of Lyons, or the society of the Midi. Perhaps that was not possible. But what was done? They were packed off to the yokels of Limoges, lowest of the low, backward, slow-witted, grasping and poverty-stricken. Those Alsatians, still quite bedazzled by the memory of their ordered, well-tended fields and their fine houses, have landed up in that countryside or those dirty towns among suspicious, ugly and for the most part dirty people. It is enough to compare the magnificent farms of Ittenheim, for example, all their buildings grouped around a courtyard (most advanced form of the peasant house), with those box-like 'two-up-and-two-down' houses of the Limousin, to appreciate the disappointment and surprise the Alsatian communities must have felt. The contrast must have been exaggerated still further by the language difference, and by the inferiority complex of the Alsatians vis-à-vis France – a complex that obviously makes them all the more critical. Their standards of clean-liness must have been outraged by little towns like Thiviers, where only twelve years ago household refuse and excrement was still being emptied into open ditches.[38]

At any rate, the result is clear: every Alsatian who writes home describes the Limousins as *savages*. The word recurs in every letter, it is really a collective description: 'We are among savages.' The Limousins, for their part, react by calling the Alsatians 'Boches'. Without any particular animosity, apparently. More as acknowledge-ment of a fact. Naturally, quarrels ensued at first, until strict edicts established order. Naturally, with those little cancers scattered throughout it, the Limousin community is becoming more fiercely self-conscious. There are two chauvinisms confronting each other in those parts today. But what makes the whole thing worse is the incompetence of the public authorities. In many regions, fifty per cent of the evacuees have not yet got beds. The sick have not been cared for. Our landlady quotes us the example of a woman forced to go twelve kilometres every day to find the milk her children need. They pack two or three families at once into a barn, which means lack of privacy is a real ordeal: 'We don't dare get dressed any more,' writes an Alsatian woman, 'Thérèse's little boy (aged 14) is always there staring at us when we wash.' Apparently the Alsatian mayors are as much to blame as the prefects: they don't do a thing. As for the local inhabi-tants, they find all kinds of little ways of making a profit: rent out bundles of straw for ten *sous* apiece, etc. 'All that's hardly calculated to discourage autonomism,' Mistler sighs. Obviously. But the really strange thing is this direct contact between two provinces remaining whole and *organized*. It had never been seen before. It should be put under the same heading as those massive transplantations introduced by Russia for economic reasons, and carried on by Germany and Italy for political reasons.

The astonishing extent to which the Alsatian evacuees are concen-trated (a village of 1,000 inhabitants has to take in 1,100 of them) is justified, it seems, by a wish to keep intact the institutional framework – municipalities, prefectures, religious framework (parish council, etc.) – and not leave the individual (ferment of revolt) to himself.

Fluchtlings geld:[39] 10 francs apiece for each evacuee. Mistler says: 'In

38. This entire passage assumes a special resonance in view of the fact that Sartre's maternal family came from Alsace, whereas his father was born precisely at Thiviers.
39. *Fluchtlings geld*: German term, as used by the population of Alsace, for the

a village, you can get by with ten francs a day, and in the case of large families' – when each individual receives 10 francs – 'put some money aside.' Paul replies: 'Well, you know, you can save money in a village if you've got roots there, but not otherwise.'

Sunday 26

I notice that a strange and somewhat hypocritical modesty has held me back from recording my change of mood in the past seven or eight days. I haven't recorded it because I didn't feel it was 'interesting'. And in point of fact there isn't anything very exciting about it; but if this journal is the wartime story of a man who's neither really unfortunate nor especially well-off either, I must record all these variations scrupulously. I have not recorded them, or found them interesting, because they did not redound to my glory. In fact, for the past seven or eight days my warrior status has been getting me down. It hasn't been a question of 'the blues', or rage, or revolt. Rather one of imperceptible changes in the world: the poetic comfort of Brumath has vanished. It's a town I have left for ever. Our departure has been talked about too much. I am no longer here. It was going to become *querencia*;[40] now it is merely a charmless stage-set. It owed its poetry partly to its proximity to the front lines. Over to the east lay a beyond, all imbued with danger and exoticism. All that has disappeared. As Mistler was saying yesterday: 'Who thinks about the Germans?' The Warrant-officer, perhaps. But that's his profession.

Brumath has become a mere *domicile* bereft of meaning, and there's something gloomy and cold about it. Certain spots like the Taverne de l'Écrevisse, which had a kind of *worldly* and *human* charm, have suddenly lost it. In the latter case, this is due less to my mood than to progressive disclosure of the truth. In the beginning, those bold, much-courted serving-girls, who rubbed up against the men and beckoned them suddenly down to the cellar, whence they returned all dishevelled; that sly, pretty landlady, who looked like Jacqueline Delubac; and then the presence of that 'gilded youth' of infantrymen or chasseurs who'd been butterflies in civilian life (one a daddy's boy who lamented his Tabarin-dancer mistresses;[41] another a film actor, a plump, handsome little man); all that effort to recon-

---

allowance paid by the state to displaced persons; literally 'refugee money'.

40. Bullfighting term adopted from Hemingway, both by François Mauriac and by Sartre, to mean 'a favourite spot'.

41. Jacqueline Delubac: actress (1910–), former wife of Sacha Guitry.

Tabarin: Montmartre vaudeville theatre opened in 1910.

struct something resembling a Montmartre bar here; that selection
effected by the prices (with the less fortunate going a little further
down to the Café de la Boulangerie instead): all this gave the Écrevisse
a strange charm, at once comical and a bit depraved. But now that I
lunch there every day, I can see through it all: bourgeois vileness of
the gilded youth; mindless immorality of the two girls, who are as silly
as boarding-school misses; mercenary nature of the landlady.
Besides, the clientele has gradually changed: NCOs have replaced the
other ranks, and sometimes captains come there for intimate parties.
Of a morning, the Taverne de la Rose still has its charm, but habit
blunts it somewhat and I shall rediscover its strange poetry only later
in my memories. So behold a withered Brumath. The schoolroom is a
bit like a cage at present, a bit like an operating theatre, and a bit like
an office.

At the same time, the future is beginning to take shape and torment
me. It is no longer the nebula it was last September. First there's the
leave I'm expecting, which peoples my days with odd images: long
sojourns in dark, cold carriages; Paris gloomy with violet stars at the
street corners, its blackish mass at the foot of Sacré-Coeur, etc. And
then, I'm ashamed to admit, I'm starting to expect the war's end. Oh,
it's an imaginary belief: I'm expecting it as I expected peace to end
during the winter of ['38-] '39, I don't believe in it. But the truth is I'm
ill at ease in war, as I was ill at ease in peace in '38-'39. I thought I'd
settled down in October, and then I suppose the Beaver's visit threw
me somewhat off balance.[42] In hoping for peace – and a not too distant
one – I think I am participating in a collective phenomenon. All the
men who left with me were raring to go at the outset – I explained
about this in my first notebook. All, except the softies and sissies,
experienced the grotesque misfortunes of the stoic.[43] Whereupon they
decreed the war would last six years, which was a way of immersing
themselves in another stoicism. More fitting, perhaps: it was no
longer a question of the impatient heroism that goes to meet blows,
but of a long human patience schooling itself to suffer daily exile. At
the time, the newspapers were helping us: the aim was to frighten
Germany. When the notorious blitzkrieg failed to occur, England
responded by announcing she was preparing for three years of war.
To which Hitler responded at Danzig: 'Five years – ten years if need

---

42. De Beauvoir visited Sartre in Alsace from 1 to 5 November 1939.

43. A reference to something Sartre had been writing in his first notebook. See *Lettres
au Castor*, vol. I, p. 302: 'I'm writing at great length in my little notebook: the
misadventures of a Stoic. You can guess what kind: the circumstances are too ironically
easy and favourable for an honest Stoic such as me.'

be.' There was no lack of wise officers, then, to shake their heads and write in inspired papers: 'It will be long, longer than people think.' It was good publicity. And also a way of thinking opposed to '14. People did not want to repeat the mistake of those men who went off 25 years ago for a 'military stroll'. They preferred to err in the other direction. And like the others, I too was imbued with that sombre conviction, even though my personal optimism slyly induced me to hope for a short war. I followed a middle course and was fond of repeating: 'I've stocked up with enough courage to last me till the spring of '41.'

And then, all of a sudden, a rumour begins to circulate that the war will be a short one. Here, the first thing is a priest who reads in the tea-leaves and forecasts that Hitler will fall in December. And then come the discreet reflections of wise men (the same ones who were predicting a long war or others), some speaking about a mysterious possibility that the war may be 'cut short', others writing more frankly: 'I have a feeling the war will be shorter than people think.' Here, even the greatest pessimists are succumbing. Partly, no doubt, under the influence of this new propaganda (Is it organized? Is the aim to raise morale, which had fallen pretty low?); partly, too, because that long human patience is hard to acquire and they are dying of boredom. All these views reflect the image of my optimism back to me, and lo and behold hope returns. This is perhaps the hardest thing of all, because our daily life then becomes inhuman and absurd. At the same time, the war loses something of its fascinating allure. And peace will be a real swindle of the most unedifying kind, benefiting the ruling classes. We shall end up duped and gagged, having lost a year out of our lives.

Once again, I have no intention here of providing *causes* that might explain a gloomy mood; simply of describing the change of atmosphere and horizon amid which my mood continues to be unresponsive. The only changes I find *in myself* are an increased irritability and bouts of passionate anguish regarding T. Yesterday, for example, at about two o'clock I received a letter from her which ends like this: 'I must stop, because I can see the top of B[lin]'s head surfacing; people clutch at him as he passes, but his gaze is fixed upon me and he is walking softly in my direction with a crab-like determination. Till tomorrow.' That serial-story ending – 'continued tomorrow' – threw me into a bout of jealous prophecy: I was sure something was going to occur between them. At once I wrote an irreparable letter, which I finished by tearing up. Today I reverted to a more balanced view. But these passionate crises signal a lack of balance. Perhaps it has a physical origin: my eyes were better, but I was feeling lousy. And this morning they're starting to bother me again. Once again, I know my state only through this slight disaster that colours everything, and through these outbursts.

It remains the case that yesterday afternoon was particularly gloomy: I was seething with jealousy, my head was on fire, while Paul, who'd been given a typhoid shot that morning, paced up and down, red and miserable, a few beads of sweat on his forehead, wrapped in his blue overcoat. Through him I could sense the discomfort of this schoolroom. Everything was gloomy. Today, I'm not sure: I'm hard and unresponsive, as always in the morning, with no liking for myself, no passion, no interest in the war and no hope of seeing a speedy end to it. This state seems to me the best way, really, of living the war in the period now beginning. While I think of it, I must record – as a sign of my lack of balance – that four or five days ago, by contrast, I had quite violent moods of poetic sentimentality. I wrote to the Beaver about them. It should be said the Beaver sensed my change of mood from my letters, before I became aware of it myself.

War, when all's said and done, is a concrete idea that contains within itself its own destruction and that accomplishes this by an equally concrete dialectic. As Romains has shown, the day people realized that the means of destruction contained within themselves their own destruction, and that mere makeshift *constructions* – infinitely less costly and more primitive – were enough to ward them off, war between *men* was practically finished and destruction shifted towards goods. It may be that future modes of transport will render blockade warfare equally ineffective (if, for example, transport takes place by air: there was some idea of setting up a system for transporting raw materials from Russia to Germany by zeppelin). In that case, war will have had its day. So it's not pacifism but its own intrinsic dialectic that should be expected to suppress war. The essence of war will be *realized* concretely the day war becomes impossible.

I advised Mistler (who's an Alsatian, billeted on Alsatians) to carry out a little on-the-spot inquiry into the condition of the evacuees, based on their letters. It interests him. This morning, after conversations with his landlady and her neighbours, he reports to me that letters from the evacuees about the Savages who are giving them shelter have provoked intense feelings of pride and fear among those who have stayed behind. They see their rich land, so civilized and opulent, with all its comfort and luxury, as a delicate, exquisite flesh at the borders of a rough, backward country. They are more terrified than ever of evacuation. Our landlady was assuring us only recently: 'I'll leave only if they evacuate me by force.' The old women whom Mistler saw were all saying: 'We're quite prepared to be shelled, but not looted.' Because evacuation, for them, means looting.

People are bandying around stories about some suspicious crates, dispatched by a *Höcher* to his wife, which were on the station at Strasbourg and which the authorities ordered opened: they were full of women's underwear. The *Höcherer* (officers – bigshots) are more dreaded than the other ranks. People are also talking about an officer who turned at up Brumath post-office to send three big parcels to his wife. The girls who worked there were suspicious and opened them up: more underwear and women's hats. This last story is wholly implausible, given that officers have no more right to use the civilian mails than soldiers do. Besides, even supposing that soldiers here and there really have sent packets containing underwear to their wives, are they not most probably those natives of Strasbourg who have recently been given leave to spend a few hours in their city, precisely in order to fetch warm clothes from their homes and send them to their evacuated families? In any case, rumours about looting are rife, and they're accompanied by an odd preamble: 'Hardly surprising those savages loot: they've got nothing like that where they come from.' (Comment from the daughter of the power-station manager.)

Absence of solid foundations or roots, combined with preservation of the social structures, must, if I'm not mistaken, provoke an outburst of social mysticism among the evacuees. The priests and parish elders are there, moreover, to confiscate this mysticism for religion. Meanwhile, the public authorities have begun to issue counter-propaganda aimed at the Alsatians left in Alsace. Not a day goes by without some evacuated Alsatian mayor, priest or whatever turning up to give a little chat in Alsatian on the radio, to explain to those who have stayed behind how comfortable and well-off they are in the Limousin. All in vain: the letters destroy the entire effect of these speeches.

Mistler comes in, and I read over to him what I have just written. He finds the comments on the last page far too categorical. The truth is I have merely reproduced his own remarks, but by the very fact of writing them down I have given them a decisiveness they weren't meant to have. He now corrects himself, and here is what he says (which is much more interesting). The fact is, there's a real obsession with evacuation and looting at Brumath. But the main thing about the rumours that feed this is that they're inconsistent. Hazy. Entirely imprecise. The true facts are as if intentionally shrouded and vague. For example, it's not true that anybody told him: 'A soldier sent boxes full of underwear by post.' No, it's vaguer and more mysterious. It takes the form: '*There have been* boxes full of underwear at the post-office.' And the connection between these packages and the *Höcherer* is purely affective. It does exist, but nobody goes so far as to say they sent them, just that they're mixed up in the business somehow, that's all. Even this is not actually said, merely implied. Furthermore, if you try to pin the rumour down, it evaporates. The Alsatians grow mistrustful and say: 'Oh, you know, I wasn't there myself; that's what I've been told.' In short, it's more of a secret nightmare, which confirmation by *facts* would crystallize into a conviction. It's a hesitant, discreet fear that mistrusts both itself and others; that is ever ready to retract or belittle itself in public; but that, when they are alone or among themselves, is doubtless all the more tenacious for having no precise object.

As if to confirm what I was saying this morning, the papers are carrying a statement by Roosevelt: 'I hope the war will be over by spring.'

The orderly of the 68th, who lives at Strasbourg in civilian life, receives numerous letters from evacuees in Périgueux. The Alsatians are very badly treated there. The population is very hostile to them, and they are blamed for being the *cause* of the war. For if Hitler declared (?) war, it's because he wants to get back Alsace-Lorraine.

Monday 27

'Conquer oneself rather than fortune.' Very well said. But a fine demonstration of the guile of stoicism. For after all, to take a precise example, if I'm passionately attached to some object that eludes me, what can renouncing it mean to me? Do people think I can continue to assert the object's value in the flesh, in short be a martyr to that value, and *at the same time* cut off all my desire at its roots? Do they not see that I grasp that value *through* my desire? So it's necessary to cause the object to undergo a certain depreciation that will favour the extinction of my desire. Little jesuitical tricks will do for this, permitting me ceaselessly to assert in word and thought the object's value (out of fidelity to myself), while diverting me from feeling it. But this is to be wilfully blind, for the object's value, though experienced only through my desire, is *truly* constitutive of the object. In this sense, all those famous Epicurean and Stoic diatribes against lovers (in whose eyes a great lump of a girl is of slender build, and one that limps has a wayward charm in her gait) are mere jesuitical stratagems and slogans. For it's true that grace is hidden in a particular woman's limping, and needs only to be discovered there; but you have to love her to discover it. Blind and deaf, that's what stoics are. On principle, because the end justifies the means. Small matter here that the end is equanimity. In any case, the stoic is a pragmatist who resorts to violence and self-deception to attain his goal.

So what should we do? Well, the best thing is to suffer and whine and weep, but never hide the value of things from ourselves. Authenticity demands that we be a bit tearful. Authenticity and true fidelity to ourselves. What I'm saying about love, I shall say of life too. It's hard to leave life. The person who strikes a sudden pose, and thinks he's leaving it with no regrets, has deceived himself in one way or another. Excellent passage in Koestler's *Spanish Testament*: 'They died in tears, crying vainly for help, and in great weakness, as men must die. For dying is a confoundedly serious thing, one shouldn't make a melodrama of it. Pilate did not say "Ecce heros"; he said "Ecce homo".'[44]

The essential thing is that this terrible weakness, which discloses the meaning of what Koestler calls *dying*, does not make it impossible for you to die, if need be. I had always dreamed, I recall, even at the time when I was barricaded within my stoicism, of portraying a grumbling, cowardly hero who would nevertheless always do what was required just right; who would die screaming and begging for mercy, yet without confessing what they wanted him to confess. For my own part, I know that in such a case the truth is that screams would be forced from me despite myself. I should strive with all my strength not to weep. I should weep, no doubt – I'm not sure – but conquered by fear and humiliated; fear would break my stoicism like a dyke, but I should no doubt strive to be stoical. Out of pride, and I condemn myself for that. Pride – human respect. And then, when all's said and done, what lies behind that fine stoicism, other than fear of suffering? Authenticity requires one to accept suffering, out of fidelity to oneself and fidelity to the world. For we are free-to-suffer and free-not-to-suffer. We are responsible for the form and intensity of our sufferings. It's very easy to be distraught – very easy too to be stoical. But during all these days I'm finding it almost impossible to *sustain* authenticity. I understand very well now that speech by one of Stevenson's

44. Arthur Koestler, *Spanish Testament*, London 1937, p. 382.

characters, who says he's a gourmet of fear, because fear is the most intense emotion – more intense than love.[45] It would be more accurate to say: the most authentic.

The motives that induce me to write this page include, on the one hand, an event in my personal life of no interest here and, on the other, at another level, always this strange, proud desire to range myself with the weak against the strong, in order to feel myself stronger than the strong. I must confess, I have a kind of spontaneous irrational repugnance for people who complain when they are suffering. I wouldn't wish to do so for anything in the world; and, in the little sufferings that sweeten the life of any average man and town-dweller, I have always – with no great trouble but with great satisfaction – preserved a discreet attitude. Amid the little bumps and bruises, this discretion used to serve magically as the *sign* of a similar discretion and sobriety maintained amid the most atrocious sufferings. Magically, I would see myself at every moment of my life just as if I had passed a test, and was on my way back from bearing the most terrible pain without uttering a word. And then, from time to time, there were lapses of pride and I wondered unreservedly what my limits were in this domain, irritated to have no proof. But, I repeat, I consider myself spontaneously to be *on the side of* those who do not moan. So, of course, I go and take my place alongside those who do moan, and this ruse gives me the satisfying impression of transcending both of them: the strong, silent ones because I am capable of their muteness and reject it; the others because I freely seek an authenticity that is imposed on them, often as a result of their weakness. And here is yet another proof of the extreme difficulty of achieving authenticity. Trickery and ruse insinuate themselves into its very pursuit.

I learn that the *Times* has published draft peace proposals based on the Federation of Peoples. 'To this end, the various nations of Europe will accept certain limitations on their independence in the economic, financial or even political fields.' This article has been virtually suppressed in France. *Je suis partout* has been given free rein to criticize it.[46] On the other hand. Francisque Gay comments in *L'Aube*:
    'As we have already mentioned, democratic journalists endeavour-

45. Doubtless refers to Mr Malthus in 'The Suicide Club': see *New Arabian Nights*, London 1904, pp.22-23.
46. *Je suis partout*: political weekly founded 1930; it moved to the far right in 1936, and became the principal collaborationist organ in occupied France 1941–44.

ing to clarify the broad outline of our war aims are being "recommended" to observe the greatest discretion. They must be very cautious not just about approving the sensational article in the official *Times*, but even about rejoicing over the similarities to be discerned between certain speeches of Messrs Lebrun, Daladier or Paul Reynaud and the even more precise statements by Messrs Chamberlain and Eden, Lord Halifax or Sir Nevile Henderson. On the other hand, the most generous liberalism is evidently being displayed towards those writers who think fit to develop the most impassioned indictments of the 1919 treaties.'

There follow quotations from articles in the *Petit Parisien, AF, Le Temps, Je suis partout*, etc. which have been censored either not at all or very little. This can be put down to initiatives by reactionary junior censors.

Today, I really don't have any reason to be joyful: this business about T. – and then my eyes are hurting, the weather's overcast and gloomy, I'm broke and I can't go out. And yet, at about half-past twelve, alone in the schoolroom with Keller guzzling beans as I eat bread and chocolate, I went to look out of the window, at the sky and the red shutters of the house opposite, and as I thought about authenticity and about Mathieu's dialogue with Marcelle,[47] a solid, robust joy – not very strong but durable, a little callouse of joy – took hold of me. I have no idea what caused it. I first experienced the joy, and am reduced to suppositions – but I know very well I owe it only to myself. It comes neither from my pride, nor from any dubious poetry of objects, nor from any questionable emotion. It is nothing like a fragile passion. It is childlike and peaceful, and as I can see no motive for it I think it pure.

I can see clearly how this authenticity I'm aiming at differs from Gidian purity. Purity is an entirely subjective quality of the feelings and will. These are pure insofar as they burn themselves up like a flame, no calculation besmirches them. Pure and gratuitous. Hence, they need no justification other than themselves, nor do they seek any other. They are only themselves and wholly themselves. But authenticity is not exactly this subjective fervour. It can be understood only in terms of the human condition, that condition of a being thrown into situation. Authenticity is a duty that comes to us from outside and

47. Mathieu and Marcelle are characters in *Les Chemins de la liberté*, of which Sartre was then writing the first volume, *L'Âge de raison*.

inside at once, because our 'inside' is an outside. To be authentic is to realize fully one's being-in-situation, whatever this situation may happen to be: with a profound awareness that, through the authentic realization of the being-in-situation, one brings to plenary existence the situation on the one hand and human reality on the other. This presupposes a patient study of what the situation requires, and then a way of throwing oneself into it and determining oneself to 'be-for' this situation. Of course, situations are not catalogued once and for all. On the contrary, they are new each time. With situations there is no label and never will be.

Mistler comes to find me. 'I want to ask you a question about soldiers with kids.' – 'Fire away.' – 'Like you, I've noticed that they all say they miss their children more than their wives. Why?' – 'To hide from themselves the failure of their conjugal lives. From the moment war is declared, they can draw a line under their past lives and tot up the balance. Everything's dead, one can look it over and say: "What was I worth?" Well, their relations with their wives now appear to them in their true light: wretched and botched, their greatest failure. So they turn away from them, take their minds off them by thinking of the child. The child is nothing as yet, there's no balance to be totted up. On the other hands, it's the future, their future as much as its own. It's the post-war years, post-war years that are *theirs* because they have made that child. It's a way of thinking: "My life's not yet over, the balance hasn't been totted up yet, there's a reprieve." The child's the only reprieve for that dead life.' – 'But,' Mistler says, 'aren't there individual cataclysms even in peacetime that may induce a person to think in this kind of way?' – 'Perhaps, but that's not the same at all. In peacetime, there's an individual system – a man's life – and its co-ordinates: the epoch. The individual system may vary, but the co-ordinates remain fixed. The system varies in relation to those coordinates. So there's never this total surcease of life. However, once war comes, the line is drawn; it's not just the individual system that comes to a halt and congeals, it's the coordinates too. Everything has fallen into the past, and one is able to judge one's life, one's epoch, and one's life insofar as it is constructed with materials provided by the epoch. This would be their chance to be free, but they don't want to. They use paternal love to hide from themselves their total freedom with respect to that failed life.'

St-Exupéry's *Terre des hommes* has a very Heideggerian ring to it: 'A spectacle has no meaning except it be seen through a culture, a civilization, a craft.'[48] 'The requirements imposed by a craft transform and enrich the world.' 'To passengers, the storm is invisible. The surface of the sea appears to be covered with great white motionless palm-trees, palms marked with ribs and seams stiff in a sort of frost . . . But the hydroplane pilot knows there is no landing here . . . These palms beneath the plane are so many poisonous flowers.' [p.21] 'The aeroplane is a machine, no doubt, but what an instrument of analysis! This instrument has unveiled for us the true face of the earth. For centuries, highways had been deceiving us . . . [they] avoid the barren lands, the rocks, the sands. They shape themselves to needs and run from stream to stream . . . We have elected to believe that our planet was merciful and fruitful. But a cruel light has blazed and our sight has been sharpened. The plane has taught us to travel as the crow flies . . . transformed into physicists . . . We are able to judge man in cosmic terms.' [pp.53-4]

I am reading *Terre des hommes* with a certain emotion. Yet I do not like the style very much: somewhat vatic, and in the Barrès, Montherlant tradition. I do not like a certain daintiness about it, nor a certain calculated bonhomie that sweeps us along from the funeral oration ('Guillaumet, you miser! You had made up your mind to deny us your return' [p.33]) to panegyrics worthy of *La Science et la vie*.[49] And above all I don't like that new humanism: ' "I swear that what I went through, no animal would have gone through." This sentence, the noblest ever spoken, this sentence that defines man's place in the universe, that honours him, that re-establishes the true hierarchy', and so on. [p.34] But there are still plenty of good, even excellent, passages to move me. And then again, there's nothing more suitable for bringing tears to a prisoner's eyes than those accounts of breathtaking journeys. Since my call-up, I have often missed the cities and landscapes of the world I know – and sometimes that's bitter. But this evening I miss Argentina, the Sahara, all the parts of the world I don't know, the whole earth – and that's much milder, more resigned and hopeless. It's a 'tender suffering' that resembles happiness. It's like missing a life I might have had, when I was 'a thousand Socrates'.[50]

48. Antoine de Saint-Exupéry, *Wind, Sand and Stars*, London 1975, p. 9. (In the following passage, portions omitted in the English version have been translated from the French original: *Terre des hommes*, Paris 1939.)

49. Popular scientific periodical which still appears to this day.

50. The phrase originated with Raoul Lévy, a former pupil of Sartre's: see *Lettres au Castor*, vol. I, p. 442.

But now I'm only one. Or maybe two or three.

Tuesday 28

Mistler is pursuing his investigation. Here are the facts collected this morning. Apparently the word *work* is of considerable importance. One evacuee's comment (reported by a fellow from Metz serving here) is fairly typical: 'Perhaps we were sent here to teach *them* to work.' A comment evidently provoked by the primitive look of farm labour and implements among those 'savages'. So they're clearly people who are proud of knowing how to work, and quite ready to teach others what they know and to give advice. The Alsatian character is very prone to giving advice. But judging by their letters, their keenest disappointment seems to come from not being able to *place* their labour power. I imagine, moreover, that if they could work they would recover a human dignity and no longer feel like an 'evacuated mob'. But they are given little or no employment. (To qualify this, however, I really must mention what a fellow from Périgord who's serving at Brumath said. In his village, one farm employs 10 Alsatians: he claims that at first they were disconcerted by how *modern* and *new* the implements were – especially the ploughs; but apparently they adapted quickly.) In any case, the majority are not working. They say: 'After all, people have been called up from the Limousin, there are people to *replace*; so how come we're not given jobs?' They are obviously coming up against Limousin mistrust: the Limousins prefer to slave away and do *everything* themselves. But now we have the beginning of a social phenomenon: some big farmers, tired of inactivity, are planning to buy land in the Limousin. It will be curious to see the results of this plan, if they go through with it.

On the other hand, we discover that, at St-Junien, a certain number of Alsatian families are so disgusted by the Périgord food ('They eat garbage') that they have decided to pool their *Fluchtlingsgeld*. One or two women with more skill than the others will take care of the shopping and cooking. I notice in this the tendency to socialize funds that are socialist in origin. They have less inhibitions about pooling the money, because they don't feel it's *theirs*. No doubt they have a perfect *right* to the daily ten-franc allowance. But they do not have the raw, intimate bond with those ten francs that a person has with money earned or inherited. At the same time, I feel I can see emerging – from beneath this rudimentary phalanstery, from beneath these shared repasts – that tendency to social mysticism I was speaking about the other day. People are coming together, closing ranks. Perhaps meals are regaining the sacred character they lost long ago. In any case, in order to generalize this new institution, the Alsatians of St-Junien invite those in neighbouring parishes to join forces with them. Here, another phenomenon comes into play: the authorities in the neighbouring parishes *refuse* permission to the Alsatians under their jurisdiction to go and take their meals at St-Junien. Why? There may be a variety of reasons for this: perhaps it's simply a local initiative on the part of a meddlesome or hostile council. But it's also possible that they don't want a broader society, or communities like those of the early Christians, to be created *outside the structures* which the government has shown such jealous concern to preserve. Perhaps, as well, they are not too eager for the Alsatians evacuated to one parish in the Limousin to know what's going on in the others. That only spreads discontent.

It is noteworthy that – since the Alsatians' contempt for Limousin food equals that of the soldiers from central France for Alsatian food – a number of charcuteries run by evacuated Jews have made their appearance, selling Strasbourg sausage and *saucissons gras*.

The Alsatians in Limoges, furious at not being able to find work, report that the Limoges shopkeepers complain about having too much work: 'It's because of those evacuees,' the Limousin tradesmen say with a groan. 'You see, they keep coming to buy things, and we keep having to replenish all our stocks.'

When I tell Hang about my investigation, he informs me that he receives letters from his gardener and the gardener's wife, whose main complaint is that they're being shamelessly exploited. But, though Alsatian, he is a conformist and does not *wish* to feel indignant, He tells me: 'I reply that they're much better off than the refugees in 1914, and that they shouldn't complain, because the war could have taken quite a different turn.' All the same, this idea that they are being exploited does worry him a bit. But he shrugs his shoulders and tells me: 'What do you expect, it's so very human!'

For a while now, the Warrant-officer has been repeating with a scowl: 'Roll on the Bang-Bang! I've got a score to settle with those Boches.' On the first few occasions, this warlike refrain showed every sign of being an improvisation. But gradually it assumed a ritual character, and some justification for it became necessary. This morning one was offered. As he was taking coffee, he told me: 'I've got a score to settle with the Boches. I want to pay them back for all the whippings I got from those bastards when I was little.' I, keenly interested: 'Oh, so you got whipped by them, did you?' – 'Well, not exactly. I was in an occupied area, when I was little. So the Boches used to give me chocolate for shouting "Frankreich kaputt". I didn't understand German, so I used to shout it. But one time my grandfather told me, in front of them: "Don't shout that". Then they threatened me with the whip.'

Paul, in a fit of anger, reproached Pieter yesterday with lacking dignity because he is always begging. And it's true that Pieter loves *making requests*: for help, a favour, anything. But it would be a serious mistake to believe that he does so out of servility. Quite the contrary. Firstly, there is a kind of lyricism of social address about him. He makes requests because he knows how to make them. He will say, as if he has some pleasant surprise in store for his interlocutor: 'Don't you know, Madame, what I'm going to request of you?', so that the person in question, when she learns what is expected of her, will be delighted and overjoyed because her curiosity has been satisfied. Or else: 'Oh, I'm afraid I'm going to bother you again . . .' With him, there's a kind of generosity in making requests. He sometimes even begins requesting something, without knowing what it is that he's going to request: just for pleasure.

But all this is not the essential thing. For him, in fact, making requests is a sacred rite of the humanist religion, a naive and almost feudal ceremony which, momentarily, re-establishes equality between requester and giver. The act of requesting sets two men face to face in their nakedness as men. Pieter puts all of himself into his request: 'You can see who I am, a man like so many others, in his dignity as a man.' The reason he's so fond of plying superiors with requests is that he has the illusion he's addressing the man. For in his request there's always something confidential and whispered, which, beneath his conspicuous respect, means: 'I'm not forgetting you're an officer, but what I want from you I want from the man, etc.' So when it's granted – and only rarely is it not granted – he is doubly happy, above all because he has the impression that the lieutenant or captain has given him what he wants *as a man*. So, with Pieter, requesting is a mystical and perpetually renewed communion between his humanity and that of others. In return, he gives as generously as he requests – even, or above all, when nothing has been requested of him.

As I get up this morning, I am still preoccupied by that thought so eloquently formulated by St-Exupéry: 'A spectacle has no meaning except it be seen through . . . a craft.' Paul shivers and says: 'It's colder than yesterday.' Yesterday it was raining. And I feel that this sharp, biting cold is not at all like the cold I might feel on certain days in Paris, in my room at the Hotel Mistral. This is *my* cold, the material of my work, a cold it will shortly be my duty to measure. It's much less hard to bear than the other, because I don't endure it passively. It doesn't bite, but strokes me and scratches a little, like a cat playing. At the same time, it's not, as previously, a little icy pool, which has flowed into my room through the gaps in the windows and stagnated there. It's a sign of fine weather. It *is* the fine weather. Into this room with its shutters all closed, through the yellow light of the electric bulbs, it has slipped, ray of sunlight, dry and rosy dawn. I have no need to open the windows: I'm already in the fine weather, and there's no longer anything sinister about these two rosy-lidded soldiers getting up, they're getting up in the fields; the walls no longer count – they haven't fallen down, but they can do nothing against this dimension of cold, my new medium.

There must be many similar transformations I could note, but I'm too lazy, I shall write them down if they occur to me. However, there's one I was thinking about that arises not from my job as a weatherman but from my condition as a soldier in wartime. At present the fine skies, so pure and cold, conceal something furred and vibrant that stretches from one end of the horizon to the other, like a moth's wing: they are skies *with* raiding German planes. It's their nature, a scenic feature that we see in them of a morning when we look up. It's not at all frightening, because the planes are not vicious; it's not even terribly interesting; it's just a fact, the sky is quietly poisonous, like those white palm-trees St-Exupéry speaks of. And rainy skies, by contrast, are solid walls that isolate us, a foretaste of peace. For our landlady, who is afraid of the air-raids, the meaning of the weather has been reversed. She opens her shutters and smiles at the rain, just as she once used to smile at the sunshine.

I was forgetting to say that the morning cold is not just a local experience of myself and my comrades. It comes from afar – these days from on high – and is pregnant with exotic poetry, like a flight of migrating birds. The Beaver, when she reads these lines, will no doubt think of the cold of winter sports, which was a humanist bond between men – a human medium – and at the same time a dense, perceptible substance one could touch with one's hands or the skin of one's face. This was not merely endured, either, since we went right to its mountain haunts to seek it out, for the pleasure of plunging into it and feeling it whistling round us, like air pierced by a missile.

Two anecdotes recounted by Hang, who vouches for their authenticity. Near Wissembourg, a French patrol is surprised by the Germans. The men get away, the sergeant is taken prisoner. He is led to a blockhouse, where a German officer interrogates him for half an hour in excellent French. The sergeant acts stupid, but begins to fear he may be roughed up a bit to make him talk. After half an hour, the German officer says to him: 'All right. Now you just bloody well clear off. Go home, and don't come pestering us again with your patrols.' The other story: again near Wissembourg, some evacuated civilians are allowed back to their village for twenty-four hours, to retrieve essential belongings. At this point, the Germans capture the village. When they see the civilians busy moving out their chattels, they help them do up their parcels and then just let them leave. This latter anecdote seems more suspect to me. But the fact is, both are going the rounds here. It has been confirmed that, on both sides, the few killed or wounded in this sector have been the victims of reprisals provoked by some ill-timed shot. Another story: one night, amid tight security, the 65th arrives to take over a new sector. The next morning, German placard on the other side of the lines: 'Welcome to the 65th.'

The truth is that volition is normally thought of as a lightning-flash, which does not modify the substance wherefrom it emanates. I, however, think of it as a total and existential modification of human reality.

As if to confirm what I was saying yesterday, according to Valois,[51] here is what I read today in *L'Oeuvre*:

'Yesterday, at midnight, *L'Oeuvre* headlined this sentence from Mr Chamberlain's speech on the aims of peace: "It would not be a question of redrawing the geography maps in conformity with our ideas as victors, but of endowing Europe with a new spirit." An excellent sentence, in full accord with the French government's reiterated statements – the "new spirit" of which Mr Chamberlain speaks obviously being the spirit of freedom, justice and peace. Yet, at two in the morning, the censorship requested *L'Oeuvre* to suppress the English premier's sentence. We hasten to add that the suppressed headline was reinstated in the following edition: the high-ups had intervened.'

51. Georges Valois (1875–1945), journalist and politician, founded a fascist movement in France in 1925, but later broke with fascism and took part in the Resistance.

The end of the article, which doubtless attacked the junior censors, has been suppressed by the censorship.

I copy here this charming, ironical letter from T. on authenticity: 'If you became authentic, you'd be neither the better nor the worse for that, it would be something else. From a social point of view you'd be worth less, and your outside life would no doubt be less successful. But in yourself, you'd be a thousand times more poetic and a thousand times purer; instead of writing, you'd be the subject of a book (doesn't that mean something to you?). I think, as you say, it must be terribly hard to achieve authenticity. I always thought people were constitutionally authentic from birth. That's a structural flaw you don't possess. And then you've made yourself just the opposite: you've thought too much, you know yourself too well, and then you write. Even supposing that a person has some glimmer of authenticity, it flies out of the window when he writes. I had a quiet laugh over what you said about being sorry you weren't intelligent when you lost, so as to benefit from it. One can't benefit from that, because authenticity can't be known. I see it as a thing where there's no middle course, whereas you just dabble, because you don't want to bust a gut or anything. As a result, you'll shortly be writing a wonderful book in several volumes on authenticity. Actually, you should drug yourself for that. The only writers at all authentic are surrealists, plus Rimbaud.'

In the evening, Pieter and I usually eat bread and chocolate or tinned stuff. Paul and Keller scoff all four portions of meat and vegetables. Yesterday evening, Pieter fancies eating a bit of potato. He tells Keller: 'I'll take a bit of potato.' 'OK', grumbles Keller. Pieter goes off, Keller and Paul eat. Ten minutes later Pieter returns to eat his potatoes: the mess-tin is completely empty, they have polished off the lot. 'Is that all that's left for me?' he asks. Keller answers coldly: 'We got small helpings today.'

It's true, I'm not authentic. With everything that I feel, before actually feeling it I know that I'm feeling it. And then, bound up as I am with defining and thinking it, I no longer more than half-feel it. My greatest passions are mere nervous impulses. The rest of the time I feel hurriedly, then elaborate in words, press a little here, force a little there, and lo and behold an exemplary feeling has been constructed, good enough to put into a bound volume. All that men feel, I can guess at, explain, put down in black and white. But not feel. I fool people: I look like a sensitive person but I'm barren. Yet when I consider my destiny, it doesn't seem to me so contemptible: it seems to me I have before me a host of promised lands that I shall never enter. I haven't felt Nausea, I'm not authentic, I have halted on the threshold of the promised lands. But at least I point the way to them and others can go there. I'm a guide, that's my role. It seems to me that, at this moment, I am grasping myself in my most essential structure: in this kind of desolate greed to see myself feel and suffer, not in order to know myself, but in order to know all 'natures' – suffering, pleasure, being-in-the-world. It is precisely *me*, this continuous, introspective reduplication; this avid haste to put myself to good use; this scrutiny. I know it – and often I'm weary of it. That's the source of the magical attraction dark, drowning women have for me: T., formerly O. And then, from time to time, I have certain innocent, pure-hearted pleasures; but these are at once recognized, tracked down, expressed, disseminated in my correspondence. I am nothing but pride and lucidity.

Wednesday 29

Since 2 September, I have read or reread:
    The Castle, by Kafka
    The Trial, by Kafka
    In Gaol,[52] by Kafka
    Dabit's Journal
    Gide's Journal
    Green's Journal
    Les Enfants du limon, by Queneau
    Un rude hiver, by Queneau
    The September, October and November issues of *NRF*
    Mars ou la guerre jugée, by Alain
    Prélude à Verdun, by Romains
    Verdun, by Romains
    Quarante-huit, by Cassou
    La Cavalière Elsa, by Mac Orlan
    Sous la lumière froide, by Mac Orlan
    Colonel Jack, by Defoe
    Volume Two of Shakespeare's Works (Pléiade edition)
    Terre des hommes, by St-Exupéry
    The Spanish Testament, by Koestler

52. *In the Penal Settlement* (*In der Strafkolonie*) is the correct title.

Thursday 30

As I have no more money, and as I don't want to burden the month of
December with debt by borrowing from Pieter, I haven't been going
to the Écrevisse for lunch for the past five days. Not being any too
enthusiastic about the idea of cooking, I'm seizing the opportunity to
semi-fast: slice of bread and cheese in the morning, hunk of bread and
piece of chocolate in the evening, yesterday nothing at all. I'm hoping
in this way to lose the two or three kilos of excess weight I've put on
since September. I've already hauled in my belt one notch. Actually,
I'd perhaps have gone to eat lunch at an inn yesterday, but I can tell
my confederates are watching me. I've reproached them so much for
their weakness; so often made it clear how greatly they irritate me,
with their resolutions a hundred times formed and a hundred times
called into question! They'd be glad to catch me *in flagrante*. They'll
not have that pleasure. However, Paul made up for this by confiding
in the strictest secrecy to Mistler – who repeated it to me – that I'd
'never been so aggressive as since that voluntary fast'. I find this
amusing and informative: I hadn't realized. But a comparison of dates
makes it clear that this nervous aggressivity is related, quite simply, to
that strange paroxysm of passion into which I cast myself over T. And
that paroxysm was itself anterior to my resolution to eat less. From
this standpoint of passion, the day before yesterday was really painful.
Yesterday much less so. The mail had brought me no letter from her,
and when I'm in that state I prefer her silence. I don't feel so strongly
that she's a consciousness. Her life in Paris seems unreal to me. A
letter is the sudden explosion of a little consciousness – faithless and
absolute – in the midst of the Paris I so much miss. When I compare
what I'm writing today with what I was writing on Sunday the 26th, I
can see I must have gone through a fit of 'the blues'. But since, out of
pride, I was unyielding in my decision not to miss my past life and not
to complain about this one, that little transient despair was channelled
into the only free path it could find: an unhealthy, jealous anxiety
about T. Not that I did not have – do not still have – reasons for
anxiety. But there can be no doubt that I should have reacted differently in peacetime.

At all events – a prisoner from choice, and fasting out of obstinacy –
yesterday and the day before I was reading a book that suited my
gloomy mood admirably, and that under present circumstances
yielded its maximum: Arthur Koestler's *Spanish Testament*. The
passionate interest it aroused in me spread to overlap retrospectively
with that aroused by Romains' *Verdun*. Hard books which speak of

cruelty, poverty and death are dear to me at present. I'd like to read only these for the moment. The mere fact of being plunged into this war – which isn't so very terrible, but which has a modest little future of destruction and death – is enough to make these gloomy tales vivid and real.

Last year, though I'd have read them with the appropriate indignation, of course, I'd have felt they didn't concern me: my indignation would have been 'generous'. The war of '14 was safely interred, and Spain after all wasn't France. I imagine that most well-intentioned bourgeois, as they perused their newspapers or other similar accounts, were unable to suppress a kind of civilized sense of security: 'That will never happen in France', 'Spain's a backward country', or again 'People have always been massacring each other in the Balkans', etc. A Frenchman always more or less thinks of France as a Kosmos in the midst of a vast, formless, violent universe. The universe is convulsed, huge storms blow across it, but this does not affect the Kosmos. But today, when in spite of everything we're at war – which, after all, is at the very least a way of calling the Kosmos into question – I am open to these gloomy books: they scour away the thin layer of idealistic optimism I have still retained. I have the impression they're speaking to me of men as they really are. A Frenchman always tends to be the kind of fellow who eats beef but would frown upon anybody who suggested he go and visit the abattoir, to see how the cattle are slaughtered. But I've approached the abbatoir.

On the first day, the account of the capture of Malaga inspired me with a mixture of horror and longing for that lazy, cruel war which at least was being waged in the sun. The next day, what struck me above all was the systematic enumeration of the tricks a man in mortal danger employs to hide that danger from himself and gain reassurance – while, in his own eyes, he is seeking only to be brave. I like very much this comment on people just before the fall of Malaga: 'I have an uneasy feeling that he is acting a part . . . that all the others, including myself, are children playing at being Walter Scott heroes and are unable to visualize the stark reality of death.'[53] I am very sensible of the kind of trick that underlies this pathetic derealization of death. And then later, when the 'heroic' moment has passed and one has to live wretchedly with the ever-present idea of death, every fit of heroism is basically a subterfuge, that conceals Heaven only knows what naive way of reassuring oneself. Generally a magical comfort we'd never accept in its naked form, but that we peek at surrep-

53. *The Spanish Testament*, p. 201.

titiously pretending not to know it. These, of course, are still the tricks of stoicism, and that way of being caught unawares – and *by oneself* – at the very moment one would swear one was keying oneself up to a desperate courage. It awakens many echoes in me: did I not use that selfsame technique to comfort myself at the start of this war while thinking myself very brave?

Consider this remark: 'I don't believe that since the world began a human being has ever died *consciously*. When Socrates, sitting in the midst of his pupils, reached out for the goblet of hemlock, he must have been at least half-convinced that he was merely showing off. Of course, he knew theoretically that the draining of the goblet would prove fatal; but he must have had a feeling that the whole thing was quite different from what his perfervid, humourless pupils imagined it; that there was some clever dodge behind it all known only to himself' [p.310]. And this other remark: 'Nature sees to it that trees do not grow beyond a certain height, not even the trees of suffering' [p.289].

But for me it's not a question of nature, it's a question of ourselves, and we're entirely responsible for those particular tricks. Besides, he recognizes he's had a few hours of authenticity: 'Most of us were not afraid of death, only of the act of dying; and there were times when we overcame even this fear. At such moments we were free – men without shadows, dismissed from the ranks of the mortal; it was the most complete experience of freedom that can be granted a man' [p.382]. This remark too: 'The constant nearness of death weighed down and at the same time lightened our existence' [ibid.]. I've already said that war could serve as a justification: it lightens, it excuses from 'being-there'. Now I see that death can too. It's so difficult just to live, without being *in any way* justified.

All in all, this paroxysm of passion is quite simply the unveiling – motivated by an external circumstance – of a whole dimension of my universe and my future; and, at the same time, the unveiling of the terrible *simultaneity* which, fortunately, remains hidden from us most of the time. I imagine if one lived that simultaneity *here* in its full dimensions, one would spend one's days with a heart that bled like Jesus's. But many things screen it from us. For example, the letters I receive take three days to get here. So I live in suspense between past and future. The events of which I learn took place long ago; and even the short-term plans about which I'm informed have already been realized (or failed) by the time I learn of them.

The letters I receive are scraps of present surrounded by future;

but it's a past-present surrounded by a dead future. I myself, when I write, always hesitate between two times: that in which I am, while I pen the lines for the recipient; that in which the recipient will be, when he reads my words. It doesn't make the 'surrounding' unreal, merely timeless – as a result of which it's blunted and loses its harmfulness. Thanks to which, my present here – my neutral present – can get some of its colour back, I can value certain things: my reading, my little mornings at the Rose, etc. Similarly, the letters I receive no longer appear to me as worrying signs of the existence of other consciousnesses, but instead as a convenient form these consciousnesses have assumed in order to travel to me. When I read the letters, I hold these consciousnesses captive in a circle around me; they cannot escape or go off to reflect other skies and other faces: they're a bit petrified, a bit out of date. But if simultaneity is suddenly unveiled, then the letter is a dagger-blow. In the first place, it reveals events that are irreparable, since they are past. Secondly, it allows what is essential to escape: the present life of those consciousnesses, which have survived their letters, which have escaped from them, and which are pursuing their lives beyond those dead messages – like living beings beyond their graves. At that moment, I don't know quite how to put it, it seems to me that it is I who am outdated, impotent, ineffective. I cannot catch hold of my future from here – it is swallowed up. Whence a state of nervousness that can then take the form of jealousy.

By the way, I don't regret those few gloomy days. It was life in the full sense: along with that sterile, painful nervousness, they brought me the 'tender sufferings' of which Exupéry speaks and the poetic evening of the 27th; they also brought me the baleful illuminations of the *Spanish Testament*. All because I was unbalanced, of course: I was flinging myself into distractions. But at least I was caught up in those distractions: at least, twice over, I was an other.

Madame Magdelin, my mother writes, is making gold braid to adorn the robes of chaplains at the front. 'And, since it's necessary to economize everywhere, embroidered outfits belonging to prefects and academicians, ball-dresses, antique materials, everything is being requisitioned by their band of sewing-girls.'

The Warrant-officer is lodged free of charge by a young woman (whose husband is German – and at present in a concentration camp).

But he suffers and 'will never forgive her because she calls her kid Willy, like the Boches do'.

It has been confirmed that round Wissembourg the French troops have looted everything.

At six o'clock the Warrant-officer comes back in and informs us that Russia has attacked Finland. Bad.

Friday, 1 December

The rumour is becoming more definite: Pieter chatted to his landlady yesterday. 'I know one fellow,' she says, 'and I could even tell you his name, who's a warden at Strasbourg specially assigned to keep an eye on evacuated houses. Well, he comes back every week with parcels full of clothes and underwear.'

Our landlady has told us that after our departure she'll agree to put up only officers, because at least they'll be able to make her some conversation.

Pieter tells me: 'We were talking about you yesterday evening, Paul and I. Watch out, old man, you're working sixteen hours a day! That way, how can you expect not to be irritable?' Flattered at first, I reflect that at most I can work only 13 hours, since I hardly reach my table before 8 o'clock and leave the school at 9 in the evening. And then the two hours for lunch (11 to 1) have to be deducted from that: no doubt I do write in my diary during those two hours, but much less. What is more, Pieter lumps together under the general rubric of work the times when I'm reading novels or answering letters. So at most I reckon 8 or 9 hours of actual work. But all the same, it's true I must do ten or eleven hours of reading and writing daily. That explains why my eyes are tired.

Struck yesterday, as I leafed anew through Gide's journal, by its *religious* aspect. It's primarily a Protestant self-examination, and then a book of meditation and prayer. Nothing in common with Montaigne's essays, the Goncourts' diary or Renard's journal. The basic thing is the struggle against *sin*. And keeping up the journal is very often presented as one humble means – one humble trick – to facilitate struggle against the Evil One.

E.g.: 'I have never been so modest as when constraining myself to write every day in this notebook a series of pages that I know and feel to be so definitely mediocre . . . I cling desperately to this notebook; it is a part of my patience; it helps keep me from going under' (7 February 1916).[54] And (16 September 1916): 'I shan't succeed without a constant effort, an hourly effort, constantly renewed. I shan't succeed without deceit and attention to detail. Nothing gained if I aim to note here only things of importance. I must make up my mind to write everything in this notebook. I must force myself to write anything whatever' [p. 143].

So his notebook is a task, a humble daily task, and it is with a certain humility that one rereads it. Of course, it is not and cannot be that alone. First, because of Gide's personality and writer's craft, and then because of the dialectical notion of notebook both imposed and executed by the writer. But the framework remains religious. Whence the austerity of that journal, and on occasion its *sacred* character. At the same time it is the journal of a *classic* author. In other words, it contains a book of rereadings, and of meditations upon these rereadings. Moreover, the severe quality of many of the notes too must be attributed to this. There is no question of that notebook being the reflection of a life. It is a kind of religious and classical offertory; a moral account-book, with a page for the credit side, a page for the debits. And almost every note, more than the faithful transcription of an act or feeling, is itself an act. *Act* of prayer, *act* of confession, *act* of meditation.

In the light of this, I returned to my own notebook and saw how different it was from Gide's, It is above all the notebook of a witness. The more I go on, the more I consider it as testimony: the testimony of a 1939 bourgeois draftee on the war he's being made to fight. And I too write anything whatever in my notebook, but I do so under the impression that I'm justified by my testimony's historical value. Let us be clear: I'm not an important person nor do I meet important people, so my journal won't have the same value that Giraudoux's or Chamson's might.[55] On the other hand, I'm not in a privileged position – on the Maginot line, for example, or on the contrary in the intelligence service or a censorship office in the rear. I'm at an artillery staff headquarters twenty kilometres from the front, surrounded by

54. *The Journals of André Gide*, London 1947–9, vol. II, pp. 125–26.
55. Jean Giraudoux (1882–1944), novelist and playright, was one of the most eminent French men of letters in the nineteen-thirties. André Chamson (1900–), novelist, though less famous, was nonetheless like Giraudoux an established literary figure by comparison with the younger Sartre.

petty and middling bourgeois. But, precisely because of all that, my journal is testimony that's valid for millions of men. It is a *mediocre*, and for that very reason *general*, testimony.

But here there intervenes what Gide would call one of the Devil's tricks: I am emboldened by the very mediocrity of my condition, I am no longer afraid of being mistaken, and I speak boldly about this war because my mistakes will have a historical value. If I am mistaken in considering this war as a swindle, etc., this mistake is not just my own stupidity, it is representative of a moment in this war. Others, more or less intelligent than me, more or less well informed, have been surprised like me, have reacted like me, without writing it down, or using other words. No more is needed to convince me that everything I write is interesting: even the confession of my sullen moods, for they are sullen moods, blues, of 1939; even that 'anything whatever' which Gide apologizes for writing – and forces himself to write. So I shall write anything whatever without humility. You can see pride's ruse. Too lucid to attribute value to *everything* I write (tittle-tattle, gossip, political soothsaying, passing moods), I still end up conferring such value upon all my notes without exception, by a detour via History. I use historical *relativity* to endow my notes with an absolute character. The advantage of this trick – for it does have an advantage – is to give me the sense of my historicity, something I'd never really had. To give it me daily in my humblest actions, whereas in the month of September I'd attained it only in the sublime – which is always to be avoided. But in consequence this journal has no humility. What is more, as I've noted somewhere, it has no intimacy. It is a proud, pagan journal.

From another point of view, and in a quite different spirit, this journal is a calling into question of myself. And there again a parallel might be made with Gide's confessions. But this is merely apparent. In fact, I don't do this calling into question with groans and humility, but coldly and in order to move forward. Nothing of what I write is an act, in the sense in which I was speaking of Gide's acts. It consists of recordings, and as I write these down I have the (fallacious) impression of leaving what I write behind me. I'm never ashamed of it, I'm never proud of it. There's almost always a gap between the moment when I felt and the moment when I write. So it's essentially a fair copy. Except, perhaps, in a few cases when the feeling has governed the writing directly. When I write, I try to establish a solid, clearly defined foundation as a point of departure. After all, among primitive peoples there are ceremonies to help the living person to die; to help the soul detach itself from the body. My 'confessional' notes have the same purpose: to help my present being slip into the past – push it in a bit deeper, if need be. There's a degree of illusion there, for it's not enough to expose a psychological constant in order to modify it. But at least that sketches some possible lines of change.

All these remarks naturally led me on to compare Gide's moral formation with my own. So that's what I have done. I shall try to record here, this afternoon and in the days to come, the various moral attempts I have made since my eighteenth year; and I shall endeavour to uncover certain moral constants I have discovered thereby, constants that could be termed my moral 'affections'. For I imagine everyone freely determines a kind of moral affect for himself, on the basis of which he grasps values and conceives his own progress. For example, from the outset I undoubtedly had a morality without a God – without sin, but not without evil. I shall return to this.

I lost my faith at the age of twelve. But I don't imagine I ever believed very strongly. My grandfather was Protestant, my grandmother Catholic. But so far as I could see, their religious feelings if decent were frigid. With my grandfather, there was a rejection on principle of the whole religious business, as a great cultural phenomenon, combined with a 'dissenter's' contempt for clerics. I think he cracked anti-clerical jokes at table and my grandmother rapped him on the fingers, saying: 'Be quiet, Dad!' My mother made me take my first communion, but I think it was more out of respect for my future freedom than from true conviction. Rather as certain people have their children circumcised for reasons of hygiene. She has no religion, but rather a vague religiosity, which consoles her a bit when necessary and leaves her strictly in peace the rest of the time.

I hardly have any religious memories: however, I can still see myself at the age of seven or eight, in Rue Le Goff, burning the lace curtains on the window with a match; and this memory is connected with the Good Lord, I don't know why. Perhaps because this incendiary act had no witness, and yet I was thinking: 'The Good Lord can see me.' I remember too that I wrote an essay on Jesus at Abbé Dibildos's catechism class (this was on the premises of the École Bossuet), and that I won a silver-paper medal. I am still filled with admiration and delight when I think of that essay and that medal, but there's nothing religious about this. The fact is my mother had copied out my composition in her beautiful hand, and I imagine the impression that seeing my prose transcribed in this way made on me was more or less comparable to the sense of wonder I felt at seeing myself in print for the first time. Moreover, the silver medal, which was a beautiful, glistening, pale-grey colour, had to be stuck on to the first page of the exercise so that the whole formed a superb and precious object. In addition to this, the abbé who'd corrected my work was very young, a pretty boy with red hair, a pale face and beautiful hands. I seek in vain, I can find nothing else within me.

Oh yes! They used still to take me quite often to church, but (and this, which comes back to me, is a pretty good indication of the type of bourgeoisie I belong to) it was primarily in order to hear fine music – the organ of St-Sulpice or Notre-Dame. It is clear to me what feelings of high spirituality were provoked, in my mother and grandmother, by this union between the purest forms of art and the most elevated forms of faith; and it is also clear to me that, with these teachers' wives and daughters, religion touched them only if it decked itself out with the charms of music. They no longer had any very clear idea, I imagine, whether the music thrilled them because it was religious or the religion because it was harmonious. And their respect for religion merged with their academic cult of spiritual values. For my own part I understood nothing of that music, those great moaning winds that used suddenly to fill the church. Yet, in spite of everything, those masses were linked in my mind with the idea of virtue. Since I used to grow very bored, my mother had discovered how to handle me by explaining that a *really* good little boy had to sit like a statue at mass. So, at little cost, I achieved that perfect goodness for the hour that the service lasted, in order to be able afterwards to ask my mother, sure of her reply: 'Have I been good, Mummy?' I even used to overdo things, intent on avoiding even the smallest creak of my chair or scuffling of my feet. But I used to hate kneeling down, since for some reason I have two rather sensitive bumps on my knees.

So there you are. It's pretty thin. God existed, but I didn't concern myself with him at all. And then one day at La Rochelle, while waiting for the Machado girls who used to keep me company every morning on my way to lycée, I grew impatient at their lateness and, to while away the time, decided to think about God. 'Well,' I said, 'he doesn't exist.' It was something authentically self-evident, although I have no idea any more what it was based on. And then it was over and done with. I never thought about it again; I was no more concerned with that dead God than I had been bothered about the living God. I imagine it would be hard to find a less religious nature than mine. I settled the question once and for all at the age of twelve. Much later I studied religious proofs and atheist arguments. I appraised the fortunes of their disputes. I was fond of saying that Kant's objections did not affect Descartes's ontological proof. But all that struck me as hardly any more alive than the Quarrel of Ancients and Moderns.[56] I think I ought to say all this because, as I have said, I am affected by moralism, and because moralism often has its source in religion. But with me it was nothing of the kind. Besides, the truth is I was brought up and educated by relatives and teachers most of whom were champions of secular morality and everywhere sought to replace religious morality by it.

I am breaking off to record a charming anecdote about Keller. At the Fort de St-Cyr in '21, he was given an injection against typhoid and handed three quinine tablets in case the injection gave him a fever during the next forty-eight hours: 'The injection had no effect on me,' says Keller with pride, 'but I swallowed the three tablets all the same, so as not to waste them.'

I note here something that is all to Pieter's credit, and that I meant to note long ago: he received only a rudimentary education, and he knows it. So he takes advantage of this enforced leisure to study algebra, for three or four hours a day, without much success but with great zeal. Mistler and I call him the Angel, or the Cherub. And he really is an angel, there's a kind of innocence in his stratagems that enchants me, and then he's quite without complexes and asks only to be happy. And so he is, moreover, even here. And then the way he fondles himself gives him the look of a seraph caressing its cheek with its wings. Those hours of algebra represent a refusal to waste this time of war, a refusal to let oneself go, a will to put this idleness to some profit: the only refusal of war that's open to us. When, beside him, I consider Keller stuffing himself because the food's free, that hunted rat Paul and all the others, it fills me with respect for him.

I don't think I'm being over-schematic if I say that the moral problem which has preoccupied me up till now is basically the one of relations between art and life. I wanted to write – there was no doubt about that and never had been. However, apart from these strictly literary labours there was 'the rest' – in other words, everything: love, friendship, politics, relations with oneself, what you will. Whatever one did, one was thrown into the midst of all these questions. What to do? I think I'm respecting the truth if, from this point of view, I distinguish

56. The *Querelle des Anciens et des Modernes* was a late-seventeenth-century literary dispute between classicists like Boileau, La Fontaine and La Bruyère, and champions of a new literature without classical models, such as the Perrault brothers and Fontenelle.

three periods in my life as a young man and as a man.

The first goes from 1921 to 1929 and is a period of optimism, the time when I was 'a thousand Socrates'. At this time I think, light-heartedly, that a life is always unsuccessful; and I construct a metaphysical morality of the work of art. At bottom, however, I'm not at all convinced; the truth is that I'm sure it's enough to devote oneself to writing and life will take care of itself in the meantime. And the life which must do so is already outlined in advance in my head: it's a great writer's life, as it appears from books. There's basically this magical confidence: to have a great writer's life, it's enough just to be a great writer. But to be a great writer, there's only one method: concern oneself exclusively with writing. So fate would owe me that moving, crowded life with its seductive pattern – the life of a Liszt, a Wagner, or a Stendhal – if only I made good books. This optimism came to me assuredly from my childhood, and also from an Aristotelean thought (a conceptual, participationist thought): a great writer has a great writer's life, so I should devote all my efforts to becoming a great writer – the rest would take care of itself.

Now, if I were asked what I most wished for at that time, to make a good book or to have a great man's life, I should be at a loss how to reply. It seems to me that I was full of lust for that marvellous life, but wanted to *deserve* it by good books. Not for moral reasons, but so that it would be truly mine. As for the content of that life, it can be easily imagined: there were solitude and despair, passions. great undertakings, a long period of painful obscurity (though I slyly shortened it in my dreams, in order not to be too old when it ended), and then glory, with its retinue of admiration and love. I admit to my shame that *Jean-Christophe*, that infamous emetic, more than once brought tears to my eyes when I was twenty.[57] I knew that it was bad, that it presented an abject image of art, that it was the story of an artist written by a philistine academic, but all the same . . . There was a way of lifting a finger at the end of each chapter and saying: 'You'll see! You'll see! That little Christophe may suffer and go astray, but his sufferings and his strayings will become music and the music will make up for everything' – which used to make me grit my teeth with irritation and desire. In a word, I'd have liked to be sure of becoming a great man later on, so as to be able to live my youth as a great man's youth.

Anyway, even though I couldn't be sure, I behaved as if I must

57. *Jean-Christophe* (1906–12), a novel in ten volumes by Romain Rolland, follows the career from birth to death of a musical genius.

become one – and was extremely conscious of being the young Sartre, in the same way that people speak of the young Berlioz or the young Goethe. And from time to time I'd go for a little stroll into the future, for the sole pleasure of looking back from up there at my young present and shaking my head – as I believed I should then do – saying: 'I never thought suffering would be so useful to me, etc.': as an old man, I'd turn back towards my youth and view it with a tenderness filled with esteem. These factitious dissociations left traces in a fat notebook that I've lost, where between dry philosophical notations I would berate Simone Jollivet, exclaiming more or less: 'You make me suffer, but I'll have the last laugh, because I am a great man.'[58]

In that particular case, I was basically amusing myself by judging my love-pangs with the sympathetic solicitude of a future academic, like Koszul speaking of Shelley's sorrows or Lauvrière of Poe's.[59] But I imagine that overlaying everything there was a very youthful confidence in the future, and also that bourgeois decision which limits the likely at will and always halts it before anything horrible, before any catastrophe. And then I was available: everything was still possible for me, since I was nothing. In view of that sturdy confidence in my star, I could tranquilly assert that life was a game lost in advance, and meditate enthusiastically upon Amiel's striking comment on Moses: 'Every man, like him, has his Promised Land, his day of glory and his end in exile.'[60] The end in exile I willingly accepted, it was far away; moreover, that pessimistic touch allowed me to accept the day of glory without being untrue to myself. Life was unsuccessful, to be sure, since it always ended with a failure. However, there was the day of glory. Contemptible day of glory, of course, since it ended in defeat. But still, it was there, like an invisible sun, and it warmed my heart.

It was those tricks, that pessimism covering and masking my basic optimism, which allowed me to tackle a more gloomy and demoralized period without my principles apparently having changed. I remained

58. Simone Jollivet (née Simone-Camille Sans), actress and playwright, was an early love of Sartre's (they met in 1925). Nicknamed 'Toulouse', she appears in De Beauvoir's autobiography as 'Camille'. She later lived and collaborated with Charles Dullin (1885–1949), the actor and theatrical producer who founded the Théâtre de l'Atelier in 1921 and who was to stage several of Sartre's plays after 1944. She remained a friend of Sartre and De Beauvoir, despite political differences during the Occupation, until her tragic decline into despair and alcoholism (d. 1967).

59. Émile Lauvrière, *Edgar Poë: sa vie et son oeuvre. Étude de psychologie pathologique*, Paris 1904; A. Koszul, *La Jeunesse de Shelley*, Paris 1910.

60. Henri-Frédéric Amiel (1821–81) was a Genevan aesthetician and moralist influenced by Hegel, and German culture in general, famous for his posthumous *Journal intime*; a new study of his psychological formation gave rise to a discussion of his work in the *NRF* in 1939.

convinced that life was a lost game, only this time I really believed it. And I believed it because I needed to believe it. There was still a degree of falsehood in all this. Here's why. I'd always thought that a great man had to keep himself free. This was a question neither of the Bergsonian freedom of the heart nor, above all, of that which I have now discovered in myself and which is no joke, but rather of a kind of caricature of Hegelian freedom: to keep oneself free in order to realize, in oneself and through oneself, the concrete idea of a great man. There was a perpetual danger of coming up against obstacles or getting caught in traps, but it was necessary to press forward ruthlessly. A lot had been written about this freedom of the great man – free-for-his-destiny – who naturally assumes the visage of fatality for all those he meets on his path. I remember a fairly silly play, *Moloch*, which develops that theme.[61] In short, I had my head stuffed full of it, and as is natural at that age I dreamed above all of asserting this freedom against women.

It was all the more comical in that women certainly weren't running after me, indeed it was I who was running after them. Thus, in the few adventures that came my way at that time, after I'd gone to immense trouble to get round some young lady, I used to feel obliged to explain to her, like some dragon of virtue, that she must take care not to infringe my freedom. But within a short space of time, as I was good-natured, I'd make her a gift of that precious freedom. I'd say: 'It's the finest present I can give you.' Nothing would be altered in our relations; but if the girl was still a bit naive, she'd be filled with gratitude – and if she was wordly-wise, she'd pretend to be. Happily for me, moreover, circumstances independent of my will would intervene in time to restore me (after a bit of a drubbing) to that dear freedom, which I'd forthwith make haste to bestow upon some other young lady.

On one occasion I was hoist with my own petard. The Beaver accepted that freedom and kept it. It was in 1929. I was foolish enough to be upset by it: instead of understanding the extraordinary luck I'd had, I fell into a certain melancholy. At the same time I left the École Normale and that amorphous, violent world of camaraderie to live alone. There was also my military service which prompted me to a very great modesty – that I later joyfully abandoned, it must be said. But this modesty finally cleansed all the last dross of superhumanity I still retained. Moreover, I was becoming a teacher. I've already said

61. Probably the unfinished play of that name by the German playwright Friedrich Hebbel (1813–63).

this was a hard blow. For, all of a sudden, I was becoming just one Socrates. Until then I'd been preparing to live. Each moment, each event, had brushed past without ageing me: they had always been rehearsals before the play. And then, all at once, I was acting in the play; everything I did from now on was done *with my life*; I couldn't take my moves back, everything was inscribed in that narrow, short existence. Each event would arrive in my life from outside and then, all at once, it would become my life: my life was made out of that. I was like the Chinaman Malraux describes in *Les Conquérants*: I was discovering late that one has only one life.[62]

I recall, moreover, that when I read that phrase in *Les Conquérants* I was struck by it as if by some pleasant intellectual game, but I did not sense its truth (that was in 1930). I really came to sense that truth only in the years that followed: '31, '32, '33. What I did dimly sense was that one can't take a point of view on one's life while one's living it: it comes on you from behind, and you find yourself up to your neck. And yet if you look round, you realize you're responsible for what you have lived – and that it's beyond repair. I felt I was deeply committed to a path which was growing narrower and narrower; I felt that at every step I was losing one of my possibilities, as a person loses his hair. Incidentally, I did begin to lose my hair – but that has stopped since, or continued at a slower tempo. When I noticed it – or rather when the Beaver noticed it with a shriek at the Trou de Bozouls[63] – it was a symbolic disaster for me. I still remained more or less indifferent to the idea of death. On the other hand, I got a taste at that time of how irreparable and tragic it can be to grow old. And for ages I used to massage my head in front of mirrors: balding became the tangible sign for me of growing old.

In short, I took the transition to manhood as badly as possible. At thirty-two, I felt old as the hills. How far away it was, that great man's life I'd promised myself. On top of everything else, I wasn't very happy with what I was writing; at the same time, I really would have liked to be in print. I can appreciate the extent of my disappointment today, when I recall that at twenty-two I'd noted down in my diary this dictum from Töpffer, which had made my heart beat faster: 'Whoever is not famous at twenty-eight must renounce glory for ever.'[64] A totally absurd dictum, of course, but one which threw me

62. André Malraux, *The Conquerors*, London 1929, New York 1977.

63. Gorge on the Dourdou river in the Tarn region, where Sartre and De Beauvoir went for a walking holiday in 1935.

64. Rodolphe Töpffer (1799–1846): Swiss aesthetician, author of *Voyages en zigzag*, etc.

into agonies. Well, at twenty-eight I was unknown, I'd written nothing good, and if I wanted ever to write anything worth reading I had my work cut out.

I had a year's holiday in Berlin, rediscovered the irresponsibility of youth there, and then, on my return, I was recaptured by Le Havre and my life as a teacher – perhaps even more bitterly. I remember that in November of that new year, the Beaver and I, sitting in a café called Les Mouettes on the sea-front at Le Havre, were bemoaning the fact that nothing new could happen to us. Our friendships were settled: Guille, Mme Morel, Poupette, Gégé; we were weary of that virtuous, dutiful life we were leading, weary of what we then called the 'constructed'. For we had 'constructed' our relations, on the basis of total sincerity and complete mutual devotion; and we would sacrifice our impulses, and any confusion there might be in us, to that permanent, *directed* love we had constructed. At bottom, what we were nostalgic for was a life of disorder, of confused yet at the same time imperious casualness; a kind of obscurity contrasting with our clear rationalism; a way of being drowned in ourselves, and of feeling without knowing that we were feeling. It was also the existential and the authentic, which we vaguely sensed beyond our petty-bourgeois rationalism.[65] We needed immoderation, having for too long been moderate. All this culminated in that strange, black mood which turned to madness around March of that year – and ultimately in my meeting with O., who was precisely everything we desired and who made this quite clear to us.

So one had only one life, and what was being offered me was that doughy, abortive existence – so far, so very far, from the 'great man's life' I'd dreamed of. Then began a patient little ant-like labour, through which I undertook to persuade myself that *every* life was lost in advance. This was all the easier for me in that I'd always *said* so (but without believing it). There was no shortage of arguments, of course. And if need be, I'd have invented some. It would have been too terrible for me to imagine that this 'life of an eminent man' was *possible* – that it had been lived by other men, at other times, in other places – and yet *I*, for my part, should not live it. Henceforth, for me, the writer was judged by his works – objectively – and his life was no different from the most humdrum lives. Racine was a petty bourgeois of Louis XIV's day. But that petty bourgeois had written *Phèdre*. It wasn't possible to move back from the works to the life: they escaped that life, rolled out of it, and remained outside for ever; they no more

65. The published version in French has *nationalisme*; presumably this is a mistake.

belonged to the person who had created them than to their readers. Less, perhaps. After this, I devoted myself to writing with a kind of fury. The sole purpose of an absurd existence was indefinitely to produce works of art which at once escaped it. That was its sole justification; an imperfect justification, moreover, which did not succeed in redeeming those long gobs of time that had to be swallowed one after another. It was really a morality of salvation through art. As for life itself, this was to be lived in carefree fashion, any old way. I was doing so well at living it 'any old way' that I was getting into a rut: I was acquiring bachelor habits.

I was at the nadir at the time of my madness and my passion for O. Two years: from March 1935 to March 1937. And yet those woes were beneficial to me. Madness pushed back the bounds of likelihood: from that time on, I abandoned my bourgeois optimism and understood that *everything* could happen to me, as much as to anybody else. I entered a world that was blacker, but less insipid. As for O., my passion for her burned away my workaday impurities like a Bunsen-flame. I grew thin as a rake, and distraught: farewell to all my comforts! And then we fell, the Beaver and I, beneath the intoxicating spell of that naked, instant consciousness, which seemed only to feel, with violence and purity. I placed her so high then that, for the first time in my life, I felt myself humble and disarmed before someone, felt that I wanted to learn. All this proved useful to me. At about the same period, and precisely because of this passion, I began to have doubts about salvation through art. Art seemed pretty pointless faced with that cruel, violent, naked purity. A conversation in which the Beaver once again showed me how trashy my attitude was detached me, once and for all, from that whole morality.

And then, at that precise moment, when I was at the nadir – so miserable that on several occasions I contemplated death with indifference; feeling old, fallen, finished; convinced, through a misunderstanding, that *La Nausée* had just been rejected by the *NRF* – everything began to smile on me. My book was accepted, *Le Mur* appeared in the June '37 issue of the *NRF*, I met T., I got a teaching post in Paris. All of a sudden I felt full of a tremendous, intense youthfulness; I was happy and found my life beautiful. Not that it had anything of the 'great man's life', but it was *my* life (I shall explain this on another occasion). And this time life won out over art, but slowly, timidly. I now think one never loses one's life; I think nothing's worth a life. And yet I have retained all my old ideas. I know a life is soft and doughy, unjustifiable and contingent, but that's unimportant. I know too that anything can happen to me, but it's to me that it will happen:

every event is *my* event. I don't want to expand on that. This division of my life into three periods is merely a preliminary. I wanted to situate the oscillations of my morality in an affective atmosphere. All I have just written basically represents only the description of my inner motives [*mobiles*]. I shall speak tomorrow of my reasons [*motifs*].

Saturday, 2 December

Yesterday, I wanted to register the affective atmosphere in which the moral problem was formulated for me. I see that it has, in a sense, always been resolved. By virtue of the simple fact that I have always thought of creating an 'oeuvre' – in other words, a series of works related to each other by common themes and all reflecting my per- sonality – I have always had the whole future before me. Whatever I may have thought at different times about my life – now embellishing its future with romantic colours, now picturing it in a black light – I was, for all that, provided from earliest childhood with a *life*. Nor have I ceased to be. A life: in other words, a tapestry-frame to be filled, with (already) a throng of rough-tacked outlines still needing to be embroidered. A life: in other words, a whole existing before its parts and being realized through its parts. To me, an instant did not appear like some vague unit aggregated to other units of the same kind; it was a moment that rose *against a background of life*. That life was a rosette-like composition wherein beginning and end coincided: maturity and old age gave meaning to childhood and adolescence.

In a sense, I envisaged each present moment from the point of view of an accomplished life – or, to be precise, I should say: from the point of view of a biography. And I considered myself bound to account for that moment to this biography: I felt its full meaning could be deciphered only by placing oneself in the future, and I always sketched out for myself a vague future that would allow me to make my present yield up its whole significance. This whole 'life', of course, was projected before me in a non-thematic fashion, and was the object of what Heidegger calls 'pre-ontological comprehension'. At least, most of the time: for it sometimes happened that I *imagined* moments of my future existence. That way of being embarked, from childhood on and without having been able to reflect, in a 'great life' – just as others were in the Catholic or communist faith – always denied me the anxieties and crises of conscience in which I used to see my comrades take such delight. I was sure of myself; I had simple faith.

I insist on the fact that this 'life' had nothing in common with the popular, biological concept of life, in which the ideas of consciousness, lived experience and fate are strangely intermingled, My life was an undertaking. But an undertaking favoured by the gods. The only risk I ran – through light-mindedness, passion or idleness – was of being diverted from it; of lingering too long here or there in some ill-omened delight. It would be my own fault if I squandered my life. In actual fact, however, my assiduity, concern to preserve my freedom and zeal gave me an incontrovertible right to bring it off. In short, it resembled a career: the brilliant young man enters a bank, he has powerful protectors, his career will take care of itself. All that's asked of him is application – and, through all his actions, to give evidence of his merits.

I never really called all this into question. Even during my gloomy years, the collapse of my youth was effected from underneath while the façade remained; every life was a lost game. But I was still the man of a life for all that. I was then in the custom of saying: 'I've had all I have wished for, but never in the way I wished.' And by this I meant that my life was as much of a success as it's possible for a life to be, but that a successful life wasn't really anything special. And it's true enough that I've had all that my naive imagination desired. And it's true that each time I've been disappointed. For I'd have wished every event to befall me as in a biography: in other words, as when the story's end is already known. This is the diappointment I expressed with respect to adventure, in *La Nausée*.[66] In short, I was always haunted by the idea of life. When I was at the École Normale, however, I still had a feeling of freedom and irresponsibility in relation to that life, my moves didn't count, I was still preparing for it. Whereas subsequently I fell in.

You can see how certain glorious excesses were always kept away from me: surrealist despair, Christian humility, revolutionary faith. I cherished an ideal of a great man's life that I borrowed from romanticism. It was Shelley, Byron, Wagner who'd had those lives I took as models. So stubbornly and without being aware of it I sought to achieve – between 1920 and 1960 – an 1830 life. This was concealed from me, of course, and I borrowed my materials from my own century: Marxism, pacifism, anti-fascism, etc. But the tapestry-frame dated from the epoch of *Antony*.[67] Nor did it ever occur to me to attempt a morality of pure pleasure, or of happiness: that was not my destiny. On the contrary, you can see how – in this perspective – the ideas of progress or superman, the admonition to master oneself, took

66. See, for example, *Oeuvres romanesques*, pp. 44–47 and 177.
67. Play by Alexandre Dumas *père*.

on a special value. I uprooted them from their own moral systems and introduced them into the framework of my life. My final goal was not to create the superman or to advance morality, but simply to have a fine life. They represented advice addressed specifically to me and valid solely for me and my career – exactly like the benevolent patron telling the young man of the future: 'Go and pay a call on the deputy director; look after Mr X., he's an important customer.'

If I now wonder which criterion enabled a fine life to be recognized, I perceive that a fine life was simply one that dampens the reader's eyes when it's recounted by a feeling biographer. I was imbued to the very marrow with what I shall term the biographical illusion, which consists in believing that a lived life can resemble a recounted life. Could I otherwise, from my adopted standpoint, have found Stendhal's life fine, with its unhappy loves and its long tedium at Civitavecchia? When one read about it, however, in Arbelet or Hazard, one did not lose sight of *La Chartreuse de Parme* – and *La Chartreuse de Parme* redeemed the entire life.[68]

What I've just explained, I never said to myself – or only very badly. But I felt it. On the other hand, I did have clear moral concerns. I didn't want just to be a great writer, or just to have a great man's fine life. I wanted to be somebody 'really good', as I used to say in about 1930, with a kind of virtuousness. These moral concerns certainly sprang from a different source than my desire to write and be great. But they combined easily with my dream of a fine life, and merged into it: I should deserve that life all the more if I lived it in a moral way; and the biography would be even richer and more moving if that man, who'd known and loved everything passionately and left fine works behind, had into the bargain been a 'really good' man.

But for long these moral tendencies, since they had merged with my desire for *life*, remained subordinated to it: it was *in order to achieve* the finest life that I'd be moral, not for the sake of morality itself. Naturally, this subordination of morality disappeared when I considered the moral problem in itself, or when I attempted to act morally. But, for the rest of the time, it was in the background without my realizing it. It was later, after the disintegration of my youth, that moral concerns became predominant.

If I leave to one side the destructive, anarchistic individualism of my nineteenth year, I see that immediately afterwards I concerned myself with a constructive morality. I have always been constructive,

68. Paul Hazard, *La Vie de Stendhal*, Paris 1927; Paul Arbelet, *La Jeunesse de Stendhal*, and a whole string of other works on Stendhal published in the interwar years.

and *La Nausée* and *Le Mur* gave only a false image of me, because I was obliged first to destroy. So I sought a moral system at the same time as a metaphysics, and I must say that for me (in this a Spinozist) morality has *never* been distinguished from metaphysics. The morality of duty never interested me, firstly for the reasons I set out on 5 November: in my eyes, it was embodied by my stepfather. But above all, however much I was told that the categorical imperative expressed the autonomy of my will, I didn't believe a word of it. I have always wanted my freedom to be above morality, not below it; I wanted this, as I noted earlier, even at the time when I was a spoiled child. And then the morality of duty is tantamount to separating morality from metaphysics – which in my eyes meant stripping it of its greatest attraction.

I see clearly today that, from my twentieth year on, the moral stance had the privilege in my eyes of conferring upon man a higher metaphysical dignity. This is what Nizan and I, in about 1925, used to dignify with the Spinozist term 'salvation'. The whole time I remained at the École, to be moral was tantamount for me to achieving one's salvation. The expression was inappropriate, but the thing itself has remained. To achieve one's salvation, not in the Christian sense of the word but in the Stoic sense: to impress a total modification upon one's nature, that raises it to a state of existential surplus-value. The expression 'existential' that I use here was then unknown to me, as was the thing itself, but I already had a premonition of it. In other words, I quite simply needed it. In philosophy, to need a notion is to have a premonition of it. In Spinoza too I found that idea of total transformation – and, properly understood, even in Kant. Hence, to be moral was tantamount to acquiring a higher dignity in the order of being; to existing more. At the same time, it was to isolate oneself. The wise man is no longer understood by other men and no longer understands them. And this existential transformation became ensconced in the wise man once and for all, nor would it budge: 'The wise man can take three tumbles.'[69]

I can see now that it was our period of incubation in superhumanity which brought Nizan and me to this point: what does mastering oneself mean, if not acceding to a higher dignity? I can see, too, that our contempt for men was decreeing we should withdraw from their ranks, so we were losing our humanity in one fell swoop. I see, finally, that the quest for salvation was the search for a means of access to the absolute. This quest for the absolute was, in any case, a fashion of that

69. Stoic saying, cf. *Being and Nothingness*, London 1969, p. 370.

period. The reviews *Esprit* and *Philosophie* (with Friedmann and Morhange), and in its own way surrealism, were also striving to achieve it. But for us that quest corresponded to a deep-lying tendency. I found it disagreeable to read, in a philosophical work, the customary arguments of relativism against absolute philosophies. I was a realist at the time, out of a taste for feeling the resistance of things, but most of all in order to accord to everything I saw its character of unconditional absolute: I could enjoy a landscape or sky only if I thought it was absolutely as I saw it.

The word intuition, and all terms designating the immediate communication of the spirit with things in themselves, delighted me beyond all measure. And the first morality I constructed, based on a few lines from *La Possession du monde*,[70] decreed enjoyment at the mere perception of anything. Which meant that perception, carried out ceremonially and respectfully, became a holy act: communication between two absolute substances, the thing and my soul. As I have said, it sometimes happened that I'd look at my table and repeat: 'It's a table, it's a table', until a shy thrill appeared that I'd christen joy. This tendency to consider perceived objects as absolutes gave rise, I think, to an idiosyncrasy of my style, which consists in repeated use of the form 'There is'. Guille used to make fun of me in the following terms: 'It was said of Jules Renard that he'd end up writing "The hen lays". But as for you, you'd write "There is the hen and she lays".' That's true: by the 'There is' I'd like to separate the hen from the rest of the world, I'd make her into a little, clearcut, motionless absolute, and I'd attribute laying to her as a property or attribute. There's something transitive about 'the hen lays' which greatly displeases me, which causes the 'substance' hen to vanish into a plurality of relationships and actions.

In short, I was seeking the absolute, I wanted to be an absolute, and that's what I called morality, that's what we used to term 'achieving our salvation'. So morality paid. I've never believed that morality didn't pay. This realism was also the affirmation of the world's resistance and of its dangers, against the dissolvent philosophy of idealism; the affirmation of Evil against the optimistic philosophy of unification. But I imagine it had another source: it derived from my wonder at the world and the age I was discovering. How could I admit that so many charms, so many pleasures to be conquered, so many fine dangers, were merely shadows, or badly unified 'representations'.

---

70. Essay (1919) by Georges Duhamel (1884–1966), novelist, essayist and poet at one time associated with the Unanimists.

There had to be something to conquer; we were hungry as wolves and dreamed of brutal conquests and ravishings. The world was a promised land and our conquest had to be absolute. Besides, idealism was expert knowledge, it was my stepfather. In that real world, there was something harsh, immoral and naked that didn't give a fig for parents or teachers. If the colours of things weren't mere appearances, then they all had secrets the experts didn't know.

In that case, to conquer the world it was no longer necessary to work one's way up the ladder or to queue up behind the laboratory men; one could possess it alone, one could think about it alone, it delivered up its secrets to the man alone, I'd not arrived too late. I looked at the trees and the water and I repeated ecstatically: 'There's work to be done. There's lots of work to be done.' And each of my 'theories' was an act of conquest and possession. It seemed to me that by placing them end to end, I should ultimately subjugate the world to myself alone. It was, besides, the period of a violent literary neo-realism. Rereading some of the works of that epoch, I have recently been struck on the contrary by their intellectual aridity. But at the time we didn't take them as such. They spoke to us of the whole world – of Constantinople, of New York and of Athens – and their glitter of comparisons, which today I precisely find extremely precious and contrived, dazzled and deafened us with a profusion of lights and sounds.

It took me a long time to understand that comparison should be kept to a minimum. At that time, every comparison seemed to me like an act of possession. Gide in his journal berates authors who are set on having images: 'A freshly shaved field. Why "freshly-shaved"?' [II, p. 385] Well, 'freshly-shaved' is a magic spell: the author has invented a personal way of saying 'to mow', has invented it *before* the meadow in question, and this verbal invention is tantamount to an appropriation. I used to put images everywhere, with a brutal intoxication. Last week I found that same intoxication in Mac Orlan, as I was rereading *Sous la lumière froide*: 'A pink and white Norwegian was holding his little glass between his two clasped hands, like a bird he was trying to warm.'[71] What's that image doing there, for God's sake? But at the time, with barbaric joy, I used to overwhelm things in a hail of images. And the invention of images was, fundamentally, a moral, sacred ceremony: it was the appropriation of that absolute, the thing, by that other absolute, myself.

71. Pierre Mac Orlan, pseudonym of Pierre Dumarchais (1883–1970), author of humorous and adventure novels.

As I have said, this quest for the absolute might have led me to the existential. But to tell the truth, the very notion of the existential was too difficult for me to have invented it alone. And then I was diverted from it at the time for another reason. There was something of the existential then floating about almost everywhere in our little world. For many students, their first contact with philosophy had expressed itself in a kind of amazement – which was genuinely existential and authentic, though pretty silly for all that – at death, time, the existence of other consciousnesses. The Beaver, precisely, didn't escape this, because she's more naturally authentic than me. At the age of eighteen, she was sitting on an iron chair in the Luxembourg Gardens, leaning back against the Museum wall and thinking: 'I'm here, time is flowing by and this instant will never return', and this caused her to fall into a state of stupefaction resembling sleep. But this philosophical poverty is, in reality, very authentic philosophy: it's the moment at which the question transforms the questioner. The Beaver on her chair was really a little metaphysical being: she had metaphysicized herself wholeheartedly, she was throwing herself into time, she was living time, she *was* time. On waking, however, it was her words – those empty, highflown words – that betrayed the strange metamorphosis: 'this instant will never return'.

The very poverty of that language obliged those student metaphysicians to borrow a richer one. They found Baruzi's hazy and abstruse, Brunschvicg's dissolvent;[72] they put up with them as best they could and attempted to cast their impressions in those new words, but they were hardly successful. The result was a kind of philosophical rhetoric disguising ecstasies; a way of chewing over problems with no solution; mere words. The gap was too great between those metaphysical hours and that academic language. As for us – Nizan, Aron, myself – we were very unjust to those poor people, who really did have the *feeling* for philosophy but who lacked tools. To us, they were the most odious representatives of loose thinking and verbalism. In opposition to them, we'd placed ourselves under the sign of Descartes, because Descartes is an explosive thinker. Nothing displeased us so much as that grey thought; those transmutations. evolutions and metamorphoses; those slow thrills. Phrases like 'Become what you are' set our teeth on edge. By contrast, we'd spend our time isolating concepts, making them incommunicable and closed each upon itself – like Descartes, separating soul and body so well that no one has been able to reunite them since. We'd have been apt to say: 'One can become

---

72. Jean Baruzi (1881–1950), historian of religion at the Collège de France.

only what one is not yet. So one cannot become what one is.' Thus, affecting to stick to strict definitions, we used to repudiate elegant, soft thoughts and had the impression we were thinking by great sword-strokes. This was what we used to call a revolutionary thought. And indeed Descartes, by refusing intermediaries between thought and extension, displays a catastrophic and revolutionary cast of mind: he cuts and slashes, leaving to others the task of re-stitching. We cut and slashed in his wake.

Something of that time has remained to me: for example, I sniggered at that extraordinary title of Chardonne's: *Love is Much More than Love*.[73] And, to be sure, the title is idiotic. But it was above all my old Cartesian indignation reawakening, for it's true that love is much more than love. Only it should have been put differently. Thus, our perception isolated things and made them into juxtaposed absolutes; our thought fragmented concepts and made them incommunicable; and in this way we gave ourselves the impression we were thinking with brutal power: that we saw grimly and to the bottom of things. For us, to think, to separate concepts, was to act as moralists and dispensers of justice. We were legislating, by those stubborn refusals to move away from concepts, and would have ended up becoming Megarians if, happily for us, we'd not been less fussy about our own thought than about that of others.[74]

The fact remains we oriented ourselves towards a neo-realist pluralism and, in order to seek the absolute in things, I turned my back on the existential absolute in myself. Yet I vaguely sensed in myself an absolute and free consciousness; as a moral agent, I considered myself unfettered by conditions. It is this intransigence, as well as my theory of contingency, that led me to adopt a morality of salvation through art, outlined in this notebook on 8 November. But you can see how many levels I was then moving on. Officially, everything was mere contingency and every life was lost; it was possible only to create fine works outside oneself. Underneath, however, I was quite convinced I should have a life that matched my works; I sought friendship, love, all the passions, pursued every kind

73. Jacques Chardonne, *L'Amour, c'est beaucoup plus que l'amour*.

74. The Megarian school of philosophy flourished at Megara near Athens between the late-fifth and early-third centuries BC. No writings have survived from it, but from contemporary references it is clear that its members were influenced by Socrates and the Eleatics and critical of Plato and Aristotle, and that they made a contribution to logic. It is possible, however, that Sartre is referring here to Theognis of Megara, an aristocratic poet of the sixth century, who was concerned to prevent intermingling of cultural values between the classes.

of experience. And to deserve that life which I was expecting – but in relation to which I was not yet committed, considered myself still to be free – I did not consider it sufficient to write, I also had to be moral. For me, this morality was a total transformation of my existence and an absolute. But ultimately I was seeking the absolute in things, rather than in myself; I was a realist for moral reasons.

At the same time, thanks to the Protestant austerity of a lover of justice, I'd adopted a harsh and trenchant thought, which distanced me from the absolute that I was myself and confined me in a rough pedantry that delighted in its own harshness. That harshness went hand in hand with the violence I unleashed upon my schoolfellows. All this drew me towards a violent enjoyment of a garish, colourful world in complete contradiction with the one I'd given myself through my theory of contingency. And I went so far as to preach a Nietzschean morality of joy, whereas in other respects all joy and all harshness were shown to be impossible in the contingent, nauseous world I'd discovered.

It's in this happy disorder that my years at the École Normale slipped by. Then came the gloomy years. Then, little by little, the aesthetic morality I'd equipped myself with – through a generous pessimism – came to assume more importance in my eyes. It wasn't good for man to know himself, or to be over-concerned with himself; one should just write and create. I didn't renounce the absolute, though; but by a very natural slippage it came to cloak man's works. Henceforth, man himself was an absurd creature, lacking any raison d'être; and the big question posed was that of his *justification*. I felt myself utterly dreary and unjustified. Only the work of art could give man that justification, for the work of art is a metaphysical absolute. So, lo and behold!, the absolute is restored – but *outside* man. Man is worth nothing.

It's at about this moment that my theoretical opposition to humanism was strongest. I say theoretical because, as I've already noted, at about the same time I was surreptitiously seeking compromises. And clearly it still remained a morality of *salvation*, but this time there was no upheaval in man's heart that could save him. Salvation came to him from outside. I have said how sullen my mood was, as I defended this thesis. At bottom, I couldn't console myself for the fact that I'd lost my 'great man's life'. I had certain bêtes noires: Benda, because his clerks had some similarity with my artists; Elémir Bourges, because he too had upheld a theory of salvation through art.[75] Proust himself disturbed me. I particularly detested Tennyson, because that English writer – of whom I hadn't read a single line – had, according to reliable reports, lived in conformity with my sermons: he had written, and nothing had ever happened to him. I used to say furiously to the Beaver: 'I certainly don't want to have a life like Tennyson's.' On the other hand, the dismal, industrious life of Cézanne impressed me by its grandeur. Obviously this was the one that could illustrate my thesis best. But all the same, I found it somewhat hard. To be like Cézanne: yes . . . of course . . . if one wished. But I couldn't help eyeing the tragic, brilliant lives of Rimbaud and Gauguin.

The question grew more complex at about that time, because reading Scheler made me understand that there existed *values*. Basically, until then, quite absorbed by the metaphysical doctrine of salvation, I'd never really understood the specific problem of morality. The 'ought-to-be' seemed to me to be represented by the categorical imperative; and since I rejected the latter, it seemed to me that I rejected the former with it. But when I'd understood that there existed specific natures, equipped with an existence as of right, and called values; when I'd understood that these values, whether proclaimed or not, regulated each of my acts and judgements, and that by their nature they 'ought to be': then the problem became enormously more complex. At about the same time, the Beaver forced me to renounce the theory of salvation through art. I'd long since abandoned Cartesian thought, with its flashing blades. I'd long since ceased to count on my 'life of a famous man'. Our common faith in the value of the constructed was shaken by the Z. story. The only thing left was to begin everything over again.

Sunday 3

This morning Mistler tells me wonderingly: 'It's comical, I've always thought of war as an immense stupidity, indeed I still do, and yet for me it will be an opportunity for immense progress.'

Gide's journal: four-fifths of it was written (at least so far as what's published here is concerned) between the ages of 40 and 67.[76] It's a

---

75. Julien Benda (1867–1956) published his *La Trahison des clercs* in 1927, arguing that intellectuals should remain above the hurly-burly of political and social conflict, defending timeless values.

Elémir Bourges (1852–1925) wrote grandiose novels influenced by Wagner, such as *Le Crépuscule des dieux*.

76. The 1939 edition of Gide's journal to which Sartre is referring covered the years 1885–1939.

journal of mature years. It reminds me of that writing-book, its cover adorned with flowers, which my grandfather showed me one day. My great-grandfather used to write in it: the main events in his family (births, deaths, marriages, etc.) – moral and pious maxims – exhortations addressed by him to himself. Isn't that what's called a 'family Bible' [*livre de raison*]? That writing-book seemed to have been chosen ceremoniously – and I see that Gide takes a great deal of care over choosing his. And one could sense a magical function of the writing: to fix, to engrave, phrases and dates; to protect them against oblivion; to give them a ceremonial character. That kind of notebook derives from the placards Protestants used to stick up on their walls, embellished with pious maxims – just as the art of mystery-plays derives from stained-glass windows. Behind all this, there lies the idea of *engraving* and a deep, mystical feeling that seems to go back to the origins of writing. I find this feeling in Gide's journal, attenuated, civilized, but real. And for me, this magical, religious feeling is at the origin of classicism: the classical author engraves a maxim on the wall, carves it into his material, then settles down before it and meditates. Classicism is the art of controlled meditations.

At the same time – and this goes in the opposite direction, but the contradiction is in Gide himself – the journal, with him, is an exercise in spontaneous writing. Learning to write all in one go. That curiosity about himself, that desire to see himself *de*-composed, will later lead him to his *Dictées*.[77] He will no longer even want to write with his pen's knowledge: his pen must no longer come between him and the paper. 'The great secret of Stendhal . . . consisted in writing *at once* . . . It would seem that his thought does not take time to put on its shoes before beginning to run' [III, pp. 361-2]. That route to relaxed and gratuitous, dishevelled thought – that value of truth conferred upon what's not clad at all – might lead to automatic writing, even has led other writers there. But one would have to lose oneself, and Gide never loses himself. He merely points. He wants to hold thought at the farthest limit at which it's composed, but not beyond. It's words he has got it in for – not thought. Of course, at the other extreme from this anxiety, there's his constant preoccupation with *working*, with writing hard and flat out. Here's what he says on 27 July '14 about a manuscript by J. E. Blanche: 'This morning I completely rewrote three pages of it, changing hardly anything, moreover, except the word-order and arrangement of the sentences, which were tied

---

77. Gide extracted a number of 'Dictated Pages' from his journal and published them in the *NRF*, July 1929, and later in the volume *Divers* (Miscellany).

together any which way. The extraordinary weaknesses of his style enlighten me as to those of his painting: he never embraces his object; his good points always spring from *impatience*; he is easily satisfied. As soon as he has made four slight changes on a page as he copied, he thinks he has "worked over it considerably" . . . ' [II, pp. 45-6]. But isn't impatience also the principal quality of Stendhal, and of that thought which runs without putting its shoes on? Why blame here what one commends there? Because of the results? But in that case a new element would appear: talent or prior exercise, which is irrelevant here.

To tell the truth, Gide's journal is the image of his hesitation between two aspects of his private life: tension and relaxation. The *acte gratuit*, Gide's sensuality, his renowned curiosity which so influenced our literature, and finally his desire to lose himself the better to find himself, are aspects of *relaxation*. It's the world that will teach him what he is. Similarly, it's the sentence he has written in haste, *instantaneously*, that will teach him what he was thinking. It's basically a question of throwing yourself into the universe, so that the universe will reflect your image back to you. Reaching the individual through pantheism. That unexpected, revealed image is also the notorious *devil's share*. Gide basically seeks to surprise himself at moments when he doesn't know he's watching.

However, is it quite certain that this way of losing oneself will allow us to find ourselves again? Sometimes Gide doubts it, Then he'll call it (15 January 1912): 'depersonalization, obtained by an effort of the will'. And he'll write, on the same date: 'Constant *vagabundance* of desire – one of the chief causes of the deteriorating of the personality,' And the orders he gives himself on that date inform us as to his vagrant habits: 'Never go out without a definite aim; hold to this. Walk along without looking in every direction. In a train choose any compartment whatever' [I, p.312]. One can see the infinite curiosity underlying the availability he extols in *Les Nourritures terrestres*.[78] But it's necessary to pull oneself together; to reassume the studied personality: 'Danger of aiming toward a limitless empire. To conquer Russia, Napoleon had to risk France. Necessity of linking the frontier with the centre. It is time to return home' [ibid.]. He also uses the expression to 'recover possession of oneself'. His diary is essentially a tool for *recovering possession of himself*. Consequently, more the witness and instru-

---

78. *The Fruits of the Earth*, Harmondsworth 1970. 'Availability' or 'unattachedness' (*disponibilité*) was a central concept in Gide's work at the turn of the century (*Les Nourritures Terrestres* was published in 1897).

ment of *tensions* than of relaxations. This is why it's rare for Gide to record in it the shows he has seen, the conversations he has had, or for him to describe there the people he has been meeting. All that is relaxation. He sometimes permits himself to indulge in it, but as if reluctantly. It seems, moreover, that for his external notes he often uses other notebooks, which he has not published in the *Journal*: 'I stupidly left at Cuverville . . . the little notebook just like this one, only four days old, but in which I had written last night, or this very morning, some rather sombre reflections about K' (25 July '14) [II, p.44].

On the other hand, since his journal is above all a tool for recovering possession of himself, it is full of exhortations and little bits of simple advice that Gide gives himself:

'In order to be more economical of it, I shall note in minute detail the manner in which I spend my time.

Seven thirty: bath, reading of Souday's article on A.S.

Eight-thirty to nine: breakfast, etc.' [I, p.315].

'1914, 11 June: Repeat to myself every morning that the most important remains to be said, and that it is high time', etc. [II, p.21].

It's at this moment that the journal most closely and irritatingly resembles the moral works of Pastor Wagner.[79] It contains childish maxims in the following style: 'Do not disdain small victories; when it's a question of will, many a mickle makes a muckle.' 'Well, of course,' one thinks, 'why does he need to write it down, everybody knows that.' It's because he writes it, not in order to instruct us, nor even to instruct himself, but in order to *repeat* it to himself: in order to *engrave* it. It's the Protestant placard hung over the bed as a rebuke. It's the little devotional trick, a habit with pious souls.

In short, hesitation for Gide between two conceptions of truth: truth is what I am (what Alain calls the loose thinking of psychologists) – truth is what I want to be.

And the journal itself becomes a duty. Gide exhorts himself to keep it up. And if he doesn't manage to, he has sinned. Thus, by inviting us to read it, he's urging us to watch him in the arduous fulfilment of his duties. We plunge straight into morality as soon as we open the book.

Another purpose of the journal: to allow Gide to write any old thing, when he doesn't feel in the mood for work – in order not to lose his touch and to sustain the momentum and speed already achieved. Hence reflections like the following: 'Rather good work, whence this

79. Pastor Wagner: Charles Wagner (1852–1918), champion of liberal Protestantism and of secular education, responsible for the moral sections of the primary-school syllabus; his numerous publications include *La Vie simple*.

notebook's silence' (18 January 1917) [II, p. 193].

That's how I explain the disappointment of those (including, at first, myself) who, influenced by having read the journals of Stendhal, Renard, the Goncourts, etc., opened Gide's in the hope of finding details there about his life, his character or his milieu. My disappointment dates from Berlin, when I read fragments of the journal in the *Oeuvres complètes*. I then judged the work to be very boring. But I was mistaken. Everything's there. Only everything's wrapped up. Gide's concern in it isn't to know at all, but to reform. So if one wishes to know, in order to arrive at one's own judgement, one must resist the natural tendency that leads one to make oneself the author's accomplice. One must read dry-eyed, remaining outside, calling into question the very principles of reform. Gide has observed himself constantly, and he always moves on the reflexive plane. Sometimes there's even twofold reflection. But he's never a psychologist, his goal is never purely and simply to register. The original concern is moral.

The sentences of Gide's journal must never be read as if they were simple, registering statements, even where they're in the indicative; they are wishes, prayers, commandments, hymns, laments, condemnations. The only proof of this I need is a very odd 'Amen', which occurs at the end of a passage one might believe to be purely informative: 'I intend to prevent its ever being said of anyone that he is imitating me or that he resembles me . . . I want not to have any *manner* . . . Amen' [I, p.329]. 'Amen' is obviously ironical. But, as it mocks, it betrays the inner tremor, the fervour, with which Gide wrote those lines,. The 'I want' is not just registered (as when I ask Keller: 'Where are you going?' and he replies 'I want to shave') but willed: it's will itself. He says so himself, moreover: 'As soon as the emotion decreases, the pen should stop' [ibid.]. Which is hardly possible, except in private diaries – and which shocks me a little: me, whose modesty is at once affronted, in this diary of my own, if I don't hold what I write at a respectful distance.

The role of *exercise* in Gide, in the Greek sense of ἄσκησις: the journal, spiritual exercise, reading English, literary exercise, exercise in thinking, exercises on the piano (and studies). At Cuverville, often whole days of exercises: piano, English, journal. Need to keep oneself on a tight rein (rather as young ladies used to be made to do tapestry-work). Constant thirst for profit, likewise. With him, exercise takes the place of a career.

Hardly have I written these lines than I come across a passage on p.389: 'I have been very busy these last few days writing a fair copy of my *Souvenirs de la Cour d'Assises*. It is, I think, a very good exercise . . . ' [I, p.340].

Journal even more curious and idiosyncratic because of what it omits than because of what it reveals. All relations with Em. are passed over in silence. And, certainly, Gide suppressed a good deal of this at the moment of publishing his journal. But we also know he tore up some of it as he went along, at the request of Em. herself, And, above all, in various places we can read that he *forbids himself from day to day* to speak of Emmanuelle. Why, since in 1939 he recognizes that, in this way, he's furnishing only a 'mutilated me'? [III, p.413]. Out of piety, I think. Thus, there are hierarchies of holiness in his soul. The logbook is holy, but Emmanuelle is holier. She must not be touched. But, on the other hand – if a few allusions to his passion for M. in 1914 are excluded – the journal hardly presents his sexual life other than in terms of vice and the remorse this inspires. There's much talk in it of solitary sin, and I can see it's because this sin is of the same order as idleness, heedlessness, lack of drive – all those faults with which one can indulge oneself.

The relations dealt with in the journal are essentially those with oneself; there's one domain that Gide never touches upon: that of relations *constructed* with others. There's no doubt at all he'd have had the opportunity, if he'd spoken about Emmanuelle. But, precisely, he doesn't speak about her. His nights of love inspire him to a few cries of joy, but he conceals them – even though he was apparently fond of recounting them. In fact, everything that relates to men, to the world, to society (whether it's Wilde, the court of assizes, or certain odd encounters), he files elsewhere – no doubt because they're literary materials and, as such, unworthy of having a place in the log.

Sometimes, however, he forgets himself, sketches a portrait, tells some anecdote, But it's *on the occasion* of some admonishment to himself, for wasting too much time in society; or else it's to enliven some dreary account of his days. So his journal is a closely supervised one, with nothing careless about it. If he has let himself go excessively, he tears it up. I remember Dabit criticizing himself severely in his journal, because he'd been tempted to tear something up.[80] But although Gide also sometimes criticizes himself, that's what he usually does. On 15 June 1916 he writes: 'I have torn out about twenty pages

---

80. Eugène Dabit (1898–1936): Novelist of popular life in Paris, notably in *Hôtel du Nord*, hailed as a 'populist novel', and author of a posthumously published *Journal intime* (1928–36).

of this notebook . . . The pages I tore up seemed like pages written by a madman' [II, p.142]. But precisely, it's that mad Gide we'd be curious to see. Even in his remorse, however, even in his emotional transports, he's still classical: when he doesn't compose he selects.

And then, at the heart of his diary, standing out from the entire fabric, the most ingenious and civilized product of that whole self-examination: the Devil. It's the Devil to whom those notebooks should be dedicated, he'd really have deserved it.

I walk out with Mistler and go for lunch with him at the Lion d'Or. He explains that he has completely changed, thanks to me; that when he was called up in September he was in despair, but now he's serene – or almost – and has understood that this war is an event in *his* life. He's intimidated, and stammers out his thanks. I'm intimidated too, but I lap it up. Moreover, I'm pleased because it's like an experimental verification of my new moral ideas. Yet, at the same time, always this odd impression that it doesn't concern me; that I'm acting a part and am really a wretched buffoon who fools everybody.

An excellent passage in the *Feuillets* of 1913-14: 'He who protests will later on make of the ability to renounce the wisdom of his whole life. (That too can be a moral code based on complacency.)' [I, p.344]

This expression 'moral code based on complacency' strikes me as rich and profound. It tallies quite well with my current preoccupations:

– resignation can be a moral code based on complacency (sad serenity; luminous, calm melancholy, etc.);

– stoicism too, as I've experienced throughout these past three months;

– naturalism: there's a certain naturalism in Gide, a certain trust in the virtues of raw nature (to be oneself without compromising; to adapt oneself to the world like the organism to its environment), which often torments him – and which he wonders if isn't inspired by the Devil;

– morality based on duty: all that's hidden beneath that shameful formula, with its Kantian ring: 'I have only the right to do my duty . . .'.

In the end, I can't really see anything but a moral code based on authenticity escaping the reproach of complacency (authenticity, not purity).

Mauriac (*Le Figaro*, 2 December): 'The eternal question that has always divided Frenchmen – whether it was a matter of some internal dispute like the Dreyfus Affair, or of the Spanish tragedy, or of the war with Germany – concerns the relations between politics and morality.'

I think I understand, and can now *feel*, what true morality is. I see how metaphysics and values are connected; humanism and contempt; our absolute freedom and our condition in a single life bounded by death; our inconsistency, as beings without a God yet not authors of ourselves, and our dignity; our autarkic independence as individuals and our historicity. I shall explain about this tomorrow or some other day; I want to think some more about it. But at least this time it will be a morality I've felt and applied before having thought it.

For a time, I let myself go, but in these past few days I've recovered the tension of the first days of war.

Monday, 4 December

We're leaving tomorrow morning for Morsbronn. This morning, great excitement all round me as I work. My confederates and the 3 from the SRA are busy with their packages.[81] Arguments and slanging matches.

Not to *accept* what happens to you. That's too much and not enough. To *assume* it (when you've understood that nothing can happen to you except by your own hand), in others words to adopt it as one's own, exactly *as if* one had given it oneself by decree, and, accepting that responsibility, to make it an opportunity for new advances, *as if* that were why one had given it oneself.

This 'as if' is not a lie, but derives from the intolerable human condition, at once *causa sui* and without foundation, so that it's no judge of what happens to it, but all that does happen to it can do so only *by its own hand* and within its responsibility.

Start off from these two ideas:
1. Man is a plenum that man cannot leave.
2. It's necessary to lose all hope. Morality begins where hope ends (future life, human perfectability, etc.)

One is totally responsible for one's life.

81. SRA = *Service de Renseignements de l'Artillerie* (Artillery Intelligence Service).

At every moment, the world is present to my life in its totality.

One never has any excuse, because events can affect you only if they're assumed by your own possibilities.

Keller collects other people's rubbish, especially the officers' – an issue of *Conferencia*; a copy of *La Revue des Deux Mondes*; an old novel that Hang abandoned because a bottle of cough-syrup had been spilt on it, so that it stank. He puts everything into his pack without looking, sometimes saying: 'It's for my wife', at other times: 'It's for the kid, I'll take it him when I go on leave.' What attracts him, here, is the object to be taken that may still be 'of some use'; he prowls round the rubbish bins, waste-paper baskets, etc. and always finds something to fish out.

No one owes you anything – and, above all, you have no rights over fate. Everything is always given, because you are always superfluous in relation to the world.

Metaphysical value of the person who assumes his life or authenticity. It's the only absolute.

We're leaving tomorrow morning at 5 for Morsbronn. To occupy a sector. The officers don't seem very happy at the prospect of these new responsibilities.

If Pieter speaks to an officer for a few moments, he always says 'I had a chat' – to evoke the trustful unconstraint of a conversation between men.

Tuesday, 5 December

4 in the morning. My confederates are finishing off their parcels, and during this time I'm noting down the main passages of an article by X. in *La Revue des Deux Mondes* for 15 August 1939: 'War-Peace'.
  'In the present state of military technique, a hundred tanks and over a hundred tons of shells are needed to be certain of breaking the resistance put up, on a single kilometre, by a single battalion well dug in and protected by barbed wire . . . On restricted frontiers like those of Europe, too narrow for the vast numbers of the levy en masse, designed for defence by permanent fortifications, there is very little hope of wrong-footing the enemy's dispositions . . . A decisive vic-

tory can be achieved only after the success of numerous offensive actions, hence at the price of a gigantic effort presupposing a considerable numerical and industrial superiority. If that were not the case, the conflict could be resolved only by the moral and material exhaustion of one of the two belligerents. In both cases, the struggle would take the form of a struggle to the death, involving such losses and destruction that the most advantageous peace conditions could not compensate for them.

'*The classical conception of war thus leads to forms of conflict that no longer correspond to the possibilities and necessities of today's Europe.* For the latter has not yet recovered from the upheavals of every kind brought about by the Great War. It needs peace in order to recover its health and reorganize its economy in the light of modern means of production . . . Furthermore, public opinion in most of the European nations instinctively rejects the idea of war . . . *This conviction is a basic fact specific to our epoch.*

'Given this, how are conflicts between nations to be resolved? . . . New methods are required . . . The problem remains the same: it consists in forcing a State to subscribe to the obligations one is seeking to impose on it – in short, to capitulate, War may change its forms, but its essential object remains the same.

'Incapable of forcing the adversary to sue for mercy by a single blow, the new war will aim to convince him to prefer capitulation to continuation of the struggle. Radical action is replaced by a *persuasive action* of force. However . . . politics formerly enjoyed only a very slight margin of pressure . . . the least error of manoeuvre, the least excess could lead to war. Politics was thus exercised only through a delicate game of combinations and compromises. The situation today is quite different: the ever-present spectre of total war, the fear it inspires, lead people to see it as nothing but a solution of despair that will be resorted to only in the last extremity. The impotence of military action has rendered the epidermis of nations very insensitive (Anschluss, Sudeten, intervention in Spain, Russo-Japanese conflict at Changkufeng): examples could be multiplied of the astonishing patience manifested by nations, compared with their former excitability.

'This repugnance for total war, by a surprising detour, thus authorizes a use of violence that goes decisively beyond the framework of diplomatic traditions . . . It's no longer peace, and not yet war as we conceive of it, but an intermediary state which we will call war-peace.

'War-peace is based on the idea of exploiting the fear of catastrophic war to exert stronger pressures than previously, while at the same time avoiding the creation of sufficient tension to lead the enemy to resort to total war.

'The first element in every combination will thus consist in calculating the critical point beyond which the adversary would prefer total war to capitulation.

'Characteristic procedure: *political war*, in other words intervention in the internal politics of the enemy country. One thus directly attacks the nerve centres upon which capitulation depends, (Ludendorff, *total war*: the spiritual cohesion of the nation is an essential factory of victory.)

'3 solutions:
– the uprising suceeeds, the goal is attained, the new government spontaneously accepts the conditions imposed;
– the uprising succeeds only partially (Spain, Palestine): civil war and intervention;
– the uprising fails utterly: in the event of a favourable international conjuncture, direct intervention (Sudeten); otherwise one washes one's hands of it (Dolfuss assassination).

'*Economic war*.

'Same insidious character, but its application in peace-war has not given decisive results. For total war requires a total reorganization of the whole economy to supply the vast needs it engenders, It is then indispensable to reduce civilian consumption to a minimum, and to make up shortfalls by imports. Thus, in the last analysis, the effort can be pursued with the desired intensity only if the nation possesses sufficient financial resources or credit, and if it has free lines of communication at its disposal. These considerations have led post-war theoreticians to attribute considerable value to a country's economic resources, when assessing its 'war potential' . . . This idea lay behind the organization of sanctions under the auspices of the League of Nations. *Their application against Italy led to a complete fiasco. Reasons: economic sanctions can have a decisive effect only against a nation that embarks on a conflict possessing the character of total war.* But this was not the case: the conquest of Ethiopia . . . was merely a war of limited effort . . . Italy never had to organize a war economy . . . Sanctions were unleashed upon a normal peacetime economy.

'Alongside the blockade – various forms of economic struggle (dumping, etc.)

'Constant use of *military forces*:
a) in the guise of a threat;

b) supplementary intervention in an internal conflict;
c) direct military actions: very frequent, but very restricted, and presenting the appearance of simple raids mostly launched by surprise.'

Arrival at Morsbronn at 7 o'clock. I am at once assigned to the telephone exchange, in a big room filled with the comings and goings of our officers and the officers we are replacing. The latter present a mirror-image of ourselves in every regard. Their division is constituted exactly like ours: that lieutenant is the replica of Lieutenant Penato; that colonel is the replica of our colonel; they're all there, right down to the replicas of us weathermen – a fat red-faced Fatty Arbuckle with glasses and an affected expression on his jovial countenance, another thin and pale with a frill of beard. We stare at these images of ourselves with curious hostility. Vague feeling of solidarity with *our* officers against *their* officers. Besides, they look very disagreeable. One of them, a glib-tongued lieutenant back from Paris, says to his colonel: 'Still raring to go, Sir!' – 'And what are they saying in Paris, then?' – 'They're saying: Bugger them for not attacking, because the war'll last longer. They're finding it no joke, Paris at night with all those lights switched off, and they'd like us to hurry up and smash each other's faces in, so that it's all over and done with.' – 'In short,' says a captain, 'just what we think.' Slight feeling of self-importance because I've been entrusted with this fearsome, ringing instrument with its score of plugs and sockets. But very pissed off, really, because around 200 calls are connected daily, and I shall no longer have any time to work. Anxieties: am I going to be left doing this job? I persuade Paul to protest: I'm a weatherman, not a telephone-operator. I'm writing this on a chair during a short break, and there are continual comings and goings all round me.

That war-peace X. talks about so intelligently helps to explain the sequel we're living through now: peace-war. The transition from one to the other is imperceptible. There are two reasons for this. 1. Germany didn't *want* war. She was above all attached to that form of international relations – war-peace – since it was particularly favourable for her. She played a tricky game in Poland, and failed to estimate the 'critical point' correctly. For her, the game is still being played on the 'war-peace' level: she refuses total war, because she can't fight one. 2. But the democratic powers are basically intent on applying sanctions. At bottom, they are sticking to the Geneva Covenant and the peaceful technique of sanctions, as at the time of the Abyssinian war. Now, as then, it's a question of punishing aggression. Taught by the

Ethiopian experience, however, they know that to use economic sanctions effectively against a nation it is necessary first to oblige that nation to put itself on a total-war footing. Thus the French armies on the German frontier have no purpose other than to force Germany to adopt a war economy destined to make their blockade effective.

Thus total war remains the spectre invoked by the belligerents, as at the time of war-peace. When Hitler threatens us with a landing in England, an air-raid on London, etc., what is he doing but summoning up the phantom of total war? And the refugees and provincials who are beginning to get used to this war, they're just as much afraid of war – real war – as if they were at peace. The methods, meanwhile, are still as before: military force remains an auxiliary; the economic war is accompanied by a political war, with each of the belligerents counting on an uprising against his adversary to save him from having to use armed force. The possibility remains of seeking victory on distant battle-fields in countries not defended by fortified barriers, where the conflict will pit one expeditionary corps against another. If, for example, Rumania were to be invaded by a German army and we sent reinforcements there: in that case, the war would once more become like former conflicts (those that occurred before 1914), in which, as J. Romains says, it's the *loser* who decides that he has lost – like, for example, Russia deciding after Tsushima that Japan had defeated her. So this war's one of Geneva-type economic sanctions on the one hand against war-peace on the other. The common concern of the belligerents is not to arrive at total war. And if it seems a 'phoney war', that's because it's a war in which the adversaries are animated, above all, by a desire not to wage war.

Wednesday, 6 December

I've more or less managed on the telephone. It really seemed like magic: all those little shutters ringing as they fell, those plugs that had to be pushed into the right holes and made voices spring up, and especially those long conversations of which I was the silent witness. It amused me. I had a strange impression of power, as if I were a conjuror who believed in his tricks. Only the stove smoked, and that gave me a violent headache.

During the rare moments of respite, I read Flaubert's *L'Éducation sentimentale*. How clumsy and disagreeable it is. How silly that constant hesitation between stylization and realism in the dialogues and portrayals. A pitiful story engraved in marble. Zola can be seen peeping through a cumbersome Parnassian style. So far, moreover, it's utterly idiotic: without a single feeling or idea or character, without even those historical comments Balzac is capable of. Its descriptions do not portray. The sentences are clumsy and laboured where they seek to etch things, to describe machines for example: 'the din was muffled [*s'absorbait*] by the hissing of the steam, which, escaping through some iron plates, wrapped the whole scene in a whitish mist, while the bell in the bows went on clanging incessantly.'[82] That din which '*s'absorbe*' – and how can the steam escape 'through some iron plates'? 'The deck shook beneath a gentle internal vibration' [ibid.]. Beneath? He means that a gentle vibration was rising from the sides of the ship and being transmitted to the deck.

Hackneyed verbs (in general, if he lacks a precise term, Flaubert uses animist metaphors: banks slip past, a pile of baggage grows higher, din is muffled) [ibid.]. Often he uses passives with the most unfortunate effect: 'A . . . stole . . . *was placed* over the brass rail behind her' [p.19]. An irritating use of the imperfect (heralding the Goncourts) to create a scene and drown whatever may be offensive about the *act*, in a kind of poetic repetition amounting to a retreat into the supernatural. 'Mlle Marthe ran up to him and, her arms clasped round his neck, was pulling his moustache' [ibid.]. It's what I shall term the Virgilian imperfect: 'ibant obscuri sub sola nocte'.[83] The most typical example (I think the Virgilian echo is striking here – Nisus and Euryale): 'Frédéric threw half his cloak over his friend's shoulders. The two of them wrapped themselves in it and, holding each other round the waist, were walking along underneath it, side by side' [p.28]. It will be noted that on each occasion the imperfect is preceded by a participle in apposition to the subject. Stylistic mannerism: to render marmoreal.

Example of negligence in his verbs: 'A pitiless energy lay [*reposait*] in his grey-green eyes' [p. 31]. It's no accident that Flaubert is meticulous about his nouns and slapdash about his verbs: this Parnassian takes care over the *show*, but neglects the *event*. The event remains shocking for him: 'I hate the movement that disorders the lines.' But his sentences are colossi with feet of clay: they crumble down into words, because the joints do not hold. Importance of Flaubert: his style is transitional. The industrial civilization of Louis-

82. Gustave Flaubert, *L'Éducation sentimentale*, ed. E. Maynial, Paris 1961; *Sentimental Education*, trans. Robert Baldick, Harmondsworth 1982, p. 15. I have provided my own (necessarily inelegant) literal modifications to Baldick's translation of the passages from this work quoted by Sartre in the next few pages, in order to make his stylistic criticism as comprehensible as possible in English.

83. 'Dim did they go beneath the lonely night': Virgil, *Aeneid, VI*, 268.

Philippe and the social movements of '48 made people want to speak about *things* (machines, tools, etc.), while the style Flaubert found at his disposal had slowly been formed for describing customs and men. Flaubert attempts to *translate*. The aim is to speak about objects, while maintaining the *quality* of style. It's the inadequacies of Flaubert which will lead the Goncourts to their verbal inventions. The truth is that Flaubert, enemy of all Louis-Philippe-style bourgeois, is himself a bourgeois, and his art is a product of the industry of '48. It's the industrial bourgeoisie curious about itself, its culture, its occupations, the men and things over which it reigns, but which wishes to know them through certain cultural mannerisms, through a classical form. The subsequent relaxation will also be a vulgarization, an abandonment of certain requirements. It should be noted that all the corrections proposed by Maxime Du Camp at Flaubert's request are conservative, in other words aim at preserving the purity of form. Flaubert is very aware of this. [84]

The worst fault of *L'Éducation sentimentale* is that the book can be read by a telephone-operator – who reads a sentence, stops, goes back to it, etc. There's no current to risk being cut off. On the contrary. I imagine an uninterrupted reading must be unbearably tedious. Each sentence stands alone, and one has real trouble ungluing oneself from it and moving on to the next sentence.

I note here a few examples of the weakness of the verb in Flaubert: 'He was always irritable, and in that state of excitement, at once natural and artificial, which *constitutes* actors' [p.48].
' . . . a hat with a turned-up brim which *made it possible to pick him out*[*le faisait reconnaître*] in a crowd a long way off' [p.49].
'He plunged his soul into the whiteness of this female flesh' [p. 59].
'The houses *succeeded each other*' – as one might have guessed! – 'with their grey façades and closed shutters' [p. 60].
'He felt a kind of penetration of all the particles of his skin' (!!!) [ibid.].
'Buildings which could not be discerned caused intensifications of darkness' [ibid.].

With many young writers, there's a triteness of the adjective which enables one to predict the qualification once the noun is given. A valley is always 'smiling', for example. With Flaubert, the congenital weakness of the verb causes its triteness, and it's still more unpleasing

84. Maxime Du Camp (1822–94): journalist and novelist, mainly remembered for his close association with Flaubert, whom he accompanid in 1849–51 on his trip to the Middle East and Tunisia.

because most of the time the noun already encloses the meaning of the action, so that the verb is stuck on to the subject like a great Norman lump. Example: 'A light breeze was blowing' [ibid.]. Well what can the poor breeze do except blow? It would be better then just to write 'Light breeze', like Loti. It's partly out of repugnance for this that for my own part I'd rather write 'there was a light breeze'; because the 'there is', vague and imprecise, doesn't prejudge the sequel, and the sentence finishes strongly. Another example from Flaubert: ' . . . damp air enveloped him . . . ' [ibid.]. That's yet another of those voluminous, useless appendices. Flaubert's sentences always finish weakly. And what a lot of crude Norman tricks to irritate one. For example: 'He perceived himself on the edge of the quay' [ibid.]. In order to eliminate the verb 'to be'.

Earlier on, a two-horse carriage is awaiting Frédéric Moreau at the station: 'the two horses did not belong to his mother' [p. 22]. In other words, just one of the two horses belonged to her – but Flaubert refused to write so clumsy a sentence. As a result, he committed a still more clumsy impropriety of thought. For 'the two horses did not belong to his mother' actually means that neither of them belonged to her.

Typical example of the weak death of Flaubert's sentences, through asthenia of the verb:

'An extraordinary talent, the object of which he did not know, had come to him' [p. 61].

'His own face presented itself to him in the mirror' [ibid.].

The secret flabbiness of that marble: the conjunctive words – where, in, by – used in vaguely connective senses (a fault he'll hand down to all naturalists and realists).

E.g. 'He was seized by one of those tremors of the soul *where* one seems to be transported into a higher world' [ibid.].

'The street-lamps shone *in* two straight lines' [p. 60].

And participles in apposition which indiscriminately mean 'because, although, given that, etc.'.

E.g. 'Sénécal, questioned, declared . . . etc.' [p. 61].

'Pellerin . . . thinking that he had found an argument . . .' [p. 62].

Actually, most of these appositions replace a *verb*, hence an act. Always that same weakness:

'Sénécal was questioned and he declared that . . .'

'Pellerin thought that he had found an argument . . .'

Educ. sentim. Chap. V: 'The conversation went badly . . . he could find no joint through which to introduce his feelings' [p.77].

A joint serves to join, not to introduce.

Fairly profound change since I've been at Morsbronn. In the first place, the hotel where we're installed is far more like a classic wartime HQ than our peaceful Brumath schoolhouse was. All the services are grouped together here. Other ranks and officers both sleep in the hotel, the colonel takes his breakfast in one of the dining-rooms – and that's where the officers eat their lunch, on a round table covered by a waxed cloth which is set with their places almost all day long, with napkin-rings on which they've used knives to carve their numbers. The hotel, standing alone by the roadside – it's five hundred metres from Morsbronn – presents all the superimposed features of peace and war. From outside it is *still* a hotel – a second-class one (apparently it's modest people – on national insurance. with friendly societies, etc. – who go to Morsbronn for treatment). But as soon as one enters, one is struck by an odour of neglect and slow decay very characteristic of evacuated dwellings. The rooms smell of fungus. They are full to bursting with a jumble of military equipment, kitbags, greatcoats, haversacks, etc. And yet a stench of civilian woes pervades them. Under the big red quilts, the mattresses are thick and the bedsprings exquisite, as befits sufferers from rheumatism. The torn, dirty wall-papers, with their flowers, are more civilian and individual than the enamelled walls of the school, where military socialism fitted in without any difficulty. The bedrooms, albeit deceptively, recall the wretched, shady hotel-rooms of Parisian workers.

The secretaries' room, where the telephone is located, has really become a very particular and individual object, in which these various layers of signification merge. It's a very dirty, rectangular room opening onto the main road, which its long bay window overlooks from quite a height. The wooden ceiling, with its exposed beams, slopes steeply down from the back wall to the bay; it's painted white, but the dirt has turned it to grey. In the evenings, the bay is screened off with blankets and rugs, which create an oriental impression – tent, animal skins, encampment – and vaguely, very vaguely, evoke the idea of Tartar luxury. A sideboard, an oak wardrobe with a mirror, and a squat little Boulle-type chest-of-drawers with a marble top, have been pushed up against the wall. A very gloomy still-life and some advertisements: Suze, Mandarin, Lithia, Pernod fils, Dubonnet, Carola table-water, Dolfi. In a gilt frame on white paper, 'Lanson père et fils. Reims', under glass. But beneath it a black slate hangs on a nail: 'Guard duty: Mistler. Orderly: Hantziger.' The words are written in chalk. In the middle of the room a German stove from Nuremberg.

Against the windows of the bay, seven rectangular tables with type-writers, card-indexes, folders: staff headquarters. But right beside the last table there's still a little round table covered with a red and white cloth. And on that cloth a big stemmed glass with artifical flowers of the iris type, which alone and unaided represents a restaurant. A restaurant for regular customers, with good plain cooking. On the wall, near the door, a coat-rack. Gas-masks and khaki great-coats hang from the pegs. Over all this, the five lamps shrouded in newspaper shed a subdued, domestic light. I was forgetting two strange objects, both mechanical, but which are to mechanical objects what Picasso's Harlequins are to men: the telephone wires that hang disconsolately from the ceiling, like hair stiff and matted with grime; and – in the middle of the ceiling, surrealistic in this season and given the difficulties we're experiencing in keeping warm – a fan which starts up mercilessly every time anyone tries to switch the lights on or off. The proximity of the officers' dining-room transmits to this room a gentle aura of food.

'Then he saaaiiiddd . . .' And with an air of self-importance Pieter repeats any old person's 'sayings'. Previously, I'd seen only the self-importance. But today – when he leaned towards me confidingly to say: 'I met Dubois, you know. So we had a chat. He saaaiiiddd . . .' – I had a sudden revelation. He's performing a social rite. He takes 'sayings' and loves them, because they have a human aroma. Whether they're to do with the complaints of the lady from the tobacconist's, or with the Alsace method of preparing *saucisson*, they're sayings of men and he's performing his function as a man by retailing them. So there are two human acts of communion here: that which occurs on the occasion of the 'saying', and that which occurs when the 'saying' is retailed. He says 'Dubois saaaiiiddd . . . ' and his voice becomes warm, he blinks his heavy eyelids, he is happy.

He irritated me this morning, because he kept insisting that every soldier he met was from the 109th, just because he has a pal who's in the 109th. And in the restaurant, pointing out a soldier who was wearing a hunting-horn on his badges, 'Look', he was saying, all excited, 'it's the 109th, it's the 109th I tell you.' He always wants to *recognize*: people and things. And if there's no way, he'll at least find some indirect relationship between them and him. It's his way of smiling at the world, of opening himself amiably to events, of assert-ing his optimism.

He's ill today, our angel, his wings are crumpled, he's feeling dizzy. He tucks his chin down into his overcoat collar, and looks utterly astonished and guileless. He didn't believe in Evil, or that a person could feel so ill. Actually, he's not feeling ill at all. 'My father, my poor father, was like me towards the end. He'd be there chatting to me and suddenly he'd turn away for thirty seconds, he'd say nothing at all or else just "Oh, my heart, my heart!", and then he'd go on with the conversation as if nothing had happened.' – 'What was wrong with him?' – 'He had angina.' And when he saw my expression: 'Oh, I'm sure he was feeling much iller than I do. But . . .' – 'But don't you feel ill?' – 'No. I just feel dizzy.'

Everywhere – in schools, post-offices or town-halls – where there are women's lavatories and men's lavatories, the officers commandeer the women's lavatories and 'Officers' is marked up under the sign 'WC'. This gives them a rather girlish air, that very well suits their uniforms with their tight waists. I am quite ready to grant that the officers are the feminine element in the army. And that we, the squaddies, with our big boots and our dumb expressions, are the males. But Pieter, reverently, always goes into the officers' toilets, so much tenderness is there in his heart and his big bum.

The mobile kitchen had been set up two hundred metres away from our hotel, but Colonel Deligne insisted that it be moved further away because it spoiled his appetite to see men going by with their mess-tins.

I didn't make a note of this in Brumath. There was a soldier at the Écrevisse , a dopy-looking little fellow with a pale face framed by big ears, who was saying with a dogged, hopeless expression: 'When my father came back in 1916, I was pushed into his arms and told "There's your dad", and I was thinking "Who on earth's this, then?" Now it's my turn: my son'll do just the same, he won't recognize me. He'll do just the same. Yes, he'll do just the same.'

In connection with Pieter and people's sayings, I forgot the following. What enchants him, and fills him with a delighted and almost mystical self-importance, is precisely the fact that they're what *'people* say'.[85] What Pieter loves everywhere and always is men, in the form of 'people'. *People* live, *people* say, *people* die. By reporting what *people* are saying, he is celebrating the mass of his inauthenticity. Pieter or the angel of inauthenticity.

85. 'People' in this passage translates the French *'on'* (the absence of a more exact equivalent is doubtless one reason why English has borrowed the French term *on-dit* in the sense of 'rumour').

Thursday 7

I must begin to set my ideas about morality in order.

The first question: morality is a system of ends; so to what end must human reality act? The only reply: to its own end. No other end can be proposed to it. Let us first observe that an end can be posited only by a being that is its own possibilities; that, in other words, pro-jects itself towards these possibilities in the future. For an end can be neither entirely transcendent with respect to the person who posits it as an end, nor entirely immanent. If transcendent, it would not be *its* possible. If immanent, it would be dreamed but not willed (see, in this same notebook, Thursday 23 Nov.). The linking of the agent to the end thus presupposes a certain bond of the 'being-in-the-world' type, in other words a human existence. The moral problem is specifically human. It presupposes a limited will and has no meaning outside it – either in animals, or in the divine spirit. But, in addition, the end has a very specific existential type: it could not be a given existent, otherwise it would at once cease to be an end. But neither can it be a pure virtuality, in the sense of simple transcendent possibility: it would lose its power of attraction. It has an existence both plenary and *to* come,[86] which rebounds from the future upon human reality by demanding to be realized by the latter in a present. Consequently, an eternal and transcendent existence – such as God or the divine will – could not be an end for human will. On the other hand, human reality can and must be an end for itself, because it is always *on the side* of the future – it is its own reprieve.

But, in addition, human reality is limited everywhere by itself; and whatever aim it sets itself, that aim is always itself. One grasps the world only through a technology, a culture, a condition; and, in its turn, the world thus apprehended yields itself up as human and refers back to human nature. Those poisonous flowers which St-Exupéry sees from his plane, traced by the winds upon the sea, are grasped by him as poisonous through his pilot's craft. But, once again, their poisonous quality refers back to him the sketch of a human reality. since it's for man they're poisonous. I wrote in *La Nausée*: 'Existence is a plenum which man cannot leave.'[87] I'm not retracting that. But it must be added that this plenum is human. The human is an existential plenum that human reality discovers on the horizon as far as the eye

86. It is perhaps worth pointing out the added resonance in the original, given by the close relation of *à venir* (to come) to *avenir* (future).

87. *Oeuvres romanesques*, p. 158.

can see. Man discovers his project everywhere, he discovers *nothing but* his project.

In this connection, the strongest argument for a morality without God is that every morality is human, even theological morality; every morality, even Christ's, is for the purpose of human reality. But that doesn't mean morality must be *either* a social utilitarianism, *or* an individualism in which the individual takes himself as end, *or* an extended humanism in the sense that *men* – singular particles of humanity – would be an end for man. It means only that human reality is of an existential type such that its existence constitutes it in the guise of a value to realize through its freedom. This is what Heidegger is expressing, when he says that man is a 'being of distances'. But let us clearly understand that this being-value which constitutes us as value of our horizons is neither you, nor me, nor men, nor a *made* human essence (in the sense of an Aristotelean eudaimonism): it is the ever-moving reprieve of human reality itself (at once, and quite indifferently, I and you and everyone). Human reality exists for the purpose of itself – and it's that *self*, with its specific type of existence (as that which awaits it in the future to be realized by its freedom), which is *value*. There exists no value other than human reality for human reality. And the world is what separates human reality from its purpose. Without a world, no value. Morality is a specifically human thing, it would have no meaning for angels or for God. It's necessary to be separated from oneself by a world, it's necessary to will, it's necessary to be limited, for the moral problem to exist. Kant used to speak of the dove that thinks it will fly higher and better if the air supporting it is eliminated. He applies the image to the use of categories – on which point much could be said. But the image assumes its full force when applied to morality: man thinks he would be *more* moral if he were relieved of the human condition, if he were God, if he were an angel; he doesn't realize that morality and its problems would vanish along with his humanity.

But if human reality is for its own end, if morality is the law that regulates *through* the world the relationship between human reality and itself, the first consequence is that human reality is obliged to account only to itself for its morality. Dostoevsky used to write: 'If God does not exist, all is permitted.' That's the great error of transcendence. Whether God exists or does not exist, morality is an affair 'between men' and God has no right to poke his nose in. On the contrary, the existence of morality, far from proving God, keeps him at a distance, since it's a personal structure of human reality. The second consequence is that there's no way to determine the prescriptions of that morality, except by determining the nature of human reality. We must take care here not to fall into the error which consists in deriving values from facts. For human reality is not a fact.

The characteristic of human reality, from the point of view which concerns us, is that it motivates itself without being its own foundation. What we call its freedom is that it is never anything without motivating itself to be it. Nothing can ever happen to it *from outside*. This comes from the fact that human reality is first of all consciousness: in other words, it's nothing that it isn't consciousness of being. It motivates its own reaction to the event from outside, and the event within it is that reaction. It only *discovers* the world, moreover, on the occasion of its own reactions. It is thus free in the sense that its reactions, and the way the world appears to it, are integrally attributable to it. But total freedom can exist only for a being which is its own foundation, in other words responsible for its facticity. Facticity is nothing other than the fact that there's a human reality in the world at every moment. It's a *fact*. It's not deduced from anything, as such, and isn't reducible to anything. And the world of values, necessity and freedom – all of it hangs on this primitive, absurd fact. If one examines any consciousness whatsoever, one will find nothing that's not attributable to it.

But the fact that *there is* a consciousness that motivates its own structure is irreducible and absurd. Each consciousness includes in itself the consciousness both of being responsible for itself and of not being the cause of its own being. This facticity is not an 'outside', but it's not an 'inside' either. It's not the passivity of a created and supported being, but neither is it the total independence of the *ens causa sui*. But if one considers things better, one sees clearly that this facticity doesn't mean that consciousness has its foundation in something other than itself — in God, for example — since any transcendent foundation of consciousness would kill consciousness with its own hands, while giving birth to it. It's merely the fact that consciousness exists *without* any foundation. It's a kind of nothingness proper to consciousness, which we shall call gratuitousness.

This impalpable gratuitousness is there, stretched out across the whole of consciousness, nowhere and everywhere. This gratuitousness could be compared to a fall into the world, and the motivations of consciousness to a kind of acceleration the falling stone would be free to impart to itself. Put otherwise, the speed of fall depends on consciousness, but not the fall itself. It's at the level of gratuitousness that the possibility of death intervenes for consciousness. And for that reason, it isn't one of *its* possibilities, or its innermost possibility, as

Heidegger claims. But neither is it a possible external to it. The mortality of consciousness and its facticity are as one. Thus consciousness, which cannot *conceive* its death, since it still conceives like consciousness, encloses it existentially within itself at the very level of the nothingness that permeates it through and through. There's no being-about-to-die in the Heideggerian sense, but every consciousness is numbed by Nothingness and by death, without even being able to turn on this Nothingness and look it in the face.

The specific structure of consciousness is to throw itself forward into the world to escape this gratuitousness. But it throws itself there for its own purpose, in order to be its own foundation in the future. To say that human reality exists for its own purpose comes to the same thing as saying that consciousness throws itself towards the future in order to be its own foundation there. In other words, it projects a certain future of itself beyond the world, on the horizon, in the illusion that when it becomes that future, it will be so in the guise of its own foundation. This illusion is transcendental, and derives from the fact that consciousness, free foundation of its possibles, is the foundation of its being to come, without being able to be the foundation of its present being. For this being-*to-come*, as we've seen, though in relation to consciousness it doesn't have the transcendence of a real possible in relation to a thing, is nevertheless charged with a noematic transcendence, Being-to-come of consciousness, it's for that very reason no longer *itself* consciousness. And, consequently, it's in fact totally relative to the latter. That's what is called will. And here my description links up with the one I was giving on Thursday 23 and Friday 24. What escapes from consciousness here is the fact that when this future becomes present, be it exactly as it *had to* be, it will be consciousness – and will consequently draw its motivation from itself, despite being numbed by gratuitousness and nothingness.

Thus the first value and first object of will is: to be its own foundation. This mustn't be understood as an empty psychological desire, but as the transcendental structure of human reality. There is original fall and striving for redemption – and that fall with that striving constitutes human reality. Human reality is moral because it wishes to be its own foundation. And man is a 'being of distances' because it's only as a possible that he can be his foundation. Man is a being who flees from himself into the future. Throughout all his undertakings he seeks, not to preserve himself, as people have often said, nor to increase himself, but to found himself. And at the end of each undertaking he finds himself anew just as he was: gratuitous to the marrow. Whence those notorious disappointments after effort, after triumph, after love. Whence the creator's effort. Whence, as the lowest manifestation of this desire, the sense of ownership. (In these last two cases, there is a transfer to objects: the *created* object symbolically represents human reality founded upon itself; the *possessed* object symbolically represents human reality in possession of itself. Love is the effort of human reality to be a foundation of itself in the Other.) Whence the deep origins of the sense of having *rights*: the right consists in covering over the facticity of human reality by choosing ourselves as existent-that-exists-because-it-has-the-right-to-exist. But this grasping of oneself as existing by right can take place only on the occasion of particular objects over which we claim to have rights.

Thus the source of all value, and the supreme value, is the substantiality or nature of the being which is its own foundation. The substantiality forms part of human nature, but only in the capacity of a project, a constituent value. And human reality differs from pure consciousness inasmuch as it projects a value before itself: it is consciousness self-motivating itself [*se motivant elle-même*] towards this end.

Life is the transcendent, psychic object constructed by human reality in search of its own foundation.

However, this search for the absolute is also a flight before oneself. To found substantiality for the future is to flee the gratuitousness given at present. Human reality loses its way trying to found itself. The *life* it secretes is a totality only in appearance, it is gnawed backwards by death, *right* is an infamous lie, love is denied by *jealousy* or gripped by the impossibility of being for the Other the foundation of human reality. Human reality remains the prisoner of its unjustifiable facticity, with itself on the horizon of its search, everywhere.

It then comes to know weariness, and to deliver itself from the torment of freedom by pleading its facticity; in other words, it tries to conceal from itself the fact that it is condemned for ever to be its own motivation, by the fact that it is not its own foundation. It abandons itself; it makes itself a thing; it renounces its possibles, they're no longer its *own* possibles, it grasps them as external possibles analogous to those of things. For example, last year war was able to appear to everybody as an external possible, a mechanical eruption that escaped any particular human reality, just as the rolling marble is escaped by the fold in the carpet that will stop it. We shall designate this state buffeted human reality, for it realizes itself as buffeted amid the possibles, like a plank amid the waves.

But this state itself is inauthentic. For human reality, out of weariness, here conceals from itself the fact that it is condemned to self-motivate itself. And it self-motivates itself to conceal that fact. It resigns functions, it makes itself a thing, but it carries out this resignation by its own act. And this resignation itself is only one episode in its search for substantiality. It resigns to escape the constraint of values, to realize substantiality by some other means, etc. etc. It will, for example, refuse to assume an event on the pretext that it has refused the principle of it. From this point of view, the classic example of buffeted consciousness is Paul saying to me the other day: 'Me, a soldier? I consider myself a civilian in military disguise.' That would be all very fine if he weren't making himself a soldier – whatever he may say to the contrary – through his volitions, his perceptions, his emotions. A soldier: that's to say, adopting his superiors' orders as his own in order to execute them himself; hence complicit down to his arms that carry the rifle and his legs that march; a soldier in his perceptions, his emotions and his volitions. He thus stubbornly continues to *flee* what he's *making of himself* – which plunges him into a state of wretched, diffuse anguish.

This state of misery *can* be a reason for consciousness to return to an accurate view of itself and stop fleeing itself. It's not a question of its seeking any value other than substantiality   if it did, it would cease to be *human* consciousness. The value that will assign it its new attitude remains the supreme value: being its own foundation. It will no more stop asserting – and willing – this value than cognitive consciousness, after Husserl's ἐπόχη,[88] ceases to posit the world. It is from the first impetus towards substantiality that human reality must draw the value-reason that allows it to recover itself. For buffeted consciousness can quite freely will, by its plenary authenticity, to accomplish its effort to found itself. And this not at all because authenticity is original value, superior to inauthenticity, but rather as one corrects a clumsy, ineffective effort by purifying it of all useless, parasitic actions. Thus authenticity is a value but not primary; it gives itself as a means to arrive at substantiality. It suppresses that which, in the search, is *flight*. But, of course, this value of authenticity is merely *proposed*. Consciousness alone can self-motivate itself to effect the conversion.[89]

Which is this conversion? The search for a foundation requires that

88. In Husserl, a 'placing in parenthesis' or suspension.
89. Conversion: in Aristotelean logic, change of one proposition into another by mutual transposition of subject and attribute.

one *assume* that which one founds. If the act of founding is anterior to the existent one founds, as in the case of creation, assumption is contained a priori in the act of founding. But if, as in the case that concerns us, it's a question of an effort to found that which already exists in fact, assumption must precede foundation, as an intuition which reveals *what* one is founding. To assume does not at all mean to accept, though in certain cases the two go together. When I assume, I assume *in order* to make a given use of what I am assuming. Here, I am assuming *in order to* found. Moreover, to assume means to adopt as one's own, to claim responsibility. Thus the assumptive conversion that presents itself as a value for consciousness is, therefore, nothing other than an intuition of the will, which consists in adopting human reality as one's own. And, by that adoption, human reality is revealed to itself in an act of non-thematic comprehension. It is revealed, not as it would be known through concepts, but as it is *willed*.

But if assumption presents itself as a value of authenticity, it is because it already exists in advance. Value really only bids human freedom to do what it is doing. Consciousness self-motivates itself: it is free, except to acquire the freedom to be free no longer. We have seen that it renounces its possibles only by acquiring others. It can *freely make itself* akin to things, but it cannot *be* a thing. All that it is, it makes itself be. All that happens to it must happen to it by its own doing: that is the law of its freedom. Thus the first assumption that human reality can and must make, when looking back on itself, is the assumption of its freedom. Which can be expressed by the following formula: *one never has any excuse.* For it will be recalled that buffeted consciousness was a consciousness that pleaded the excuse of its facticity. But we should be clear that facticity has no relevance here. Granted, it is thanks to facticity that I'm thrown into war. But what war will be for me, what face it will reveal to me, what I shall myself be in war and for war – all this I shall be freely and am responsible for.

There is something intolerable here, but which one cannot complain of since it is also elusive: this obligation to *shoulder* what happens to me. This, no doubt, is what gave birth to the religious notion of *trial* sent me by Heaven. But, by refusing excuses and assuming my freedom, I appropriate it. Of course, it's a question not just of *recognizing* that one has no excuse, but also of *willing* it. For all my cowardices, all my stupidities, all my lies, I bear the responsibility. The point is not to say, with the saint: 'It's too much, O Lord, it's too much.' Nothing is ever too much. For – at the very moment when I lose my grip, when my body 'overcomes me', when under physical torment I confess what I wanted to keep secret – it is of my own accord, through the free consciousness of my torment, that I decide to confess. Jules Romains says that, in earlier wars, it was the defeated party who himself decided he'd been defeated (for those were not totalitarian wars, and he still had resources in men, weapons and wealth at his disposal). Well, similarly, it is always upon me that the terrible responsibility falls of acknowledging I am defeated; and, at whatever point I stop, it is I who have decided I couldn't go on any longer – hence, I could have gone on a bit longer still. But if I admit – and wish – never to have any excuse, my freedom becomes *mine*, I assume for ever that terrible responsibility.

The assumption of my freedom must, of course, be accompanied by that of my facticity. Which means, I must will it. And, no doubt, will it *in order to found it*. But we shall see what the result will be. What does it mean to will one's facticity? First, it is to acknowledge that one no more has rights than one has excuses. I grant myself no right for anything to happen to me other than what does happen to me. And, there again, I am only willing what is. All that happens to me has a dual nature: on the one hand, it is *given* me by virtue of my facticity and gratuitousness – and whatever it may be is still too much, in relation to what is due me, since my existence itself is *given*; on the other hand, I am responsible for it, since I self-motivate myself to discover it, as I noted above. Consequently, I have no *right* for it not to happen to me. For example, in the case of war.

NOTEBOOK 5

DECEMBER 1939
MORSBRONN

'. . . and we scratched our heads a bit. It's purely a question of sleeping and eating and not being cold. That's all. One can hardly think of anything else . . . All that I imagined from stories and books falls short of the reality. We're exactly like animals. It's incredible.

'I'm trying to keep up my journal as well as possible, but it's not easy. But I'll do it after the event, and in any case I forget nothing of what I see and do at present.

'When I think that at this very moment there are people in the cafés or in restaurants, clean and in mufti, who will go to sleep in beds, it makes me laugh and really doesn't make me envious; I can't imagine it happening to me and, if someone offered with the stroke of a magic wand to put me in their place, I should accept but with a sceptical, unenthusiastic shrug of the shoulders. I've never before been in a situation like it.'[1]

Sunday 17

For the past fortnight Pieter has had dry lips – the result, he imagines, of a slight digestive fever. He licks them all day long to moisten them a bit. At least, in the beginning it was for that. But, little by little, the habit has got a grip on Pieter and become downright obscene. He licks his lips now in order to touch himself, like young boys who fiddle with themselves through their pockets; he offers himself this succulent contact of mucous membrane like a sweetmeat. As he listens to you, even as he speaks to you, he assumes a furtive, sensual air and, protruding his upper lip like a gutter, entices his lower lip into his mouth like a seducer enticing a little girl to his home. He sucks it in, he sips at it, and in obedience to his bidding it swells and thrusts deeper into his mouth, vast and dilated – and there, Heaven knows all that he

1. Sartre is quoting here from a letter he had received from a friend, who had also been called up.

117

does to it in the way of tonguings and quivering caresses! He nibbles it a bit as well. But his principal pleasure, I think, is that most primitive of sensual delights, the rapture of the naked, splayed, mucous membrane laid upon another mucous membrane like one dried fig upon another – and the pleasure, like a thick oil, passes from one mucous membrane to the other by osmosis. For the enjoyment to be complete, however, it has to be accompanied by noise. Pieter is always surrounded by a host of little sounds – sharp or soft; plaintively melodious or a bit raucous – which are like the perpetual, angelic song of his self-abandon. While he masturbates his lip, he utters a thousand slurping smacks – reminiscent of the greedy suckings and lappings and 'yum-yums' of a nursing infant, or the pantings of a male on the job, or the consenting groans of a woman satisfied – and then the lip re-emerges, obscene and slack, glistening with saliva, and hangs down a bit, enormous and female, spent with bliss. When I see him do it – when I see on his face that furtive, naughty look of a depraved child or a dotard – the organic and infantile depth of his narcissism almost makes me afraid. Thanks to this little game, moreover, he has acquired a big shining white spot at the base of his lower lip and is really unhappy this morning. He's still licking himself a bit – because he's absolutely incapable of taking reponsibility for, or checking, his greedy pleasures – but circumspectly and without pleasure.

Pieter has invited a pal in, a travelling salesman, who happens to be billeted 3 kilometres away. He's a chasseur, and apparently things are none too funny out there. Pieter leaves us for a moment, and the fellow says to me with a conviction that makes him lower his voice a couple of notches: 'Oh, that father of his! He was a really brainy chap! What a mind!' He transfixes me with an embarrassing stare that demands my vigorous approval – which I should certainly give if I'd known Pieter's father. But what's to be done? I say: 'Yes, yes, he's told me . . .', imbuing my voice with as much respect as I can for Pieter's opinion. But it's obviously insufficient. The fellow resumes: 'You could ask him any question at all, he had a way of coming up with the right dilution (?) that I've never known in anybody else. I can tell you, he's one of the few real men I've met . . . the only one, to tell the truth. And a real Hercules! You see this table, well, if he'd banged on it, it would've just collapsed. And I've seen him, with my own two eyes, bang on a wall with his fists – I was still just a kid – and the wall collapsed!'

I like to picture that legendary father, through his son, my great, greedy angel. He was a Pole under Russian rule and, in about 1898,

serving as a private in a *sotnya*.[2] A lieutenant slapped him a month
before his discharge, and Pieter senior thrashed him so badly he laid
him out cold. It was court-martial for him; but the military doctor,
who'd taken a liking to him, told Pieter: 'All I can say, you poor fool, is
that if I could by any chance discover that you had a burst ear-drum,
I'd be able to say that the slap ruined your ear and you acted under the
sway of a fit of crazy rage.' Pieter senior went back to the barrack-
room, took some spirits of salt and poured it into his ear. As a result of
which, the military authorities preferred to hush up the whole business
and Private Pieter was discharged with a pension. He came to settle in
Paris in 1900; my Pieter was born there in 1902. The Pieters used to
live in the Rue des Rosiers, and the kid went to school in the Place des
Vosges; his mates were toughs who dreamed of one day going dancing
in the Rue de Lappe, and lording it over a tame string of girls. 'Oh, the
Rue de Lappe,' Pieter likes to say, 'it's not what it used to be. In those
days, they were the real article.' Often for a couple of *sous* he would
keep watch in the Place des Vosges, while the big bosses from the
Bastille played Faro in the square-gardens with blankets over their
knees. The war gradually eliminated all those great names, and
Pieter's pals sported leather caps and began to act high and mighty;
the oldest ones already had a woman or two working for them. Pieter
used to follow them into the brothels, where they were making a shot
at talking big. From time to time there were punch-ups.

All this, especially at the beginning, endowed that fat body with a
poetry for me that it hardly deserved. First, Poland and the similar
destinies of the Jew V. and the Jew Pieterkowski.[3] Similar, but at
different levels: V. abandons Vienna and his medical studies, summoned to Paris by a diamond-merchant cousin, and after the latter's
death he and his brothers take over the management of a big jewellery
business; Pieterkowski establishes himself in the Rue des Rosiers and
struggles to start a business, then moves and goes to live in the Rue du
Faubourg-du-Temple. There's some Jewish and Polish destiny there,
which I've already sensed through L., and which moves me a little in
Pieter.[4] In the beginning, when people believed the war was for real,

2. *sotnya* = company: military unit originally of a hundred men.
3. V. = 'Védrine' or Bienenfeld, father of Bianca Bienenfeld (see following note), a
former pupil of De Beauvoir (to judge, at least, from a repetition of this same comparison with Pieter in *Lettres au Castor I*, p. 483).
4. L. = 'Louise Védrine', or Bianca Bienenfeld, friend of De Beauvoir with whom
Sartre had a short love affair in July/August 1939: see the handful of letters to her
included in *Lettres au Castor I*, pp. 228 ff., in which he addresses her as 'My darling little
Polack . . . '

Pieter careful as ever used to say: 'My name is Pieterkowski, but I prefer to be called Pieter, because if the Germans took me prisoner and saw I had a Polish name. they'd kill me at once.' And then, I sense around him the very specific poetry of a neighbourhood in Paris which I love just as much as the more beautiful ones. How many times have I wandered with the Beaver, with T., with O., with L., with Little Bost, in the Rue des Francs-Bourgeois and the Rue Vieille-du-Temple and the Rue de Rivoli, behind the Lycée Charlemagne, in the Rue des Rosiers. I have hundreds of memories there: a little, gloomy café in the Rue des Rosiers, opposite a second-hand clothes stall, where I used to drink rum with T.; a close, summer afternoon on which, back from Laon, I walked those narrow, gloomy streets with O., at a time when my feelings for her were not yet dead; a 14th of July too; and some evening or other of deadly boredom with old F., when, in the darkness, not far from the Rue des Rosiers, I discovered a charming arcade chock-a-block with costers' barrows.

All this haloed Pieter – how unjust it was! – because, in my eyes, he wore the glory of having *lived* in that neighbourhood, where I was never anything but a tourist; of having lived in it, a Jew among Jews, a hoodlum among all those other little hoodlums who hang round the Dupont café at the Bastille of an evening. Another thing too, at a deeper, more secret level: his adolescence is bound up with that poetic, mysterious Paris of the '14 War; that dimmed Paris, in which before-the-war was being transformed imperceptibly, under the pressure of horrors, bereavements and prohibitions, into after-the-war – just as a gas, cooled and compressed by a piston, passes insensibly into the liquid state. (Now that I'm speaking of liquefied gas, I must admit it's not the first time I have made use of this comparison. I was filled with amazement, in the fifth form, when I was told about a certain state of such gases – invisible, hidden by the solid walls of the piston-chamber – that was neither the solid nor the liquid state, but intermediary between the two. I felt that was mysterious and perverse; the paradox of it was a spur to my mind and it has remained an intellectual schema of ambiguity for me – to be set beside 'death in the sun' and 'dirty china'. So that ambiguity which would have been shocking to a systematic mind (and yet, I have a systematic mind) – that ambiguity which Kierkegaard calls to his aid against Hegel – first appeared to me through an experiment in physics: or, at least, this experiment in physics established *against physics* that idea of ambiguous states.)

In any case, to close the parenthesis, only very recently did that Paris of the last war start to seem poetic to me: precisely when it began to shine with its dark fire between two dead periods – 1900-1914 and 1918-1939 – and when I learned to dream of the home front a little, in order to gain some momentary respite from the pressure of the real front. It then rose before me in all its ambiguity as a dark little dimmed jewel. It must be said, moreover, that Pieter contributed greatly to revealing its charm to me, his stories portraying it as a great city of the night abandoned to unruly children. For example, I had certainly heard people speak of war-widows street-walking in their weeds; but for me this had remained a trivial historical and literary fact, a social trait. Pieter, however, lost his virginity with one of those women. He'd just delivered a parcel to a customer and was waiting for the bus, somewhere in the neighbourhood of Clichy. This woman was waiting too. They walked together up a long Montmartre avenue, unlit and melancholy, she chatting away strangely in a manner at once pathetic and suggestive. She gave herself to him in a hotel-room, accepted a hundred *sous*, but wanted to hold him at her side and kept begging him 'Stay, stay!'. He was the one who wanted to leave. He never knew whether, above all, she had sought some tenderness and pleasure with a little profit into the bargain, or whether a sad eroticism was her professional speciality.

So there you are, he has all that: all those memories and atmospheres. I've seen an old photo of him aged twenty, which shows him sitting on a boat at the seaside, slim and good-looking, with fine, velvety eyes and heavy lids with a woman's lashes. He is fond of portraying himself as a dare-devil, always raring for a fight. He had money in 1920, when he was twenty – that's classic too, it's typically 'post-war' – and says: 'I was rich too soon'. A car; women; a splendid attack of the clap, which from time to time still sends him its kind regards. I imagine he exaggerates his former adventures a bit. But all the same, how has he become *that*? That: his greedy, stay-at-home softness, his masturbated sensuality, his radical-socialist inauthenticity.

I said in notebook 3 I'd describe myself some time *performing an act*. As yet, I don't think the time's ripe. Even though I can already perceive several little things: for example, objects becoming sorcerer's apprentices' brooms in my hands and developing initial whims with a rigour that terrifies me and frustrates all my plans.[5] For me, objects

---

5. Sartre and De Beauvoir had enjoyed the Walt Disney film *Fantasia* when it was shown in Paris before the war: one of its episodes was based on Paul Dukas's *The Sorcerer's Apprentice*. (It is also, perhaps, of note that Georges Bataille published an essay with the same title in the *NRF*, July 1938.)

are neither machines nor living beings, They are mechanisms out of order, which in their behaviour retain a hint of the evil spirit, but conceal this wizardly malevolence beneath a show of corpse-like stiffness. I'm immensely distrustful of them. As soon as I touch them, there's always something jocular about them: they're in the habit of coming apart if I seek to grasp them bodily; but as soon as I fall back on particulars, the whole reassembles without my noticing, and whatever least change I may effect in the element repercusses in an unpredictable way upon the whole.

But let us leave all this. What I should like to signal today – and it's not so very far away from the act – is the way I'm faithful to a decision once it's taken. For example, I can by and large say that I've been faithful, yesterday and today, to my decision to take just one meal daily and not to drink wine or eat bread. But seen close up, this triumph breaks down into little specific defeats, just as battles if they're seen close up are always defeats for the victor. In the first place, once the decision was taken I regretted it and added a postscript: 'Well, actually, for my breakfast I shall eat bread after all.' Not so much because I considered this unimportant, but because, after a rapid inspection of my possibles, I saw I couldn't help doing so. When one wishes to take any decision, one takes a good look all around and inspects one's possibles. There are some which are hard as rocks and must be skirted, while others form soft, jelly-like masses and that's where one must direct one's efforts. Those are the ones to smash through.

My breakfast every morning is a rock. I don't at all mind missing the midday meal, or even both main meals; eating just bread, or alternatively salad with no bread; or actually fasting for a day or two. I can also go without sleep for a night or two. At the time of my passion for O., I often used to stay up for forty hours,. But I have the greatest difficulty in going without breakfast. I don't really know why. It's an hour when I'm surly and just barely alive; I like to keep my own company, but some pretext is needed: the pretext is the bowl of coffee and the slices of buttered bread. If I'm given these, I'm in seventh heaven, I feel poetic and fragrant. I don't like company at this moment. I can hardly endure even the Beaver. I have been known, when she'd be waiting for me at the Rallye, to pop in to the Café des Trois Mousquetaires and quickly gulp down a coffee and croissants, in order to remain for a moment still wrapped up in myself and last night's dreams.

At such moments, my thought is lively and affable, I tell myself stories, I find ideas. A day begun with a breakfast is a lucky day. And in these last few years, if ever I happened to get up around eleven because I'd gone to bed at four in the morning, I'd prefer to take a couple of black coffees and some croissants at the Dôme, rather than wait an hour and eat meat. I suppose it was a way of prolonging the morning. Even on those days, I wanted to have had my morning. At Brumath I tortured Paul, who's a great sleeper, by setting the alarm every evening for six even though we could have stayed in bed till seven, just for the pleasure of cycling through the cold to eat a couple of plump rolls and drink a glass of chicory brew at the Taverne de la Rose: it was an enchanted moment. (Though, towards the end, Mistler used to disturb it by coming to talk to me about Heidegger.) So my courage failed when I realized something would be missing from that breakfast. For it has to be made up of coffee and bread (or croissants). T. vainly insisted on countless occasions that I should take tea and fruit. I preferred to go down in the morning before her, to the Café de la Poste in Boulevard Rochechouart, and secretly gorge myself on croissants.

(I'm recounting all this with a touch of complacency, *feeling* rather ridiculous but rather nice: I'm laughing at myself.) In short, first little defeat. I note that the draconian nature of my decision was itself another. Every four or five months, I look at my stomach in a mirror and get unhappy. I decide there and then to follow a strict, even barely endurable, diet. The horror of growing fat came upon me quite late. When I got back from Germany, I was a real little Buddha: Guille used to grasp handfuls of my paunch through my jumper to show Mme Morel I had enough and to spare, and I used to laugh with pleasure – it didn't bother me especially being fat. But when I got to know O., I conceived a horror of fat people and began to dread the idea of becoming a bald little fatty. To tell the truth, I would have a slight tendency in this direction if I didn't watch myself. But precisely, I'm incapable of watching myself. That Lady[6] and the Beaver have often pleaded with me to follow some gentle permanent diet. But I'm absolutely unable to keep a check on myself without lapses. Furthermore, I'm always in a hurry to see the effects of my diets. So I always choose the extreme course and prefer to torture myself a bit, because then it seems to me I can *feel* the progress of my slimming through the protests of my stomach.

Also, of course, if I crack down on myself a bit roughly I have the impression of being my own master, hence free. Mme Morel once told

6. *Cette Dame*: pet name for Mme Morel. See the second and third volumes of De Beauvoir's autobiography, where she figures as Mme Lemaire.

me: 'You're really fond of forcing youself to do what you don't like.'
Yes, but in fits and starts. A month of constraint, with me looking at
myself every day in the mirror to see my progress and weighing myself
every day on those automatic scales which chemists place in front of
their doors, and then – the target reached, or reckoned to be – I go
back to living as I please, I no longer watch myself, I grow fat, until
the day I begin looking anxiously at my belly again and reflecting on
what measures must be taken to deflate it. Hence, there's weakness in
the decision itself, in its brutality and its excess. I realize, too, that I
have recorded it here because I can't shout it from the rooftops as I
usually do – not out of boastfulness, but in order to burn my bridges
and commit myself more fully. Furthermore, there's also an image at
the back of my mind which usually makes me stick to these decisions
to the bitter end: it's the holy terror I have of all those fellows who
decide at three-monthly intervals to stop smoking, keep it up for a day
or two with a hell of a struggle, and then give in and start smoking
again. Sinclair Lewis wrote very well about this in *Babbitt*, and
Babbitt became for me the archetypal example of such cowards. What
I'd like to show here is that my way of standing fast is not noticeably
different from their way of giving in.

So I went off on my own to have lunch at the Restaurant de la Gare,
and since my newly-made decision remained merely superficial, I
preserved a kind of deep and happy conviction – albeit unformulated –
that I was going to eat a good lunch without constraint, eating and
drinking as I pleased. Once I'd arrived there, I recalled my morning
resolution – and it struck me as an objective impossibility. I said to
myself 'Oh, I'd forgotten I mustn't drink wine or eat bread', in the
same spirit in which one might say 'Oh, I'd forgotten that So-and-so' –
whom one has come to see – 'is never at home on Monday mornings.'
And immediately, quite naturally, precisely because in all innocence I
was taking that decree as an *objective* impossibility, I looked for ways
of getting round it – just as once one has recalled that So-and-so is not
at home on Monday mornings, one looks for ways of reaching him: at
his office, at his parents', etc., etc.

This reflection lasted only for an instant; immediately afterwards,
it disclosed to me what was certainly the most dangerous and terrifying thing: the total absence of *objectivity* in that decision; its immanence and my absolute freedom with respect to it. If Kierkegaard is
right to call 'the possibility of freedom' anguish,[7] it's not without a

7. English translations of Kierkegaard render *angst* as 'dread' (or 'anxiety'); but the
French standard rendering *angoisse*, which Sartre incorporates into his own termi-
nology, seems best translated as 'anguish'.

touch of anguish that I discovered once again yesterday morning that I was entirely free to break the piece of bread which the waitress had placed beside me, and free also to convey the fragments to my mouth. Nothing in the world could *stop* me doing so, not even myself. For to refrain is not to stop oneself . . . To refrain is merely 'to put off', to remain in suspense, to pay close attention to other possibles. In the idea of 'stopping' there's the image of a sturdy arm coming to check my arm. But I do not possess an inhibiting arm; I cannot personally erect barriers in myself between me and my possibles – that would be to abdicate my freedom and I cannot do it. All that's left me is the possibility of an internal diminution of my freedom, gnawed away from within until it collapses and freely re-forms a little further on towards some other possible. So that my fidelity to decisions taken was nothing like a sharp check, nor did it have the nobility of a *No*. It was, rather, a sly way of impregnating my desire to eat bread with flabbiness; a way of saying to myself, very feebly: 'Oh well, is it really worth while eating bread? Do I really want to? Will it give me enough pleasure for me not to regret having broken my pledge?' So that the would-be 'sharp check' is as weak as water; it's merely a way of perpetuating hesitation until the world changes, suppresses the object of your desires, and so gets you out of trouble by itself depriving you of one possible.

So there I was having lunch, more spineless than usual, with the disagreeable impression of being in a 'weak form', in Köhler's sense,[8] of belonging to an open unbalanced whole; whereas, on other days, the restaurant at midday was a perfectly round, hard, plenum, closed upon itself, where I had my place. There remained the *wine*. What helped me was that it isn't very good in this restaurant: it has a pink cloudy colour that doesn't tempt me, and also a sugary acidity that reminds one of apples more than grapes. But there now occurred the kind of event one should always reckon with, the kind one never thinks about and whose specific character is to lead you into transgression by offering you a ready-made excuse: 'I couldn't do anything else.' Before I'd ordered anything, the maid went off with a smile to fill a flask from the barrel and placed it on my table, as if saying 'You see, I know your tastes.' She looked happy at being acquainted with her customers' preferences, and I didn't have the heart to disabuse her.

So there I was, with that full flask on the table and an empty glass

---

8. Wolfgang Köhler (1887–1967), one of the founders of Gestalt theory, was lecturing at Berlin at the time of Sartre's stay in 1933–34.

next to my plate. But it's not ended, for if I leave the flask untouched, she'll express surprise at the end of the meal, she'll say 'Wasn't it good, then?, etc.' What am I to do? Drink up, thinking: 'I'll start my diet tomorrow, today it's impossible, nobody's obliged to do what's impossible'? Drink up, out of human respect? In short, I was almost resolved on doing so and was on the point of giving in. For the fact was, I had made my decision as if there were only a bottle, a glass and me in the world. My decision concerned only those material objects in a dead world: 'Of my own accord, I shall never order a bottle of wine.' But I hadn't foreseen the case where somebody might bring me the bottle without my ordering it. Because I'd not envisaged that eventuality, I hadn't made any preparations for the case in which it might occur. I was in virgin territory, and my commitment was failing. I was even vaguely thinking how, with that draconian decision, I was giving myself enough personal bother without into the bargain running the risk of saddening a waitress's heart – that wasn't part of my contract.

Here, downfall is due to the decision having been made with a very simplified situation in mind, and to that situation not being *recognized* in the real event that presents itself, which is always more complex. Salvation lies in spinelessness. I postponed deciding until later: there was a gap in my attention, and I found myself reading *Colomba* a hundred leagues away from both bottle and waitress. Then, when the question was posed anew, I found an expedient: I would pour a little wine into my glass so that the waitress, seeing the flask half-empty, would simply think I hadn't been very thirsty, and wouldn't notice that the contents of the glass corresponded precisely to what was missing from the bottle. In addition, to complete the illusion, I would take just a sip of it.

So there I was, pouring the wine into my glass: an ambiguous act which from a certain point of view was exactly suited to the present situation, but which from another point of view simply placed me in the shoes of the merry toper pouring himself a beakerful. And that act, justified by particular circumstances, certainly offered me a symbolic satisfaction: it mimed what I was forbidden to do. Weakness again. And weakness likewise that permission I at once grant myself to drink a gulp, in the belief that it doesn't count since it isn't inspired by thirst, it's 'for a good motive', and I can't do otherwise. So I drink that gulp, but stingily – for I'm afraid, all the same, of allowing myself to be drawn too far.

My courage at once fails me and I stop, But at the same time, 'while I was about drinking it', I tried to enjoy it as much as possible: I concentrated my attention on the wine's bouquet, on the fresh taste of that gulp of liquid – a furtive, sly pleasure reminiscent of a doctor who 'takes advantage' of auscultating a beautiful patient to transmit all his sensuality to his fingertips, and who enjoys her via his fingers without halting his professional explorations. Weakness again. And weakness likewise that sudden check, that abrupt way of setting my glass back on the table, for *fear* of breaking my word. In short, I flirted with the Devil, without having the courage to go right through with it. It reminds me of that passage in Gide's journal: 'Yet last night I did not quite yield to pleasure; but this morning, not even benefiting from that repulsion which follows pleasure, I wonder if that semblance of resistance was not perhaps worse. One is always wrong to open a conversation with the devil, for, however he goes about it, he always insists upon having the last word.' [II, pp.200-201]

This morning, same conjuncture: Pieter had a visitor (the one I spoke of earlier), he'd ordered a bottle of good wine and was insisting I must sample it. To refuse point-blank would have been impolite, so I drank a few drops. Why record all this in such detail? Because, from the outside, in spite of everything it's a *successful* act. From the outside, one sees a fellow who has decided not to drink wine, and who does in fact, in each of the cases quoted, drink only a practically negligible quantity – for example, a tenth of a glass instead of the two full glasses he was used to. He said he wouldn't eat bread, and he hasn't eaten any. So, a victory – but a Pyrrhic one. I shall have another five or six like that, then the habit of eating meals without wine will come back to me, and in that way I shall *in effect* have kept my word. But when all those backslidings disappear, consciousness too will disappear and the act will become automatic. That's why, when I receive any kind of praise, I always have the impression it's really directed at somebody else. There is no act without secret weakness. The others see only the style, I see only the weakness. In short, I shall keep my pledge – and that better and better – until my leave. That is what's called having will-power, You can see how much it's worth.

Monday 18

Men, it is said – Maheu was saying in his last letter – do not *deserve* peace. That's true. True quite simply in the sense that they *make* war. None of the men at present under arms (I make no exception for myself, of course) deserves peace, for the simple reason that if he really did deserve it he wouldn't be here. – But he may have been obliged, forced . . . Fiddlesticks! He was free. I'm well aware that he set off in the belief he could do nothing else. But that belief was decisive. And why did he come to that decision? Here's where we find the motives, and the complicity. Out of inertia, spinelessness, respect for authority, fear of condemnation; because he computed his chances and reckoned he was risking less by obeying than by resisting; out of a taste for disaster; because his life didn't *hold* him sufficiently (in this sense, to *succeed* in one's life – insofar as the nature of the object permits – is to work for peace: I've seen people who, because their marriage had failed, declared in October 1938 that they viewed the approach of war with indifference, without seeming to understand that their situation as *historical men* gave weight and consequence to that indifference and brought war nearer – not enough to cause it to break out, but enough to make them its accomplices); because he needed some great cataclysm in order to carry out his task as a man; out of self-importance, folly, naivety, conformism; because he was terrified of thinking freely; because he was a fighting-cock.

That's why, in war, there are no innocent victims. Were they such at the outset, moreover, they'd adopt the war as their own by innumerable ways of making themselves complicit with it in the routine of their military life. So that the myth of redemption here assumes its full moral force: the nature of historicity is such that one ceases to be complicit only by becoming a martyr. Only those men who have accepted to be the martyrs of peace do not deserve war. They alone are innocent, since the strength of their refusal is great enough for them to endure unhappiness and death. So it is true that, by accepting the consequences of their refusal, they suffer in all innocence for other people and pay their debt. So there's no way of assuming one's historicity other than by making oneself a martyr and redeemer.

This is what made me admire the foreign journalist Koestler, who's present as a spectator at the fall of Malaga. His friends bundle him into a car and they all set off for Alicante amid the general panic. At the first traffic hold-up, however, he jumps out and remains alone in Malaga. Though he doesn't say so, one can tell he wants to pay. To pay for the generals who've betrayed, for the soldiers in disorder, for the cowardly democratic governments that haven't dared intervene. To pay, because he feels responsible for human reality and because he wants to assume his historicity. Accomplice or martyr, that's the alternative. And your decision makes History. By refusing war, I'd have paid for others. By accepting it, I'm paying too, but just for myself.

We shan't be responsible for the telephone any longer. They're sending some lad from the Engineers to relieve us.

I should like to note down here – as an exercise and example, and in order to give the pages that precede and will follow their proper tonality – the principal characteristics of what Lewin would call my 'hodological space':[9] that's to say, in effect, the conformation of the world such as it appears to me from this Hotel Bellevue, the paths that criss-cross it, its holes, its traps, its perspectives.

First of all, it's a world that I've *appropriated*. In the early days it was cold and inert, but behold it's *mine*: this countryside, this cold, this particular vantage-point from which I can see stretching out around me France, Germany, Europe – all this is mine. *Querencia*. I'm on a ridge of the world, on the roof of the world (= on top of a hill). The world is a plain, dominated by this ridge (the Alps, the Pyrenees are *down below, underneath*, dominated by the roof: synthesis here, obviously, of this slight elevation's real height with the fact that on a geographical map it would be located above the Alpine and Pyrenean massifs). This elevation, which makes itself out to be a roof of the world, certainly represents symbolically my will to *dominate the war*. Hence, here I am atop this fine, serenely dominant sugarloaf. Over-topping all the rest, since upon this roof of the world there stands a house and I live on the first floor of the house. Materialization of my scorn for the secretaries: I look down upon them. Whirlwind of icy grey wind about the house: the house is now a ship atop a wave, now a lighthouse. Of an evening, when I'm alone in the warm room where we spend most of our time, it's a lighthouse: I *know* that I'm in a round tower. The wind and cold isolate me. For me, cold has always had the affective resonance of 'purity' and 'solitude.'

Germany has moved further away – I don't know why. At Brumath I used to feel it right next to us, warm and poisonous. Here – although I can *see* it in fine weather (the grey hills to the north-east) – it has only an abstract proximity. Instead, I'm at some end of the world, with the warm and clamorous cities, the people and the *lands*, all behind me. This is certainly a transposition of the direction rear-front, which presses me from behind towards the forward lines. And this trans-position appears to me through that poetical schema which, I think, acts upon all childish imaginations: lighthouse at the end of the world, *finis terrae*, etc. *Vanguard* position: there again, the symbol is visible. Whence a slight discrepancy in directions. I see the road which passes

9. Kurt Lewin (1890–1947), founder of topological psychology, influenced by the Gestalt movement, was lecturing in Berlin until just before Sartre's stay there. He distinguished a threefold series of concepts: topological (representing the structures of activity); vectorial (its causal determination); hodological (representing the paths whereby tensions are resolved).

in front of the hotel and comes from Morsbronn as the road from the rear forwards, since Morsbronn is the final advanced post of the world (= there are still civilians) – so it must continue forwards, in the direction of Germany and the front line. In actual fact it goes to the *north*, and the front is really on my right when I take this road. But since, in other respects, the north represents for me: purity, isolation, cessation of life, *finis terrae* – the result is that I sometimes think the road goes to the east, while at other times it does indeed go to the north but then Germany is at the other end. Germany (as I have said) like a dark sea rather than a danger.

That last advanced post of the rear, Morsbronn, I feel far away behind me like a menacing, poisonous (tropical) but colourless growth. Colourless, in the first place, because Pieter has been there sometimes and told me: 'It's rubbish.' Secondly, because it's there one's 'treated like a soldier'. There the offices are located where my fate is settled, there too the infirmary where I can be made to strip naked at the drop of a hat and where I'm soon to be given an injection (the injection is a danger – not in itself, since it confers the right to 48 hours rest, but because it's given in three goes at 8-day intervals and one can't go on leave in between). Yet in that same place, at the heart of that envenomed flower, there's a warm, civilian blood: I imagine drawing-rooms with pianos – because Hantziger said he'd go and ask the mayor to lend him some albums of music. Between the village and the Hotel Bellevue there are isolated outposts: the hotel where the mails officer has his premises, and the farm that shelters the mobile kitchen. When I go for some grub with Paul, or when I go to fetch a parcel from the mails officer, I am *reversed*, I am going the wrong way, I am turning my back on my natural direction – the north – and I feel a sort of shocked resistance of the air.

In the hotel itself, on the first floor, two holes: a hole of light and heat – our 'Home',[10] the room reserved for the weathermen (captain's cabin); and a black hole where the wind swirls and whistles, an icy hole (because Pieter leaves the window open all day long) – my room. It repels one: one plunges into it as if into cold water, doggedly clenching one's teeth. Poetic, because it's a kind of gash onto the countryside: the moor comes in through the window. Outside, the cold: which is a substance, as in winter sports – a pure, metallic substance that one can *touch*, as soon as one goes out in the morning, like a beautiful wall of burnished steel, The sky – my vertical dimension (because of the little balloons I send up there). Grey and motion-

10. English in original.

less, with air-currents whose curve can be traced. The sky that is divided into 'layers'. At one and the same time, my domain, the object of my technical expertise, and what dominates me. A vertical prolongation of myself, and also an abode beyond my reach. I know that, even on sunny days, like milk it has its secret, frozen blackness. Because its vertical temperature is telephoned through to us every day. For example: minus 50 at 8,000.

Such is the outline of my present situation: symbolic directions, orientations that reflect my worries, my preoccupations and my job. I regret not having done this work for Brumath and Marmoutier: it's in one's interest to determine these affective sites and perhaps compare them. This topography shows pretty clearly how the mind takes possession of sites and lays them out. At present, if I wish to determine precisely at what level of existence this geography is located, I shall say that it's at the lowest, at the pre-thematic level. It's the reef-bottom. If I thematize it, I make it into a madman's delusion – but the fact is, it's never thematized. It's in the gesture I make, in my reluctance to place the east where it ought to be, etc. At Brumath, despite repeated experiments, Paul could never manage to put the north in the right place. He used to complain about it, he'd say: 'Try as I will, I always put it in the east.' At the root of this error, I'd swear there was a resistance of the affective topography.

Kierkegaard (*The Concept of Dread*, p. 85 [39]): ' . . . the relation of dread to its object, to something which is nothing (language in this instance also is pregnant: it speaks of being in dread of nothing) . . .'[11]

The influence upon Heidegger is clear: use of the stock phrase 'to be in dread of nothing' is found word for word in *Sein und Zeit*. But it's true that for Heidegger anguish is anguish-at-Nothingness, which is not Nothing but, as Wahl says, 'a cosmic fact against which existence stands out.'[12] Whereas, for Kierkegaard, it's a question of 'a psychological anguish and a nothing that is in the mind'. This nothing, in short, is possibility. Possibility that is nothing as yet, since man in the state of innocence does not yet know *of what* it's a possibility. But it's there, nevertheless, as a sign of freedom: 'That which passed innocence by as the nothing of dread has now entered into him, and here again it is a nothing, the alarming possibility of *being able*. What he is able to do, of that he has no conception . . . There is only the possibility of being able, [as a superior form of

11. Sören Kierkegaard, *The Concept of Dread*, London 1944.

12. Jean Wahl, *Etudes Kierkegaardiennes*, Paris 1938.

ignorance] as a heightened expression of dread . . . ' [p.40].

Anguish at Nothingness, with Heidegger? Dread of freedom, with Kierkegaard? In my view it's one and the same thing, for freedom is the apparition of Nothingness in the world. Before freedom, the world is a plenum which is what it is, a vast swill. After freedom, there are differentiated *things*, because freedom has introduced negation. And negation can be introduced into the world by freedom only because freedom is wholly numbed by Nothingness. Freedom is its own nothingness. Man's facticity is to be the one who nihilates his facticity, It is by freedom that we can *imagine*, that's to say at once nihilate and thematize objects from the world. It is by freedom that we can, at every instant, establish a distance from our essence, which becomes powerless and suspended in Nothingness, ineffective. Freedom establishes a discontinuity, it is a breaking of contact. It is the foundation of transcendence, because – beyond what is – it can project *what is not yet*. It denies itself, in fact, because future freedom is negation of present freedom. I cannot commit myself, because the future of freedom is nothingness. Freedom creates the future of the world by nihilating its own. And once again I cannot commit myself, because my present-become-past will be nihilated and put out of action by my free present-to-come.

I'll explain on some other occasion how these characteristics of freedom are simply those of consciousness. But, precisely, if Nothingness is introduced into the world through man, anguish at Nothingness is simply anguish at freedom, or, if you prefer, freedom's anguish at itself. If, for example, I experienced a slight anguish yesterday before that wine which I *could* but *should not* drink, it's because the 'I shouldn't' was already in the past – it was on the wane, out of circulation like petrol – and *nothing* could prevent me from drinking. It was before that particular *nothing* I was so anguished: that nothingness of my past's means of acting on my present. *Nothing* to be done. And the common phrase 'I don't trust myself' [*j'ai peur de moi*] is precisely an anguish at nothing, since *nothing* allows me to foresee what I shall do and, even if I were able to foresee it, *nothing* could prevent me from doing it. So anguish is indeed the experience of Nothingness, hence it isn't a psychological phenomenon. It's an existential structure of human reality, it's simply freedom becoming conscious of itself as being its own nothingness. Anguish at the Nothingness of the World, anguish at the origins of the existent – these are derived and secondary. They are problems that appear in the light of freedom. The world in itself *is* and cannot not be. Its nature as a *fact* doesn't allow one to deduce it, or imagine its having a *before*.

There's a problem of the world's origin only through the effect of freedom upon things. Thus the existential grasping of our facticity is Nausea, and the existential apprehension of our freedom is Anguish.

Tuesday 19

'Dread of sin produces sin. If one represents that evil desires, concupiscence, etc. are innate in the individual, one does not get the ambiguity in which the individual becomes both guilty and innocent. In the impotence of dread the individual succumbs, but precisely for this reason he is both guilty and innocent' [pp.65-6].

Anguish at a possible one doesn't want to realize is, in fact, anguish at the Nothingness which separates one from that possible, at the fact that one is prevented by *Nothing* from realizing it. It aims, therefore, to suppress this Nothing by realizing the possible. From the moment when, instead of refusing this possible, it makes it into its own possible, there will be full adherence of freedom to the act's possibility, project and outline. At that moment, the Nothing disappears and there is plenitude. Thus the transgression provisionally causes anguish to disappear, by replacing the Nothing with plenary facticity. It must also be noted that, if *nothing* prevents us from *doing* the incriminating act, *nothing* obliges us to do it either. And this other *Nothing* is likewise given in anguish. It is the positive Nothing in freedom, from which responsibility derives. This Nothing is grasped in the fact that the motives which might encourage one to realize a possible are always separated from this possible by a hiatus of nothingness. Motives, human essence, affectivity, past, are retained within freedom, they're in suspense; and, at the same moment, freedom outlines in the future the possible to be realized. But there's never any *contact* between the motives thus retained and the possible thus outlined. The motives only ever encourage.

Thus, at the heart of consciousness, a link is missing – and it's the absence of this link that deprives us of any excuse. But let us clearly understand that this Nothingness is not a hole, purely and simply given. If it were thus, this Nothingness would be a datum, which would bring us back to Being and to Facticity. A Nothingness that was a Being – that would be meaningless. In reality, this Nothingness is a Nothingness that we are. Existence, for consciousness, is nihilation of self. The origin of responsibility is this primary fact that we realize ourselves as a discontinuity between the motives and the act. That's what we're above all responsible for: responsible for the act's not flowing naturally from the motives. But the possible itself can be only a certain concretion of Nothingness, since its existence as *my* possible does not consist in being foreseen as a reality that *will be* – but maintained as a reality that *would be*. Thus, in the urgency of the possible, there's a certain nothingness-ness [*néantité*]. It can also be seen that the possible couldn't be anterior to being. Quite the contrary, the original possibles are my own possibles and flow from my 'facticity-as-being-which-is-its-own-nothingness'. The possibles of the World, connected to things by external relations – as when I say, for example, that 'it's possible the fire may go out . . . the wind may drop . . . the bottle may break' – are derived possibles, quite obviously: reflections of my own possibles onto things. So we find again here the trinity: Nothingness – Possible – Being, but in a new order. There is priority of Being, and the Possible appears only at the horizon of a Nothingness. Moreover, this Nothingness must be Nothingness of a being which is its own Nothingness.

It can be seen that the transgression is an attempt to fill Nothingness with Being. The transgression is always impatience with anguish, flight of Nothingness into the Real.

Consciousness is alleviation of being. Being-for-itself is a disintegration of being-in-itself. Being-in-itself numbed by Nothingness becomes being-for-itself.

One can see the origin of the third cardinal category of modality: Necessity. There's priority of the possible over the necessary, as was clearly seen by Kant, who defined the necessary as: a being such that its possibility implies its existence. This is what we shall call the specific object of freedom. Freedom is Nothingness, once again, because it aims to suppress itself by nihilating the Nothingness it contains. The ideal of freedom is thus a possible that would be realized without needing the assistance of responsibility, a possible that would immediately be an *excuse*. The intimate dream of all freedom is suppression of the hiatus between motives and act. Let us suppress the hiatus by thought and we haven't thereby rejoined pure existence, since we keep the temporal discrepancy between motives and possibles. But here those possibles are now, being realized right from their own conception. From this moment on, 'it's not my fault'.

Thus every excuse invokes Necessity. But Necessity naturally remains on the terrain of values, and never descends to that of existences. From this point of view, one can see what is the Ideal of all possibles: it's a human reality that would be its own necessity – in other words, for which being its own possible would be enough to become its own existence; a human reality in which the void of the 'for-itself' would be filled, and which would be its own foundation. Necessity is thus a category of action, a *moral* category, and it's only through the effect of freedom upon things that it can appear as a structure of the real. The primary meaning of Necessity applied to things is always that of *excuse*. 'What's *necessary* to me' ('I'm taking what's necessary', 'Let us distinguish what's superfluous from what's necessary', 'To reduce one's expenses to what's strictly necessary') is anything whose absence would constitute a provisional or permanent excuse for me. For example, lack of what's *necessary* might, in the case of a 'necessitous' person, constitute an *excuse* for the theft he has committed. Thus all the sciences of the Necessary are normative sciences, because they study all the cases in which consciousness can retire. And, of course, these cases remain strictly ideal.

By dint of living on the defensive with the same people, one ends up being filled, overwhelmed despite oneself, with the style and the meaning of every movement they make – no way of avoiding it. The way in which Pieter takes a chair is peculiar to Pieter, and in it I find the whole Pieter. He approaches the chair with huge, stealthy strides, a bit hunched, vastly silent and crafty, just like a child wanting everyone to notice how silent he's being, and at the same time quite astonished to be performing an act that takes time and yet is not expressly intended for the social sphere. But he guards against that astonishment – that kind of unease which grips him, as if the air were growing thinner around him – by imagining what he's doing from the social point of view. One can sense how he's setting himself up in judgement, and giving himself a congratulatory acquittal, for the discreetly successful way in which he has taken the chair. But there's still something sly and mulish about him, as if he were playing a fine trick on us and really knows he's making a noise. In short, he can't prevent himself from taking a chair *for us*, even though we're absorbed in our reading or writing. He puts on a show of taking a chair at the very moment that he takes it. A virtuous, right-thinking show, moreover: 'I'm taking a chair. I've a perfect right to take a chair. Everyone will approve of my taking a chair, etc.' However, there's tenderness in the way he creeps furtively up to the chair, looking like some greedy old woman who 'whips up nice little dishes for herself'. He gives himself a tender little assignation in the future: how he's going to love himself, before long, on that chair! And satisfied with himself and his fellow men, communing with us on the occasion of the little surprise he's about to give himself, he grasps the chair with a virtuous look and scampers with it over to the stove, before which he proceeds to sit down.

It's precisely *this* I'd like to succeed in catching and describing in myself: the style of my actions, as it may appear to someone who has frayed nerves and whom I've been irritating for the past three months. I'm afraid it may be impossible, but I'll try.

My confederates are becoming more and more like K.'s assistants in *The Castle*. I have too often preached at them – which they accept, at the time, with shifty looks and without saying a word. At present they're on watch to catch me out, obliging me to behave. Pieter calls me a 'war-profiteer' because I'm profiting from the war to write; he suspects me of trying out arguments, moral principles and experiments on them that will provide me with copy. Paul, counterattacking in turn, reproaches me for my bad faith – because I began by reproaching him for his own. Both of them bristle up when I berate them, and affect to believe that I'm speaking from pure aggressiveness. At the same time, they keep a close eye on me. At the first lapse, what a triumph!

Yesterday, precisely, I'd gone for lunch with Pieter, and since he was surprised to see me refusing bread and wine, I explained my diet to him. Well, it so happened that there were veal cutlets with Brussels sprouts on the menu. The cutlets were very thin, and I don't like Brussels sprouts. As a result, I ate hardly anything. I felt, moreover, as I chewed the few little mouthfuls which did come my way, that I was accumulating excuses and rights – for the sole purpose of being able to use them that evening, if I felt like it. I was in the situation of that saint who said 'It's too much, O Lord, it's too much!', turning vaguely over in my mind such thoughts as: 'Yes, I did decide to eat nothing in the evenings, but on the assumption that I'd get a proper meal at midday. I'm already not eating bread . . . etc. etc.' And my complaints would have been all right if they'd been the fruit of a sincere indignation; but they were busy and provident, they saw far ahead. A great deal could be said about the patient art of establishing excuses for oneself: in other words, of arranging a set piece in such a manner that one may deem it *necessary* to yield to the pressure of circumstances. In this way, one will as far as possible compress the weak layer of nothingness separating the motives from the act. But one always forgets that it's freedom which will deem that the relationship between motives and act is necessary, so one displaces Nothingness but doesn't suppress it – and remains without excuses.

As it was a matter of a dirty little internal manoeuvre, I was discreet enough to say nothing about it to Pieter, and even took care not to let him know that I'd hardly eaten anything, which was the strict truth. At about five in the afternoon, I began to feel hungry. I fidgeted about on my chair for an hour at most, then stood up, took a ration-loaf and thrust my knife into it: hunger had roused the complaints and rights so carefully stored away at noon, and had breathed new life into them. Yet I have a horror of excuses, and I've always taken pride in not having any: if I'm caught out, either I say that I have no excuses, or else – if my excuse is ready as it was yesterday – I alter it, strip it of all sense of an excuse, and present myself in my own eyes as deciding freely on sight of the evidence. The excuse then becomes simply an objective argument which I examine impartially, my sole concern being to decide in favour of the best.

I therefore faced the Assistants and declared, in an objective tone: 'I ate very little at midday, so I'm deciding to make a little exception to my diet this evening.' I said it quite innocently, more for myself than for them, too much absorbed in my own little internal swindles to be watching out for their judgement. So I was quite bewildered by the result: there was a dreadful hullaballoo, they doubled up in unison and began to guffaw, stamping their feet on the floor, pulling faces and giving me knowing looks. Pieter tried to speak, but he couldn't because he was laughing too much. Finally he managed to get a few words out, whose sense was that I was putting on an act and couldn't resist my appetites any more than anyone else. Still grasping the bread with the knife stuck in it, I replied with dignity – but without assurance – that I'd really eaten very little that morning. At which Paul – who hadn't been at the restaurant – turned to Pieter and asked: 'Is that true? Didn't he eat much?', in the severe tone of a judge requesting information. 'Well, I like that!' said Pieter. 'He had a normal lunch.' I was fuming, but what could I do? I adopted the course of laughing it off, and said: 'You're right, you've shown me what I must do. Oh, it's so lucky I've got you!' Whereupon I put the bread down, placed my knife back in my pocket and returned to work.

I was expecting their laughter to continue: I certainly wouldn't have let an adversary go myself under similar circumstances; I'd have 'followed up' as they say in boxing parlance. But they were disconcerted by my acquiescence, didn't breathe another word and, when they'd been to fetch the grub, even offered me beans and pressed me to eat some. I think they were afraid I might starve myself out of vanity. I refused everything, of course, mortified and absolutely famished. But today, for lunch at least, I've got used to it: it seems *natural* to me not to take wine with food and not to eat bread. And it's already almost *natural* not to have any supper: that's to say, by diurnal time – which yesterday was still traversed by two parallel bars, lunch and supper – today ends in free folds; the afternoon floats supple and unbroken below lunch, like a flag at half-mast below its pole. I'm not expecting anything that could 'cut it short'.

Thus do the Assistants force me to be free.

The Beaver writes to me (dated Saturday 16): 'I have the impression you are far more cut off from the world at Morsbronn than before, far more confined in solitude . . . You seem quite cocooned in solitude, quite confined with the telephone, the nice warm stove and your moral thoughts.'

Is that true? I don't know. It seems to me that I was already growing accustomed to war and to Brumath when the Beaver arrived there at the beginning of November; and that her coming had the effect of a time-bomb, disrupting my calm a few days after her departure and leading me finally to late November's palpitations of passion. And I think that immediately after the crisis, as always happens with me in such cases, I withdrew into my shell again and began as a reaction to concern myself only with my own little affairs. In fact, at the moment I'm extremely calm and happy. In any case, I don't entirely understand that month of November; there was some strange ground-swell there.

This morning, when I wrote in this notebook that I'd like to try and catch the style of my movements, I reminded myself of some maniac for analysis of the Amiel type.[13] Yet I went more than fifteen years without looking at myself living. I didn't interest myself at all. I was curious about ideas and the world and other people's hearts. Introspective psychology seemed to me to have yielded its optimum with Proust; I'd tried my hand at it rapturously between the ages of 17 and 20, but it had seemed to me that one could very quickly become a dab hand at that exercise, and in any case the results were pretty tedious. Furthermore, pride deflected me from it: it seemed to me that by prying into trifling acts of meanness, one inflated and reinforced them. It has taken the war, and also the assistance of several new disciplines (phenomenology, psychoanalysis, sociology) – as well as a reading of *L'Age d'homme*[14] – to prompt me to draw up a full-length portrait of myself.

Once launched upon this undertaking, I go at it with a will, out of

13. See note 60 on p.74 above.
14. Michel Leiris, *L'Age d'homme*, Paris 1939.

systematic spirit and a taste for totality; I yield myself up to it entirely, out of obsession. I want to make as complete a portrait as possible, just as when I was little I wanted to have the entire series of *Buffalo Bill* and *Nick Carter*, just as a little later I wanted to know everything about Stendhal, etc. etc. There's certainly a lack of moderation in me: indifference or obsessive enthusiasm, it's one or the other. But I don't think there's any advantage in spending one's whole life delousing oneself. Far from it. I used to have a horror of private diaries and think that man isn't made to see himself, but must always keep his eyes fixed before him. I haven't changed. It simply seems to me that on the occasion of some great event, when one is in the process of changing one's life like a snake sloughing its skin, one can look at that dead skin – that brittle snake image one is leaving behind – and take one's bearings. After the war I shall no longer keep this diary, or if I do I shall no longer speak about myself in it. I don't want to be haunted by myself till the end of my days.

Read (since the last review of my reading):
Mac Orlan: *Sous la lumière froide*
Paul Morand: *Ouvert la nuit*
Marivaux: *Théâtre choisi*
Mérimée: *Colomba*
Flaubert: *L'Éducation sentimentale*
Mac Orlan: *La Cavalière Elsa*
Kierkegaard: *The Concept of Dread*
Dorgelès: *Les Croix de bois*

Received today:
Lucien Jacques: *Carnets de moleskine*
Maurois: *Les Origines de la guerre 1939*
Mac Orlan: *Quai des brumes*
Mac Orlan: *Maître Léonard*[15]
Lesage: *Le Diable boiteux*
Larbaud: *Barnabooth*

Wednesday 20

Fine preface by Giono to the *Carnets de moleskine*.
'When one doesn't have the courage needed to be a pacifist, one's a warrior. The pacifist is always alone.'

---

15. Sartre is mistaken about the title of Mac Orlan's book: it is *Le Nègre Léonard et maître Jean Mullin.*

'The warrior is sure of being in agreement with most people. If it's a majority he wants, he can set his mind at ease, he's in it . . . If, like everyone, he needs greatness, it's in the mess that a greatness "in his own size" is found for him. Everything is prepared for him in advance. If a man trembles at the idea of one day surpassing Man, let him tremble no longer but become a warrior; or, simpler still, just surrender and let himself go – he'll be set among the warriors as a matter of course . . . The whole game of war is played out on the warrior's weakness . . . The simple soldier: neither good nor bad, recruited into it because he's not against it. He'll suffer the warrior's lot there without causing trouble, until the day when, like Faulkner's hero, he discovers that anyone can stumble blindly into heroism by mistake, as easily as he can fall down a manhole left open in the middle of the sidewalk. It's absurd to claim that an army made up of millions of men is the personification of courage: that's the conclusion of a facile mind.'[16]

The diaries themselves are drab and grey, they convey nothing new. Retrospective view of the 1914 war through all these books. I no longer see it, in the way I did last year, as the image of war *itself*; but as a particular war, a particular disordered slaughter, that took place because the generals had not yet invented the technique of what Romains calls the 'million men'.

Ville, a sub-lieutenant in the artillery, writes to the Beaver: 'The situation is so stationary that every now and then some people wish it would change. But then, suddenly reflecting that if it changes we'll be fired at, they recant their incautious words and declare for the status quo. Whereupon someone else retorts that the status quo condemns us to stay here till we grow old. Then everybody talks about something else. The problem is a very awkward one; in the meantime the days go by, unhappily.

'I'm not too sure what's going on back home; the papers are so stupid nobody reads them, though we buy them out of habit. What we are thinking, for the moment, can be summed up in a single word: nothing. We wait for spring, dig, bury ourselves under layers of timbers. Perhaps we'd have a few private ideas, if we could sometimes be alone. But the soldier is never alone; or if he is he has wet feet, which paralyses the intellect.'

16. Jean Giono (1895–1970), novelist sharply critical of modern civilization and its attendant horrors: well-known for his pacifist views.

Barnabooth sells all his goods, 'castles, yacht, cars, huge properties . . .' and he calls that 'dematerializing his fortune'.[17] The gesture is inspired by that of Ménalque or of Michel in *L'Immoraliste*.[18] Gidian. That word 'dematerialize' made me dream. For when you come down to it, it's really a question of detaching oneself from *goods*, as the concrete aspect of wealth, and of keeping only its *abstract* aspect: money. Here, moreover, in the guise of bundles of shares and cheques. In short, that's the advice given by Gide and followed by Barnabooth: to swap real possession for symbolic possession, to swap property-wealth for sign-wealth, It's no accident that Gide preaches *disponibilité*.[19] Basically, the Gidian *homme disponible* is the one whose capital isn't tied up. And what I saw clearly was that Gide's moral code is one of those myths that marks the transition from big bourgeois property – concrete ownership of *the* house, fields and *the* land; private luxury – to the abstract property of capitalism.

The prodigal son is the rich grain merchant's child who becomes a banker. His father had bags of grain, he has bundles of shares. Possession of *nothing*, but this nothing is a mortgage on everything. Do not, O Nathanael, seek God anywhere but everywhere:[20] reject material possession, which limits the horizon and makes God a withdrawal deep into oneself; swap it for symbolic possession, which will permit you to take trains and boats and seek God everywhere. And you'll find him everywhere, so long as you put your signature on this little bit of paper, in your cheque-book. I'm not exaggerating: that's exactly what the Gidian Barnabooth, on page 18, calls a 'burning quest for God'. And Gide himself, now a traveller and now head of the patriarchal community of Cuverville, is a great transitional figure between the propertied bourgeoisie of the 19th century and the capitalism of the 20th.

It must further be noted that the exoticism of the 20th century – thoroughly Gidian – signifies capitalism. It no longer even has the true meaning of *ex*-oticism (in short, to move away from home).[21] Earlier exoticism was understood in relation to fixed coordinates: *property* owned in one's place of birth: 'Happy who like Ulysses,

17. Valéry Larbaud, *A.O. Barnabooth: His Diary*, London 1924, p. 22.

18. Ménalque appears in both *Les Nourritures Terrestres* and *L'Immoraliste*, Michel only in the latter.

19. See note 78 on p. 90 above.

20. Nathanaël: imaginary youth to whom *Les Nourritures Terrestres* is addressed.

21. 'Exoticism' is formed from 'exotic', which in turn comes from the Greek ἐξωτικός, adjective derived from ἔξω = 'outside'.

after a lengthy voyage . . .'²²

Contemporary exoticism starts off by asserting the equivalence of all coordinates. Which means that one can 'change' a pound sterling everywhere. There's no privileged viewpoint for seeing the world. That means you can consider the pound sterling as an abstract purchasing power, which can be broken down at will into marks, francs, öre, pengö, etc. The classic exoticism is the Lyons silk merchant sending his young son to China to train him for business. The young man, in the midst of his Chinese life, will remain Lyonnais: he is in China the better to be Lyonnais; the better to be able, later on, to enjoy his Lyons wealth. Capitalist exoticism lacks any mooring: the traveller is lost in the world. He is at home everywhere or nowhere. Whence this new aspect of literary exoticism: to reduce everything one sees to common structures – instead of *contrasting*, as formerly, the alien with home. To show, beneath the motley appearance of local mores, the universal and everywhere similar constraint of capitalism. To insist upon the crumbling, moribund aspect of mores and to draw poetic effects therefrom (whereas the earlier exoticism used to draw poetic effects from the spontaneous exuberance of local customs). To write, for example, like Larbaud in *Barnabooth*, that Florence is 'a curious American town built in the style of the Italian Renaissance' [p.9]. It is in this sense that a Muslim woman I encountered one day between Agadir and Marrakesh, straddling a bicycle in her veils, seemed to me the perfect embodiment of contemporary exoticism.

The *Graf von Spee* affair. Caution and guile on the part of the allies. It is announced to the whole world that *Renown* and *Ark Royal* are waiting for the German ship to leave harbour. It takes fright and scuttles itself. *Renown* and *Ark Royal* were a thousand miles away. To be compared with our secret withdrawal at the beginning of October: the Germans, deceived by the resistance of a few outposts, advance into empty space and are caught in a hail of fire. To be compared with the principles of '14: heroism, fair-play warfare. This time we mean to wage a war of tricksters and cheats. A war against military honour. The Germans are doing the same, moreover: the *Graf von Spee*'s suicide. Hitler said to Rauschning: 'I have no use for knights.'²³ Not scrupling to do so, the French papers have the ef-

22. Sartre misquotes this famous line from Joachim Du Bellay: 'Heureux qui, comme Ulysse, a fait un beau voyage . . . '

23. Hermann Rauschning, *Hitler Speaks*, London 1939, p. 21. Rauschning was a personal friend of Hitler who turned against Nazism in 1935, after local Nazis established a dictatorial regime in Danzig where he was president of the senate.

frontery to criticize him for this and to mock the abandoning of the *Graf von Spee*. But this is because it's necessary, for a time, to maintain the legend of military honour in the eyes of the home front. In fact, the war's being waged against military honour, as it is against the war of '14. It will emerge forever ruined. Luckily. Granted, there have always been stratagems of war. But this one seeks to use only stratagems. Another two or three years of this stamp, and the notion of courage will become associated with peace, the notion of cowardice with war. Moreover, it's in this guise of boredom without grandeur that the war is seen in other countries, apparently. My pupil Christensen writes to me from Norway: 'There is a Mannerheim line which defends Helsinki. That region is reminiscent of the war of position which you know, and there people die of boredom – at least figuratively speaking. But I hope that compiling a few books is occupying your time a bit.'

Thursday 21

Enchanted by *Barnabooth*. It is noble and graceful. Very much influenced by Gide, whose themes permeate the book through and through. The word 'fervour' is even uttered. And the critique of Barrès and his school, in the name of life: refusing to go to the Uffizi and losing oneself joyfully in some low music-hall. We were all trained in *that* way of travelling. We were all as scrupulous about visiting the Barrio Chino in Barcelona, the closed quarter in Hamburg, or simply the working-class neighbourhoods of Trastevere, as the Germans used to be twenty years earlier about checking through print collections, Baedeker in hand. We too had our Baedekers, but they weren't visible, And that fag-end of an evening I once spent in a Naples brothel where some sailors had taken me – that was still grand tourism.

In books and in the spirit of the age, in short, I found the same tendency to democratize objects which thirty-five years ago provoked violent literary battles and tremendous scandals – and which presents itself as a sequel to the romantic battle to democratize words. The same work was being carried on around 1910 against fine-art work or rare pictures and architecture as in 1830 against the old words of the classical repertoire. Gide too could have dubbed a stained-glass window at Chartres or a portrait by Chardin a 'has-been'. But when we came, for our part, the battle was over. The right had been won for us to roam around the London docks, instead of going to the National Gallery; the right to go and see belly-dancing at the Bushbir in

Casablanca; the right to spend whole days in the dingy bars which surround the Alexanderplatz in Berlin. We travelled quite naturally in this way, 'seeking God everywhere', without even being aware of it. Nobility – which had left men to take refuge in words, then words to take refuge in things – pursued everywhere, had disappeared from this world. Capitalist democracy.

All that I find in Barnabooth – and it's all Gidian. Yet I can also see an idea taking shape in him that doesn't exist at all in Gide, and that we have all been deeply influenced by: the idea that things have a *meaning*. And that one must know how to read it. This idea comes from Barrès: in Barrès, however, it was very comprehensible and even rational, since it came down to saying that the objects of *Kulturwissenschaft*, human products, were imbued with signification and that this signification could be revealed to the artist.[24] To be sure, this signification always transcended what the craftsman had consciously *put* into them, but it was nonetheless based upon the conscious intentions of the creator. There was a signification of Aigues-Mortes as Aigues-Mortes, which is nature recovered by men; a signification of Lorraine, because Lorraine is a cultivated land; a signification of Toledo, because Toledo was the product of the unflinching, constant application of the Toledan nobility. A popular neighbourhood, the product of chance and destitution, had no signification.

Gide, wholly concerned with conquering new lands for literature and overly preoccupied too with pleasures of the senses, neglected this side of the question. I vainly seek in his oeuvre some effort to grasp those fugitive, loosened meanings that settle furtively upon a roof or in a puddle, But Gide's descendants have managed to make the synthesis. The work Barrès used to do conscientiously on a few aristocratic products, they're going to do on any old thing. For Barrès, Toledo alone has its 'secret'. For the traveller of 1925, there's nothing in the world that doesn't have a secret. Barnabooth seeks the 'air' of Italy; Duhamel, alighting one evening at Cologne, speaks to Aron of the 'smell' of Cologne; Lacretelle seeks the *keys* to Madrid.[25] To uncover these secrets, all means are fair: the most vulgar objects and the noblest are equivalents.

Barnabooth, for example, seeks to grasp the meaning of Italy in 'the singing of the great poets . . . the directory principles of the Ris-

24. Maurice Barrès (1862–1923), novelist, essayist and politician of mystical-nationalist views (anti-Dreyfus, etc.), but who had in his early works developed a 'cult of the self' which had wide influence.

Kulturwissenschaft: approximately 'philosophy of civilization'.

25. Jacques de Lacretelle (1888–), novelist, published *Lettres espagnoles* in 1927.

orgimento . . .'. But he adds: 'That is much less important than the dreary pink with which the docks at Naples are painted' [p. 52]. I recognize myself in Barnabooth: I too, as I ate the Caflish pâtisserie's garish little iced cakes, thought I could sense through my mouth the same Italian redolence which the 'dreary pink' of Neapolitan houses or the sad, dry exuberance of the gardens of upper Genoa allowed me to sense through my eyes. For me, too, the Italian secret was contained in every Italian thing, and the toothpastes of Bologna had a secret affinity with d'Annunzio's prose and with fascism. What charms me about Barnabooth is that this 'hermeneutic' tendency is still faltering. He writes in apology: ' . . . the Italy for which I am trying to find the definitive formula (instead of these fumbling assessments) . . . .I have heaped up words without being able to render the Italian *air* which I can feel so well' [pp.50, 52]. People have done better since – but nothing so graceful. When one reads these pages, it's as if one is studying a naive literary premonition – like when one discovers a few descriptions of nature in Mme de Sévigné's letters. Larbaud himself has done better – but not so well.

For my own part, in *La Nausée* I pushed the passion for secrecy – against Barrès – to the point of trying to catch the secret smiles of things seen absolutely without men. Roquentin before the public garden was like myself before a Neapolitan alleyway: things were making signs to him and it was necessary to decipher them. And when I decided to write some short stories, my aim was quite different from that which I subsequently achieved. I noticed that pure words let the meaning of streets and landscapes escape – just as Barnabooth noticed that. I understood it was necessary to present meaning still adhering to things, since it's never entirely detached from them, and – in order to exhibit it – to show rapidly some of the objects that secrete it, and to make their equivalence felt; in such a way that these solids would drive away and annul each other in the reader's mind, just as one event drives away the memory of another, and there would eventually remain on the horizon of this motley chaos only a discreet, tenacious meaning – very precise, but escaping from the words for ever. And, in order to escape from logical connections – and from the defect of a disconnected enumeration besides – the best thing, I thought, was to unite those heteroclite things by a very brief action. In a word, I was going to write short stories of a similar kind to those of K. Mansfield.

I did two of these: one on Norway, *Le Soleil de minuit*, which I subsequently lost in the heart of the Causses, walking with my jacket slung over my arm; the other, which didn't come off at all, on Naples: *Dépaysement*. And eventually the inherent logic of the 'short-story' genre led me to write *Le Mur* and *La Chambre*, which no longer bore any relation to my original intentions.[26] In short, I'd pushed the tendency for secrecy to the point of dehumanizing entirely the secret of things. But I hold that the vast majority of secrets are human. And I see the culmination of Barnabooth's 'fumblings' in the Heideggerian pages of *Terre des hommes* which I was quoting in my third notebook, where St-Exupéry says more or less: 'An object has no meaning except it be seen through a civilization, a culture, a craft.' So we're back to being-in-the-world. And the world once again becomes that complex of significations 'whereby human reality discloses to itself what it is.'[27]

So it seems to me that a new page has been turned in the literary history of 'feeling for nature'. Barrès, or secrets; Gide, or the democratization of things; Larbaud and the whole postwar period, or the democratization of secrets. And finally that broader humanism of '39: the return to action, and the *craft* conceived as the best organ for grasping secrets. I'd be inclined to say that the Larbaud epoch – when there seemed to be an artistic intuition of secrets accessible to any man of good will – forms part of the capitalist abstraction I was speaking about yesterday. The man who picks up secrets is here an abstract antenna – he's that notorious 'abstract man' of the democracies. Whereas, in St-Exupéry's assertion that secrets are an outcome of the craftsman's action, I sense some kind of secret revolt against capitalism: a desire to find the concrete man again, and to reattach him by some new means to the soil, since the bourgeois house has collapsed. This time, it will be the craft. We should be in no doubt, there's a vague nostalgia here for fascism in its various forms. And I recognize myself that there's a hint of fascism in my current thought (historicity; being-in-the-world; all that binds man to his time; all that roots him in his land and his situation). But I hate fascism, and I'm using it here only as the pinch of salt one adds to a tart to make it taste sweeter.

This contrast between the labourer and the abstract tourist in St-Exupéry is so strong that for him, though the traveller (in other words, Barnabooth) can *see* the white flowers of the sea, the pilot alone *feels* their poisonous nature. And the cultured man will certainly not be surprised to find in St-Exupéry those sudden transitions

---

26. 'La Chambre' is included in *The Wall and Other Stories*, see note 13 on p. 15 above. 'Dépaysement' has not been translated, but is published in *Oeuvres romanesques*.

27. See pp. 40 and 54-55 above.

– from the Sahara to Tierra del Fuego, from Paris to the Andes – to which contemporary writers have accustomed us. If he does not watch out, however, he will miss the essential difference. For Barnabooth, Norway, France and Italy are lands and cultures placed end to end, which by their inherent inertia would tend to separate: there is juxtaposition. But for the pilot St-Exupéry, there is first of all the unity of *his* world, He is-in-the-world by virtue of the primordial act of *flying*. And it's against a background of world that cities and countries appear, as *destinations*. In this sense, it's the death of exoticism: those cities with their magical names – Buenos Aires, Cartagena, Marrakesh – are laid beside him so that he can *make use of them*, just as nails or a plane are laid on a work-bench. Tangiers is first and foremost a landmark, a means to find one's bearings, a radio-centre; then it's a mission, a task grasped through the craft. Finally, as one draws closer, the flower opens and behold the dry, yellow town with its impoverished, haughty Spaniards and its handsome Kabyles. But it's that – that sweetness – only *in the last instance*. St-Exupéry is the anti-Barnabooth.

So things are human, and we can do nothing about it. They disclose man to man. But we shouldn't understand by this that their human meaning has been deposited on them in successive layers – in the course of generations and in the course of the individual life. It's enough to exist, to throw ourselves once into the world through a gap of nothingness, and to throw our human reality to the horizon of the existent as an ideal to found, for each thing to reflect back to us and proclaim that human reality – but refracting the latter with its own particular sign. Thus do we learn about ourselves through things. But the human meanings they reflect back to us are all encumbered, all enriched, by their own particular substance. Hence, what we read in things is by no means limited to revealing ourselves to ourselves: it *creates* us.

It shouldn't be thought, for example, that we first constituted our psychological nature – 'sly, disturbing softness, baseness which belimes through self-seeking flattery and taste for self-humiliation, etc.' – then *afterwards* constituted gluey sliminess as a physical image of this mental trait.[28] That would be to believe that the image is always

28. Sartre's famous concept of *viscosité/le visqueux*, here making its first real appearance, is strictly untranslatable, combining as it does in a way no English word can encompass the pejorative charge of 'slimy' referring to persons and the senses 'sticky', 'glutinous', 'viscous', 'viscid', 'gluey', 'treacly', etc with reference to the material world. The translator of *L'Être et le néant* opted for 'slimy' throughout (keeping 'sticky' for the

a metaphor, gripped by abstract relationships; that the moral of the fable was conceived before the fable itself. In reality, by virtue of the fact that I throw myself into the world, every object rises up in front of me with a human expression even before I know how to make use of it and understand that expression. Glueyness disturbs me and pierces me even before I can know that among men there exists a soft, cringing baseness. There is no *Einfühlung*[29] here, no animation of nature *afterwards*, but quite to the contrary: before any psychological feeling, before any empirical *Einfühlung*, gluey sliminess presents itself as an existential category; it is its thick, clayey pitchiness that is going to orient us towards other, inasmuch as this stands out against the background of a human world, Gluey sliminess is human inasmuch as it receives the formal, pragmatic category of resistance to man; of distance between man and man; of means utilized by human reality to catch up with itself. But its own particular nature does the rest and reflects back a 'human-sliminess'.

This is what explains disgust. Disgust is always disgust of man for man. The child who accidentally thrusts his hand into some gluey pitch, and pulls it out with tears of disgust, has just undergone a human experience. Not that he has sensed man's baseness *through* gluey sliminess – he has experienced only a *thing*. But this thing is human in its deep structure: it has an undifferentiated depth in which a thousand indistinct human possibles are mingled, a thousand possibles belonging to the child who cries. Gluey sliminess is *haunted*. The fall from there into fetishism and then into animism will be easy, but nature is neither fetishist nor animist. Things are sorcerous, but only because they are inexhaustibly human; they conceal human meanings that we sense without understanding them. There is no baseness hidden in gluey sliminess, there's only human-sliminess, sliminess-for-man, mother of all basenesses. A slimy human reality is on the horizon of this gluey sliminess, and this human reality that we do not even understand is ourselves. Ourselves: possible beliming of ourselves in gluey sliminess. Possible slimification of ourselves –

---

more inert *pâteux*): but this presents Sartre applying the term inappropriately to pitch, birdlime or honey. The origin of the image for Sartre seems to have been a childhood world where he poked his fingers into honey or dough in the kitchen, into birdlime or pitch in the backyard. After discarding 'viscosity' as over-technical, 'gooeyness' as too colloquial and endearing, 'stickiness' as too inert, etc—quite apart from the fact that none of these can replace 'sliminess' as a human quality—I have reluctantly fallen back on the inelegant portmanteau 'gluey sliminess' for *viscosité* here: repeated thereafter as 'sliminess' when referring to persons, as 'glueyness' when referring to things.

29. *Einfühlung*: empathy.

which we sense with anguish, without even being able to understand what it would be. That's why there would be good grounds for making an inventory of these real categories whence man comes slowly to himself: gluey sliminess, elasticity, flakiness, etc. etc.

In respect of this, it should be said that I can now see more clearly something that I've long guessed at: pre-sexuality. The Freudians rightly saw that the innocent action of the child who plays at digging holes was not so innocent at all. Nor that which consists in sliding one's finger into some hole in a door or wall. They related it to the faecal pleasures which children take in being given or administering enemas. And they weren't wrong. But the core of the matter remains unclear: must all such experiences be reduced to the sole experience of anal pleasure? I shall point out that this supposes a mysterious divination of instinct: for the child who hold back his faeces in order to enjoy the pleasure of excretion has no means of guessing that he has an anus, nor that this anus presents a similarity with the holes into which – immediately – he seeks to put his fingers. In other words, Freud will consider that all holes, for the child, are symbolic anuses which attract him as a function of that kinship – whereas for my part I wonder whether the anus is not, in the child, an object of lust because it is a hole.

And certainly the arsehole is the most alive of holes, a lyrical hole, which puckers like a brow, which tightens in the way a wounded beast contracts, which finally gapes – conquered and ready to yield up its secrets. It is the softest and most hidden of holes, what you will – I have nothing against the Freudians composing hymns to the anus – but it remains the case that the cult of the hole is anterior to that of the anus, and that it is applied to a larger number of objects. And I'm quite prepared to grant that it gradually becomes imbued with sexuality, but I imagine that it is initially pre-sexual: in other words, that it contains sexuality in the undifferentiated state and extends beyond it. I think that the pleasure a child takes in giving enemas (numerous are those who play at doctor to have this pleasure: in my own case, one of my earliest memories is of my grandmother's arms raised to the heavens in a hotel-room at Seelisburg, because she'd just caught me in the middle of giving an enema to a little Swiss girl of my own age) is pre-sexual: it's the pleasure of poking into a hole. And the 'poking into a hole' situation is itself pre-sexual. By this we mean it is neither psychological nor historical; it does not suppose any connection, realized in the course of human experience, between orifices and our desires.

But as soon as a man appears in the world, the holes, the cracks, all

the excavations that surround him become human. The world is a
kingdom of holes. I see, in fact, that the hole is bound up with refusal,
with negation and with Nothingness. The hole is first and foremost
what *is not*. This nihilating function of the hole is revealed by such
vulgar expressions heard here as 'arsehole with no buttocks' – which
means 'naught' or 'nothingness'. To call an enemy an 'arsehole with no
buttocks' is to annihilate him, to treat him as an empty idiot, a zero.
For in popular imagery, of course, the buttocks form the rims of the
anus. I notice, too, that people are bothered by the idea of the *bottom*
of the hole. They talk about a 'well of stupidity', and about 'bottomless
stupidity'. There is a seductive ambiguity here, a kind of shimmering
of the finite and the infinite: in every hole one expects to find a bottom
– since it has rims – but on the other hand Nothingness is an infinite,
since it could be bounded only by itself. So there is a lure of Nothingness – an ambiguous lure. Whence the game of *hidey-hole*. To enter a
hidey-hole is originally to bury oneself in a hole, to annihilate oneself
by identifying with the void that constitutes the hole. To protect
oneself, it will be said. No doubt. But to protect oneself by annihilating oneself, by withdrawing into the invisible.

Thus the hole's nothingness is a nothingness of man; it's at once
death and freedom, negation of the social. One day I saw a Freudian
mother gazing tenderly at her little daughter crouched on all fours
under the table. She was convinced that this liking of the child's for
dark hidey-holes was a desire to return to the pre-natal state; she felt
flattered, as if the child were knocking at her door and wished to
return to the intimacy of her womb. I suppose she was already
preparing to part her legs. But this is all nonsense, The vertiginous
thrill of the hole comes from the fact that it proposes annihilation, it
rescues from facticity. This nothingness is the attractive element in
what is properly termed 'vertigo'. The abyss is a hole, it proposes
engulfment. And engulfment always attracts, as a nihilation which
would be its own foundation. Of course, attraction for the hole is
accompanied by repulsion and anguish. But the hole's nothingness is
coloured: it's a *black* nothingness, which causes another nature to
intervene here, another cardinal category – Night. The nature of the
hole is nocturnal. That's what confers upon it its shady, mysterious,
sacred character. And precisely because it is nocturnal, it conceals.
Daytime holes are slashes of night. In the depths of the night there is
something. The hole is sacred because it conceals. It is, moreover, the
occasion of a contact with what one doesn't see. The particular
situation of the man who delves into a hole is that his hands meet
enemies which his eyes cannot see. His eyes are still in the kingdom of

light, but a whole blind part of himself has already gone down to hell.

I have already mentioned that the hole is often resistance. It must be forced, in order to pass through. Thereby, it is already feminine. It is resistance by Nothingness, in other words modesty. This is obviously why it attracts sexuality (will to power, rape, etc.). But at the same time, in the act of poking into a hole – which is rape, breaking-in, negation – we find the workman's act of *plugging* the hole. The child who stick his finger into a hole in the ground experiences the joy of (ful-)*filling* the hole. In a sense, all holes plead obscurely to be filled, they are appeals: to fill = triumph of the full over the empty, of existence over Nothingness. What is involved here is a craftsman's act. Expressions like 'plugging the gaps' or 'stop-gap' indicate clearly enough the human concern to achieve plenitude – in contrast with the vertiginous thrill of annihilation that is black magic.[30]

To plug a hole is to transform the empty into the full, and thereby, magically, to create material possessing all the features of the holed substance. If I plug a hole in a brick wall with earth, I have made brick out of earth. Whence the tendency to plug holes with one's own substance, which brings about identification with the holed substance and, finally, metamorphosis. The child who sticks his finger into a hole in the ground becomes one with the ground which he plugs; he transforms himself into earth by his finger.

At the root of these sorceries I rediscover the craftsman's idea of *fitting-together* – primitive aspect of necessity. Two bodies which fit together are made for each other. Fitting together magically entails fusion. One can see that the nature of the hole (pre-sexual) will be very well suited to polarize almost all of sexuality, when the child will be able to think that he himself is the hole which is penetrated, or on the contrary that he can penetrate and plug with his own flesh a hole which lives hidden in a living body. But one can also see that – far from sexuality giving to holes its appeal for the child – it is, on the contrary, the categorial nature of the hole that will constitute the basic layer of signification for the various species of sexual hole: vagina, anus, mouth, etc. And this doesn't at all mean the hole is not in itself an object of sexuality. It must be noted, however: 1. that this sexuality is undifferentiated, fused in the ensemble of human tendencies and of the human attitude towards the hole; 2. that it isn't directed to the hole derivatively, because of the latter's analogy with the anus, but

---

30. I have translated *boucher* by 'plugging', *combler* by 'filling'—but it should be noted that *combler* also means 'to overwhelm' or, more specifically, 'to satisfy sexually'.

directly as constituent of its very structure. The hole – nocturnal female organ of nature, skylight to Nothingness, symbol of chaste and violated refusals, mouth of shadow which engulfs and assimilates – reflects back to man the human image of his own possibilities, like sliminess or flakiness. There can be – there is – human enjoyment that is not properly speaking sexual in filling a hole, just as there's a human enjoyment in scratching a flaky substance and breaking pieces off.

The Freudians have made themselves the hole's sexual poets, but they haven't explained the nature of its appeal. To do so, it is necessary to see man's shadow projected on to the cracks and craters of nature. The Beaver was telling me of the dreadful fright she'd had reading a book entitled, I think, *The Jungle Trapper*. Among other gruesome stories, one was recounted there which, if one thinks about it for a moment, highlights admirably all the properties of the hole. Two prisoners discover the entrance to a narrow, dark, underground passage, and escape by crawling into it on all fours. As they proceed, the gallery closes in until finally the one who's in front – a big, jolly, likeable lad apparently – finds himself wedged fast between the sides, so that he can no longer either proceed or retreat. At this juncture, a boa constrictor appears and literally swallows him, despite his desperate screams. His companion, who is the one telling the story, is an impotent witness to the wretched fellow's engulfment.

The whole horror of the story – which often prevented the Beaver from sleeping – obviously comes from the fact that it takes place in a hole. Granted, it's never pleasant to be swallowed by a boa. But when the operation unfolds in the open air, it's an example of the kind of atrocity with which children's books teem, and which children read about unconcernedly as they munch a slice of bread and jam. Here, however, the anecdote serves to awaken the dread, filled with horror and lust, that we experience before the hole. What's the point of going looking for arsehole connotations here? The episode speaks for itself. Isn't it the very essence of *hole*, that dark orifice which is violated, and which yields at first, and which is nothingness and night, and which then closes slowly like a mouth or a sphincter, and which contains something at the bottom of itself, conceals – what? – *another* hole endowed with a devouring and annihilating power: a boa. And I'm not sure whether, right at the back of the Beaver's terror, there wasn't an obscure enjoyment. Because that engulfment, followed by deglutition – that man swallowed bodily by the powers of darkness – there's something satisfying to heart and mind about it.

Of course, what I have tried to do for the hole, one could do for a dozen or a score of pre-sexual objects: for the finger, for the curve, for cementation,[31] for positions (positions of things with respect to each other – juxtaposition, superposition; positions of wrestlers, warriors or players; and lastly, mutual positions of the man and woman in games of love). I wished only to signal the human origin of the meaning of things: understanding by this, not at all that man is anterior to the meaning of things, but that the world is human and it's in a human world that man appears. For we may note here that gluey sliminess is by no means *first* glueyness and *then* human-sliminess; nor is the hole *first* hole and *then* nocturnal nothingness, engulfing power, etc. It is by a single movement that they constitute themselves as natural objects and as human objects; for, without man and his nihilating power, there'd be neither glueynesses nor holes, there'd be only a blossoming of undifferentiated plenitude. It is by projecting his nothingness into that plenitude that man, by negation, causes there to be holes – and these holes to be holes-for-man.

This evening Klein, the colonel's driver, pays us a visit. He heard our raised voices – I was explaining to Pieter that he had a feminine temperament and he was getting angry – and that attracted him: light, warmth. We offered him a slice of tart and he told stories. He's the first fellow I've met who has really *seen* the state the evacuated villages are in. The other day they stopped in a frontier-village, and while the colonel was going to the gun-emplacements, he asked a sergeant to open one of the houses for him and show him the state of the furnishings. It was edifying. Mirrors smashed on the wardrobes; pieces of furniture split by bayonet-strokes; bed-linen looted – what couldn't be carried away is torn. The tiles on the roofs are smashed, the silverware has disappeared. In the cellars, the lads drank what they could and then, when they could drink no more, went off leaving the spigots of the barrels open; the cellar is flooded with wine. A sewing-machine is split in two. By axe-blows? 'And yet it was cast-iron,' says Klein sadly.

Not long ago, some evacuees returned to this village and its neighbours on a 24-hour pass, to fetch bed-linen, When they left their houses, most of them were weeping in despair: they'd found nothing left. They complained to the commandant. But what could be done? The people responsible don't come from our division, nor in all probability even from the division which preceded us here. It goes

---

31. Cementation here has the technical sense used, for example, in metalworking, where a metal such as iron is hardened through incorporation of some other substance under heat.

back to the earliest days of the war. As Pieter rightly said, that was the time when everyone believed the war would be a cataclysm. The soldiers made haste to loot, thinking that the first artillery bombardment would wipe out all trace of looting, along with the very existence of the looted houses. And then, lo and behold, the war became a long tedium, a long wait, and the looted houses remain – shocking and indiscreet.

'It's not possible,' the sergeant was saying, 'it's not possible to give them back in that state; it'd cause trouble. They'll have to be told the Boches looted everything. But for that, the Boches would have to attack . . .' It seems that the officers set the example. At Herrlisheim, some wagons supposedly containing damaged ammunition were unsealed: they were stuffed full of underwear, sewing-machines, silverware. It's impossible to know whether the civilians who come to fetch warm clothes don't loot too. They have a free pass and that's all. Impossible to tell whether they really go to their own houses or into their rich neighbour's instead. Only the mayor could say, but the mayor isn't there, he's in the Limousin.

We talk about Strasbourg. He says the police there, by contrast, is well organized and strict. One old eccentric he used to know, an umbrella-merchant, wouldn't allow himself to be evacuated; he hid in his house and let the others go off, then lived alone, feeding himself from tins. In the end, he grew bolder and switched on the lamps of an evening. One night, as the constables were doing their rounds, they saw a light. They called and shouted, but the old man didn't reply. They called three times, but the old man still remained silent, terrified no doubt that he'd be evacuated forcibly. After the third time, they fired through the window and the first volley killed him stone dead.

Friday 22

I have been on a 'pilgrimage' to Pfaffenhoffen, cradle of my mother's family if I remember rightly. In any case, I spent the summer holidays of 1913 there at the house of my aunt Caroline Biedermann, who had a lingerie shop – the richest in town. (Incidentally, how did my grandfather, such a stickler on the score of intellectual nobility, come to terms with his sister's misalliance?) I vaguely recall having seen, on that occasion, the silvery flash of a German regiment parading beneath our windows to the shrill, piercing music of the fife.

It's at Pfaffenhoffen that my first 'literary' memory occurs. I was writing an adventure novel – *For a Butterfly* – sitting at a writing-desk with my back turned to the window. The paper I was using was ruled, but the divisions were more like stripes than lines: every two centimetres, two parallel rules were drawn, a quarter-centimetre apart, and intended to hem in my schoolboy handwriting above and below: it created an unpleasant impression of stinginess. I used to buy those thin German exercise-books at Rosenfeld's, a dingy stationer's whose little shop just opposite the vast Biedermann emporium also provided me with pens and sweets. A strange connection had formed in my mind between those sweets and the pens and exercise-books, and as I ate them I used to have the impression of chewing paper. To my mind they were studious sweets, a bit boring but all the more attractive for that: work sweets. I spent all my time hanging round that stationer's, and my Aunt Caroline – who was a real old cow – was forever making disagreeable comments: 'Don't bother Mr Rosenfeld for things that only cost a few pfennigs.' To tell the truth, so far as I can recall, Mr Rosenfeld – bald and kindly with spectacles – was not the man to scorn a few pfennigs.

After the war, I went back to Pfaffenhoffen with my grandfather, probably in 1920 or '21. Aunt Caroline was still just as disagreeable. I can still remember the garden, where I used to find games to amuse her great-nephew Theo; her stepdaughter, with whom I used to play duets on the piano; and her daughter Anna, who was hunch-backed and used to make me say 'Pipele' and 'Ripele' in order to poke fun at my French accent.[32] A trip, too, to the castle of Lichtenberg, in a horsedrawn carriage. We had supper on the way down in an open-air café: Cousin Mathilde and Cousin Anna ate heartily Alsatian-style, and the heady fumes of the meal coloured their faces brightly. That shocked me – or rather I'd have liked it to shock me. I was at the age when one's prone to do an Alain-Fournier number:[33] when one feels refined, because one demands of women a graceful unreality – which allows one, if one's handsome and already sought after, to show oneself profoundly tyrannical and capricious with them, in order to make them pay dearly for their terrible crime of being made of flesh and blood; and, if one's ugly, to read Laforgue with bitterness and scorn.[34]

32. I am unable to explain either these names, or their special suitability for showing up the Frenchness of Sartre's accent.

33. Alain-Fournier: pseudonym of Henri-Alban Fournier (1886–1914), author of *Le Grand Meaulnes*.

34. Jules Laforgue (1860–87), symbolist poet who employed irony and commonplace elements to puncture poetic fantasy. He was a major influence on T.S. Eliot, for example.

I had a little stab at that kind of delicacy, but only a feeble one. It was one possible direction, but almost at once Nizan and I took the other path: the cult of the body. I remember how we used to enjoy ourselves – on principle, too – at the Cluny snackbar, watching some strapping blonde rend a cold-meat sandwich with her splendid teeth. We could very well have written, with Larbaud: 'I find that there are not many things more agreeable to watch than a pretty woman in a low-cut gown eating fine red meat with a good appetite' [p.53]. And perhaps, at the source of the many conversations we held on this subject, there lay that little text of Larbaud's. But it was above all in keeping with our Cartesianism: a body is a body, one likes the female body, it must be accepted totally, the body hasn't any 'weak points', etc. The whole thing seasoned, of course, by a dash of paganism: it was the period when we were reading Montherlant's 'hymns to the body'.[35] Naturally, we were unsure enough to relapse every so often into seraphic delicacy – and the memory of those two women with their glowing cheeks was the one I evoked in such instances. It served as bullion backing for my judgements. For my main concern at the time – since I was building faster than I could provide foundations – was, in each case, to assure myself of a memory backing. I made Mme Morel really laugh a few years later, by declaring to her in that peremptory tone of voice I affected at the time (the one Guille used to call my 'Frederick voice'[36]): 'I have a horror of women who get flushed when they're eating.'

Such were the sole memories that remained to me of Pfaffenhoffen. Nevertheless, I felt myself obliged to make a pilgrimage there. Why? Basically, I had some vague hope that this sudden contact with a town where I'd lived would cause a cloud of memories abruptly to crystallize. And then it struck me as poetic – that little city buried at the back of my memory, like the town of Ys at the bottom of the sea (there's a whole production in Renan about it, I think).[37] So when someone had to go and fetch a hydrogen cylinder from the balloon-unit, I begged Paul to get me sent. This morning before leaving, though, I was almost regretting my decision, simply because I always have to force myself a bit to get moving. Moreover, it was necessary to take my rifle

35. Henri de Montherlant (1896–1972), novelist and playwright; his earlier works exalt war, sport, bullfighting and the cult of the body.

36. In his youth, Sartre had written a novel inspired by the relations between Frederick Nietzsche and Wagner.

37. See Ernest Renan, *Oeuvres complètes*, vol. II, Paris 1948, 'Souvenirs d'enfance et de jeunesse: Préface', pp. 713-23: the legendary drowned city was in fact called Is, at least by Renan.

and helmet and that offended me: those are not the classic pilgrim's accessories. And, it must be admitted, I was furious at having to give up the poetic hour of my breakfast.

We left on a lorry, big Grener and I. I was sitting beside the driver, a moustached Alsatian in his forties, and Grener was in the back. 'Perfect weather' – as that 'Joseph Prudhomme'[38] of a Courcy had told me when I left, in just the tone of voice needed to disarm the words spoken: a kind of good-natured, level emphasis, a careless deliberation, embellishing the phrase with invisible quotation marks and implying that it's a question of saying what has to be said, but not by any means of thinking it – especially not of thinking it – whether it concerns the weather or the music of Beethoven: with Courcy, speech is the best remedy for thought. The ground was hard as rock, cracked and yellow, whitened by frost. A charming, pale sun illuminated wakening villages: Eberback, Schweighausen, Niedermodern. In the fields, there were heavy Percheron horses harnessed to artillery-caissons; but the countryside adopted them as its own, making them into plough-horses and the soldiers into peasants. Dry, sharp winter countryside. It was minus 9°. I recognized nothing. In a café, I found a lad from the Met. who was going on leave that evening and insisted on standing us a round of schnapps. After which I stood a round of my own, so did Grener, and so did the driver. From there I went to the BNC,[39] where the Corps met. section has its quarters behind a counter. We drank some rum. I left feeling rather hazy and wandered round that solid market town, prosperous but rather dismal, which held no message for me. All that particular past is well and truly buried – nothing can resurrect it.

I bought some terry towels for Captain Orcel and some writing-pads for Lieutenant Ulrich. Round a bend in the road, I found myself in front of a big ochre construction, very ugly, with slate roofs, turrets and gables: it was the Biedermann emporium. There, too, my memory remained dumb. I went into Rosenfeld's opposite as of old, and as of old I bought some paper. The shop has been modernized, it's not showy, it has the austere discretion of a Protestant store, but it seems full of nice little accessories, handsome ledgers, Omo-ring books, fountain-pens, etc. No more sweets. On leaving, I mused for a time in front of the Biedermann store. Caroline is dead, Mathilde too. Anna has doubtless been evacuated (she lived in Strasbourg). Theo must have been called up. Only old Georges must be left, whom the

38. M. Joseph Prudhomme: personification of the banal, prosperous bourgeois under the July Monarchy, created by the caricaturist Henri Monnier.

39. Banque Nationale de Commerce.

family usually spoke of with a meaning tap on the forehead.[40] I certainly had no wish to go in, but I saw shapes – a woman's face which suddenly appeared and was pressed up against the windowpane. I don't know why, for an instant that struck me as heartrending. No doubt, it was my symbolic wish to go into a home; once again to see civilians going about civilian occupations; to bury myself in the soft, dark heart of Peace; to speak to a woman. In short, my wish to get the hell out of here.

I went back to the café, where Grener was waiting for me. The lads from the Met. had given me an armful of newspapers, including the *Lumière* for 15 December, where Émile Bouvier writes of me: 'I doubt whether M. Sartre will become a great novelist, for he seems to have a dislike for artifice, and in artifice lies "art". It is to be feared lest – taking his mission too seriously and perceiving that the means of expression at his disposal must needs involve some trickery – he may leave literature for philosophy, mysticism or social preaching.'

I was flabbergasted: I'd never have believed that anyone would consign me to mysticism like that. And as for social preaching, M. Bouvier can set his mind at ease. And what strange idea has he got of me, if he thinks I have a dislike for artifice? Heavens, I'm perfectly well aware that in a novel it's necessary to lie in order to be true. But I like such artifices, I'm a liar from choice, otherwise I wouldn't write at all. I found it pretty disagreeable, especially since – by one of those coincidences which are so common in my life – it came on the day following a letter from L., who was telling me Lévy respects me more 'as a philosopher than as a novelist', because I lack imagination. A little further on, that same M. Bouvier reproaches me for forgetting that the novel is an 'entertainment'. He's the one who says so! There's no dispute about the object of the novel being an unreal. But it takes a pretty crude kind of utilitarianism to conclude that the novel itself is an entertainment. The same fellow, under the rubric of 'commendation', declares that in my books 'a fine density of life is displayed with calm immodesty'. A sentence which bothered me even more than the rest: when anyone starts talking about 'density of life', I think of Rabelais or Crommelynck's *Tripes d'or* or what have you.[41] But 'life' – in a cold fish, a stockfish, like me? And there's nothing calm about my immodesty! Besides, it's not even immodesty.

After this, Grener pays for a round, I pay for a round, the driver

---

40. Sartre's maternal uncle.

41. Fernand Crommelynck (1888–1970), Belgian playwright, author of farces such as *Le Cocu magnifique* (1921) and *Tripes d'or* (1925).

pays for a round and we return home rather merry. The countryside is redder, the sun yellower. It's noon. I can't understand noon's reputation for sharpness, on the pretext that it doesn't cast things into shadow.[42] The true, keen, clarity of mind is that of early morning. On the way back to Morsbronn – a bit queasy; vaguely astonished at having an afternoon to spend – I was bitterly regretting my joyful morning clarity. The driver said to me: 'I like making friends: it's my nature. Can I drop in and spend Christmas evening at your place?' – 'Of course': but I'm counting on Paul and Keller to amuse him.

It's true we're only two days away from Christmas. For most of the fellows here, this is important: for them, it will be a time for regrets. Christmas is one of the moments in the year when the family smells stuffiest – that's the smell they all miss. Concerned for their morale, the military authorities arrange a little surprise for them on that particular day. And there'll be a Christmas tree for us at the Restaurant de la Gare. Perhaps I'll go along. I'd like to see that soldiers' Christmas. But it will be as a tourist, whereas one would really need to be caught up in it. Incidentally, Paul got me to bring a bottle of good wine back from Pfaffenhoffen, because it's his birthday tomorrow. So we'll celebrate it and there'll probably be a tart, He'll return the favour, so we'll be celebrating mine on 21 June. I find it ridiculous and rather touching.

Letter from Paulhan. Aragon 'is still MO in a "workers' " regiment (several suicides), and thinks that while we're "pretending", the USSR is squeezing Hitler more tightly every day.'

Saturday 23

Minus 10° this morning. An antiseptic, charming cold: the kind of cold of local anaesthetics, chilled meats, liquefied gases. One can feel its density when one walks on the road, powdery with frost. Objects are smaller and sharper, but seem separated from me by a refractive medium: going down the frozen road, on my way to eat breakfast at the Restaurant de la Gare, I have the impression I'm plunging into a pane of glass. At present the cafés are out of bounds to troops in the morning, so as a great favour I get breakfast in the restaurant kitchen, off a dirty oilcloth, amid a great din of water and a sickly smell of meat

---

42. The reference must be to Paul Valéry's 'Le Cimetière marin': 'ce toit tranquille, où marchent des colombes/Entre les pins palpite, entre les tombes;/Midi le juste y compose de feux'—though *midi juste* in everyday speech simply means 'noon'.

(it's there behind my back, the meat – a ragged mess of tea-rose pink, with blueish bones like eyes). Slung over a stick propped between the edge of the sink and a window-cornice, thick blackish sausages swarm like maggots. There I hold my morning conversation with the patrons of the place: the cook from the officers' mess; the military butcher, who's waiting for his van to go and buy meat at the Carrefour des Tziganes; the helmeted chasseur, with his long horse-face, who comes to pick up soldiers returned from leave as they alight from the coach.

Always the same sentences, but always 'felt' – which gives them a bit of new life and a remnant of freshness: 'It's nippy, this morning.' – 'Right, minus nine.' – 'We'd be better off at home.' – 'And that van of mine's still not here: what the fuck's that lad of mine doing?' – 'Well, in these conditions, you know, radiators . . .' – 'Oh yes, that big fellow from the horse-meat firm, the driver, they had to fetch a car in yesterday to get his going. They towed it along for five hundred metres, and it still wouldn't start.' They look at my books: 'Still reading?' And I make my excuses shamefacedly: 'Well, yes, as there's nothing else to do.' And they excuse me indulgently, even encourage me with good-natured superiority: 'You're right. As you've got the chance . . .' Every so often the restaurant idiot, a tall thin fellow with a shaggy countenance, goes by sniggering. The other day, I'd made my way towards what's called the piss-hole here, German-fashion. One of the cubicle doors was open and one of the waitresses was relieving herself, sitting comfortably, her skirts spread all about her. The idiot was sitting outside on a stool and chatting to her as he peeled the potatoes. At the sight of me she cried out 'Sorry' and slammed the door shut.

Second letter from Bost: 'What astonishes me – it already struck me a few days ago, but you don't get much time for thinking, round here – is the extent to which the life I'm leading appears natural to me. There was some slight astonishment the first day . . . but that passed at once – and it only comes back on rare occasions. The funny thing is that this evening it hit me when I'd finished reading your letter. I put it back in the envelope with a stupid giggle, and it's the stupidity that struck me. That's what staggers me at the moment, the extent to which my life seems normal to me. One is no longer surprised by the mud; one is no longer too cold; one finds it quite natural to sleep on straw, and it's the idea of washing oneself that appears abnormal. Here, the state that corresponds to being "serious" in civilian life is despondency. It doesn't go any further than a 'Can you beat that?' and one doesn't feel really gloomy or oppressed, just alone and abject.

'I say abject, I don't know why, because one doesn't, of course, pass any moral judgement, but that does seem to me to be what one feels. The rest of the time, one yells, talks total bullshit, smokes and swears. I'm afraid I may be giving a tragic impression, but that's not at all what I intend. It's not tragic at all, it's lousy, but the main thing about it is that one never manages to get really indignant. I say one *feels* abject, but that's not right. One really feels nothing: one knows certain things, but it doesn't affect you. At this moment I'm not sad; I'm *never* sad and *never* tired. When I write that I'm tired, it is false. I'm simply empty and fagged out: this is often the case, but one isn't fagged out by fatigue – one's simply fagged out.

'I think that what saves me is the fact that what I'm seeing at the moment interests me – in fact I'm sure of it – and that one feels a bit puffed up with self-importance. I don't know if I've told you how Lavice and Vala were, for example. They're bursting with pride. And not in a rotten way – because they feel interesting, for example, or because they'll be war veterans one day. It's a naive pride at seeing themselves – they who've never been out of their own·backyards – participating at close range and actively in a world event. This delights them, and makes them endure everything with seriousness and dedication. With me, when it comes down to it, it's exactly the same thing – which makes me laugh, because I became aware of it when I saw them. For at the moment I have the impression I'm seeing something famous and memorable. When my chemist brother wrote that he was sorry to go back home, because he had the impression he was missing something like the Pointe du Raz in a storm, I mocked him cruelly – but he wasn't far wrong. I'll remember that. It's something.

'Do you know, I'm often in a good mood? Since I've been in the woods, that's what predominates. Except in the mornings, or when they bugger us about – but they don't bugger us about too much. It's a stupid good mood, but that doesn't matter . . .

'Nothing's happening, of course. We get up around eight, we do a bit of work building blockhouses or laying out huts, we go and fetch our grub (in the evenings, when it's pitch dark, that's a dreadful chore). This afternoon we went to the showers: we had to do 4km wading through the mud, it was a real sight I can tell you. Have you read *Memories from the House of the Dead*?[43] Well, everything he says about the convicts' mentality holds true for soldiers. Everything

43. Dostoevsky's *The House of the Dead*.

he says about the men's relationships with each other; about their
relationship to their work, their cash and their tobacco; or about the
way they adapt to their discomfort – all that can be applied without
changing a single comma, even though it's about Russians. It staggers
me actually that it should be so similar. I think that from the moment
you cram people together, it'll always be the same. Exactly the same.
It's all play-acting and poses and distraction.'

All that he says is true. First, it's true that war, as Giono says, plays on
the warrior's weakness; in other words, on a certain inertia of the heart
and a certain tendency to reduce everything to what's *natural*. A
fortnight of wartime life changes the coordinates of the world. Barnabooth writes à propos a visit he makes to the prison at Florence:
'Through the gratings of the cells I saw a hundred times the same
pierrot in green-and-yellow stripes, lying on the same bench under a
rectangle of bright blue daylight. The punishment seemed to me
useless, and even more useless the act which had led to the punishment. Life had taken that form here and that was all' [p. 117]. This is
what predominates among the prisoners we are, we khaki or navy-blue
pierrots: 'life has taken that form and that's all'. At this particular level
of life one seeks nice little pleasures and poses for oneself, with the
same avidity as before. Like Bost, since the beginning of the war I
have seen around me only poses. Poses and distraction, as he says so
well. Surreptitiously, moreover, the little predatory plant delves
avidly into the hard earth and gets a hold. It will live there.

It's true, moreover, as Koestler says more or less, that at a certain
level sadness coils in on itself and becomes deadened. Sadness is not
capable of infinite growth – like Einstein's world it is indefinite. Once
a certain degree is passed, one does not get free of it but relapses into a
lesser sadness – the world of sadness is unbounded yet finite. And
then again, it is perfectly true that war provides justifications. We are
all justified in being there, doing bugger all, getting bored, granting
ourselves a thousand craven little allowances. As he says, we are all
deeply imbued with the feeling of participating in a world event. In
fact, we have always participated in world events and not an instant
has gone by when we were not historic; but war makes everyone feel
his historicity. Then one diverts the 'seriousness and dedication' that
are appropriate for historic creatures onto stupid, petty fatigues
imposed by some warrant-officer's idiocy. Fools' game: it's *during
peacetime* that we should have had that dedication and that seriousness – we'd perhaps have avoided the war. But peace will return, with

permission for each of us to feel 'achronic'; all peaces to date have been mere dispersals.

What's so right in Giono's preface is that he explains how man has a tendency at once to greatness and to facility, and how war brings greatness through facility.

Keller comes back from leave. We hear his slow, heavy tread on the stairs and he comes in changeless and serene, looking pleased. His leave has slid over him without leaving a trace. Faint, joyful excitement at seeing him, because he comes from Paris; but irritated too, because Paris is obscured behind him, blocked off by his great opaque bulk. He has been there; he has *seen*, seen everything as I'd have seen it; he has been in direct contact with the air of Paris, with its streets and its light. This contact was total: despite all my avidity, I couldn't have *been-in-the-middle* of more things than he was. All Paris was given him, only he chose otherwise than I should have done – which suffices for all the vast experience that was his 'being-in' Paris to be left behind him, unusable and lost. Yet it has been.

He says the soldiers returning from leave in Paris are full of complaints against the 'young fellows shirking in the factories'. His entire compartment was a chorus of indignation. 'The one complaining most was a bloke who lost two fingers on his left hand in the last war, and who caught two bullets in the lung too. He still has them: 65 per cent disabled. They took him all the same. He was fuming, I can tell you. He was saying: "I've caught on now, tomorrow I'll be reporting sick." But there was a Metro worker there too, who used to be a boxer and who broke a finger on his right hand in a fight in London. When they wanted to invalid him out, he'd refused his discharge, "because I'll lose my job".'

At Port d'Atelier on the outward journey, a drunken soldier on leave was kicking up a rumpus.[44] A lieutenant comes up, a very young one: 'Get into line with the others.' The soldier: 'Just fancy, when I was back there they didn't make me line up.' They argue and the lieutenant, feeling that he's getting out of his depth, says: 'Obey orders, or I'll call the guard and have your leave cancelled.' Then all the men going off on leave crowd round their mate and shout at the lieutenant: 'The guard – just let 'em try! We'll chuck 'em on the tracks

44. Under war-time conditions, passenger trains were routed from the Alsace front to Paris via the stations of Port d'Atelier or Aiguevilliers in the department of Haute-Saône—i.e., a considerable detour.

double quick!' Whereupon the lieutenant goes off without pressing the point.

Apart from that, it's stories about the cost of living and how dear oil and coffee have become. He spouts it all in a calm, indifferent voice, with long, unpredictable pauses between the sentences.

'The rumour was going round yesterday at Port d'Atelier that a leave-train had gone off the rails at Chaumont. I'm sickened by all this indignation of the men on leave against the shirkers back home. It's always the same: this indignation can't – or won't – rise to its rightful target, so it makes do with their peers. They don't want to see the revolting ignominy of war, except through the petty privileges of people like themselves'. Yet they do suffer from the war, they are bored by it, and – what really lies at the root of their fury – they're down in the dumps because they're returning to it. But instead of feeling glad that some people have had the luck or cunning to escape it, they'd like to drag them all into the soup and drown together.

In this sense, wishing war for their fellows, they're indeed fit to wage it: they *deserve* it. The further I go, the more I see that men deserve war – and deserve it more, the more they wage it. It's like the sin of Adam that each individual, according to Kierkegaard, freely adopts as his own. The declaration of war, which was the fault of certain men, we all adopt as our own, with our freedom. This war – we have all declared it at one moment or another. But then instead of paying for it, instead of saying 'It's *my* war' and trying to live it, they all take refuge from it in poses. They refuse it with bad faith, exactly as one refuses a fault one has just committed. They cover it over with a veil of *natural* and *normal*. And when peace comes, all those bastards will by turns benefit from the innocent victim's aureole and from the war veteran's laurels.

In short, to date I have encountered the following assorted figures of men at war: the 'leftovers and strays' as Lanson calls them in his manual [45] – those who (in their warm shelters) recreate the dream of the '14 – '18 war; those, at the other extreme, 'who aren't having the wool pulled over their eyes', who are convinced this war is a clever trick played by the governments on their citizens, and who aren't far from believing in a secret understanding between Hitler, Stalin, Daladier and Chamberlain; the bulk of the discontented, most of whom set out with an attitude they have not been able to sustain and

45. In his famous *Histoire de la littérature française* (Paris 1894), Gustave Lanson (1857–1934) used the rubric 'Attardés et égarés' as a chapter heading for the confused, transitional period in French literature at the beginning of the seventeenth century.

who have made themselves *retailers* of discontent, since, remaining uncertain about the general principles of any revolt, they bob about from one grievance to another, taking refuge from themselves in grievance; the civil-servant types, who after a spell of disorientation have peacefully resumed their petty civilian habits, speak of their future leave in the same terms as their paid holidays, and grow attached to their paperwork and to little habits; Courcy – smoking his pipe of an evening on the hotel veranda, and saying with a smile of rapturous vanity, placing the word between inverted commas: 'So we've got our "living-room" ';[46] the terrorized – those . . .

46. English in the text—did Courcy, an Alsatian, perhaps mean *Lebensraum?*

NOTEBOOK 11
FEBRUARY 1940
MORSBRONN/PARIS
BOUXWILLER

[Paul] used to imagine [that] our profession would unite us: he's one of those teachers or civil servants who feel immediately drawn to their colleagues.[1] We could stick together, debate professional matters, assert – in the midst of this war – the durability of the mind. But, precisely, I blame him for being a teacher. I don't like the fact that, in the middle of wartime, I've been forced to see a caricature of myself at every hour of the day. I don't *feel* myself a teacher in his way, and each time he used to try to draw me close, I'd imagine that world he's so fond of – its colleagues, colleagues' wives, unions and cups of tea: [the conversations] with the ladies, the [profess]orial surrender to nature, the socialist spirituality, the fear and hatred of the headmaster. So I repulsed him with all my strength. He for his part, seeing my resistance, explained it to himself in his own way. He's the son of a schoolmistress, the husband of a schoolmistress, and himself a lycée teacher with just his *licence*.[2] Everyone knows of the base pretence by teachers who have their *agrégation* that they're a superior elite in comparison with those who hold a mere *licence*. Most *licenciés* hardly deserve any better: in their hatred and their jealous claims, there's an acknowledgement of that superiority – they've never raised themselves to the point of contempt.

Paul attributed [the reserve] I was displaying to a difference in [our situations] within the teaching profession. One day when Pieter was talking about the astronomical difference that separated Captain Orcel, a rich industrialist, from Lieutenant Munot, the lowliest of

1. Some of the pages of this notebook were damaged by damp. Words between square brackets have been reconstructed by the editor, with a greater or lesser degree of certainty.

2. The *licence* is roughly equivalent to an ordinary university first degree, whereas the *agrégation* is awarded through a yearly competitive examination to candidates who already hold a *licence*. *Professeurs agrégés* are better paid than *professeurs licenciés*, and are appointed to a select range of teaching posts in lycées.

engineers, Paul said in an ironic, resigned tone of voice: 'The same difference, you mean, that separates me from Sartre.' And the other day again, as I was pointing out to someone or other that he was a bloody idiot, he interposed in honeyed tones: 'Don't you think, Sartre, that the exclusive company of Normaliens has made you over-exigent?'[3] To which I retorted that I mixed with hardly any Normaliens. But this shows pretty clearly how he conceives of my [situation:] the same as his, [basic]ally, but in a super-institute, collegial relations with the 'upper crust', Paris instead of the provinces, etc. In short, to his way of thinking I'd shown I despised him.

And there you have the real structure of our relations within the group: an irritable distaste, on my part, for the member of the teaching profession which he is to the very core; and for his part, in return, a resigned, mistrustful dignity – which doubtless stops short of envy, but which is certainly wounded. I am 'too proud', too insistent on the 'elite' to which I belong, and this excessive pride means I'm [restricted to] my profession. [That said], however, if he notices some amusing little physical phenomenon in his surroundings, he can't help turning to share it with me, deliberately excluding Pieter and Keller – in order, for a few seconds, to realize that intellectual community which he doubtless enjoyed with the third-year geography teacher, and which allowed him to feel the rights of intelligence. He's unlucky: I don't understand a thing about physics and it doesn't interest me. He perceives this, and it confirms him in his belief that I hold him in contempt.

But the essential structure of my relations with Paul – that which forms the pivot [of our relationship] – is different. Paul represents authority. In a sense he's ashamed of being leader. On the other hand, he tries to exert his authority in a thousand sly ways, not from any taste for command but from fear of the responsibilities he holds. Well, I resist, from a horror of being commanded. Someone only has to give me an order and I bristle up, and this craze for independence means that I smell out the order concealed or enwrapped in Paul's civilities. With all the more irritation, the more it is enwrapped. Of course, I refuse to obey it. But my refusal doesn't just irritate Paul [because of his] fear of responsibility. It always casts up against him that by his own free choice he regrets being leader, so consequently he should be my accomplice when I resist him. With his moral code under attack, Paul resists through bad faith.

And there you have our essential relationship, which runs through

3. Normaliens: graduates of the École Normale Supérieure in Paris.

our organic group. He's ashamed of being leader, but nevertheless wants to make me obey him; and I'm an undisciplined soldier, who doesn't want to obey him and appeals to the socialist in him against the military superior. Around this rigid and chronic relationship (he won't give in and neither shall I) the entire group is ordered. For, since he is a democrat, I have dreamed up the idea of resisting him [by appealing to] the majority. And I can [rally] a majority against him. Pieter – who's naturally peaceable, and who though he grumbles a bit at Paul does so like a wife at her husband, taking care not to 'go too far' – nevertheless, surprisingly, allows himself to be roped into the majority: it's necessary to force his agreement a bit, looking at him in amazement and taking loud account of the 'Yes' he whispers before he has had time to take it back. Keller grunts a hoarse 'Yes' for the pleasure of taking the piss out of the corporal. So an opposition abruptly reassembled in each new set of circumstances holds in [check the ineffectual authority] of [Paul, who] is invariably at a loss, given that he can't object to the majority principle. He is under no illusion, and dubs me 'the opposition'.

However, he endeavours slyly to constitute an exactly contrary line-up of forces, which, though it no longer has the significance of a majority, aims to isolate me in the face of public opinion. Since I've set myself up – unasked – as their moral conscience, they try as I've already mentioned to nab me: to catch me red-handed committing the very misdeeds I criticize them for. They watch me [constantly]. It's Pieter who calls the [tune], snapping fairly innocently at my heels. But Paul waits for the right moment, then suddenly takes his side with some little fact or argument, when he feels a helping hand is needed. Keller remains absolutely neutral or goes away. But the fact remains, the other two are against me. On the other hand, the combination Paul, Keller and I against Pieter never occurs. So our group is much like a movable tray, inclining now to the right and now to the left, with balls that roll to one side or the other depending on the slope [imparted by the move]ment which [the] internal tension that runs from us to Paul or from them to me maintains. This is what defines the essential role of Pieter – 'the Plain, the Marsh' – who reverses the structure totally, depending on whether he rebounds towards me or runs off towards Paul.[4]

But there are other relationships: particularly the one between

---

4. *La Plaine* or *Le Marais*: names given to the centre group of deputies in the Convention Nationale, who went sometimes with the Girondins to the right, sometimes with the Montagnards to the left.

Pieter and myself. Something unites us and establishes between us the connection which, according to Paul, should have existed between Paul and me: our shared curiosity about the *outside*. In a sense, we are the pseudopods that our group projects into the world and extends into restaurants, cafés and other people's homes. Then [after all there's] Paris which we have in common – [and] also, I must confess to my shame, money. It's not that Paul has any less than I do; but a timorous propensity to save holds him back, even though he expects bankruptcy to ensue after the war. Hence, we represent a gilded, madcap youth that spends. We introduce great slabs of outside life when we return to the group.

This alliance in spending and excursions daily produces another, parallel alliance between Keller and Paul: the ones who stay at home, the guardians of the household; or who eat at the mobile [kitchen], as against [those] who go to the restaurant; or again, the big eaters (for they eat everything indiscriminately and in vast quantities) against the dainty gourmets. However, the Paul-Keller group lacks cohesion. Paul isn't at all jealous of us, he even accompanies us sometimes. Keller, meanwhile, who's stingy and hard up, envies and hates us whenever we leave. In such a way that he welds our twosome t ogether, by giving us a guilty class consciousness against our will. We feel we go to the restaurant together against him.

Besides, Keller represents the proletariat in our group and Pieter the capitalist. Keller – right at the bottom, [penniless,] thrust to the lowest depths by his massive inertia – looks mutely up at us with distrust and jealousy. He feels no solidarity with any of us. Every evening, one or other of us pays a round, offers cakes or fruit or whatever. Keller accepts everything without in any way feeling in honour bound to repay it, as he certainly would in his own milieu, for all his stinginess. It's a kind of individual compensation. Vis-à-vis us, especially Pieter and me, he *feels his class*. Vis-à-vis Paul, as I was saying just now, he's like a worker vis-à-vis a foreman. He [establishes an] additional structure [within] the organism: the class structure. Which results in a kind of reciprocity of relations between him and me, for I have a bad conscience. He impresses me by his brutality, and I treat him with a sort of consideration which he repays to the best of his ability. We are afraid of each other. He doesn't hold himself outside the group, but the relations one can have with him – apart from the hidden class relation – are destructured. It's a kind of amorphous immanence: he steeps in the group, and is permeated by it through cementation.

Likewise, the relations between Paul and Pieter represent a weak form. Except when they [try to] nab me. Besides, the help they give each other at such times involves a degree of mental reservation: for each of them feels a greater solidarity with me than with his ally; each thinks that he is right against me in his own way, and on the terrain that's specific to him; so I generally have no trouble in dividing them, and uncoupling their attacks. Pieter likes to think of Paul as a kid who's still wet behind the ears – a 'virgin': he likes to tell him 'When you come to Paris, *we* (i.e., Sartre and I) will introduce you to some women.' As a provincial too. Whenever he has some piece of meanness to reproach [Paul with, he says]: 'What can you expect? Provincial life!' Paul reproaches Pieter for a kind of tactless exuberance – they never make a couple.

So, when the question arose of giving some practical structure to our group, it quite naturally split up into two groups of two: Pieter and I; Paul and Keller. Each group sees in turn to the meteorological soundings, while the other takes care of the housework. This belatedly arrived-at technical structure has considerable importance. It has really compartmentalized our unit and softened its other structures. For example, the struggle between Paul and me is less bitter, because we unburdened him smartly [of responsibi]lity for our soundings. By contrast, the link between Paul and Keller – foreman and worker – was reinforced. Of course, all these structures dissolve and are replaced by a provisional homogeneity when we're fighting for our common interests against the outside world.

The final touch to complete this hotel where we live. Since yesterday, the radio-operators who live in the room next to mine have had the itch. Two of them are seriously affected, the third is under observation. They replaced three other radio-operators a fortnight ago, and one of those apparently also has the [itch. The doctor] asked them 'Where are you billeted?' – 'At the Hotel Bellevue.' – 'Oh, now I understand: that's where they used to treat scabies patients in peacetime.' The hotel's customers were sufferers from rheumatism and skin diseases. I must admit that for a while I've been feeling nervous itchings on my hands, face and scalp.

In the two last Romains novels published before war was declared, Jallez and Jerphanion take delight in prophesying the death of God.[5]

---

5. The novels in question are *Vorge contre Quinette* (1939) and *La Douceur de la vie* (1939) (hence the reference below to the 'sweetness of life'). Jallez and Jerphanion are *normaliens*, one a novelist, the other a politician, who play the main linking roles in the entire novel sequence—of which these are Numbers 17 and 18.

Jerphanion makes gloomy forecasts for the year 1937 (Romains had the decency not to put 1939). He compares the '14 war to one of those excessively severe storms that can wreck an entire summer. To Jallez, the Dada movement appears highly symptomatic. Romains sees Europe as 'delivered over to the forces of internal disintegration'. His book, which takes place in 1919, would no doubt have sounded quite different if the war hadn't broken out. Similarly Drieu, in *Gilles*, presents us with a Europe in its death throes between the years '17 and '37: 'The war killed France; she will not recover from it.'[6] It's going to become fashionable to search – in the light of present events – for all the signs of decomposition in the France of 1920–35. It will be seen as a sinister period of exhaustion and disorientation, [punctuated by infrequent] little [feverish] lulls: an epoch of demoralization and destruction. Particular stress will be laid on surrealism because of its negative charge, and the picture will be painted of a wild, crazy, unstable epoch.

This must not be allowed. It isn't true. Granted, the '14-'18 war led to the war of '40 – for a host of reasons, most of which are well known and the remainder of which will be uncovered by historians. Granted, there were disturbances, convulsive shocks and instability. But that's not *all* there was. In France, at least, it was possible to experience – I experieneced – the 'sweetness of life'. Happiness was possible, [calm too]. Between '25 and '33 I was often happy. I knew hosts of happy people round about me, and there was nothing frenetic or unhealthy about their bliss. Truly and calmly happy. Perhaps some things were more difficult to do than in the old days, and some moments were harder. But that wasn't really a problem.

Furthermore, perhaps people like Drieu or Montherlant may have been knocked groggy by the war, but I would reply that my own generation – which was about to take over when this war broke out – was in full possession of its senses. If I look for unstable individuals among the people I knew, I find some to be sure, but not many of them; their weak characters, moreover, suggest that they'd have been unstable at all times. But before the war, were there many young people more *solid* than us? More solid than Nizan, than Guille, than Aron, than the Beaver? We were seeking neither to destroy, nor to achieve wild ecstasies of excitement. We wanted patiently and wisely to understand the world, to discover it and find our own place in it.

6. Pierre Drieu la Rochelle (1893–1945), novelist of right-wing and later fascist views: he became editor of the *NRF* under German occupation, and committed suicide at the end of the war. *Gilles* (1939) was a despairing work, expressing the futility of commitment to any cause.

We wished to acquire knowledge and wisdom. Maybe the place in the world that we were after wasn't very modest. Maybe we were in rather more of a hurry than our predecessors to secure it. But there was nothing very excessive there. Those of us who wanted to change the world, and who for example were communists, became so in a reasonable way after weighing up the pros and cons. And what I remember best – what I shall always regret – is the unique atmosphere of intellectual power and gaiety which enshrouded us.

People have said we were too intelligent. Why 'too'?' I have never recognized – in any of those who came into close or more distant contact with me – the image of those cynical boys bragging of their vices that the (bad) literature of those days strove to popularize. We did have considerable sexual freedom, but we strove to think honourably about the minor sentimental circumstances of our lives. We were tougher than our elders – than a Fournier or a Rivière:[7] this was partly through affectation and partly, too, because there had after all been the war and we didn't conceive of life as a holiday. But it's unfair to blame us simultaneously for that affectation of hardness, whose result was a real self-discipline and a healthy cynicism, and for helpless swoonings which we never indulged in . . . Examples drawn from the half-confessions of this very notebook will be brought up against me: my fit of childish pride with Nizan, my political indifference, etc. I shall reply that self-control and so-called 'moral health' have nothing to do either with being a shrinking violet or with public spirit. I know that I'm entirely in control of myself, with no aberrations; and that I can endure hard blows. I know, too, that I have a concern for morality. I've tried to destroy plenty of old ideologies, but my concern was to build. I may have lacked 'roots', but I've never lacked stability.

Why do I feel I have to [write] all this? Because I can see that our epoch is busy constructing an image of itself to cut the ground from beneath the historians' feet: it wants at least to have had the glory of judging itself, and to hand them ready-made work. And it's this one-sidedly black picture I'm protesting at. I fear it may persist. I'm worried to see that people are already affecting to view the admirable burgeoning of ideas and works in the '18-'28 period as a proliferation of decay: the true freedom people then enjoyed as anarchistic licence. All these simplistic views are deceptively neat. Forget about Drieu, who's an idiot; but there are far too many others wanting to draw a balance-sheet. In my view, one must wait. The epoch is most cer-

7. Jacques Rivière (1886–1925), friend of Alain-Fournier and editor of *NRF* 1919–25.

tainly dead, but it's still warm. Let people have the decency to wait till its corpse cools off a bit.

The problem of negation has always been veiled like that of being, since 'not being' seemed the judgement of a mind conjuring two objects up before it and asserting their alterity. If, for example, I say that paper *is not* porous, [I] do not ascribe this negation to the paper, which in itself has no relation whatsoever with porosity, but to my mind. Let's be clear about this: isn't negation a mode of being of my mind, which in negating performs a *plenary act* of judgement – and which, for most philosophers, is pure act, plenitude of existence, at the very moment in which it negates. Thus negation becomes a Λεκτόν, a *nothing*.[8] It is *neither* mind, *nor* in the mind, *nor* in paper, *nor* in porosity, *nor* a relationship that exists like a repulsive force between paper and porosity. It is basically just a category that allows the mind to make a synthesis between porosity and paper – from a distance, without altering their nature in the slightest, without changing their respective positions, without either drawing them closer together or driving them farther apart. Thus philosophy's endeavour has been to slim negation down to the point where it becomes a thin film between the mind and things – a nothing. And it must certainly be acknowledged that the negations I mark in the world are not at all basic, substantial relations between things. Cooperation from my consciousness is required in order to produce the negation of inherent porosity in paper. It is not *in the being* of paper not to be porous.

But the problem becomes quite different when, for example, we say of consciousness that it *is not* extended.[9] No doubt, if we limit ourselves to delivering this judgement upon the consciousness of other people – viewing it as a datum revealed by experience – we shall tend to classify it in the same category as the aforementioned judgements and say that we deny the extension of consciousness just like the porosity of paper. However, when it's a question of the consciousness that we *are*, matters turn out quite differently, since it *is* its own nothingness of extension. In other words, there's no third party here to observe that two inert substances – consciousness and extension – have no relationship of inherence. But it is in the being of consciousness not to be extension. In other words, the *not* is an existential

8. Stoic concept meaning a purely abstract, incorporeal notion.
9. The distinction between consciousness and extension in this passage is that made by Descartes between *res cogitans* and *res extensa* (and much discussed by Heidegger).

characteristic. This will be understood at once if the following two judgements are compared: extension is not consciousness, and consciousness is not extended. In the first case, what's involved is quite obviously a relationship established after the event by a contemplative consciousness; for it is no part of the nature of extension either to be or not to be consciousness: it is simply extension. In the second case, on the contrary, all spiritualists will be at one in saying that it's a characteristic of consciousness not to be extended.

Because it has seemed contradictory to grant negative qualities in any being whatsoever, people have tried to get round the problem by forging positive concepts to take account of this property: for example, the concepts of unextendedness or immateriality. But a verbal examination will suffice to show that 'unextended' is a mere word, hiding a shamefaced negation in its womb. For consciousness, to be unextended does not signify a positive virtue; it is purely and simply an elided way of denoting the fact that consciousness *is not* extended. So it belongs to the inner structure of consciousness *not to be* extended. This 'not being' is neither observed nor judged, but – in the term we were employing the other day – it *is been*.[10]

However, my reflections had so far led me above all to envisage the case where consciousness was not what it was: in other words, where negation exploded in the homogeneity of one and the same existence; and where the negated referred back from itself to that whereby it was negated – since it was one and the same being. But here – behind the appearances of the simple principle of non-contradiction – the problem grows more complicated, since consciousness is now what it is not. For if this apparent truism is scrutinized, it can be seen that one of the negations destroys the other. For if consciousness *is not* extension – which, according to the classical theory, would imply the total absence of any relation between consciousness and extension – and since, moreover, there's no third party to establish the wholly external relation of negativity between consciousness and extension, one doesn't see how this consciousness could, in and of itself, contain in itself sufficient relations with extension to make itself precisely the negation of extension.

Yet such is the case, and our previous comments should clarify one

10. The translator of *l'Être et le néant*, perhaps understandably, shrank from 'is been' to render 'est été'. However, it is not really any more shocking in English than in French, and is merely Sartre's modification of the 'est Ayant-été' which Corbin had used in his translation of Heidegger for 'ist gewesen' (the English translators of Heidegger likewise prefer 'is having been'). Said of a being 'of which the *present* is constituted essentially as *past* of a *future*' (Heidegger).

point for us: every negation presupposes a certain mode of synthetic unity of the realities it negates. When negation is a λεκτόν, as in the case of the judgement 'paper is not porous', the unitary synthesis is likewise a λεκτόν: it's a pure categorial comparison, which leaves the objects entirely intact. When negation *is been* by at least one of the two beings, it appears against a background of real synthetic unity of those two beings. In a word, for consciousness really to be able – of itself and by its nature, without the contemplative intervention of a third party – *not to be extension*, it is necessary for it to secrete in the innermost depths of its being a unitary relation with that extension which it is not.

But this primary relation could not express itself through the terms of repulsion, production, projection, etc. – which all presuppose a constituted world and elucidated problem of being. What's involved is quite obviously an original relation of being between two beings. It's necessary for the connection to be as intimate as possible, in order that consciousness should not be precisely *that*. It's necessary for extension to be present to consciousness on all sides, and even cross its entire breadth, in order that finally consciousness should be able to escape from extension – which threatens to belime it on all sides – only by *not being*. Not only by *not being* extension, but by *being nothing*.[11] The unity of consciousness and extension is such that consciousness *is not* extension only insofar as it *is not itself*, is nothing. Nothing positive comes to make up for *not-being-extended*. It's because it is its own nothingness that consciousness is not extended.

This relation of extension's being to consciousness is what we may call vesting [*investissement*]. But precisely because consciousness is defined as being what it is not and not being what it is, it cannot quite simply *be* that which is not extension. Its mode of being that which is not extension is wholly numbed by Nothingness; it *is* that which is not extension, in the nihilating mode of the reflection and the reflected. In other words, the formula 'consciousness is not extended' should be emended to 'consciousness is not extension',[12] which means: 1. that this negation implies the vesting of consciousness with extension; 2. that this vesting can be for consciousness only insofar as consciousness is consciousness of itself as unextended – in other words, as vested by the extension it is conscious of not being. In other terms, if consciousness were what it is, that's to say existed in the mode of the in-itself, it

11. The original has a force here, derived from the double negation *n'étant rien*, which cannot be reproduced in English.
12. Throughout this passage, 'extended' (referring to consciousness, which is of feminine gender in French) is *étendue*; 'extension' is *l'étendue*.

would be extended. But it's insofar as it escapes from itself – by not being what it is – that it's not extension but consciousness *of* extension. Thus consciousness is nihilation of extension, and this nihilation can be accomplished only in the guise of consciousness *of* extension. Extension is only an example here, of course. In a quite general way, there is no annihilation possible of an existent in itself, other than by the apparition of a consciousness *of* that existent.

Thursday, 1 February

The apparition of Nothingness can occur only against the background of being that it *is not*. The absence which a consciousness is can be absence only *before a presence*. Unextendedness appears against a background of extension and as negation for itself of this extension. In a quite general way, the *for-itself* can arise only in connection with the totality of the in-itself that encloses it. The for-itself retains the in-itself before and around it, as what it is not. It needs being in order not to be. The for-itself nihilates itself with respect to the totality of the in-itself. This primary connection between the for-itself and the totality of the in-itself, as what it is not, is what we call being-in-the-world. Being-in-the-world is making oneself into absence *from* the world. The unity between consciousness and the world pre-exists both consciousness and the world. To be consciousness is to make onself into non-world in the world's presence; it's to make onself, precisely and concretely, into what is not *that particular world*.

One should not, however, grasp this negation as a flight outside the world. The for-itself's movement of nihilation is not a withdrawal. If nihilation were accompanied by withdrawal, it would be *nihilation of nothing* and would relapse back into the in-itself. This, perhaps, is how death must be understood. By contrast, nihilation implies an immediate, distanceless adhesion of the world to the for-itself. This presence of the world to consciousness – which is separated from the world by *nothing* save that it is itself a nothing – is transcendence. The in-itself vests consciousness in order to be surpassed by it in Nothingness. But not, as Heidegger believes, in the Nothingness which retains the world in it, but in the Nothingness which consciousness itself *is*. Consciousness, in its for-itself, transcends the world towards itself. It is vested by the in-itself precisely insofar as it is numbed by Nothingness.

Let us take a simple example. We may say, for instance, that perception of *that* tree is above all an existential phenomenon: to perceive the tree, for consciousness, is to surpass the tree towards its own nothingness of tree. One must not, of course, see in the word 'surpassing' [*dépassement*] any indication of an *act*. It is merely a mode of existing. Consciousness exists for-itself beyond that tree as what *is not* that tree; the nihilating connection between reflection and the reflected ensures that consciousness can be for itself only by reflecting itself as being, precisely, nothingness of the world *where* there is that tree. Which means it is non-thetic consciousness of itself as thetic consciousness *of* that tree; the tree is the transcendent theme of its nihilation. Thus, for example, intuitive knowledge is irruption of the nothing into immanence, which transforms the immanence of the in-itself into the transcendence of the for-itself. Thus the pure event which ensures that Being is its own nothingness makes the world appear as totality of the In-itself transcended by self-nihilating being. Being in the world and being numbed by Nothingness are one and the same thing.

I should like to show, on the basis of a precise analysis, the irreducible necessity we are in to have recourse to this idea of *nothingness*, and I shall take as my example the idea of *contact*. I want to show that this apparently simple idea – 'the table is in contact with the wall' – necessarily refers us to being-in-the-world and to Nothingness.

If, in fact, I want to grasp the meaning of this notion to the full, I observe that I am tossed about between two opposite ideas: the idea of the immanent plenitude of the in-itself, and the idea of absolute withdrawal into Nothingness. For when I say of the table that it *touches* the wall, I can't mean that it's *beside* the wall – even as close as possible to it, even separated by an infinitesimal distance. I mean by *contact* an intimate relation of being between the two objects. But this relation of being leads naturally to the in-itself: in other words, to immanence. But that slippery notion of contact aims to stop in mid course. I want to maintain the total separation of the two individualities: contact is not fusion. So behold I am referred back to the idea of a distance which, however small it be, at least separates the two objects. But thereupon the idea of contact vanishes.

For if in fact I try to grasp what it entails, I see that in order for there to be contact between the two individualities, it is necessary that they be without distance for each other at one point at least of their area, and that they yet be separated. But separated *by what*? By *nothing*. But this nothing here is indispensable. In geometry, for example, when two curves (tangent and circle, for example) are in contact, they have common points – so they would now seem to make but a single curve. Yet we rightly maintain their independence. At the very spot where they touch, they are separate. Yet there are not *two* series of points there, but a single series. So the separation takes place within each point. This separation is not a splitting, for the point is indivisible, nor a dissociation. And yet it exists. I can hear a Köhler saying that each form – the form 'straight line', or the form 'circle' closed upon itself – draws to it all the points which make it up.[13] And that's quite right. In this sense, it is the individuality of the pregnant form that keeps contact from culminating in fusion. But this is itself possible only if a discreet negation comes to differentiate the forms where necessary. The points of contact have to be separated from the ensemble of points constituting the other form, precisely by *nothing*. They have to be *numbed* in a way by Nothingness. Exactly like a consciousness.

But precisely these conditions, in themselves, would have no meaning at all if they were not posited by a consciousness. In and of themselves, they would lead to absolute separation or to fusion if there were no consciousnesses. For contacts to be given in the world, in general, consciousnesses have to be given as vested by the world. For the notion of 'touching', as Heidegger clearly saw, belongs to things only by reflection. In fact, a chair does not touch the wall unless it is carried off into the unity of a world transcended by human reality. Originally, it is human reality which *touches* objects, which *takes* them, which *rejects* them, etc. Contact is by its nature contact between the hand that takes and the object taken. However, the notion still remains obscure if the hand is viewed as a material object amid other objects. The hand itself cannot produce the Nothingness which separates it from the knife it takes. It is necessary for itself and the knife – in the guise of secondary structures – to belong to a *primary totality of contact*. This totality can be only consciousness's transcendent relationship to the world. Consciousness is *in contact* with the world.

Considered on this level, the notion of contact becomes clear. For in relation to consciousness the world is given without distance, since consciousness is negation of distance. It is even still more pressing than a distanceless presence, since it vests consciousness and rejoins *itself* through the latter. But at the same time consciousness escapes the world precisely insofar as it is nothing. In fusion with the world insofar as it *is*, consciousness escapes it and separates itself from it insofar as it *is not*. Thus the world's relation to consciousness is a

13. See note 8 on p. 125 above for Köhler's lectures in Gestalt theory. It should be said that Sartre's geometrical remarks in this passage seem somewhat odd: a tangent, for example, is not a curve; and a tangent and circle touch at a single point, not at a series of points.

relation of contact. The world exists for consciousness insofar as it is concretely and singularly what consciousness is not. Consciousness touches the world in the sense that its partial nihilation can establish only a distanceless exteriority between the two of them. The world is neither subjective nor objective: it is the in-itself vesting consciousness and in contact with it, as surpassed by the latter in its nothingness.

An excellent expression of Julien Green's in *Le Figaro*, to denote the week that preceded the war: 'a catastrophe *in slow motion*'.

How the women keep their men's morale up: fragment of a letter from a doting, Christian fiancée, found in the latrines:
    'When you tell me it's three days since you had a wash, what does that matter, it's of minor importance, you'll certainly look much better as soon as you've cleaned yourself up. For my own part, I gave my stove a good clean-out this morning, I was as black as a real chimney-sweep. I'd have given you quite a fright if you'd caught me like that.'
    She's a bit worried too, because a little further on she's praying to God to keep her fiancé's 'spirits up'. The aforesaid fiancé, thus entrusted to the hands of God, didn't hesitate to wipe his bottom with this love-letter.

If I want to understand how much there is of freedom and how much of fate in what's termed 'being influenced', I can reflect on the influence exerted upon me by Heidegger. This influence has in recent times sometimes struck me as providential, since it supervened to teach me authenticity and historicity just at the very moment when war was about to make these notions indispensable to me. If I try to imagine what I'd have made of my thought without those tools, I am gripped by retrospective fear. How much time I gained! I'd still be marking time before great finished ideas like France, History or Death – perhaps still fuming against war and rejecting it with all my being.
    But when I reflect further, I see there's much less chance in this conjuncture than at first appears. Granted, *if* Corbin hadn't published his translation of *Was ist Metaphysik*, I shouldn't have read it.[14] And if I hadn't read it, I shouldn't have undertaken last Easter to

14. Martin Heidegger, *Qu'est-ce que la métaphysique?* ed. Henri Corbin, Paris 1937.

read *Sein und Zeit*.[15] And granted, it might at first seem that the appearance of *What is Metaphysics?* absolutely didn't depend on me – that it really represented a simple encounter. But in fact it wasn't my first encounter with Heidegger. I had heard him spoken of long before I left for Berlin (I'd read *What is Metaphysics?* without understanding it in 1930, in the journal *Bifur*). He was usually classified among the 'phenomenologists', and as I'd started off with the plan of studying the phenomenologists, I was determined to study him too. I bought *Sein und Zeit* in Berlin in December [1933], and I'd resolved to begin reading it after Easter, reserving the first semester for studying Husserl.

But when I came to tackle Heidegger, in about the month of April, it turned out that I was saturated in Husserl. My mistake had been to believe that one can *learn* successively two philosophers of that importance, as one learns one after another the external trade patterns of two European countries. Husserl had gripped me. I saw everything through the perspectives of his philosophy – which was in any case more accessible to me, thanks to its semblance of Cartesianism. I was 'Husserlian' and long to remain so. At the same time, the effort I'd made to *understand* – in other words, to break my personal prejudices and grasp Husserl's ideas on the basis of his own principles rather than mine – had exhausted me philosophically for that particular year. I did begin Heidegger and read fifty pages of him, but the difficulty of his vocabulary put me off. (In fact, this difficulty was not an insurmountable one for me, since I read him without any trouble last Easter: without trouble, and without having made any progress meanwhile in my knowledge of German.)

I should add that spring has always been the occasion for a total relaxation of my efforts. I work when the dormice are sleeping, then as soon as they wake up I go out for a stroll, in quest of some little adventure. Fate was so kind as to give me one in that particular year. But the essential thing was certainly the revulsion I felt against assimilating that barbarous and so unscientific philosophy, after Husserl's brilliant, *scholarly* synthesis. With Heidegger, it seemed as though philosophy had relapsed into infancy. I no longer recognized the traditional problems in it – consciousness, knowledge, truth and error, perception, the body, realism and idealism, etc. I could *come* to Heidegger only after I'd exhausted Husserl. For me, moreover, to exhaust a philosophy is to reflect within its perspectives, and create

15. Martin Heidegger, *Being and Time*, Oxford 1962.

my own private ideas at its expense, until I plunge into a blind alley. It took me four years to exhaust Husserl. I wrote a whole book (apart from the final chapters) under his inspiration: *L'Imaginaire*.[16] Against him, granted – but just insofar as a disciple can write against his master. I also wrote an article against him: 'L'Ego transcendental'.[17] Whereupon, encouraged, I sought in the autumn of 1937 to elucidate my ideas by beginning a big book: *La Psyché*.[18] I enthusiastically wrote four hundred pages of it in three months, then stopped for a reason: I wanted to finish my book of short stories.[19] But I was still so steeped in my researches that, for more than two months, my literary work seemed entirely motiveless.

Gradually, however, without my fully realizing it, the difficulties were piling up and a deeper and deeper gulf was separating me from Husserl. His philosophy evolved ultimately towards idealism, which I could not accept. Above all, like every idealism or kindred doctrine, his philosophy had its *passive matter* – its *hylē*[20] – which a form then comes to mould (Kantian categories of intentionality). I thought of writing about this notion of *passivity*, so essential in modern philosophy. At the time, as I drew further away from *La Psyché* it was ceasing to satisfy me. First because of the problem of *hylē* that I'd evaded. Then because of numerous weaknesses for which I was responsible. I reverted to seeking a *realist* solution. In particular, although I had numerous ideas concerning the knowledge of others, I could tackle them only if I had solidly assured myself that two distinct consciousnesses did indeed perceive *the same* world. The published works of Husserl brought me no reply. And his refutation of solipsism was inconclusive and weak. It was certainly to escape from this Husserlian impasse that I turned towards Heidegger.

I had already on several occasions reopened his book, which I'd brought back from Berlin; but I hadn't had time to finish it – or any firm intention of doing so either. So it's evident that I *could* not study Heidegger any earlier than I did. Read him with an amateur curiosity, perhaps – but not come to him with the intention of learning. Where-

16. *L'Imaginaire: Psychologie phénoménologique de l'imagination*, Paris 1940—*Psychology of Imagination*, New York 1948.

17. The exact title was 'La Transcendance de l'Ego: Esquisse d'une description phénoménologique', in *Recherches philosophiques*, 1936; republished in book form 1972. See *The Transcendence of the Ego: an Existentialist Theory of Consciousness*, New York 1957.

18. Never published.

19. *Le Mur*, Paris 1939, contained the five stories translated in *The Wall and Other Stories*, New York 1948.

20. ὕλη = matter; the first matter of the universe.

upon, however, the threats of spring and then autumn '38 slowly led me to seek a philosophy that was not just a contemplation but a wisdom, a heroism, a holiness – anything whatever that might allow me to hold out. I was in exactly the same situtation as the Athenians after the death of Alexander, when they turned away from Aristotelian science to incorporate the more brutal but more 'total' doctrines of the Stoics and Epicureans, who taught them to *live*. Furthermore, *History* was present all round me. First, philosophically: Aron had just written his *Introduction à la philosophie de l'histoire*, and I was reading him.[21] Secondly, it surrounded and gripped me like all my contemporaries, making me feel its presence. I was still ill-equipped to understand and grasp it; nevertheless I keenly wished to do so and went at it with such means as I had at my disposal.

That's when Corbin's book appeared. Just when it was needed. Sufficiently detached from Husserl and wanting a 'pathetic' philosophy, I was ready to understand Heidegger. 'Well and good,' people will say, 'but it's still the case the book might not have appeared.' In the first place, I'm not so sure I wouldn't have had a go at reading *Sein und Zeit* anyway. Secondly – and above all – the publication of *What is Metaphysics?* is a *historical* event that I precisely contributed for my own part to produce. For around the time that I was leaving for Berlin, a movement of curiosity about phenomenology started up among the students. I participated in this movement, exactly as I participated in the movement of Parisians towards winter sports. That's to say, I seized hold of words that were floating about everywhere; I read a few isolated French works dealing with the question; I mused about notions that I ill understood and wished I knew more about them. Whereupon I left for Berlin. Numerous students and young teachers followed the same path I did. When I got back, I knew a bit more and taught what I knew. So I increased that interested audience. One of my old pupils, Chastaing, even published an article on 'das Man' in Heidegger.[22] I certainly don't mean to say I'm responsible for that article. I just want to show how I inserted myself as an *active* and *responsible* member into a community of interested people and scholars which designated itself spontaneously as an audience. It was *for us* that Corbin made his translation. That initial curiosity was necessary.

It had been the lack of that curiosity, moreover, which had meant

21. Raymond Aron (1905–83), friend of Sartre at the École Normale in the twenties, his instructor in meteorology during his military service in 1929; always an intellectual antagonist and, after 1945, a political one as well.

22. The impersonal 'one': see note 10 on p.11 above.

that one had to wait twelve or fifteen years in France. It gradually emerged around translations like the one in *Bifur* (1930) or the one in *Recherches philosophiques* (1933), until at last it became properly organized and *demanded* information. At a still deeper level, that surge of interest for which I had my share of responsibility, and which first produced books like Jean Wahl's *Vers le concret*, had its origin in an obsolescence of French philosophy and a need we all felt to rejuvenate it. Thus if Corbin translated *What is Metaphysics?*, it was because I (among others) freely constituted myself as an audience awaiting that translation – and in this I was assuming my situation, my generation and my epoch.

But why was this first translation one of Heidegger rather than of Husserl, it will be asked, since serious study precisely had to begin with the master Husserl before coming to the dissident disciple Heidegger. Here I can answer, since I have seen the question discussed in the *NRF*. It was the success of Corbin's book that made Groethuysen think of translating Husserl. For Husserl is not a popular taste. Heidegger's 'pathos', though incomprehensible to most people, is very striking with all those words like Death, Fate or Nothingness scattered about. But above all it arrived just at the *right moment*. I have explained how I was vaguely waiting for it – longing for somebody to provide me with tools to understand History and my destiny. But, precisely, there were many of us who had those longings – and who had them at *that particular moment*. It was we who dictated that choice.

In other terms, it was my epoch, my situation and my freedom that decided my encounter with Heidegger. There's neither chance nor determinism here, but historical conformity. However, one might think that the question 'Why, after all, was there a Heidegger?' remains outside the cycle. And to tell the truth, in a sense it does fall outside it, insofar as Heidegger is the apparition in the world of a free consciousness. Yet from a quite different angle it doesn't strike me as so 'eccentric'. For Heidegger's philosophy is a free assumption of his epoch. And his epoch was precisely a tragic epoch of *Untergang*[23] and despair for Germany. It was the postwar period, the epoch when, for a multitude of people who had hitherto found it entirely *natural* to be Germans, poverty and war were making Germany seem like a contingent reality with a destiny. As Rauschning wrote in a passage I have quoted before: 'that was when . . . the unique character and the solitude of this nation was revealed, its mission and its damnation'.[24]

23. The reference is to Spengler's *Der Untergang des Abendlandes* (*The Decline of the West*), published in 1918, with its theory that modern civilization was doomed.

24. Quoted, presumably, in one of the lost notebooks (VI or VII).

And Heidegger's attitude is obviously a free surpassing towards philosophy of this pathetic profile of History. I don't mean to claim that circumstances are identical for us at the present moment. But it's true that there's a relationship of historical conformity between our situation and his. Both, moreover, are the development of the '14 war; they hang together. So I can rediscover Heidegger's assumption of his destiny as a German, in that wretched Germany of the postwar years, in order to help me assume my destiny as a Frenchman in the France of '40.

Keller is leaving us. Tomorrow or the day after, probably. Because of his age, he's being transferred to a territorial unit.

I have tried to show how notions like contact, seemingly plenums, actually envelop the idea of Nothingness. But vice versa, it's necessary to show how other, apparently purely negative notions refer back to the in-itself's transcendence with respect to consciousness. If, for example, one takes the notion of *absence*, in its most everyday form – our absent loved ones; I absented myself; someone came to see me during my absence; the absent are always wrong – one immediately notices that absence is not pure negation: it presupposes the unity of the absent in *being*. There is a being of absence. For it is wrong to confuse absence with simply 'being away from', in the sense in which one might say that two towns are 20 kilometres away, or distant, from each other. Being away belongs to those negative syntheses which consciousness establishes between things without modifying their nature, and which I was speaking of yesterday. Without consciousness, the distance from A to B wouldn't exist; it's by transcending the world that consciousness causes distances to arise in it.

But absence belongs to the very heart of things; being absent is a particular quality of an object. In vain will one seek to reduce this quality to a purely mental perspective – for example , by saying that Pierre is not *absent* from home, that he *is* simply away from his house, and that the everyday term 'absence' is used for all the feelings of regret his being away inspires in his wife and himself. This is to put the cart before the horse. In fact, those feelings of regret presuppose that there exists something like absence, which is a certain *way of being* – even though in other respects it's a pure negativity. The truth is that absence is a way of being of the for-others. Something is only ever truly absent insofar as it is momentarily assimilated to some 'Other'.

But absence is a certain relationship between my being and the Other's being. It is a certain way I have of being given to the Other.

This way of being given to the Other presupposes a prior unity: the unity of *presence*. In presence I *am* in my current concrete reality inasmuch as I am for the Other, and vice-versa; and at the same time I grasp the world not just as world in which *I* am, but as world defined by the being-in-the-world of the Other. But naked presence cannot be the foundation of absence; it would not suffice, since the *presence* of a mere passer-by cannot found his absence if he moves away. This presence has to be given not only as presence, but also as constituting the essential and constitutive being of a concrete for-others.

There can be *absence* of Pierre only in relation to his wife, for example, because here Pierre's existence alters the very being of his wife's for-herself – and in an essential manner. Pierre's presence is constitutive of the *being* of his wife as for-herself, and vice-versa. It is only against the background of this prior unity of being that absence can be given between Pierre and his wife. But it isn't pure annihilation. Even if it were, it would be annihilation *of* those relations. But in reality it's not. It's a *new* mode of connection between Pierre and his wife, which appears against the original background of presence. That original background of presence is *lifted* and denied by absence – yet it's what makes the latter possible. And absence itself is a kind of special unity between Pierre and his wife – so long as it is not thematized. For any thematization of absence refers us back to another freely nihilating power of consciousness, which it possesses only inasmuch as it is itself numbed by Nothingness: imagination. But absence lived and not thematized can be understood only as a concrete relation between two existents against a basic background of unity of contact. Pierre's wife is immediately given to Pierre as *not being there*.

Thus absence, which is a negation, has two characteristics of being. 1. It appears against the background of existential unity that it denies, and retains this positive unity as the essence of its negation. It draws its *being* from this positive unity; borrows its being from it. Absence is been. 2. It establishes between two beings a synthetic unit of negation: in others words, it brings them together precisely by denying their presence. Pierre and his wife are given to each other by that negation; or, if you prefer, that negation is a particular mode of the unitary connection between Pierre and his wife. In other terms, from the moment when Pierre and his wife form a whole, the only mode of unitary negation which will *nihilate* this whole without *destroying* it (divorce, forgetting, etc. are destructions) is absence.

But this *at one and the same time* concretely explains to us the nature of the original nihilation or apparition of consciousnesses –

which is precisely an absence in relation to the in-itself's whole, and which *nihilates* without destroying the in-itself's original relation of immanence, indeed is even able to nihilate only against this original background of immanence – and *simultaneously refers back* for its primary explanation to the original absence, which is precisely the absence of consciousness with respect to the world that vests it. Without this primary and metaphysical absence, all the absences we have just described couldn't exist, indeed there wouldn't even be any distance. The origin of all absences is the metaphysical absence of consciousness as the type of synthetic and unitary connection between consciousness and the world.

Friday 2

The division is leaving in three or four days. Probably for Bouxwiller, to rest up.

Yesterday met Nippert back from leave. I ask him: 'Did it go all right, then?' He replied with conviction (a conviction which I found all the more surprising because he'd gone off in despair): 'Oh yes! It was a beautiful leave!' I can't describe the tone of voice in which he pronounced these last words. It had a kind of edifying and apologetic ponderousness about it – the tone of a *Naturfreund*[25] praising a violet – something like: 'See, my child, what good and beautiful things God has made for man.' Of course, it's the married man – the domestic priest – who speaks with such assurance: he is delivering the lesson that it is good to 're-immerse' oneself in the bosom of one's family. And leave joins the family in the category of *natural* things created by God for his glory: since the creation of the world, there have been families and leaves. But at the same time, beneath the doctrinal intonation a sincere, childlike and almost charming wonder showed through, putting me in mind of that young Arab girl on the deck of the *Théophile Gautier*: 'We had such lovely things to eat.'[26] He added 'Too short, alas!' – and then, to avoid being suspected even for an instant of criticizing the handiwork of God and the high military command – 'Like all beautiful things.' As if the leave's brevity were not governed quite simply by external circumstances and by events, but were its most quintessential and exquisite quality, the very source

25. Lover of nature.
26. Sartre and De Beauvoir travelled back from their Greek holiday in 1937 aboard the *Théophile Gautier*.

of its beauty and that secret death which used so to touch Barrès on young faces.

At first this only made me laugh, but then I realized that in my own way I too took leave like that. As something given, not as a right. Also as a beauty. I envisage it with its specific time of ten days, which does not strike me as an arbitrary limitation but as a personal quality of that beauty, exactly like the rhythm and duration of a melody. The flat, amorphous time of every day – it's here I live it, here that it piles up;[27] *there*, it seems to me I shall know another time, the time of music and adventures, wherein the end is already present in the beginning. It's as if I were introducing myself into a merciless little short story, that doesn't end very well but that's beautiful. And I'm rather indignant at the thought that all the so precious material that will fill it – the Beaver, Paris, T., leisure – was once an everyday affair. I used to live all that with the carefree, indefinite time, copious and doughy, full of little sly collapses, which is my time here. It seems to me that I used not to treat all those exceptional blessings with the consideration they deserved; that the only right way to treat them was by absence, punctuated by rare, dazzling presences. As if that *absence* with respect to all he loves formed part of man's condition. I would like those ten days to have a certain quality, in their very fabric, that one ordinarily finds only in books: in K. Mansfield, in *La Chartreuse de Parme*, in Barrès's best short stories. To have, rather than a harsh frenzy, a kind of distant and somewhat cruel sweetness – a sort of aristocracy too – that my days have never known.

I have had many moments of happiness, but it was rough, copious happiness, heavy as rough red wine: it had no 'quality'. And this was not due to the nature of my fortunes, which were very good (wouldn't you term good fortune an awakening at first light beneath the theatre steps at Epidaurus, with the Beaver by my side; a hasty return as evening falls over the alleyways of Fez, while the first lamps are being lit and the little dark streets to right and left along our way are being barred with chains; or a walk round the ramparts at Aigues-Mortes with T.), but because my personal character, besides a certain thinness of the blood, involves a certain cynical mistrust of the precious: a fear of being taken in, of doing an Alain-Fournier number, of the magical. Then there are always details which clash, but which nevertheless *also* belong to the moment. Then, despite everything, it's in a quite everyday time: that walk in the streets of Fez intrudes into the

27. It should be borne in mind when reading this passage that the French *temps* means not only 'time' but also 'tempo'.

annoying wait for a money-order which doesn't arrive, the one at Aigues-Mortes between two flaming rows with T.

Pieter was reproaching me just now for wasting money. Well, it seems to me I'm also wasting my life. Not through a thirst for living life to the full – which, precisely, wouldn't be a waste – but through a certain carelessness about letting moments flow into the past, sure as I am that none is irreplaceable; through a total lack of desire to say like Faust: 'Time, suspend thy flight!' I lack that sense of the irreplaceable and specific which even the wretched Drieu possesses, or claims to possess (granted it was the fashion, when he was starting out). Perhaps, in many instances, I should have clung on. But even so, it seems to me that it's not the thing to do; that it diverts the natural flow; that one becomes insincere. At Mycenae – alone with the Beaver under a fine, stormy sky, amid those strange tombs and those rocks – it wouldn't have taken much for me to have a precious moment. But I'd have had to think about Agamemnon – that was absolutely indispensable. To explain why here would take too long. The fact remains I refused to do it. The ruined palace demanded the presence of the Atridae, but I had no wish to people it with legendary heroes. So it remained in ruins, and I lost something thereby. It's always like that: depending on my mood, I call it thinness of blood or intellectual honesty.

What I mean is I'm a bit afraid of that intellectual honesty for this time that's coming. From afar, those ten days look so precious to me: for once, I feel I might know a noble happiness. But I'm a bit afraid of finding, in the very midst of those ten days, the copious, lymphatic foam of my time here; I'm afraid of having fits of careless generosity; I'm afraid of being too intellectually honest. Certainly, I want to live them as *authentic*. But in that very authenticity there's room for something rarer, something exceptional. In short, I'm being given this leave, but it's necessary for me to take it. It's an undertaking. I've already often thought about the difficulties awaiting men on leave 'back home'. I've already thought how leave is *difficult*. It's not so easy being reunited with a wife, for example. For me, those particular difficulties don't exist, but there are others I've just mentioned. I shall record here whether I've 'pulled off' my leave. I already have the impression that Mistler and Nippert have 'won' theirs (astonishing as it may seem for the latter), and that Courcy and the Warrant-officer have lost theirs. As for Pieter, he passed through without realizing there was any match to be played (except insofar as his business is concerned); but his natural affability, his kindliness and his luck – and the thickness of his hide, too – prevented him from losing: a draw.

Sudden disorganization of our group; it was high time I described it, tomorrow it will no longer exist. Tomorrow Keller is leaving for Paris and I'm going on leave. In four or five days we're being relieved and the whole division is moving to Bouxwiller. Paul and Pieter will be alone together, in a new town. These abrupt upsettings of the balance, which suddenly shatter forms at the very moment when they seem best organized, are typical of military instability.

Saturday, 3 February

Set off on leave.

Sunday 4

9:30 hrs. After spending all night in the train, I disembark with Keller loaded down like a pack-mule at Aiguevilliers (Haute-Saône), the assembly-centre. An odd place. Wooden huts (similar to the renowned Vilgrain huts) below the railway embankment, in the middle of a little wood. The town and civilian station are a good twenty minutes march away. Thirty-odd hutments arranged with a certain eye to symmetry, their doors facing. No snow seems to have fallen in Haute-Saône; the ground is black and muddy, a real quagmire, the air sweet and luscious. Thin, twiggy trees as abundant and irregular as weeds. One *first* feels that one is in a wood. And then all of a sudden, in that wood, a human gathering with a strong human smell.

Despite the uniforms, this gathering has nothing really military about it. There's a certain leisure about the faces, and a vague, distraught melancholy that's nothing like the empty expectation one can read when soldiers are under orders. Uniforms are loosened, greatcoats opened, lots of men are leaning on big sticks carefully trimmed and carved, others are holding dogs on leads, others again are carrying clanking tins which give out little squeaks. With those sticks and their pear-shaped outlines – which packages, helmet, water-bottle and gas-mask thicken round the waist, causing them to splay out at the bottom – they're more like those 'soldiers' in Andersen who, when discharged, used to come home semi-brigands. They look as if they've 'seen a thing or two', with an air of peaceable toughness that contrasts with the sheeplike look they wear as serving men. A few drunks – but not many. Fewer than yesterday. They've slept it off on the night train.

But the very particular character of this gathering (whose members may come from anywhere and be going anywhere) derives from the blasts emanating from the loudspeakers installed in every hut – and on the roof of most of them. From time to time there's music. Rarely – just now it was *Plaisir d'amour*. But most of the time it's information, exhortations, advice, etc. All of it dispensed according to the best principles followed by Radio announcers. The voice is distinct and steady; an attempt is made to find the striking turn of phrase; catchwords, witticisms and gags are not excluded. The way we're treated is more civilian than military. Midway, really, between the 'Attention all Passengers' of the state railways, and the 'Men!' of the Captain or the daily parade.

We are summoned: 'Army personnel on leave! Please pay careful attention now. For the Green Train only, assembly behind the sorting-hut. For the Green Train only. Hullo, hullo! Will those not on the Green Train kindly return to their billets, in order to avoid congestion. There's no point in getting soaked for nothing.' The striking thing is that an appeal is made to our *reason*. Admittedly still a childish reason, that has to be impressed and convinced through repetition. But nevertheless a reason all the same. The thinking behind the orders is *explained* to us. And the order thereby becomes merely a piece of advice. The very title 'Army personnel on leave' – which is the only one we're given here – denotes an intermediary reality between civilian and soldier. Something like 'Passengers!', or better still 'Holders of large-family travel-cards', or again and especially: 'Those in possession of cheap weekend excursion fares for the Loire châteaux'.

This quite new synthesis of civilian organization (it's genuinely very well organized), uniforms, command with veiled threats, and appeals to individual initiative (but an initiative whose only possible direction has been strictly predetermined) – this effort towards a crude modern mass comfort (possibility of sending telegrams; snacks at the Soldiers' Home; free cups of coffee at the canteen) – all this is what gives the whole thing the character of a *fascist festivity*: I recognize a tone of voice on the microphone that I've heard before, in Germany, at the Tempelhof festivities, etc. An impression shattered, it should be said, by the tough, silent, indifferent, inward look most of the lads are wearing.

What's really striking, in fact, is that the men don't look as if they're enjoying themselves. They're calm and even a bit gloomy. I'm just the same. Yet there are some of them who've battled for a fortnight (I'm one) to be able to set off today. But they appear reflective, as if it were both an undertaking and an ordeal. They seem not to be free from apprehension. I understand this anguish very well and share it. Apart from the very young ones, they'd like things 'to go *all right*' and aren't sure they will.

All the same, a brief little outburst of joy in our hutment when the loudspeaker announces: 'Army personnel on leave taking the Blue Train, fall in!' There are a few shouts from the lads, but these soon die away. Few other demonstrations: just a couple of whistles when the tannoy mentions the police.

The very particular aspect of this gathering obviously comes from the fact that it has been organized by civilians under military control. Signs, services, tannoy, etc. etc. are, I'm sure, the work of the state railways. And it's for these that we're 'Army personnel on leave'. In other words, people 'having the right' to a free journey on specified trains.

The hutments: about thirty metres long and eight wide. Wooden floor, deal walls, three frosted-glass windows and eight transoms on the two longer side-walls. Four electric bulbs on the ceiling; deal benches with backs, crammed close together; between these benches, from one end of the hut to the other, a corridor that runs between the two facing doors.

Example of the tannoy's *tone*: 'The canteen opens at nine o'clock, for army personnel on leave taking the Pink Train only. Any individuals slipping into the squad without having a pink pass . . .' A silence. One expects: ' . . . will get four days in the glasshouse'. But no, the voice proceeds in a fatherly tone: ' . . . will not be allowed into the canteen. And the canteen is a long way away. It takes twenty minutes to get there, twenty minutes to get back. They will have lost forty minutes for nothing.'

Around 10.30 the tannoy transmits *Ta main dans ma main* sung by Charles Trénet. I see myself anew with Bost and the Beaver in some popular neighbourhood of Marseilles, on a fine August night, trying to recall the tune of that song. A violent, abrupt emotion, quite unrelated to my considered moroseness of the instant before, brings tears to my eyes. I fight them back, pretending to wipe my glasses. In all this there's certainly a pretty abject relapse into gushing over myself. Plus sentimentality due to a pretty tiring night. But it's also because all those past things – all those blessings I was still thinking of as dead only yesterday – for an instant appeared wonderfully and illusorily *accessible*. They were *restored* to me.

I am writing this comfortably ensconced in the Pink Train, which leaves at 11.16. It's eleven o'clock, I can still hear unrecognizable scraps of tear-jerking music. And then, from time to time: 'Last-minute passengers for the Pink Train, hurry along now' – which has a tiny hint about it of 'Workers of the world, unite'.

16 February

Back from leave. I didn't touch this notebook during my stay in Paris, and that was quite right. All that happened to me there really didn't concern it. It's a war notebook and only as such has any meaning. Furthermore, I wanted to let myself go; to live without thinking – or rather without immediately defining and settling my thoughts, without knowing what I was thinking. I shall, however, record here what may be of interest in relation to 'being-at-war', since in any case leave is an episode of war.

First of all, I must say I was overwhelmed. Nothing but the finest. There were no wasted hours. I don't think it could have been improved on. I saw the Beaver and T., I wasn't alone for an instant, but I'd sampled enough solitude at Brumath and Morsbronn to earn the joys of being a twosome. People didn't disappoint me, quite the contrary. There was even a happy surprise – which belongs to my private life. But now that I've stressed the perfection of that leave, I must say it wasn't at all as I'd imagined (especially on Friday 2). It wasn't *precious*. And this was due primarily to the nature of time, which, back there as here, was time writ large. One can do nothing about it. There's just one time: the time of Existence. The fact that from the moment I arrived I felt those ten days must come to an end – be-ten-days – changed nothing. For, especially at the beginning, Paris seemed workaday. I wasn't much aware of the war there. On the streets, perhaps, in the evenings. But in the carefully selected places where we went, the Beaver and I, the war had disturbed almost nothing. All my old habits had repossessed me against my will, and I felt at home. The five months I had just spent in Alsace appeared like a dream.

Towards the middle of my leave, I began to notice the large proportion of old and infirm people, and felt Paris as a bloodless town that some haemorrhage had drained of all its men. The sadness of the evenings, above all, affected me. Montmartre was dead and desolate. The Place St-Charles in the night's mirage struck me as having the gloomy vastness of some major road junction in the suburbs. Going down the Rue Pigalle I here and there perceived, like vitreous fissures, the dying gleam of the dance-halls through the curtains. I knew the jazz-spots had gone downhill, and these words of T.'s told me all that was needed about their death-throes: 'Let's not go to the Chantilly, it's too cold there.'

There was something more subtle in the air, moreover, which the Beaver made me feel very distinctly: it was a town of men without futures. 'A domestic existence,' she'd tell me. For what used to separate people entertainingly in peacetime was the fact that every man and every woman seemed like a door opened upon the outside, upon unknown futures. Each of them was waiting for something that I didn't know, and that depended partly on them; and it was that unknown future which cut them off from me, not the bus platform or patch of pavement which united us by contrast in the present. All that has disappeared. Most of the people I saw in the cafés, streets and dance-halls look very ordinary, don't talk about the war and occasionally even enjoy themselves. Yet I know their fate is settled, like that of the dead: they have nothing left to wait for but the end of the war – which does not depend on them. In the meantime, they occupy themselves as best they can; they let the war flow over them, arching their backs.

Yes, Paris had the same effect on me as a family vault, and this too helped quite a bit to strip my leave of its 'precious' quality. That city I'd so wanted to find again: either it was quite prosaic, and I no longer even maintained sufficient distance to feel I'd found it; or else I discovered it suddenly at my feet, but it was dead and gone – and most mournfully so. So mournful, indeed, was the effect that the only two strong impressions I drew from Paris were exactly the opposite of what I was expecting. I'd imagined I would feel myself lost in an alien city, immense and teeming – as has befallen me in Berlin, London or Naples. But just the opposite occurred.

On one of my last evenings, the Beaver had gone into a café on the Champs-Elysées – the Rond-Point – and I was waiting outside for her, seduced by that new, padded discretion which after dark gives the cafés the clandestine look of brothels; seduced by a sky that was taking an age to fade away and a few precious stones attached to the gas-lamps which shone without illuminating – by a whole night, blue and filled with whisperings, which brought summer to mind. And suddenly I was overcome by a kind of joy at the thought that I, alive, was there in that proud, dead city. That I was alive precisely because I didn't belong to it: because my destiny was being played out elsewhere and yet, inasmuch as I was *waging* war, I was its architect. At that particular moment, I felt like a traveller who gives himself up to a city, while something awaits him elsewhere. And it was bitter, no doubt, because I was soon going to leave those whom I loved the most – and whom, precisely on that particular day, I loved more fiercely than ever. But in the midst of that bitterness, it was a real sop to my pride not to be caught up in it all. I can compare my impression only to the one we had, the Beaver and I, before splendid Greek or Moroccan cities peopled with corpses. At Sparta, for example, seeing the Greek youth drinking apéritifs in the city's principal café, or at Fez in the souks. We were fascinated, almost to the point of letting overselves fall right in; yet also relieved and comforted because we were people from elsewhere.

Another time, with T. at the Jockey, I had a similar though less pure impression. I loved T. very much and she seemed to love me. And there were other couples, very young (the men must have been below call-up age), who seemed to love each other greatly too. And I felt that against my will I was escaping that love, because I was going to leave. They only loved. Whereas I, though I perhaps loved even more than they, was alone and could only lend myself to that love, because I had to leave again.

Apart from those two little moments, I lived as of old – satisfied, to be sure; happy; interested by every moment. But the rare quality I was hoping for failed to materialize. I am decidedly not cut out for rare emotions.

What I also learnt – and I note it down here without further elaboration – is that it's much easier to live decently and authentically in wartime than in peacetime.

17 February

All in all, that leave formed a whole – a solid, round shape which I glimpsed from afar and thought in January I'd be able to appropriate. But in the event I managed only to aim at that object and miss. At the very moment when I thought I almost had it, it escaped me. To conclude from this that it only ever existed in my imagination, there's but a short step – which Proust, for example, would have soon taken. But I shall take care not to do so. For the Beaver has taught me something new: in her novel, one sees Elisabeth complaining about being surrounded by objects she'd like to enjoy, but that she can't 'realize'.[28] It's unfortunate she gave this reflection to Elisabeth – a disagreeable, tense character who diminishes its scope. For most of the time, Elisabeth really only feels *in appearance*. But the Beaver was looking beyond that. She meant that we are surrounded by *unrealizables*. These are existing objects, that we can think from afar and describe, but never *see*. Yet they are there, within reach; they attract

28. The novel in question is *L'Invitée* (1943): *She Came to Stay*, London 1949.

our gaze, we turn towards them and we find nothing. They are generally objects that concern *us*.

The example chosen by Elisabeth is excellent: one can never truly live the relation between what one has been and what one is. For example, I sometimes say: 'All that I used to want in my youth, I have had – but not in the way I wanted it.' I *think* this, by comparing what I remember having wanted with what I've obtained. I think it, but I don't *see* it. It always seems we could redouble our joy at having brought off some undertaking, by looking at this success through our past hopes and fears: I wanted it so much and, behold, I have it. But, in most cases, that's quite impossible. Our great hopes are dead, and far from our being able to see our success through them, it's them we look at through our success.

Thus that most stirring of all objects, which we can grasp perfectly when it's a question of other people, escapes us on principle. Yet it's *there*. Aron would say that it's an illusion: a way of invoking the viewpoint of God (that's to say, the being for whom unrealizables are realities). But no, I'm much more modest. Those objects exist because one can think them *truly*. My leave exists because society has conferred a real existence upon it; because it's the signification of my stay in Paris; and because, in spite of everything, it gives a particular nuance to all the instants – even the most insignificant – of that stay. And yet it's out of my reach. Similarly, the relation between my youthful ambitions and my mature years can exist, for example, for the Beaver. But not for me. Of the same type, I'd say, is the 'adventure' which always eludes the adventurer, amid the most extraordinary circumstances, and which is nevertheless an essential category of human action. I appeared to be saying, in *La Nausée*, that it didn't *exist*. But that's wrong. It's better to say that it's an unrealizable. Adventure is an existent, whose nature is to appear only in the past through the account one gives of it.

The disturbing thing about these unrealizables is that I can think them right through and in detail, and by means of words cause them to be realized by others. For example, if I were concerned to write a short story entitled 'The Leave', I could compose that leave as it ought to have been, with its pathetic, precious nature. I could ensure that the reader would realize it, like a melody flowing inexorably towards its end. But that would be art. Art is one of the means we have to get our unrealizables realized vividly and 'imaginarily' by others. I take this opportunity to note that unrealizables are not at all of the same nature as imaginaries: they are real, they are everywhere – but out of reach. Others can grasp them in the realizing mode or in the imaginary mode. But authenticity, I think, conduces to reserving them a place all round us as unrealizables. We must neither deny them nor seek vainly to realize them, but assume them as unrealizables. The failing that the Beaver and I have often recognized in others, under the name of 'pretence' ('making pretences', 'putting on a show'), consists essentially in a kind of bad faith whereby we present as realized what is in principle unrealizable.

By contrast, T.'s purity is based upon a blindness – on principle – to unrealizables. She'll never dream of thinking the time I spent with her as a *leave*. It's a presence between two absences, quite simply. She won't call her countless escapades at the Bal Nègre adventures. Each time, she was fascinated by the instant. Yet, in spite of everything, she lacks those objects; her activity lacks incentives. In each case, it's advisable to determine what the unrealizable is, and what can be realized. For example, Paris is a real existent, there's no doubt of that. But is it a realizable existent for me? I can think that I'm in Paris. But can I *be-in* Paris? The Beaver and I had a very long argument about this two years ago, arising out of an article by Caillois on the myth of the great city. In that instance, I think I was right against the Beaver. (We were posing the question wrongly, in any case, since we precisely lacked this notion of unrealizable; we were merely wondering whether Paris existed or was just a myth.) I think one can *be-in* Paris.

It goes without saying that I don't call '*realizing* an object' the mere fact of visualizing that object with more or less intense feelings. One realizes an object when that object's presence is given us as a more or less essential modification of our being, and through that modification. To have an adventure isn't to visualize oneself having an adventure, but to be-in the adventure – which, as I showed in *La Nausée*, is impossible. Unrealizables can always be visualized, but they can't be *enjoyed*; and that's what gives them their bothersome, ambiguous character. I think that half men's actions have the aim of realizing the unrealizable. I think the majority of our most subtle disappointments come from the fact that an unrealizable appears to us in the future – and then after the event in the past – as realizable; and from the fact that we then indeed feel that we haven't realized it. And I indeed feel at present that those ten days which lie behind me – contracted, squeezed in such a way that their end touches their beginning – are already in my memory becoming *The* Leave: precisely the one I wished to have when I was dreaming about it on 2 February.

I want to recount my return journey. The day before yesterday, 15

February, at around eight-thirty I donned anew my military uniform, all tidied up by a civilian tailor. I had new puttees, ski shoes (those I'd worn till then belonged to the Beaver), and was neater than I'd ever been since the war began. At nine o'clock I arrived on the platform at the Gare de l'Est, where I found a corner-seat without any trouble. There were many women seeing off soldiers, very few men. The women were clinging to their arms and looking at them with a kind of ferocity. But most of the soldiers, washed and shaved and likewise neater than they'd ever been before, weren't looking at them: they'd already left and were gazing into space or else looking at the other soldiers.

I'm not making hasty generalizations. I walked the whole length of the platform and everywhere I was struck by those odd little groups. By that smaller, clinging shape in motion which would be seeking to close the group and make it into a whole against the outside, and by the larger shape – silent, heavy, almost passive – which would be turned slightly away from the former, displaying itself full-face when the former was in profile. By those two looks : one of them wishing to maintain and preserve; the other, perpendicular to the first, fleeing towards the future. From time to time a woman would burst into tears; her companion would notice and tell her clumsily 'You mustn't cry' – but then he'd stop, not knowing what to add, deeply convinced that on the contrary she had every reason to cry. One woman and her companion started to sob in unison, but that wasn't taken too well by the crowd. A soldier running past shouted out 'An' didn'it rain!', so people started laughing. Strange social event, in dirty grey and smudged khaki: that utterly primitive separation of the men, who were all being taken away, from the women – ill made-up, disfigured by the sleepless night, hastily clad – who were going to stay there.

There were two trains opposite each other and mine was leaving second. At 9.30, when the other one left, I saw a parade of women. The couples whose males were taking my train had retreated a little, and watched the parade in silence. The women clasping their men's arms were doubtless thinking that, a quarter of an hour later, they'd be like that. It was a slow, silent parade with a kind of hesitant grace. With two or three exceptions, all the women were weeping, it was almost comical: old women and young ones, tall ones and dumpy ones, blondes and brunettes intermingled, with the same red, dark-ringed eyes. One or two of them caught my attention – one in particular, a tall elegant blonde with a fur coat and face past its prime, who wasn't weeping but walking with long strides, her head turned to one side and gazing at our train with a look of kindly distraction: that one struck me as being groggier than the rest. Another one too: a little girl with just the same bearing and expression as women returning to their seats after communion. At the sight of her vague inward smile and lowered eyes, it seemed to me she could feel her memories within her like a consecrated wafer.

Someone shouted 'All aboard!' and we climbed into our carriages. In my compartment, the soldiers came to the door one after another, and each in turn – after he'd shaken the hands that stretched towards him or hoisted a woman up to him by her shoulders – would say politely as he withdrew: 'Next one'. The train drew away. The lads were silent and gloomy. In the corridor, a handsome fair-haired lad was laughing in angry derision. Someone told him: 'No point in getting worked up, what's the use?', and he replied with sibilant irony: 'Oh, sure! It's just a matter of getting used to it. In ten years it won't bother me a bit.' A soldier mentioned our next leave and was met by a black look from another: 'Oh yeah, let's all talk about our next leave, then!' And one wearing a moustache concluded, as if just for his own benefit: 'That's our lot for four months.' Someone knocked an entire kit down on the head of a small Jew with glasses. There was an apology, and the small Jew said with resigned gaiety: 'Oh well, now or later! But the later the better, all the same.'

They spoke for a moment longer, in vague, rambling phrases directed at no one in particular and requiring no reply. From those rambling phrases, I got the impression that they were all terrified of a spring offensive; that's what gave their departure that tragic aspect. After a quarter of an hour, everybody fell silent. There were some who read and others who slept and others who sat staring. I read Ludwig's *Bismarck*. Occasionally, I'd put down my book and go for a smoke in the corridor. I wasn't sad but very shaken, in a state which could very accurately be termed pathetic – and which must be that of insects when they're metamorphosing. I'd manage from time to time to interest myself in my reading, and then I'd communicate my pathetic state to Bismarck, who almost brought tears to my eyes.

The train stopped. It was 16.30. We climbed down into the snow and grasped the situation at once : a loudspeaker began to bawl away at us the moment we set foot on the platform. We were no longer 'Army personnel on leave' but 'Men': and there was no longer any question of reasoning with us politely as at Aiguevilliers, but just of threatening us with the most dire punishments: 'It is strictly forbidden . . . Any man contravening . . . will be liable to the strictest penalties.' I felt unaffected, merely amused – I was braced. 'It's their way of saying Hullo to us,' my neighbour commented.

Hutments. It's Port d'Atelier. I drank a beer from the bottle, and picked my hut. Why choose between all those identical huts? Last remnant of civility.

I entered a large gloomy room with wooden walls. Men were sleeping on benches, others were sitting with bowed heads, others were eating. I wrote to T. and to the Beaver, then I read *Hitler Speaks*.[29] Night fell, it was beginning to grow cold. There were three benches arranged in a triangle round the stove, in the shadows. I sat down. There were a score of us soldiers, sitting thigh to thigh, with fixed stares. I recalled a host of memories and knew that each of my neighbours was likewise conjuring up memories. Some fellow came in: 'Hey, how about that, a world without women! Where've all those women gone to, then?' From time to time the loudspeaker would inform us of a train's imminent departure. It announced the departure of ours prematurely, and there was a moment of confusion. At half-past seven I left the hut: they were announcing a talking picture show. I queued with the others and then, when my turn came to go in, I went away. I didn't want to distract myself from that strong, sinister world; I didn't want to let myself be fascinated by the imaginary. I returned to my hut.

At twenty past nine, we ran to our train in the snow, in the dark, in disorder, clambering over wires, leaping across the tracks, while sergeant-majors barked in the distance behind us. I can't really understand the reason for that disorder; for my own part, there's nothing I'd have liked better than to follow the prescribed route. Was it due to mistakes by our superiors, panic, impatient heroism? That departure resembled a rout. Four of us found ourselves in an unlit and unheated compartment: the steam had frozen in the pipes. We had to use our torches for light, as we stowed our packages on the racks. I tried to sleep, but it was very cold and we were plagued by a sickly smell of disinfectant. My neighbours tossed and groaned: 'They want to kill us off, the bastards! Christ it's cold!' In the end, I told them we might perhaps try getting out at the next stop and going up to the front of the train, where we'd have more chance of finding heated carriages. But they preferred to groan.

I got out all the same, as soon as the train stopped, and they followed me. We ran the whole length of the train in the snow, two lads got lost on the way and dived in anywhere. I found myself alone with a tall, fair-haired fellow, in a pleasantly warm compartment; then two chasseurs got in, and I fell asleep like a log. We were

29. By Rauschning: see note 23 on p. 142 above.

supposed to arrive at 4.37, but when I woke up at around 6 the train was still moving. One of the chasseurs, very young with a pleasant face and ruddy complexion, told us with an objective air that his captain was a diviner. With his divining-rod, he'd determine from his office whether his machine-gun units were really in the positions to which he'd assigned them; and if they weren't, he'd ring up to ask for a explanation. The fellow spoke slowly and carefully. When he'd finished, he added in the same tone of voice: 'He's a stupid cunt.' Wherever I've gone, I've found the same hatred of officers: a restrained but profound hatred, which has nothing to do with anti-militarism, which on the contrary is entirely concrete and empirical, and which is always accompanied by an 'I don't say there aren't any good ones, but I haven't come across one.' The two chasseurs had been in the Saar.[30] They spoke wide-eyed of those first days of September, when the mines had been exploding beneath their feet. They'd seen an incautious lieutenant being flung into the air and falling back with his eyes lacerated. They'd seen a big lorry go up: its driver had been found, not much the worse for wear, hanging in a tree with his clothes scorched.

At six thirty, arrival at Dettwiller (my division has left Morsbronn for Bouxwiller). Hutments. A fellow near me is grumbling away and the others applaud him: it's still about officers. A captain apparently punished some men by making them stand to attention for two hours, with their noses to a wall. This penalty angers them, in a way that remains fairly incomprehensible to me. I'd rather that than four days in the clink, but it injures their dignity as men: 'Christ, we're not kids any more!' Another one, a big lad with a peaceable air, says in a sleepy voice: 'Cool down! We won't always let ourselves be pushed around, maybe it won't last for ever.' Yet they all recognize the necessity for the war. There's one of them who says: 'In the beginning, the war was for an ideal; but it'll all end up in a battle of interests, just like the other one.' A short while later, the same fellow speaks of getting himself invalided out, because of his heart: 'I'm so tensed up because of my heart, believe it or not, that when I meet someone I haven't seen for five months, I quite lose my wits for several minutes.' At about eight o'clock we're packed into coaches, and at twenty to nine I'm at Bouxwiller.

Hang, who has been to Saumur on leave, has come back fuming at

30. Immediately after the declaration of war, in September 1939, the French army had briefly occupied a few square kilometres of territory in the Saarland, before being driven out and settling down to the 'phoney war'.

civilians. He tells me about a certain Deck, who after he'd got back from leave said to him: 'If it hadn't been for my wife, after two days I'd have asked to come back here'; and about another fellow who said: 'The Parisians deserve to be bombed twice a week.' I don't share his opinion at all: the Parisians struck me as shapeless and sad. I imagine that what's beginning is the slow, inevitable transformation of the soldier into a misunderstood individual.

Sunday, 18 February

The two chasseurs Pieter knows came back to see us. Two months ago, they were complaining about a pretty foolish taste for heroics among their comrades. If they didn't volunteer for dangerous missions, they used to be accused of shirking. Today, they say the morale of the troops is very low. It's what I've had occasion to observe everywhere, lately.

The relativists' razor-stroke is the accusation of having secret recourse to God. For example, any effort to grasp a historical event *as it was* (and not as it appeared, through layers of technical or cultural significations, through prejudices themselves historical, or through postulates of an individual philosophy) appears to Aron as a recourse to God. The event in itself is the event as it would appear to God. In this sense he could tell me his *Introduction à la philosophie de l'histoire* was a plea for philosophical and methodological atheism. I readily admit the argument has both a technical value (it's true that *technically* the historian is historical) and a psychological one (it's true that most of the time a quest for the occurrence *as it was* is psychologically equivalent, for the searcher, to a surrender to God). But the secret weakness of this idealist razor is that it contains within it an enormous postulate, which turns it into a vicious circle. That postulate is idealism itself. To say that any search for the in-itself is a recourse to God is quite simply to assert that *esse est percipi*:[31] it is to dissolve being into knowledge, the in-itself into being-for. The question has been doctored by a pretty clever trick. If I ask what a fact is absolutely, I receive the answer that a fact can be absolutely only 'for' an absolute being – so I'm referred back to God. But I precisely refuse this reduction of the in-itself to being-for; on the contrary, I think I have shown in the course of these notebooks that being-for can appear only

31. 'To be is to be perceived': tag applied by Berkeley to sense data. The full epitome 'esse est aut percipere aut percipi' ('to be is either to perceive or to be perceived') makes room for both experiences and experiencers.

against a background of in-itself of which it is the nihilation.

But it's necessary to go further and show there's a certain in-itself not of the *for-me* but of the for-others, for example. If I suppose one of those reciprocal presences – of two for-itselfs constituting a for-others – as I've explained, this presence is given against a background of in-itself. But we'd fall back into the idealist error of the primacy of knowledge if we were to admit that this for-others exists only *inasmuch* as it's a modification of being for each of the for-itselfs. Doubtless, there's a *for-others* only as a reciprocal existential modification of two (or more than two) *for-itselfs*. But if each of the for-itselfs realizes its for-others through *its* own existential modification, what precisely shall we say of the *reciprocal* existential modification? Is it only the *sum* of the two individual modifications? But this sum can be made only against a background of prior unity. Does it exist only *for* a third party? That's possible on the face of it, and we'd fall back into idealism and finally recourse to God, since in reality the reciprocal existential modification would exist absolutely *in itself* only for the absolute being *causa sui*.[32] Or rather, is there a specific existence of reciprocal existential modification – an existence that would be posited neither in terms of *for-itself* nor in terms of *for-others*.

Here, for example, is Pieter coming in: he sees me, he speaks to me, at once he cuts into my very existence and I thrust myself like a knife into his. There we are, embarked upon a conversation. I wonder if this 'conversation' has an existence only for me who am conversing *and* for him who is conversing. Or else if it exists beyond – not, of course, independently of him or me, but independently of the being-for-itself of each of us. That's not simple, since the for-itself exists only as nihilation of the in-itself. But the in-itself precisely grasps afresh what escapes it in nihilation, by giving to that very nihilation the value of a *fact* appearing in the midst of the in-itself. By facticity, consciousness – in its nihilation of the in-itself – is grasped afresh from behind by the in-itself which it nihilates: that's what should be understood when I say that the in-itself is its own nothingness.

Not that it is itself a foundation for Nothingness: but for Nothingness to nihilate the in-itself, it's necessary that it leave the in-itself itself – necessary that it *be-been*. And that slender film of existence, by which the in-itself covers over its own nihilation – that's precisely the facticity or limit to the transparency of consciousness. Not that there's nothing *behind* that transparency; but the simple *fact* of being-as-if-for-itself is the opaque limit of that translucidity. In other terms, *it's* a

32. *causa sui*: 'cause of itself' (or 'himself', or 'herself').

fact *in itself*, escaping any nihilation, that there exists at this very moment a *for-itself* which is nihilation of the in-itself. Reflection will be able to overcome this facticity, by nihilating the de facto existence of the reflected consciousness; but this will be only to fall beneath the sway of reflexive facticity – the facticity will only have been displaced. This fact does not exist-for anyone. Consciousness, if it looks back towards it to interrogate it, doesn't *see* it – but sees only the infinite and nihilating freedom of its own motivations. The fact *is*, quite simply. Not in God's eyes – in itself. This brings us to the fringes of the question of time, which I'll attempt to examine in the next few days. It's that same film of facticity which confers an existence *in itself* upon my conversation with Pieter.

The characteristic of Nothingness is not just to nihilate [*néantiser*] being, but to nihilate [*néantir*] itself towards the in-itself. That's why the transcendence of consciousness consists in surpassing the world towards an ipseity which it wants as an *in-itself*. But that in-itself which it projects beyond the world holds in itself the essential features of consciousness. It's an in-itself which is to itself its own foundation, just as consciousness is to itself its own motivation; an in-itself which enwraps facticity, surpasses it and retains it in its womb. An in-itself that to itself is a for-itself. This hybrid projection of the in-itself and the for-itself is the only way in which consciousness can give itself the in-itself as an end. It's exactly what is termed the *causa sui*. An in-itself that was for-itself would be a *causa sui*. Transcendence is the being of consciousness inasmuch as it is-to-be-*causa-sui*.

We have lunch with five chasseurs, Pieter's two and three others. The usual rough bitterness against officers. They've all had a hard time of it, and recall without conceit – but with a kind of cynical toughness that appeals to me – the hardest places, over our heads. They're always talking about bumping off their officers. None of them will do so, of course; but the striking thing is that it isn't said mutinously, with clenched fists, but in a leisurely conversational tone, as something that goes without saying. They don't even claim they'd bump them off themselves, but observe objectively, as a fact, that if Colonel Deligne comes to visit the outposts at night he'll 'get himself bumped off'. Certain of their officers have slept rough with them, but they're no longer at the stage to be moved by that; they merely say: 'That's crafty.' More than anger, they feel contempt for them.

One from Épinal, whom I've not seen before – bullet head, fair moustache – gives a vivid account: 'The Captain works himself up into a rage all by himself as he speaks, and in the end he tells us: "Anybody who smokes, I'll put a bullet through his head. I value my skin." ' Little pitying shrugs of the shoulder. Description by another, who's a music master, of his captain: 'He's a primary-school teacher; no idea about how to command. I don't blame him, but what's he bloody doing here? He's scared, always scared. When he punishes us, he snivels: "I've got nothing against you, nothing against you at all. Fifteen days in the cooler, you'll find that pretty hard: but what can I do, it's not just up to me?" Before a spell of front-line duty, he calls us all together: "Attention! Stand easy! Until now we've just been servicemen; now we're going to be fighting troops. Perhaps I'll be the first one to fall. I'm sure ninety per cent of you . . ." We turned pale: we thought he meant "ninety per cent of you won't come back". But no: "I'm sure ninety per cent of you would go and find me in the enemy lines, if I should fall there. I ask one thing only, that's not to close my eyes on German soil. Vive la France!" Colonel Deligne was furious with him, he told him: "Consider yourself morally punished." Eight days later, when there was some cock-up, he flew off the handle and swore: "Christ in Heaven, I don't want to be punished twice. I've already been punished morally, and that's quite enough!" ' I can just picture Paul – an officer torn between his fear and his socialist conscience.

Speaking of Paul, apparently he twice broke into sobs after I left. On the evening I left, he received a letter from his wife informing him that his son was a bit over-tired. First sobs. The next day he receives a telegram, turns pale, and fidgets about with it for ten minutes without daring to open it. Pieter says to him in annoyance: 'Open it.' He ends up tearing it almost in half, before reading a few anodine words: his wife has landed a secondary-school post, at Châteauroux, I think. He'd feared the worst. He collapses and sobs 'like a woman', says Pieter indignantly.

To return to my chasseurs, someone asks if they've been under attack. 'We thought we were. Once there was a tremendous fusillade, we dived for our weapons, orders were screamed at us, and then afterwards we were told it had all been in another sector. But we found the real story out next day, from a sentry who heard the Captain saying to a warrant-officer: "What rogues! Fifteen hundred rounds loosed off, just to create the right atmosphere for them." '

I don't say it's true. But what's certainly true is that they all think so. Same impression yesterday evening, having supper with some other chasseurs. They don't really believe in a spring offensive, but they're fed up. Most of them say: 'The collapse will come from within. On both sides.'

The Warrant-officer has changed his tune. He imagines an expeditionary corps will be sent to Finland and he'll be with it. 'I'll go,' he says, 'and trim Uncle Joe Stalin's whiskers.'

My comment yesterday about unrealizables could give rise to confusion. What is unrealizable is never an *object*. It is a *situation*. It's not Paris, but being-in-Paris, with respect to which the question of the unrealizable is posed.

A warrant-officer, who seeks out our company because he has an unfortunate taste for intelligence, tells Pieter how he used to have a 'lovely interior' in a region of Alsace that is now evacuated. 'I'd bought some fine pieces of furniture and made myself a lovely little boudoir, with couches and twelve dolls. Oh, my dear fellow! When I went back there, just the other day, I wept to see it. They'd wrecked everything — if I'd found a soldier, I'd have strung him up. And they'd sat my lovely dolls down in a circle, and crapped in the middle!'

Hang has lost his morale, his leave has laid him low. He wants to report sick and says, shaking his head: 'If things go on this way without any real fighting, we'll be having a revolution and it'll start with the Army.'

Violent frenzy of gloom caused by a letter that wasn't what it should have been. I go for a walk to calm down. Crossing the village, I arrive at the top of a broad, winding road with a steep slope. Soldiers, girls and children are careering down it at top speed on toboggans. Often four or five toboggans are joined together to make a little bobsleigh. Half these conveyances overturn, amid laughter, on the way down. Both sides of the road are thronged with soldiers, like spectators at Chamonix for the ski-jumping events. When the toboggans go by, they laughingly pelt them with snowballs. Pang of regret for ski-ing. I return home quite calmed down. I take this opportunity of noting that such black fits recur often enough with me to constitute a character trait.

I feel strangely bashful about embarking on a study of temporality. Time has always struck me as a philosophical headache, and I've inadvertently gone in for a philosophy of the instant (which Koyré reproached me for one evening in June '39[33]) — as a result of not

33. Alexandre Koyré (1882–1964), philosopher of history, was editor of *Recherches philosophiques*, which in 1936 had published Sartre's essay on the transcendental Ego.

understanding duration. In *La Nausée*, I assert that the past is not; and earlier I tried to reduce memory to a true fiction. In my lectures I used to exaggerate the share of reconstruction in remembrance, because reconstruction operates *in the present*. This incomprehension perfectly matched my lack of solidarity with myself, which led me to judge my dead past insolently from the vantage-point of my present. The difficulties of a theory of memory, combined with the influence of Husserl, decided me to endow the past with a certain kind of existence: to wit, existence in the *past*. And I accepted this new idea all the more easily in that I was extremely embarrassed and put out to see myself as the sole instantaneist cast among contemporary philosophies which are all philosophies of time. I tried in *La Psyché* to derive time dialectically from freedom. For me, it was a bold gesture. But all that wasn't yet ripe. And, behold, I now glimpse a theory of time! I feel intimidated before expounding it, I feel like a kid.

Let me first observe that time is not originally of the same nature as the in-itself. So it is neither an environment, nor a framework, nor an a priori form of sentience, nor a law of development. It is, in fact, entirely numbed by Nothingness. If I consider it from one point of view, it *is*; and if I consider it from another point of view, it is not: the future *is not yet*, and the past *is no longer*, the present vanishes into an infinitesimal point, time is now but a dream.

I see clearly, too, that time is not – as contemporary theories would have us believe – of the same nature as the for-itself. I'm not *in* time, that's for sure. But I'm not my own time either, in the way that Heidegger means. Otherwise there would be a temporal translucidity coinciding with the translucidity of consciousness; consciousness would be time, inasmuch as it would be consciousness of time. But it's not the same with time as with pleasure, which can only exist for consciousness if it is consciousness. I have no need to make myself into time in order to be temporal. Time is the opaque limit of consciousness. It is, moreover, an indiscernible opacity in a total translucidity. All our acts presuppose a preontological understanding of time; on the other hand, one can thematize time – make it the object of a theory. But time is neither *before us*, like an object from the world, nor ourselves, inasmuch as we are *for-itself*. It cannot be the object of an intuition, as Bergson would have it; but nor can it be a situation, in the sense in which the situation exists only to be surpassed. Yet we *are* time, but do not *temporalize* ourselves. In fact, time appears to us only thanks to the *past* or the *future*: it is not given us to live it in its continual flow. Thus, to the extent that we *are* time, we *are* something in another mode than that of the for-itself. And yet this something is *nothing*: if we turn towards it to grasp it, it is atomized into a punctiform present, into what is no longer and into what is not yet. It first appears as the nothing separating consciousness from its motives and its essence. It does not seem distinct from the process of nihilation of the in-itself into a for-itself: I escape *in time* from my own motives; *in time* from my essence, since it is *what has been*: 'Wesen ist was gewesen ist'.[34] Yet it obviously is not the same thing, since I am my own nothingness while I am not my own time. If you prefer, there is no difference between nihilation and temporalization, except that the for-itself nihilates it*self* but *is* temporalized. And yet, though existentially distinct, nihilation and temporalization are given in one and the same movement. Time is the facticity of nihilation. Our temporality and our facticity are one and the same thing.

I'll go on tomorrow.

Civilian's view. Madame X says to my mother: 'They shouldn't allow them any leave, really, because they only go back with lower morale.'

19 February

Mistler isn't here any more. He was in the '22 enrolment, and they transferred him out soon after Keller, as a secretary at the 5th Army HQ at Wangenbourg.

I'm reading higgledy-piggledy (having begun them all simultaneously):

    Plutarque a menti: Pierrefeu
    La Siège de Paris: Duveau
    Bismarck: Ludwig
    La Guerre de 70: Chuquet

I've also begun Goethe's *Dichtung und Wahrheit* in German, discovered in our hosts' bookshelves. In reserve: a *Marat* by somebody or other picked up fom the Beaver's bedroom, and some extracts from Saint-Simon on the Regency.[35]

I return to time. The irruption of the for-itself into Being as nihilation

34. 'Essence is what is been' or 'is as having been'.

35. *Dichtung und Wahrheit* (1811–33), autobiographical work, translated as *Poetry and Truth: From my own Life*, London 1908.

Louis de Rouvroy, duc de Saint-Simon (1675–1755), memorialist; hostile to the bourgeois administrators of Louis XIV's reign, and sympathetic to the interests of the nobility, he played some role in the political life of the Regency of the Duc d'Orléans (1715–23), but then withdrew from public life to concentrate on the preparation of his *Mémoires* (1740–50), which covered the last years of Louis XIV's reign and the Regency.

of the in-itself is characterized as an existential mode irreducible to the in-itself. The for-itself is being which, in its being, is not what it is and is what it is not. It would be fruitless to seek, by expressions like 'state of consciousness', to *reduce* the for-itself's mode of being: it escapes the in-itself in every direction; it is the in-itself nihilated. And – though appearing against a background of in-itself; though synthetically bound to the in-itself by the very negation of it that it effects – it escapes it precisely because it nihilates it.

For example, the for-itself could not be grasped without the extension of which it is negation. It is dependent on the in-itself, by virtue of the very fact that it exists as escaping from it. From another point of view, however, this dependence is nevertheless total independence, since the for-itself is constituted with respect to extension as that which is not extension. It *makes itself* unextendedness; it is its own non-extension. All this we have already explained. But the in-itself recaptures the for-itself as a by-effect, by virtue of the fact that *it is* of a certain in-itself that the for-itself is nihilation. In a word, the for-itself (which is nihilation of the in-itself and nothing other than this nihilation), inasmuch as it is for-itself, appears in the unity of the in-itself as a certain existent belonging to the totality through a phenomenon of synthetic connection.

The *outside* of the for-itself is to *be*, as negation of the in-itself, in the same way as the in-itself. This is what we termed facticity. But this very facticity, which is only a necessary reflection of the in-itself upon the for-itself, could not have the same substantiality as the in-itself on pain of clogging the for-itself. It frolics on the surface of the for-itself, and is a kind of insubstantial phantom of in-itself. In a word, in order to make itself nihilation of the in-itself, inside and outside its own self, it's not enough for the for-itself to have solely the synthetic relation of negation with the in-itself; it's necessary for it to be recaptured by that in-itself, in the guise of a synthetic unity *coming this time from the in-itself*. These conditions are realized since nihilation occurs in the midst of the in-itself, and the for-itself can not be seen as constituting itself by a leap *out* of the in-itself, but rather *within* the in-itself like a canker.

I shall compare this 'in-itself', that comes to tinge the for-itself and constitute an exterior for it, to those reflections one can see on a window-pane when viewing it from an angle and which suddenly mask its transparency – only to vanish as soon as one changes position in relation to the pane. This description seems to me most accurately to convey the fact that it is always permissible for me to assert that Pieter's consciousness *exists*, and that it is bound by a certain relationship of coexistence with these tables, these glasses and my consciousness, even though it hasn't at all the same mode of existence as the tables, the glasses and the walls. However, that evanescent, iridescent, mobile reflection of the in-itself, which frolics on the surface of the for-itself and which I term facticity – that totally *insubstantial* reflection – cannot be viewed in the same way as the opaque, compact existence of *things*. The being-in-itself of the for-itself, in its indiscernible reality, is what we shall term the *event*.

The event is not an accident, or something that occurs within the framework of temporality. The event is the existential characteristic of consciousness inasmuch as it is recaptured by the in-itself. For example, this pleasure I feel exists only inasmuch as I am conscious of it, and its deep existence is that of the mirror-play of reflected-reflection. But *the fact that* this pleasure, which is such that its being is involved in its being – should be in the mode of the for-itself – now that's what we shall call the event. And the connection of being which, in the unity of the in-itself, joins from without *this* for-itself to the inner depths of the in-itself, is *simultaneity*.

Simultaneity is not – any more than the event is – something occurring within constituted time: for example, the contingent fact for several objects of finding themselves in the same present. On the contrary, it is an existential characteristic that will be constitutive of time: the necessity for a for-itself to coexist, inasmuch as it is tinged with in-itself, with the totality of in-itself whose negation it makes itself. The in-itself of the nihilation of the in-itself is the event; the unity of the nihilated in-itself with the in-itself of the nihilation of *that* in-itself, is simultaneity.

Yet with respect to the in-itself which it is, the for-itself can be only in the guise of nihilation. This means that the facticity of the for-itself is at once nihilated; or rather, that the for-itself cannot be a for-itself without giving itself to itself as separated from that facticity by *nothing*. Facticity is never *given* to the for-itself as forming the outside that the for-itself *is*; it is present to the for-itself only insofar as the latter already negates it, in a very special way, as what it itself is *no longer*. The for-itself can be only by escaping the being that it is; and this flight of nothingness before the in-itself constitutes temporality. For if we consider this in-itself, which can never take shape without the for-itself escaping it, it is surely necessary to conceive that the for-itself can never escape it without being recovered by the in-itself of the event and of simultaneity. The for-itself can escape from the in-itself only into the in-itself.

Thus what is termed the present – in other words, the event in simultaneity – never has any substantiality; it is on the point of vanishing, its being coincides with its evanescence – otherwise, the in-itself would belime the for-itself entirely. In this sense, every present gives itself as *negated past*; my present is the negation of what *I am*; every present defines itself as separated by *nothing* from a 'has been' – the 'has been' being as close to the present as you like. But by virtue of this the rejected for-itself, posited as having-been, is recaptured bodily and totally belimed by the in-itself. The past is an in-itself which was once for-itself. It's here that we can understand the meaning of 'which *was*'. The difference between the negation of extension by the for-itself, and the negation of the for-itself by itself, is entirely given by this fact: that in the former case consciousness is not what it is not, whereas in the latter case it is not what it is.

However, it is necessary to distinguish further: the *present* being of the for-itself is characterized, in its existential actuality, as not being what it is. It is in the midst of the for-itself that nihilation *is been*. The case of the past is different: it is intermediary between the nihilation which escapes, for example, from extension and the interstructural nihilation of the for-itself. To say of the for-itself that it was, is to say that it is not what it is in the same way that it is not what it is not. In other words, it *makes itself* in the totality of its for-itself other than what it is in totality. In that case, the former for-itself is entirely preserved, it still exists: it even gives its meaning to the present for-itself as that which is negated, that which is surpassed, that and not anything else – and the present for-itself precisely escapes the former for-itself only by *being nothing*.

However, this negation maintains the deeper unity of the for-itself: I can escape the past only by not being what *I* am. And, concurrently, the former for-itself undergoes an essential modification. It is not annihilated, quite the contrary: only a consciousness can be nihilated, and this nihilation precisely defines its present. It is not annihilated, but it is recovered by the in-itself. Not at all for any mystical reason, but because – *before* the pure event or nihilation as *afterwards* – there is everywhere only the in-itself. So the past has over consciousness all the superiority of substantiality and solidity – of opacity too – which the in-itself confers upon it. It is only in the past that consciousness can exist in the mode of the in-itself; and the past is nothing other than the for-itself's existence in the mode of the in-itself.

Yet the existence of the in-itself (formerly for-itself) and of the present for-itself is not *co*-existence, precisely because the present for-itself, in its totality, excludes the former one. Thus the mode in which the for-itself is vested by the for-itself which it was isn't '*presence*', in the sense in which we defined it for the world. It is precisely the *past*. And since this immediate past is negation of a more distant past, and so on and so forth, it is by this nihilation of the total bloc of the past it *has been* that the present for-itself defines itself, in its presence. Thus the question cannot arise of knowing why freedom cannot escape this past, or give us another past – since, precisely, we are free *with respect to* this past. If it weren't freedom with respect to something, freedom would no longer mean anything.

Thus a first description shows that the for-itself could not irrupt into the world, without coexistence in the present with the totality of the in-itself, and without a precise connection with a having-been that it simultaneously *is* and *is not*. What about the future at present? The for-itself can be vested by the in-itself only by surpassing it towards the *causa sui* that it is-about-to-be. The for-itself flees the in-itself through the in-itself towards the in-itself. The *causa sui* is given as soon as the for-itself irrupts into the in-itself: not as an *object*, nor as a *representation*, nor as a thematized *value*, but as that towards which the for-itself flees its facticity. Impossible synthesis of in-itself and for-itself, of total opacity and total freedom, the *causa sui* is at once that towards which the flight is made, whereby the for-itself tears itself away from itself, and that towards which the surpassing of the in-itself constituted in this world is accomplished. The *causa sui* is the *meaning of the world*: the world discloses it and makes itself world by disclosing it; it's by it that, as soon as the for-itself irrupts into the in-itself, the in-itself is *humanized* and *worldified* (which comes to the same thing). Yet the *causa sui* does not belong to us as forming one body with our pro-ject. It is the transcendent unity of the project whereby the for-itself escapes-from-itself towards . . . But of its essence it must remain out of reach.

As I have already said, the nihilation of the in-itself into for-itself is not a *withdrawal* in face of the in-itself. It is, rather, a collapse – a decompression. The for-itself is unextended insofar as it is *nothing*. But it *is* not even this nothing; it will not be found to possess even the substantiality of being *nothing*. The nothing is flight of the nothing towards the *causa sui*, nihilation of the nothing towards the in-itself. The future is the world inasmuch as it is human; it's the world inasmuch as the *ens causa sui* is its meaning, as that towards which the for-itself flees from itself. One must not confuse the world with the in-itself. The world is the in-itself *for* the for-itself. Similarly, the future is not the in-itself. The future is the world. A for-itself, whatever it may be, grasps an aspect of the world only as an opportunity to annihilate in the in-itself the lack that it itself is. Whatever the object considered may be, it is a plea to the for-itself to project itself beyond it as *causa sui*. Were it an armchair that 'stretches out its arms to us', to have the project of sitting down in it is to project oneself into that armchair as the existent which has determined itself to exist as seated in an armchair, and which will exist as seated with the plenitude of the in-itself. The for-itself can project everything ahead of it, except the fact that – wherever it goes and whatever it does – it will still be a for-itself.

Thus the irruption of the for-itself into the in-itself at a stroke causes temporality to appear, with its triple dimension of present, past and future. Temporality is neither in-itself nor for-itself; it is the way in which the in-itself recaptures itself from the for-itself – or, if you prefer, the for-itself's existence in itself. It is insofar as the for-itself in flight – fleeing towards the future from the facticity that has recaptured it – is nonetheless facticity, that without being its own temporality the for-itself *is* nonetheless temporality. It is in-itself nihilated between an in-itself that it is no longer (one mustn't say that the past is no longer, but that *we* are no longer the past in the mode of the for-itself) and an in-itself that it is not yet (same remark for the future). And its nature is to be nihilating present ceaselessly escaping from itself towards the future, ceaselessly recaptured by the in-itself.

The exact mode of being of the past and future remains to be determined. In any case, we can say that temporality irrupts into the world with the for-itself. If consciousness is, as Valéry says, an absence, temporality is the adherence of this absence as such to the world.[36]

36, Perhaps refers to a passage in 'Fragments du Narcisse' (*Poésies*, Paris 1942, p. 105): 'Gardez-moi longuement ce visage pour songe/Qu'une absence divine est seule à concevoir!'

NOTEBOOK 12
FEBRUARY 1940
BOUXWILLER

Tuesday, 20 February

I rather think I was authentic before my leave. Probably because I was alone. In Paris, I was not authentic. At present, I'm no longer anything. This leads me to clarify a few points regarding authenticity. First of all, the following: authenticity is achieved en bloc, one either is or is not authentic. But that doesn't at all mean that one acquires authenticity once and for good. I've already pointed out that the present has no purchase on the future, nor the past on the present. According to Gide, one does not 'benefit by acquired momentum' in moral conduct, any more than in the novel. And the authenticity of your previous momentum doesn't protect you in any way against falling next instant into the inauthentic. The most one can say is that it's less difficult to preserve authenticity than to acquire it. But, in fact, can one even talk about 'preserving'? The instant that arrives is novel, the situation is novel: a new authenticity has to be invented. It's still the case, people will say, that the memory of the authentic must protect us somewhat from inauthenticity. But the memory of the authentic, in inauthenticity, is itself inauthentic.

This leads me to clarify also what I said about the desire for authenticity. It is customary to consider that this desire for authenticity is 'something, after all – better than nothing'. In this way, the continuity at first set aside is reintroduced, unobtrusively and by a roundabout route. A distinction will then be made between inauthentic beings wallowing in their inauthenticity, those whom an already meritorious desire torments in their mire and, lastly, those who enjoy the authentic. But this detour will bring us back to the morality of the virtues. It must be said, there are just two alternatives: either the desire for authenticity torments us in the midst of inauthenticity, and then it's itself inauthentic; or else it's already full authenticity, though it's unaware of itself and hasn't yet taken stock of itself. There's no room for a third estate.

I see, for example, how L.'s desire for authenticity is poisoned by inauthenticity.[1] She'd like to be authentic, from affection for us, from trust in us, in order to join us – and also from an idea of merit. She suffers at seeing a supreme value posited that is alien to her; she'd like to be authentic, just as she might want to become a good skier or a clever philosopher. It seems to her, too, that if she acquired this authenticity she'd *merit* more from life and from men. And doubtless she has clearly understood that the authentic man rejects a priori any idea of merit; but she cannot rid herself of the idea that he's all the more meritorious in his very manner of refusing merit. I see only a totally poisoned desire there; one which, whatever plane of reflection one views it on, remains poisoned through and through. And I don't even say that, given the right circumstances, this desire might not be the occasion for a total transformation that would precisely confer authenticity. I say only that it cannot of itself lead to the authentic. It must be recovered and transformed within an already authentic consciousness.

On the other hand, I can very well imagine how authenticity acquired through a free mutation may first manifest itself in the guise of a desire for authenticity. So this expresses merely the fact that the cause is won. For though authenticity is all of a piece, it isn't enough to have acquired it once, in respect of a particular, concrete circumstance, in order for it to extend itself spontaneously to all the situations into which we are plunged. For example, I can imagine someone being called up who was a highly inauthentic bourgeois, who used to live inauthentically in all the various social situations into which he was thrown – family, job, etc. I can grant that the shock of war may suddenly have induced him to a conversion towards the authentic, which leads him to be authentically *in situation* vis-à-vis the war. But this authenticity, if it is *true*, needs to conquer new territory. It first presents itself in the form of a desire to revise old situations in the light of this change. It first gives itself as anxiety and critical desire. Here, this way of *extending* authenticity mustn't be confused in any sense with an increase in authenticity. The authenticity *is already there*. Only it must be consolidated and extended.

The question wouldn't present itself in that way if the previously experienced situations were present. But they've receded. The person who has been called up is no longer 'a family man', he's no longer practising his profession, etc. He's led to *think* about those situations,

---

1. L. = 'Lise Oblanoff', or Nathalie Sorokine (see De Beauvoir, *The Prime of Life*, pp.347–8 and *Lettres au Castor*, pp.484, 503, etc.); or 'Louise Védrine', see p.119n.

to make resolutions for the future, and to establish guidelines for *keeping* authenticity as he moves on to other events. The desire to acquire authenticity, ultimately, is only a desire to see things more clearly and not lose it. And resistance comes, not from residues of inauthenticity which may remain here and there in a badly dusted-off consciousness, but simply from the fact that his previous situations resist the change as *things*. He has lived them until then in a certain way, and by living them he has *constituted* them. They have become *institutions*: they have their own permanence outside him, and they even evolve in spite of him. It is necessary to *call* into question. The desire to call into question, if it is sincere, can appear only against a background of authenticity. And it's not enough to call into question: it's necessary to change. But the revolutionary changes revealed by a struggle against the solidity of institutions are no different, in nature, from the changes a politician wishes to introduce into social institutions – and they encounter the same resistance.

So it is by no means enough to be authentic: it's necessary to adapt one's life to one's authenticity. Whence that deep desire, that fear and that anguish at the heart of all authenticity – which are apprehensions *before life*. Yet it must be clearly understood that authenticity cannot be divided. This fear is due to the fact that the situations envisaged are on the horizon, out of reach; to the fact that one will encounter them later, without being immersed in them for the time being. Whoever one is, there are always a large number of faraway situations on the horizon, about which one 'worries' in the authentic. But if one of those situations is assumed to re-form unexpectedly around me, and if I'm authentic, I shall show myself to be authentic without stopping to think of this restored situation – without needing to prepare any transition – simply because I *am* so.

If, for example, the wife of this person who has been called up comes to visit him at the front, he'll be *different* with her – without any effort or premeditation or thematic preparation – simply because he *is* different. But, you may say, she'll very soon present him with the image of his former inauthenticity. Yes – and that will be the touchstone, not of his actual authenticity, but of how determined he is to cling to it. Perhaps he'll yield, but he can't revert to his old errors vis-à-vis that woman without, at a stroke, tumbling headlong into inauthenticity – and even his very being-in-war will thereby be affected. For, presumably, a being who expects the inauthentic of us will freeze us to the marrow with inauthenticity, by reviving our old love. It's an imposed inauthenticity, against which it is easy but painful to defend oneself.

If the war doesn't last too long, I'm very afraid, since my leave, of finding myself just as I was last year, at the rendezvous I'd fixed with myself for after the war.

Pierrefeu, agreeing with Gide, writes in *Plutarque a menti*: 'I assert it as a fact that any man of average intelligence, without possessing any special aptitude, but simply by the exercise of his intellectual faculties, can easily grasp the points of any military problem. He, as well as a specialist – and perhaps better – can perceive what is true and what is false in a tactical or strategical situation, provided that no particularly technical questions are raised. And, in any case, these latter only lead the mind astray on points of detail and obscure a view of the whole problem and its main issues.'[2]

He shows very well, moreover, how the '14 General Staff defended itself against the ruinous, Cartesian right of free inquiry by resorting to Bergsonian intuition. Being unable to base its superiority upon technical expertise, it sought to ground it upon priestly infallibility. In one way or another, the General Staff had to be a body of initiates. The '14 war caused it to lose its infallibility. The men nowadays no longer have that religious trust in their generals. To tell the truth, they have no trust of any kind. They're convinced that a total war is won for economic and political reasons; and as for military victories, they think that superiority of armaments alone decides them. I've never heard anybody mention Gamelin, here.[3] Never – not even to say something bad about him. He doesn't exist at all. It's not that there's any mistrust towards the leaders. They're accepted democratically as elected functionaries. There have to be some. Those or others . . . And our right-thinking people of today probably have no idea of the blow they're inflicting on the military priesthood, when they write that in modern warfare organization is far more important than strategy. For a man of average intelligence, dedicated, hard-working and well backed up by subordinates of the same kind, can always organize. Since, moreover, routine organization is always scandalously bad in the army, the conclusion is soon drawn.

One marvels that in the *Revue de Paris* for 15 February 1920, an anonymous follower of military doctrine (a senior officer, obviously) should still have dared to write: 'Progress in armament itself favours the offensive at the expense of the defensive.'[p.40]

2. Jean de Pierrefeu, *Plutarch Lied*, London 1924, p. 58.
3. Maurice-Gustave Gamelin (1872–1958), General, Commander-in-chief of the allied armed forces from September 1939 to May 1940.

This excellent passage on p. 119 [106] (the German generals are beating the retreat after the battle of the Marne): 'The military convention compels any army whose flanks are threatened to regard itself as in an inferior position, and without delay they conformed to the rule, thus assuring our complete victory and the safety of their own army. We shall see, in what follows, that all convention was abolished and that the struggle lasted for years without a thought being given to any rule. The fatal principle of the war of attrition was substituted for the idea of manoeuvre and marked the most astonishing retrogression in military art that has ever been seen.'

Oh yes, military art is dead and war is dying. It's a largely impossible war, this 1940 one. Hitler felt this, but he saw in it only the death of a *certain form* of war, since to his eyes war is in effect the eternal form of human relations. And at once, his self-taught inventor's mind turned towards invention: inventing a new form of war. I must admit, what he said to Rauschning about 'his' war didn't much impress me. It's all just puerilities and well-worn methods. Propaganda warfare was already intensive in '14–'18, espionage was intensive as well. As for attacking the enemy from within, the German General Staff had this idea too when it introduced Lenin into Russia.

Elsewhere he indicates that a war of all-out offensive was required for domestic political reasons. The author of the 15 February 1920 article writes: 'Was it not agreed that the national enthusiasm must not be depressed, nor the general confidence shaken, by adopting a timid, hesitating attitude at the beginning of a campaign which it was felt would be decisive?' [ibid.] Well, I read in Duveau and Chuquet that in '70 like considerations prevented MacMahon's army from falling back on Paris, where it could have waited at its leisure for the enemy to attack.[4] Marching on Metz was madness; but the country would not have tolerated a withdrawal and endless wait before the walls of Paris. The same anxiety – repeated at the distance of half a century, and in both cases provoking disasters – allows one to gauge the alteration in public opinion over the past few years.

Granted, everyone is convinced today that it's easier to sustain defensive than offensive operations; and this somewhat abstract thought is illustrated for the simplest of minds by the existence of two lines – the Maginot and the Siegfried. But all the same, the old civil wisdom of military men – which used to impel them into military follies – taught them that there's an enormous risk in confining a

4. Georges Duveau, *Le Siège de Paris*, Paris 1939; Arthur Chuquet, *La Guerre 1870–71*, Paris 1899.

nation one has unleashed for war to inglorious waiting and defensive operations. It's necessary for blood to flow, in order as quickly as possible to put something irreparable behind the soldiers, to block their way. It's necessary to impel men despite themselves, taking advantage of their first impetus, into the intoxication of victory or the complicity of defeat. It's now known that those useless, arduous raids from trench to trench, which so angered the soldiers between '15 and '18, were aimed primarily at keeping up morale: in other words, fierceness of temper. Alain has shown convincingly how the enemy is quite indispensable to the smooth running of the military machine. He is the target of the forward rush. His pressure, by counter-balancing the pressure which the domestic front exerts upon the soldier, determines the *tension* in him which is, precisely, the military spirit. So long as blood has not flowed, the domestic front doesn't take the war seriously.

Well, it's been six months now that our army has been on a war footing. The men are being held far away from their homes and their jobs, and are subject to military discipline. A dictatorship is exercised over the press, over speech and over thought. Our whole life has the external aspect of war. But the war machine is running in neutral; the enemy is elusive and invisible; the men stand waiting at attention. The whole army is waiting, in that 'hesitant, timid' attitude that the generals wanted to avoid like the plague. Or rather, the attitude isn't even defensive, since to be on the defensive it's necessary for the enemy to attack, or think of attacking. But for six months now the Germans have been resting. Intent on exploiting the situation to the maximum, they've displayed placards everywhere protesting their desire for peace. Besides, they didn't declare war on us; on the contrary, they were declaring peace as they invaded Poland – and we're the aggressors. We simply sent an ultimatum, and on receipt of a blunt rejection went to war. What is one to say of a war in which the aggressor doesn't attack? Much worse, as soon as the enemy showed his teeth – in other words, as soon as he'd finished with Poland – we made haste to return those few square kilometres we had been occupying in the Saar. Waiting, timidity, hesitation, withdrawal: the General Staff has deliberately accepted it all. The tenth part of it wouldn't have been required to bring on the revolution in '70, to unleash patriotic or socialist passions in 1914.

And the truth is, this waiting – which isn't even waiting for anything, since many people think the Germans won't attack – hasn't failed to have its effect: the civilians are losing interest in us; we ourselves are hardly thinking about the Germans with offensive intentions. Many people are hoping for an 'arrangement'. Only yesterday a sergeant was telling me, with a gleam of inane hope in his eyes: 'What I think is, it'll all be arranged, England will climb down.' Most of the men are fairly receptive to the Hitler propaganda. They're getting bored, 'morale' is sinking. And yet, just imagine the amazement of the soldiers in '14 if, two or three days after their clamorous departure, they'd found themselves plunged into interminable, inglorious waiting. As for us, we accept it and nobody protests. On the contrary, it's never on that score that we do protest. Most of us resignedly envisage spending three or four years in this way; whereafter, if to try them out I tell them 'It's still better than a massacre', they all say 'Oh, of course'. Nothing shows better that the war mentality is on the way to disappearing in France.

It would be wrong to conclude from this, as some imbeciles do, that we're degenerating. The men have had a very tough time of it from the first, and they've borne everything without complaining, or even thinking they had any right to complain. They weren't sustained by any patriotic or ideological ideal. They didn't like Hitlerism, but they weren't wild about democracy either – and they didn't give a bugger about Poland. Into the bargain, they had the vague impression of having been tricked. Yet they endured everything with a kind of undemonstrative dignity, simply because it was there. They had no impatience for victory, simply a profound desire for 'it all to end'. To this new situation – this elusive war that can surprise them in their *thoughts* – they are profoundly *adapted* in their *being*. It really is *their* war: this war of patience – with no military art, nothing holy, no carnage (so far, of course) – in which they have the impression they're not even the main element, they're simply makeweights, devoid of the warrior's glorious status.

Regarding the passage from Pierrefeu quoted earlier (*Plutarque*, p. 119), I imagine that's what inspired a number of remarks by Romains which I must have recorded in my notebooks, and which contrast the conventional *game* of war, in the days of military art, to total war conceived as an effort without convention – without any convention – and without art.

All happiness has to be paid for, and there's no affair that doesn't end badly. I don't write this in the pathetic mode, but simply and bluntly, because I've always thought it and because I really had to say it here. It hasn't prevented me from throwing myself into affairs; but I was always convinced they would end sordidly, and happiness has never befallen me without my thinking at once about what would come to pass *afterwards*.

Pierrefeu 200 et. seq.: 'It is true that there can be no military art without a minimum of conventions which must be accepted by both sides. But from the day when war ceases to be a game between professionals, that is to say, when it becomes national, conventions are no longer respected and military art ceases to exist' [p. 179]. With the continuous front, 'the whole edifice of past experience crumbled away and became no more than rubbish – useless and objectless. Of what use now was manoeuvre? There were no longer flanks. What use to guess one's adversary's plans? There were no plans. What meaning now had those laborious treatises on the approach battle, or the rules governing the employment of advance-guards, rear-guards or main bodies? Troops established face to face along hundreds of kilometres of front and shooting at each other at close range – it was to this that military art had been reduced' [pp. 155–6]. 'From all evidence modern war has not found a form which suits it and which will make it less murderous and shorter . . . We have reached the opening phases of a new military art, a fresh beginning. The Great War will appear to people in the future as an unshaped model, a first rough proof, as it were, of the industrialized war which the progress of science and industry has imposed upon the nations' [p. 180].

No doubt, but there's a contradiction in these lines. A military art like any other art, as Pierrefeu tells us, rests upon conventions. But a *national* war rejects every convention on principle. What results is the end of military art beyond all chance of resurrection, far more than any possible transformation. It would be better to say: the era of national wars has rendered military art impossible.

And where does that leave us, in this present war? Well, we're starting off with a continuous front, just as in 1915 – it's simply better laid out and more inhabitable. Only we've recognized on both sides that it's quite useless *fighting* on a continuous front, since there are no wings to outflank or breakthrough to be achieved. So we no longer do anything at all.

Two scouts and two infantrymen, who do not know each other, are having lunch next to Pieter. They start off by scoffing sourly at the 35th Division which replaced ours at Wissembourg: 'Those buggers from Bordeaux, we held the sector for two months, and all they've been able to do is lose two kilometres (?) as soon as they arrived!' Strange corporate and regional pride. Whereupon they fall out among themselves, the scouts saying to the infantrymen: 'We're the ones who've got most to do!' and the infantrymen retorting: 'It's us what's in most danger!' They almost come to blows, but Pieter says to them sharply: 'You're dead right, we're all in the shit, aren't we!' Then they calm down abruptly and offer him a drink.

Klein's wife, a nurse at the Strasbourg hospital, which has been moved a few kilometres back from the front, goes down with a sudden attack of appendicitis. But there's only one surgeon in this mixed hospital, where they treat both civilians and soldiers – and his situation is somewhat odd. Disabled and declared unfit for service, he's not been called up, though very young, he's been requisitioned. This makes him very gloomy, moreover: if he was an M.O., he'd get army pay; as a civilian, he operates all day long for the army – and for nothing. For every operation, he has to request authorization from the military command. He examines Mme Klein and decides on an urgent emergency operation. But the authorization takes 48 hours to come through and Mme Klein dies on the operating table.

The past could exist only as a for-itself's past. Only for-itselfs can have a past, and the mode of being of this past is very particular. No doubt, it's first and foremost an in-itself. The in-itself has here entirely recovered the for-itself, to the point of suppressing it. But it has nevertheless been a for-itself fleeing the in-itself towards the world and towards the future. So it has the dual character of being an immobilized, paralysed for-itself – a for-itself become a thing, in other words a petrified event – and a 'having-had-a-future' (whether or not that future has been realized). In this *real* guise, the existence of the past becomes non-thematic. And we carry all our past behind us, as that which we are no longer. If we thematize that past, it becomes imaginary.

Wednesday, 21 February

How this present war does resemble the '14 one, more than at first appears! Pierrefeu 204: 'The attrition of Germany! So it was that upon which we were depending! It was at this moment that the formula was evolved: "Time works for us." The superiority in resources of all kinds of the nations of the Entente was so evident that final success seemed evident, too. And the statistics of losses compiled by military intelligence showed that an effort was being made, even at the cost of a few mistakes, to give a solid foundation for this belief. The attrition of the enemy – that was the sole outcome which the Staff perceived in this interminable war . . . But here is a conception which is destructive of military art and which, in fact, totally denies its existence' [p.182].

But what is our hope in 1940? Just the same: we're hoping the enemy will wear himself out. I've just read an article by Pierre Cot in today's *L'Oeuvre*, in which he writes: 'France and England, connected by sea to the United States, are better placed for a war of attrition than Germany, connected to the Soviet Union by the Baltic and a poor network of railroads . . . I am convinced that we shall win the long war . . . Preparing for a long war of attrition is the best way of making this war of attrition as short as possible . . . '

The very term is borrowed from the earlier war, as well as the thing. Attrition is simply no longer attrition in men and matériel, but (so far) only attrition in matériel. At the same time, more concern is shown (and this is the meaning of Pierre Cot's article) about organizing resistance to attrition inside the belligerent countries: 'One can see how necessary it is to have an economic policy oriented towards exports. Any policy that consisted in saying: "Everything – credits and specialists – for the war industry; nothing for exporting industry" would be madness.' But the essential principle remains the same. And it couldn't be otherwise, since in national wars there are no longer any rules of the game. Each country can hold out – to the point of ruin. So it's this slow ruin that both sides are indeed seeking to achieve.

Reading Pierrefeu's excellent book confirms me in an idea I had in October. It shows how in the '14 war military art lost its conventions. Well, for my part, reflecting on the beginnings of the present one, I thought that we were waging a war in the manner of non-Euclidian mathematics, in which one first recognizes the arbitrary character of every postulate. The '14 war really showed, by a reductio ad absurdum, the existence of a certain number of postulates underpinning military art; postulates which could without difficulty be replaced by others, provided that the adversary adopted these others at the same time. The '15–'18 war was waged without any postulate, but it was also unable any longer to *think* itself. Pierrefeu puts it very well: 'The High Command, in its desire to intellectualize the shapeless matter with which it had to deal, created many such abstractions during the war, but each in its turn proved to be no more substantial than a cloud' [p.270]. At a distance of twenty-five years, the High Command rethinks this war, understands the arbitrary nature of the postulates and makes the concepts more flexible: either by trying to construct them without any postulates, or by utilizing the most *convenient* postulates without deceiving itself about their purely arbitrary value. Whence that expression 'expert war' which I was then using: an 'expert war' which, moreover, when and if the shock of arms occurs, could degenerate into a barbaric mass struggle.

Since I saw Paris again, I feel as though I've buried it. My most recent and tender memories now come to me from this dying Paris. As to that other Paris – the one of my past life – I really think my last links with it have been broken. It's the first time since the beginning of the war that I've been harsh with my past. I no longer care, except about people; and when I think of seeing them again, it's in wartime Paris that I place our meetings. My leave consummated the rupture with my past. So I'm getting things in perspective and one day – perhaps tomorrow – shall be able to say what Paris once was for me. I realize that if I wasn't a patriot, at least I was a communard and a regionalist. Paris was my village, as the song says. As a citizen of Paris, I'd have been a chauvinist.

Reading my notebooks, T. says: 'That surprises me. I'm so used to idiots trying to prove something, that I'm disconcerted by gratuitousness.' That charms me and it's true. Utter gratuitousness of this diary, as of thought in general. I shall write tomorrow about Paris. But why? For no reason, because it amuses me. And nothing here has any reason; it's all a game. Above all, I never force my thought. If I were writing a composed book I should press on, like soldiers in war who are always made to hold out a little longer than they're able. Whereas here I break off as soon as I'm ready to force myself.

Thursday, 22 February

On the nature of the future. The future is a transcendent existent which draws its origin from the for-itself. The in-itself has no future because it is totally *all that it is*, so there is nothing outside it that it could be. The principle of identity as existential law of the in-itself rejects any possibility of a future. The future could exist only as complement of a lack in the present. It is the very signification of this lack. But it's still necessary to define this notion of lack. It's quite astonishing that, in all philosophies and in all psychologies, it should have been possible to describe at length will, desire or passion, without being led to see the essential fact: namely, that none of these phenomena can even be conceived if the being which wills, suffers or desires is not gripped in its being as afflicted by an existential lack.

It is perhaps Christianity which has come closest to this necessary recognition, by showing the human soul as 'animated' by lack of God; and the writings of the mystics abound in striking descriptions of this inner nothingness there is within the heart of man. Yet it must be noted that most Christian thinkers, led astray by their monist conception of being as an *in-itself*, have confused – like Heidegger, moreover – the existential nothingness of human consciousness with its finitude. Now finitude, being an external limit of being, cannot be at the root of lack, which is found at the very heart of consciousness. Whether the latter is to itself its own finitude is a question I don't have to consider here; but what is quite apparent is that desire will never be explained without one having recourse to an existential lack.

If, for example, I look again at those psycho-physiological descriptions of hunger or thirst which have become classic, I see that one must be either very naive or very pig-headed to be satisfied by them. What are we actually shown? A thinning of the blood, for example, as in suffocation; irritation of the bulb by veinous blood, provoking spasmodic contractions of the diaphragm; in the case of hunger, contractions of the tunica, salivation, a nervous erethism provoking chewing motions, etc. This is all very fine, but we're not moving forward, since we're persisting in describing *states* existing in the guise of in-itself, which may well govern each other, but which absolutely could not, in and of themseles, give themselves as *desires*: which no more resemble desire than a vibration of the ether resembles the colour red. And it provides no satisfactory reply to say that consciousness *transforms* this bodily state into desire – apprehends this state in the guise of desire – since, unless a magical power is conferred upon consciousness, we still have to explain why it does not apprehend these bodily modifications in the guise of a *state*. For one would need to be blind not to see that the essential difference between desire and the physiological *state* that is supposed to be its basis is of an existential nature. It's not a matter of saying that desire is something thought, a representation, spiritual, unextended or whatever. If you make it into a *state*, you no longer understand anything. Now, the parallelism is based on the absurd idea that a psychic *state* corresponds to a *state* of the body. But the state thus conceived will never move out of itself to 'need' any transcendent object whatsoever. If we conceive of an organism as a certain type of physiological chain, I can see that if it's deprived of water it will pass through various states to end up in the terminal or dead state. But I don't see how desire comes into this. (I think, incidentally, that there's a profound error in this conception of the organism; but here isn't the place to go into it.)

For there to be desire, it's necessary that the desired object should be concretely present – it and no other – in the innermost depths of the for-itself; but present as a nothingness that affects it or, more accurately, as a lack. And this is possible only if the for-itself, in its very existence, is susceptible of being defined by these lacks. Which means that no lack can come from outside to the for-itself. Just as, in the case of bad faith, lies to oneself are possible only if consciousness is by nature what it is not, so desire is possible only if the for-itself is *by nature* desire – in other words, if it is *lack* by nature. The absurdity of the Schopenhauerian or Nietzschean 'will to power' is that, by conceiving of it as a force, one will never be able to understand that it expresses itself through *desires* or *wills*. It will remain a force and be counterbalanced by antagonistic forces, quite simply. It will be no use saying the forces are 'spiritual', unless one has precisely defined the spirit as the in-itself numbed by Nothingness. So if, at the source of all desires and of will, it's really necessary to posit existential lack as characteristic of consciousness, then we must ask ourselves the two fundamental questions: what is a lack? what is lacking?

Lack obviously belongs to the category of 'not being', in the sense in which 'not being' is a concrete and, so to speak, positive link between the for-itself and some other existent. But it is a particular case of 'not being'. When we say that consciousness is not extended, we don't mean that it *lacks* extension. Let us first observe that lack mustn't be envisaged in the way we may register it from outside – as, for example, when we say that the chair 'lacks' a leg, or that a leg is lacking from the chair.[5] This lack, hypothetical in a certain sense, leaves the chair totally intact with its three legs. It's only if we'd like to sit down that the chair 'will lack' a leg – or rather, at bottom, it's we who'll lack the leg.

This way of envisaging lack has the disadvantages of presenting it as an outside, and ultimately as an aspect of the chair's finitude. We hesitate between the practical conception of the chair, as a tool that lacks an essential part, and the theoretical and contemplative conception of that chair 'in itself': an object which is as it is, with three legs, and which lacks nothing. It's in such terms that we normally conceive

---

5. In this passage, *manquer de* has been translated as 'to lack', though it could also be rendered 'to be missing' something transitively; *manquer à* has been translated as 'to be lacking' or 'to be missing' from something—but, when persons are involved, the one who is the indirect object in French becomes the subject who 'misses' the other in English.

our psychic states: we see them in full as in-itselfs, and from this point of view they lack nothing. But if one replaces them in a complete process, one will observe from outside that they lack something (for example, a person who is away lacks or 'misses' somebody or something). In other words, one thinks: in order to attain the ideal state which they should attain (happiness, ataraxia, etc.[6]), they lack something. But taken as they appear, they are complete. Thus lack is hypothetical, and in a certain way *ad libitum*.[7] They lack something for a third party, who might objectively observe it.

But this is to forget that the for-itself is a being such that its being *is involved* in its being. Nothing comes to it from outside, and a lack for consciousness is consciousness of a lack. Through the interplay of reflection and reflected, the for-itself can only *be for itself its own lack*. So it is existentially defined as lack. To be for-itself is to lack . . . And to lack . . . is defined as: to determine oneself as *not being* that of which the existence would be necessary and sufficient to give one a plenary existence. The for-itself *is not* extended, but it does not lack extension; because, although extension belongs to the in-itself, it is not such that the existence within it of extension could confer upon it the plenary existence of the in-itself. But, on the other hand, the for-itself lacks the *world* (inasmuch as the world *also* comprises extension), because, for the for-itself, the world is the concrete totality of the in-itself that it *is not*. Let us be clear that the for-itself, which is not the world inasmuch as it nihilates itself, determines itself by nihilation as lack of the in-itself – and by so doing determines the in-itself as world. The world is the totality of what the for-itself lacks to become in-itself. And the for-itself's irruption into the world is tantamount to an existential and constitutive auto-determination of the for-itself, as that which *lacks* in-itself in face of the in-itself.

Thus to be consciousness of . . . (in the sense in which Husserl says: 'All consciousness is consciousness *of* something') is to determine oneself for oneself by the interplay of reflection-reflected as *lacking* . . . something. And as I've already said (in my Notebook 3, I think), every consciousness is consciousness of the world, first and foremost. As for the world, it's the in-itself present as being able by absorption to transform the for-itself into *ens causa sui*. The unity and meaning of the world are the *ens causa sui* as ideal synthesis in the in-itself of the for-itself and the world. For it should be noted that the idea of *cause* is drawn from itself by the for-itself; the causal link is

6. Ataraxia: total spiritual calm.
7. *ad libitum*: at one's pleasure.

originally the existential connection between the reflection and the reflecting. But let's be clear, *lack* mustn't be understood in the idealist sense. That which the for-itself lacks is *there*, before it. It's that, precisely, which it lacks: namely, the in-itself inasmuch as it's present to the for-itself; inasmuch as for-itself and in-itself are separated by *nothing*. Lack is not creative; but the for-itself constitutes itself in face of the in-itself as that which by nature *lacks* the in-itself. Nevertheless, precisely by this, the in-itself becomes present to the for-itself – which in no way affects it in itself and in its existence qua in-itself; but which constitutes the for-itself as that before which the world is present qua that which it lacks to become *ens causa sui*. It's on this basis that we can define the future.

Insofar as it nihilates itself, the for-itself is lack. But *that which* nihilates itself in the for-itself is the in-itself. Lack, like every form of Nothingness, *is been*. In its negative guise, inasmuch as it is nihilated nothingness, lack is intentionality: *consciousness of*, in the Husserlian sense. Inasmuch as it is nihilation of *in-itself* – in other words, inasmuch as it is the *in-itself* that *is* its own lack – lack in its positive aspect is *desire*. Or, if you prefer, will. Thus the perpetual flight of the for-itself before the in-itself which freezes it might be compared to the mobility of a swift stream, which in intense cold spells may – thanks to the swiftness of its current – escape freezing. If it halts, it is caught. But the stream is oriented, it runs towards something. Similarly, the for-itself flees the in-itself in the world towards the *ens causa sui* it wishes to be.

Here we hold the open totality that the for-itself is. The for-itself is to itself its own nothingness, qua in-itself which nihilates itself in the guise of for-itself. And that which the for-itself is to itself is a lack: precisely, lack of the totality of which it is negation – or world. The in-itself is present in face of it as that which it is not; and the for-itself precisely *is nothing* – nothing in itself but a total translucidity that is also degradation of the in-itself. But this nothing is grasped, precisely, in the total translucidity of the for-itself as *lack* of something. The for-itself, recaptured by the in-itself in the guise of event, constantly escapes from itself at the moment when it is going to be caught; and this flight is effected towards what it lacks – in other words, towards the world.

Thus the past is the for-itself recaptured by the in-itself; and the future is the world, inasmuch as the for-itself lacks it as that which, being absorbed, would transform it into *causa sui*. The in-itself, insofar as it appears to the for-itself, is already future. This glass, inasmuch as it gives itself as having to be taken; this chair, inasmuch as it gives itself as what I shall sit down on, etc., etc. – all is *in the future*. The for-itself is contemporary with the in-itself, inasmuch as it is vested by it; but the world is in the future for it, inasmuch as it *lacks* the world. In other words, if the for-itself could determine itself by existence pure and simple, it would be contemporary with the in-itself. But inasmuch as it is lack, the world appears to it as future on a basis of present vestedness. What I'm trying to say is that it's a sleight-of-hand to claim that this pen I'm about to pick up is entirely in the future. Granted, it's in the future qua pen. But qua in-itself vesting my for-itself, it's present – it's *a* presence. Each thing is an immediate presence that we can reach only in the future. Such is the meaning of the transcendence or surpassing of the vesting present towards the 'thing-to-come' of the world.

Confidences from Pieter: 'Oh, the fun I did have before I got married, old man! We had some proper little adventures, my two mates and I! In the end, we'd sometimes meet and go over them all, one by one, for the sheer pleasure of remembering. Every Saturday, we used to take the car and go out on the prowl. And at one time, I even had three official girl-friends all at once: well, it didn't make a bit of difference, I went out hunting all the same – just for the pleasure of adding one to the collection. Oh, we didn't spin them any yarns; we'd ask them out for an evening at the dancehall and then, if they were emancipated, well, they'd spend the night with us – and the next morning we'd take them by car to Le Touquet and offer them a good meal. And then, in the evening, we'd just say goodbye; and if they'd been good pals, they could always come along and have supper with us afterwards.

'We weren't jealous: we used to work things out between us. There was only one time, when one of them wanted to keep a girl for himself. He wasn't sweet on her, but he reckoned he'd made a hit; he said, serious as you please: "That one's not like the others." And on top of that, she was really stuck up, so we decided to play a trick on her. One evening he says to us: "Go and see Hélène instead of me, I'm busy, I'll be an hour." OK, we go along to the café, and instead of telling her he's coming in an hour's time we tell her, I dunno, that he's gone off with another woman. Well, old man, that woman, out of jealousy, in order to get her revenge, she wanted to go to bed with me right away. So I got up to her room, and I go to bed with her. But she got on my nerves: I was only doing it to fuck things up for her; I can't recall everything I came out with, but in the end I told her: "You're a slut just like all the rest, you've been unfaithful to Jules." – and I tell her about the trick. You'll never guess what she answered. She said: "To start with, I haven't been unfaithful to Jules, because I didn't come!"

'But apart from that, you know, we used to go shares, we'd take them as they came. Once we stayed in a room for forty-eight hours, with some kids who'd come along for a bit of fun; we each took our turn at banging them – we weren't into orgies, you know, no, it was just for fun – then we made them go to bed together in front of us; we were getting food sent up. It's only when we saw they wanted dough, oh, we'd be real terrors then! That's when we'd enjoy ourselves most, you see. We wouldn't exactly promise, but we'd drop hints – d'you get the idea? – then they'd fall for it and our big kick would be dumping them without a penny. One time, we took a tall, classy blonde for a ride in the car, to the Bois. I was driving, my pal's in back; he shows her a 500-franc note by the light of a gaslamp, and then he bangs her, and afterwards he gives her a blank piece of paper he'd got specially prepared. She sticks it in her garter without suspecting anything. Next I hand over the wheel to my pal, I get into the back with the woman and it's my turn. Afterwards she wanted more money, but I said no. Then she got in a rage, she made us take her home, and when she got out she told me: "Your friend is a gentleman; but as for you, you're a lout." You can just imagine how we were laughing afterwards. We were telling each other: "She's in for a big disappointment."

'In those days, I used to hang out a lot with a fur-salesman from Lyons. We didn't know him all that well, but he used to come along; he'd pay his whack and we'd share the women. From a practical point of view, old man, that fellow was a nobody. But a first-rate hunter! He was a real psychologist: he used to say that with nine women out of ten, their weak spot was money. So he went about it the right way, he made promises, and he got them all. You'd go out with him, he'd say to you: "Do'you want a woman?" Abracadabra, and before you knew it, there she was! But a bit too cocky, you know. As he never used to give them anything, when it came down to it, he had trouble with all the little ladies. There was one who followed him all down the street the next morning, screaming at him – can you imagine that? – a respectable-looking woman, they must have whoring in their blood. He doesn't get flustered, he spots a policeman and tells him: "I don't know this lady, please run her in." Another time, some angry woman rips his shirt to stop him going off without paying. Like a shot, he picks up the woman's boots and throws them out the window!

'He got me into some fine scrapes! Worth putting in your novel! That's why I wasn't too keen on going on the prowl with him: he used to take things too far. Oh yes, one time he was on bad terms with his pal, so in the end it's me he goes out with. "Shall we go on the prowl?"

he says. "OK," says I, "the prowl it is." We go off to the Latin Quarter in his Rosengart, we go to the dancehall, you know, the old one underneath the Soufflot.[8] At the dance-hall, the trick was to delay the little lady until you'd made her miss her last train. After that, you'd suggest taking her home by car – you'd have it all worked out, you see.

'We meet two kids, they take a lot of persuading. My pal starts promising that if they come with us, we'll take them next day to Fontainebleau; we'll buy them stockings and hats, five hundred francs' worth at least – of which, of course, we haven't got a single penny! They resist, we insist. We leave the dancehall with them, they still wouldn't agree. In the end, they refused for so long that at four in the morning, can you believe it, we were still outside the doors of a hotel in Montmartre jawing away. Finally, they let themselves be tempted, my friend puts his car in a garage nearby, and we all four go into the hotel. Then there was another whole production. They wanted one room for themselves and another for us. We say "All right". We go upstairs; once we're up there, we tell them: "Won't you let us sleep beside you? We'll be good." – "All right then, but with your clothes on!" You can just imagine what uphill work it was!

'In the end, I go to bed in one room with one of them, my friend in another room with the other one. I screw my one and go to sleep. The little bitch! She wakes me up at seven in the morning! I rub my eyes: "What's the matter?" – "It's time to leave, it's time to leave!" – "What's that?" – "To Fontainebleau." – "Oh, yeah", says I. I was in a spot. You can just imagine, there'd never been any question of going to Fontainebleau – especially since we'd promised them heaps of things and didn't have any money to pay for them. "OK," says I, "get up and let's go and find my pal." We go and wake them up. And now my pal has to go and notice, when he wakes up, that he's screwed the plain one and I'd got the pretty one. That really gets up his nose. Wow! That bastard could've just been satisfied with what we'd got. Oh, no! He tells me: "You're going to go and do the shopping with Renée" (Renée was the one he'd slept with). That way he wangled it so as he'd stay with my one – and I found out later he'd screwed her without any trouble.

'As for me, I go downstairs with the other one, I couldn't say no, but I was grumbling. "What shall I do now?" I say to myself. I buy a paper at a kiosk and pretend to cast an eye over the headlines, so as to give myself time to think. Then I remember a café not far from there, which had two entrances. I tell the woman: "We're going to go and

8. Rosengart: popular make of French small car in the thirties.

have breakfast. No need to hurry, they'll wait all right." We go off, I order two breakfasts, and I pay right away. We chat a bit, then all of a sudden I tell her: "Pardon me, call of nature!" And I get the hell out by the other entrance, pretending I'm just going to the toilets. Well, old man, I found out the sequel next day. After half an hour's wait, the little lady smells a rat, she goes back to the hotel, and there's my mate with both women on his hands! He put all the blame on me as best he could, said I was just some lout he hardly knew. But they'd got suspicious, and it was four in the afternoon before he could shake them off. He'd say: "I'll go to the garage and fetch the car." – "OK, we'll come with you." In the end, he was forced to have a breakdown in the middle of the Bois. He told them to get out and look for tools in the boot, and then once they were down – Hey presto, off he went!

'Well, you know, when you've lived through all that, at my age, affairs don't interest me any more. I've had too much fun, d'you get . . . the idea? The sort of fellows who have affairs at my age are ones like Paul, who won't have had anything up till then. But not me. It just doesn't interest me, I'm faithful to my wife.'

To complete the portrait, I must add that Pieter has meanwhile always had a moral horror of living off women. He has no words insulting enough for pimps. So on one side, at least, he applies a strict moral code to sexual relations. And precisely today, by a comical coincidence, he has just given renewed proof of it. It's in connection with Hantziger, that sad, lanky Pierrot, romantic, hypocritical and greedy, who's been between two women since the outbreak of war. He's manager, or assistant-manager, of the French subsidiary of an American film company. When the war came, he lost his livelihood. Well, two months before the attack on Poland, he left his pious, charmless wife, whom he'd wed too young, and was planning to get married to his mistress, a young English girl who I think was a typist. Hardly affected by military events, even seemingly unaware of his situation in the field, he spent his time wondering: 'Which one?' Should he divorce to marry the English girl? Should he return to his wife?

He used to spend whole days eating sweets, rummaging in his dull-white, albino hair and staring into space with his great, red, rabbit eyes; and in the evenings, to keep his spirits up, he used to go and play little, light waltzes on the piano – pounding them out on the keys. People thought of him as a nincompoop. But they also tended to think that his nincompoopery must be profitable to him; he seemed to have a discreet and affectionate sense of his own interests. He'd move from person to person, asking each of them: 'Which one should I take? Here, read this letter.' The whole headquarters was in the know. The right-thinking ones advised him to take his wife back, the others to go rather with the young one.

He remained in communication with his wife, because he needed to settle the matter of the divorce. She used to send him tearful letters, worthy of her line of argument – a very clever one it should be said – which was: 'Ask for a divorce if you want to, and I'll agree to it out of love for you. But don't ask me to take any steps myself against my religion or against my love.' Which amounted to making things enormously more complicated for him, since he was at the front. But she thought up still cleverer methods; she sent him little treats, pots of honey or fruitcakes, which he would devour with unhealthy greed – and finally a fifty-franc note. At once he came to look for me: 'Hey; Sartre, you're a philosopher, do you think I ought to accept? Or do you think there's some trap concealed in it?' I replied that I didn't know his wife's character (he showed me some very high-faluting letters, which positively reeked of low cunning); that, what is more, it wasn't up to me to decide whether he should get divorced or make up with her; but that in the event of his deciding to break with her, he should make haste to return the money. He nodded his head, said I was quite right and I never heard another word about the fifty francs. Today, I'm convinced that he kept them.

As his leave drew near, he became more and more anxious: where was he to spend it? The young English girl held him through his senses. 'But,' he'd explain to us, 'at my wife's I'll find a set of furniture which I'd only just bought when we separated; big, spacious, pleasant rooms; and a piano.' I don't know what he'd finally decided when he set off, since I was in Paris myself. The fact remains, he came back yesterday reconciled with his wife – who earns her own living – and really rolling. He has a whole crate of fruitcakes, honey, jams, sausages, dried figs, etc.; and he has a thousand francs – he who never used to have a penny. So his first thought was to get himself dispatched to Saverne yesterday, carrying orders. There, he bought a pair of 140-franc breeches at the military cooperative, and some 300-franc boots. He finally decided against buying a jacket too, but says that he'll see later. What delights me – even more than his air of triumphant, angelic modesty – is the indignation displayed by the worthy Pieter. 'He's nothing but a pimp!' he burst out at me just now when he came in. 'Damn it, it's too much! If I'd been thinking about getting divorced, and then had a reconciliation with my wife, perhaps I might have gone and stayed with her during my leave; but 'I'd have made a point of not accepting a sou from her, at least at the beginning.' He reflects for a moment, then has the honesty to add: 'Or only a hundred francs.'

One must never try to explain Nothingness by finitude, since finitude taken in itself alone seems a characteristic external to the individual under consideration. If, on the contrary, as sometimes seems to be the case with Christian philosophers, finitude is considered as an inherent characteristic of human-reality, then it's indeed necessary to resolve – by contrast with the accustomed method – to ground it on Nothingness. A being which *is* its own nothingness is thereby finite. If one finds it surprising that the in-itself, as soon as it's nihilated, should degenerate into finite individuality, the answer is simple: a consciousness that is coextensive with the infinite totality of the in-itself cannot exist on principle. Negation condenses. It's precisely because the for-itself *is not* the in-itself, is not extension, is not resistance, force, etc., that it is an individual. Each new negation squeezes it in upon itself; and, in the end, it's precisely *in relation* to the totality of the in-itself that the for-itself constitutes itself as a finite individual – it's precisely from the midst of the total in-itself that consciousness arises – and it would be absurd to see in it only a little bit of nihilated in-itself. However, the nihilation of the in-itself in its totality can be effected only in the guise of the irruption into the world of a particular consciousness. Only *being* can be infinite or indeterminate. Negation is by its nature finite.

Friday, 23 February

A chasseur returning from Paris: 'I got the impression back there that people see us as out of work.'

How can lack – or consciousness's primary relation to the world – lead to particular desires? Let us first note that every particular desire is a specification of the desire for the world. Or, if you prefer, the desired object appears at the tip of the desired world and symbolizes the desired world. To desire an object is to desire the world in the person of that object. Now, what does one desire of the object? One desires to *appropriate* it. What is appropriation, then? It's odd that so many social conflicts have had ownership as their object, and yet no one has ever dreamed of describing phenomenologically the act of appropriation and the situation of ownership.

One may first note that appropriation cannot be conceived as an external relation between two substances. A 'realist' theory of appropriation encounters the same difficulties as a dogmatic, realist theory of knowledge: how, between two plenary substances existing in themselves, can there be an intimate relation like that of knowledge or like that of ownership?[9] That's obviously not possible. Idealism resolves the problem by putting *Unselbständigkeit*[10] on the side of the world; for my part, I put a new type of *Unselbständigkeit* on the side of consciousness. Hence, a substance cannot appropriate another substance. Appropriation has a quite different meaning from the physical meaning. What does possessing an object mean?

I see clearly that, in our present-day societies, it's a negative right: the right that nobody except myself should appropriate it. But let us set aside this negative view and get back to the positive. I see, too, that to appropriate an object is to be able to *make use* of it. Yet I'm not satisfied: I see that I make use of the table and glasses here, and yet they aren't mine. Shall we say that it's when I have the right to destroy it that an object belongs to me? But, in the first place, that would be very abstract and I have no such intention. Moreover, a boss can possess his factory, yet not have the right to close it. Nor shall I concede that ownership is a simple social function; for although the social may confer a de jure character – a sacred character – on ownership, there's *that which* is capable of becoming sacred, that which is beneath the social bond: the primary bond of the man to the thing, which is called possession. Any explanation in terms of buying and selling, of course, has only a juridicial sense, and doesn't settle the question at all. So if I set aside as secondary all these definitions of ownership, the problem remains in its entirety: what is possessing?

Well, I note that in this question, as in so many others, magic can guide us. I observe that one says of a man that he is possessed, when his body is inhabited by demons. But I see, also, that in this case the demons are not merely in him, they *are him*; they end with him. Ultimately, it's a certain quality of the possessed man to be possessed – he's in himself given as *belonging to* . . . . And I see, also, that in primitive burials the objects belonging to the dead person are buried with him. The rational explanation 'so that he can use them' is obviously invented post facto. It seems, rather, that there's no question but that the dead one and his objects form a whole. There's no more question of burying him without his customary objects than

9. Note that the French *propriété* may be translated as either 'ownership' or 'property'.
10. *Unselbständigkeit*: failure to stand by oneself; dependence. A Heideggerian concept.

there is of burying him without one of his legs, for example. Beyond the discontinuous existence of all these objects, there lives a great organism which is buried as a whole. The corpse, the cup from which he used to drink, the knife he used to employ, etc. make up a *single dead person.* That's why the custom of burning Malabar widows, though barbarous in its result, can very easily be understood in its principle. The woman has been *possessed.* So she forms part of the dead person; she is legally dead; all that remains is to help her die. Those of the objects which are not capable of being buried are haunted. It's true that the ghosts which haunt manor-houses are debased household gods. But what are household gods if not ghosts? The ghost is nothing but what's left of the man in the house he possessed. To say that a house is haunted is to say that neither the money, nor the efforts, of its second owner will efface this metaphysical, absolute fact of *possession* of the house by its original purchaser.

Thus supersititions, and even religions, present property to us as a prolongation of the owner's being. The man is linked metaphysically to his property by a relation of being. It would be pointless to object that superstitions have no basis. On the contrary, they have their basis in human-reality. Every superstition, every magical belief, if interrogated properly, reveals a truth about human-reality – since man is, in essence, a sorcerer. All this has been said already; but what interests us – we who have already distinguished the in-itself from the for-itself – is that ownership is the prolongation of the for-itself in the in-itself. *To appropriate something is to exist in that thing in the mode of the in-itself.* (The case of possession of a beloved individual is more complicated, but we'll leave that voluntarily to one side, since it's not primary.) This latter formula remains to be explained. It has no meaning save the following: the for-itself's will is nothing but to hold an in-itself of oneself, which is symbolically the for-itself itself.

This brings us to the origin of the symbol, about which I'll speak tomorrow. But for the moment we're in the presence of the actual fact of trans-substantiation. Ownership is trans-substantiation. To be an object's owner is to be, in this object, the for-itself itself as in-itself. In this sense, a possessed object is an object that reflects in the world the vicissitudes of the for-itself which possesses it. A possessed object is the representative of the for-itself in the in-itself. And, at the same time, the possession – the possessed object – represents for the for-itself the world in its entirety. Thus the possessed object, symbol in-itself of the for-itself, is for the for-itself – symbolically – the world. The person, for example, who remains at home and cultivates his garden – for that person, the garden is the world. It's the furthermost tip of the world, and at the same time the world in its entirety is in it. Thus, the basic relation of possession is that of the for-itself to the world. Against the background of the world, however, there appears a particular object which is possessed *qua* world. It *reassures* human-reality, since the latter sees itself exist in it as permanence, as in-itself. That which I possess is me – as opaque, as *in itself*. And since it's necessary that I *procure* what I possess, the in-itself presents itself here as motivated by the for-itself; in other words, every possession reflects an *in-itself* the image of the for-itself as *causa sui*. The fact remains that I, personally, don't have any sense of property. That's what I shall attempt to describe and explain tomorrow.

What this present notebook hasn't been reflecting properly (since 20 February) is the state of enervation and anguish I'm in, because of something that's going very badly, back there in Paris. Yet my cause is just. This evening (after a few libations, it must be said) I've been gripped by a kind of enthusiasm at the idea of defending so just a cause. What has seduced me here is the idea of action. On countless occasions, caught red-handed by some individuals or other, out of amiability or out of spinelessness, I've expended the full flood of my eloquence and my explanations. I used always to be convincing. Today, the cause is difficult – but I'm not guilty. Furthermore, T. is very precious to me. In this desperate case, from far away and opposed by perfidious friends, I must find golden words – just as in those many cases when I did so carelessly. That both excites and exasperates me. I'm almost joyful at having to undertake this action – and for two pins I'd say, like the Emperor during the French Campaign: 'Bonaparte, save Napoleon!'

T. sees me for the moment as some kind of obscene goat. I find this just as shocking as when I myself, on the basis of numerous anecdotes from those who knew him, came to see Jules Romains as a miser. Before myself, as before him, I have this same impression of an inexcusable failing – but one which is surpassed on every side by freedom. I'm a bit disgusted at myself – though I know that reproach isn't really fair – and I want to change.

Saturday 24

For the past three days, thaw. Mud, slush; the roads have an oddly female smell this morning. This soft, gentle, grey weather saddens your heart. I was a bit drunk yesterday evening, when I wrote the last two notes. Not that I got drunk on purpose; but Pieter, who was going on leave, bought me a drink and then I was thirsty and drank a bottle of wine and, in short, I was so on edge the alcohol went to my head. Just enough to give me a vision of myself. Basically, that's what drunkenness is with me: when I'm drunk I have a vision of myself. This morning I'm dry and dismal, with something I can feel right down inside me all ready to be unleashed – and which undoubtedly will be unleashed at about one in the afternoon.

There's a kind of constancy, and fatality, about wartime canards and rumours. I recorded in my first notebook the following catchphrase from '14: 'The German Army sucked in by France.' Well, I find the same catchphrase in 1870. In the *Journal d'un officier d'ordonnance* (Hérisson), I read on p. 38: 'We would hear serious, level-headed, rich, intelligent officers declaring that our defeats on the Rhine were in a way providential, in that they were drawing all the Prussian armies onto our territory and these would find their tombs in France.'[11]

I should imagine the origin of this catchphrase was the retreat from Russia, and perhaps also the difficulties encountered by Napoleon in Spain.

I tried to show yesterday that the sense of appropriation was an essential structure of man. This, moreover, irrespective of any political theory, since one can just as well thereafter be a socialist or a communist. But if that were true, how to explain that I, who am writing these lines, have no sense of property? And firstly, don't I have any?

The easiest thing to verify is that I don't have any sense of other people's property. Those looters, whom I mention in the earlier notebooks – I'd certainly be among their number, if there were not in the *action* of looting something profoundly base, quite apart from the sacred character of property. I have signalled elsewhere that I used to have no scruple about opening a letter which wasn't addressed to me. How often have I leafed through private papers, that someone had carefully concealed and I had just discovered. What is more, I often stole when I was young. I'd steal again if I needed to. Three years ago, at the Gare du Nord, I had no money left to buy myself a detective story, so I stole one from a newspaper kiosk without the least scruple. I'm always ready to borrow, and if I return – and I'm always puncti-

11. Comte d'Hérisson, *Journal d'un officier d'ordonnance, 1870–71*, Paris 1885.

lious about returning – it's because of other people's consciousness, not because of their property rights: I wouldn't like people to *think* I'm a dishonest sponger. But I couldn't care less about *being* one. If someone I love prizes an object, I'll take care of it. But that's only because I can clearly visualize my friend's distress, if he found the object broken. There again, it's consciousness I have in mind, not property.

So far as I'm concerned, it's true I've never wanted lots of money. All I could do with is just a bit more than I've got. This is quite simply because I waste the money I earn. I can never manage to spread my resources over the whole month. On about the twentieth, whatever my needs may be and whatever sum I've had at my disposal, I'm near the end of my tether and have to borrow. If this state was beginning to disgust me before the war, it was more because I'd find it necessary to run anxiously to all my friends in search of next day's lunch, than because I found it impossible to have any 'money of my own'. Notes and coins in my pocket give me a sort of confidence: they *set me up*. But, to tell the truth, this pleasure hardly lasts any time, the money soon disappears, and even if it remains I grow disgusted by it. I need to spend. Not in order to *buy* anything, but in order to blow up that monetary energy: get rid of it in some way and dispatch it far away from myself like a hand-grenade. There's a certain kind of perishability that I like about money: I like to see it flow from my fingers and vanish. But it mustn't be replaced by any solid, comfortable object whose permanence would be even more solid than that of money. It must disappear on insubstantial fireworks – for example, on an *evening out*: going to some dancehall, spending big, going everywhere by taxi, etc. etc. – and, in short, nothing must remain in place of the money but a memory, sometimes *less* than a memory.

Usually, the very evening I get my salary I've already spent a third of it. Moreover, I never keep count – at least for the first few days. It's necessary that money be nothing but the prolongation of my gestures, that I spend as I breathe, that it represent merely the efficacy of my gestures. Then, after a few days, I'm dismayed because there's almost nothing left and I have to start laboriously keeping count again. When I was young, Guille purchased a little notebook in which he studiously marked down his daily expenses, and he used to urge me keenly to buy one like it. But I could never make up my mind to do so. I admired Guille for keeping his accounts in that way, but it would have struck me as unpleasant and base to submit to it. Wherever I go, I shock people by my way of spending – and this among the most generous people. Guille couldn't have been less of a miser, but he used to shrug his shoulders when he saw how I carried on; and Little Bost must have told me at least a hundred times, in mirthful reproach: 'Your affairs are always in a mess.'

The most striking thing is that this money which I spend, I spend *on nothing*. I've known fanatics like Albert Morel who'd convert their liquid assets into a thousand flashy baubles – compasses, patent corkscrews, ingenious little gadgets. Such people want to possess: they find money too abstract and put all their reliance in those innumerable little trinkets, which protect them and enclose them within a domestic circle. Others, like Nizan, give themselves presents. He sets off mysteriously to buy himself a beautiful pair of shoes, and this purchase is like a sacred and propitious celebration of his relations with himself. Nizan's relationship with *his* objects is absolutely charming: he fingers them with malice and tenderness, they're at once little pet animals and good tricks played on other people. He has as much affection for an umbrella duly paid for as if he'd stolen it.

I know, too, what a rare, laborious and sacred undertaking it is for some people – like Keller, for example – to make a purchase. They think about it for a long time beforehand, dream about it, find out about it, go into several shops without buying anything. Then, once the object has been acquired, they regard it with a somewhat sulky seriousness – even with a slight apprehension – like an unexpected, unknown companion of whose vices and virtues they're still ignorant. How often have I seen Keller looking reproachfully at the flints he'd just bought from the tobacconist and declaring severely, before so much as using them: 'They're not as good as in Paris.'

For such people, purchase and appropriation are the moments of an uncertain pact, pregnant with dangers, that will have to be concluded sooner or later with a certain object, without your really knowing where it will lead you. Keller, having broken his pipe, had to think in terms of buying a new one and was in Pfaffenhoffen with me for that purpose. But hardly had he set foot in the town than his courage failed him; he wandered from one tobacconist to another like a soul in torment. From there we went to Haguenau and it was just the same. In the end, he preferred to twist some wire round the stem of his broken pipe, saying: 'I've got another one at home, I'll get it sent me.' I'm aware there's a great deal of miserliness in this. But what exactly is miserliness? More than any fear of having less money after his purchase, I discerned in Keller a kind of terror in face of the new. It involved an anguishing 'changeover' of objects, and he just didn't feel up to taking part in it.

Others still, like the two Z. girls, surround themselves with a tiny living world, which oscillates between a graceful surrealism and a mere toy universe.[12] A thousand tame fairies, elves, goblins and sprites surround and protect them, filter the real world for them, are *theirs*. Toulouse took things to the point of holding conversations with her objects – scolding them, teaching them or taking lessons from them.[13] But neither the world of goblins which the Z. sisters possess, nor those few mediaeval objects which converse with Toulouse, have been bought. Their value derives from the giving. And perhaps this is precisely the most primitive and sacred form of property: all these objects are *given* possessions; there have been a transfer ceremony and relations between consciousness and consciousness. The two Z. girls, moreover, are not strictly speaking spendthrift; they're totally unaware of the existence of money, which doesn't prevent them from being fiercely proprietorial.

I see the birth of luxury in all those ways of possessing, since luxury resides not at all in the number or quality of the objects possessed, but in a relation as profound, hidden and intimate as possible between the possessor and the object possessed: it's not just necessary that the thing be extremely rare, it's necessary that it be born in its possessor's household and have come into existence especially for him. But, for my part, I'm just the opposite of the luxury-lover; since I have no desire to possess objects, I wouldn't know what to do with them. In this, assuredly, I 'am of' my day; I feel money as an abstract and fugitive power; I like to see it vanish into smoke, and feel out of my element faced with the objects it procures.

I've never had anything of my own, in civilian life – neither furniture, nor books, nor trinkets. I'd feel very awkward in a flat; moreover, it would very soon turn into a pigsty. For ten years, all that I've had of my own has been my pipe and my fountain-pen. And I'm profligate even with these objects: I lose pens and pipes; I don't grow attached to them; they're exiles in my hands, and live in an atmosphere hardly any more intimate than the cold light which bathed them when they were ranged alongside their brothers in the shop-window. I don't positively like them; a new pipe may amuse me for a couple of days, after which I use it without noticing.

When anyone gives me a present, I'm always very embarrassed and ill at ease, because I feel obscurely that I'm not taking it as I should. Granted, I'm perhaps more touched than another would be by the attention. (All the more so, since I'm almost never given presents;

12. Z. = 'Zazoulich', i.e. Kosakiewicz, see notes 5 and 32 on pp.4 and 30 above.
13. 'Toulouse' = Simone Jollivet, see note 58 on p.74 above.

people must feel they'd be coming to the wrong person – they may be as fond of me as can be, they still give me nothing. Similarly, it's rare for anyone to photograph me. That goes together.) But it's the immediate attention, as portrayed on the tender countenance of the man or woman who's giving – it's that attention which moves me. I give too many thanks, because I have a bad conscience; I know I shouldn't feel the kindness being done me so much on the person's face, but more in the object.

It's a pleasure to give to T., who never says thank you, because the gift is inscribed in the given object. She hardly gives a thought to the person, but the object at once becomes very precious to her. For my own part, I see nothing but a useful or agreeable object which, like all the others, is going to live a dull life with me, and which I'll end up losing or breaking. Not so much from clumsiness or inattention, as from the absence of that concrete bond which, as I was saying yesterday, meant that dead pharaohs were buried with the cup from which they used to drink – and which is ownership. Just as nobody thinks of giving me presents, no more would they dream, I'm sure, of burying me with my worldly goods if I were to die. My heirs, if I had any, would scatter them to the four winds – repelled by a certain glacial aspect of those objects, which would be the sole memory of their dealings with me.

For a while I was in love with fine shirts, silken underwear, elegant suits: quite an unhappy love, be it said, since I didn't have the wherewithal to buy myself such things. But it wasn't in order to possess them. It was merely in order to be at my best and to please. For some time now, even that has disappeared. I manage perfectly well with quite ordinary shirts, and with wearing my suits for ages. Of late I had just one a year, which I wore on all occasions. I put all my coquetry – if, that is, I had any – into being slovenly. The fine shirts, the dapper little man – all that belonged particularly to the time of the 'Corsican warrant-officer'; when the 'tall, blond Norwegian' intervened, I turned instead to old garments: to rags preserving a trace of former elegance.[14] However, I still refused to buy two off-the-peg suits for the year, which would have allowed me always to be neat. I preferred, for the price, to have just one – soon much the worse for wear – made for me by a good tailor. Perhaps one should see in this some vague rudiment of a taste for property, like a ludicrous and imperceptible gesture towards luxury.

Yet, even if I possess nothing of my own accord, and have no

14. 'Corsican warrant-officer', 'tall, blond Norwegian': presumably, these were models for masculine fashions in the thirties.

respect for other people's goods, I still have a strong indirect connection with property: I'm fond of endowing others. I often give my own belongings away, sometimes with a kind of passion. When I see beautiful objects in a window-display, I may look at them covetously as if I wished to take them for myself. In reality, however, the covetousness is *on others' behalf*. As I contemplate them, I say to myself: 'How beautiful they are! If only I had any money, I'd give them to X. or Y.' And what's involved here is assuredly, first and foremost, a certain imperialist taste for acting upon others; for pricking people's consciences; for forcing them, in one way or another, to remember me; for insinuating myself indiscreetly, like a splinter, into their inner being.

This would lead me on to consider my relations with other people. And I think I'll do that before long, since – especially at the present time – it's an open wound. But there's something else still deeper. I have as if a deep regret at not knowing how to possess; and by giving – by dreaming of giving – I delegate my powers to others and possess in the only way that's within my reach: by proxy. When giving something to T., when seeing the fuss she makes about my gift – a fuss that's not directed at all at the object because it comes from me, but because it's beautiful – I'm rather like the impotent gangster in *Sanctuary*, who used to force another man to sleep with the woman he desired.[15] I have something of that morose, solitary, voyeur's joy. I'm delighted because it's *through me* that she possesses the object: it's I who have created that relation of ownership. I stop on the brink of the rite of appropriation; but I see it from afar, enjoy it with my eyes and know myself to be its author. It is an actual relationship I have with the object.

Similarly, I couldn't put up with an 'interior', but I like other people's interiors. There are two apartments which, to my eyes, have the most poetic charm imaginable – and in which I like to tarry at length: Mme Morel's apartment in Rue Vavin, and Toulouse's apartment in Montmartre. I enjoy them because I feel them to be *possessed*; and it's that atmosphere of possession which I like – and wherein I like to dwell. I like the fact that all the objects there belong to someone who's also my friend, and who allows me in a certain degree to use them. To tell the truth I soon grow weary of them, and what I prefer – or at least what never wearies me – is to sit on chairs which belong to nobody (or, if you like, to everybody), in front of tables which belong to nobody: that's why I go and work in cafés – I achieve a kind of

15. William Faulkner's *Sanctuary*, which Sartre read in 1934 in French translation.

solitude and abstraction. Yet, from time to time it pleases me to bury myself in that luminous warmth, which does not belong to me, but which for an instant is for me. There's no doubt at all, however, that nobody would adapt better to a collectivization of property than I would, since I'd lose nothing by it save the pleasure of giving – and I could still give in a thousand other ways.

To give an explanation in terms of history and upbringing, this total lack of any taste for ownership seems to me to come, above all, from the fact that my family background was one of public service. The money that poured into the house each month, with the regulated monotony of the menstrual flow, seemed to my grandfather to have no direct relationship with the work he provided. And, indeed, an amelioration in the quality of this work would not have been rewarded. Moreover, he made it so much a matter of honour to teach as a sacred mission, that he entirely forgot the relationship between that work and his emoluments. He was as naively astonished at those banknotes he used to receive each month as Pacific Island natives are at their wives' pregnancy – which they ascribe to everything under the sun save their own efforts. My grandfather became miserly in his old age, when he was senile; but for a long time he used to walk about with his pockets stuffed with gold coins, without having any notion of the quantity of gold he was carrying. My grandmother used to go and steal it from his jacket at night, and he never noticed.

A member, like him, of the teaching profession, I have never had the impression of *earning* money. My job strikes me as a gratuitous social obligation, sometimes amusing, often boring, but without any relation to the money I'm given at the end of the month. That money has always been a sort of gratuity for me. I don't have the impression it's owed me. So it sits lightly in my purse and I sow it carelessly to the four winds – assured, as I am, that the miracle will be repeated at the end of the month. In this domain, I experience neither torments nor any great delight. That doesn't count – it's like the air I breathe or the water I drink. There again, I have no *roots*. Nothing roots one better than a harsh, tough, pecuniary *situation*. During my childhood, I never saw anyone sweating away in torment to earn a few coppers: money used to drop from the sky like ripe fruit – it was a respectable shower of gold.

I recall a trainee teacher called Delarue, who also studied drama under Dullin, bawling out my pupils and telling them (he was working himself up as he spoke, not looking at them out of shyness, and ended up losing his temper completely): 'You laugh at savages, because they think that by beating tomtoms they make the rain fall.

But what d'you think you lot are? You turn the switch; it's an imperious, magical gesture whose meaning is unknown to you – and you wait like a savage for the light to pour forth. Which of you has ever thought about the human labour it took to put the electric current into the wires?' Well, so far as money is concerned, I'm certainly like the savage. The gesture with which I place a note on the table appears like a ritual to me, like a magical gesture, like a ceremony – and I almost never think of what that note represents. Certainly Keller, when he makes a purchase, must have the impression he's exchanging his labour for an object. Not me! I make the series of gestures necessary for the object to be born. That's all.

Let me add, I belong to a family which has no real-estate. It's true that when I was about twenty I did come into a small legacy, which I squandered in a few years. But, apart from that single circumstance, none of us ever owned anything – neither land nor worldly goods. A rented apartment and that's all. From the apartment rented by my stepfather or my grandfather to the hotel-room where I live, the distance is less than from a house in the country duly owned – a patrimony – to a rented apartment. Basically, although my stepfather chronically reproaches me for living in a hotel, I am following in the footsteps of my whole family: no worldly goods; I expect no inheritance and shall leave none; I don't own the room where I live. The great transformation was made before my time, when the Alsatian peasants who were my grandfather's grandparents moved from the fields to the town, whereupon my grandfather's father became a primary-school teacher. As for me, I have only accentuated the movement. In that, moreover, I'm no 'bohemian' – as I would have been, perhaps, in 1848. All I'm doing is drawing closer to that whole petty bourgeoisie in America, for example, whose habitat is intermediary between our apartments and our hotel-rooms. In that sense, the great-grandchild of peasants, the grandchild of public servants and a public servant myself, I am collectivized to a more advanced degree. I mean, so far as property is concerned – since this material collectivization has the effect of reinforcing my individualism and taste for freedom.

For that explanation couldn't suffice. There's no shortage of public servants, children of public servants, who have a taste for 'a place of their own', a taste for possession. It's even the norm. At least they'll want to possess books. And, of course, one can take the explanation a bit further by saying that I've been formed by an impersonal rationalism, which gave me a sense of impersonality regarding ideas. It's because, as soon as I know some idea of Pascal's, it's as apparent to me as it is to Pascal or to my neighbour – or rather, it's because it seems to me collective property – that I have no need to possess a leather-bound Pascal in my library. Other people must have more intimate relations with books. They must see them as still inhabited; fondle them; think that they have an inexhaustible secret and must be possessed at home, for fear lest that secret escape: paper, binding, typeface and ideas form a whole. But, for me, a book read is a corpse. All that remains is to throw it away. And if I want to recall certain passages, I've nothing against going to reread them in a public library. At Le Havre, I used to achieve the maximum degree of collectivization: sleeping in the hotel, dividing my days between the Café Guillaume Tell and the municipal library. I even have a taste for libraries, and I really find it a matter of utter indifference to me that the book is not mine; that it has been leafed through, and will be again, by thousands of hands. On the contrary, that seems to me to be its true nature.

But, in order to find the genuine explanation, one must nonetheless turn to that being-in-the-world which, with me as with every man, surpasses his historical situation towards solitude.

The first reason I don't want to own anything is metaphysical pride. I'm sufficient unto myself, in the nihilating solitude of the for-itself. I should find no comfort in those substantified substitutes for myself. I'm not at ease except in freedom, escaping objects, escaping myself; I'm not at ease except in Nothingness – I'm a true nothingness, drunk with pride and translucid. Yet that doesn't resolve the metaphysical question, since, proud or not, I'm a *lack* and I precisely lack *the world*. So it's the world I want to possess. But with no symbolic substitute. That, likewise, is a matter of pride: I should never accept to possess the world *in the person* of such and such an object. I, as an individual, am in face of the world's totality, and it's that totality I want to possess. But this possession is of a special type: I want to possess it qua *knowledge*. My ambition is myself alone to know the world – not in its details (science), but as a totality (metaphysics). And, for me, knowledge has a magical sense of appropriation. To know is to appropriate. Exactly as, for the primitive, to know a man's secret name is to appropriate that man and reduce him to slavery. This possession consists, essentially, in capturing the world's meaning by sentences.

But metaphysics is not enough for that. Art is necessary, too, since the sentence which captures satisfies me only if it is itself an object; in other words, if the meaning of the world appears in it, not in its conceptual nakedness but via a material. The meaning must be captured with the aid of a capturing thing, which is the aesthetic sen-

tence: an object created by me and existing by itself alone. Furthermore, my desire for possession of things is masked and braked by a
more complex desire, which would be worth describing for its own
sake: my desire for possession of *others*. Here, of course, the possession is of quite another kind; but it seems certain to me that one cannot
have both desires at once – the desire to possess things and the desire
to possess people. Thus, the world seems more single and uniform to
me than to many people. It doesn't have those hollows of lukewarm
shadow, those havens of grace, that possessed objects comprise. In a
certain sense, I'm more forsaken in the face of it and more alone. And,
in another, more proudly conquering. Thus, metaphysics is desire for
appropriation.

Sunday, 25 February

Daladier's famous 'Not An Acre!', which had its hour of fame in '39,
recalls most unfortunately a no less celebrated declaration by Jules
Favre, in a circular of 1870: 'Not an inch of our territory, not a stone
from our fortresses.'

I have mentioned Hantziger's sudden good fortune. It has made him
unctuous. Yesterday, when someone was talking to him about
'picking up girls', he was saying, with lowered eyes: 'Oh no, my dear
fellow, marriage is the only thing worthwhile.' I must admit, to be
honest, he does claim that his money comes to him from his director,
who supposedly gave him a month's salary when he was in Paris. It's
possible, but I hardly think so. Why suddenly give him that money,
after six months of war? At all events, he's really saintly. He's going to
be made a corporal, and he'd like to take advantage of that to avoid
little chores like sweeping up or fetching the grub. But Klein won't
take any nonsense from him; he told him yesterday: 'As long as you
don't go and fetch the grub, you won't eat with us.' Hantziger held out
yesterday. At midday he came to eat in the restaurant, and in the
evening he had supper from tins. But Klein is stubborn and will starve
him out. Klein is a tough guy. He lost his wife three weeks ago, but
nothing in his attitude shows it. Either he doesn't give a damn or he
has staggering self-control. But personally I think he does give a
damn.

Today I received some poems from a young man called Alain Borne; I
read them and I must admit I haven't a clue about them. Out of
irritation, and to find out if I could – and also because all these days

I've been plagued by a disagreeable but poetic frame of mind – I tried to write a poem. I give it here, for what it's worth – out of mortification.

> Melted the rustlings of light under the dead trees
> In water the thousand lights of water that hid their name
> Melted the pure salt of winter, my hands wither.
> Among the houses I strain the soft greasy wadding of the air and
> The sky is a botanical garden that smells of new plant growth.
> At the windows of the great deserted market-halls
> Powdered phantoms see the slow black glue flow in the streets.
> Melted the needles of white joy in my heart
> My heart smells of fish.
>
> Poisonous spring that is beginning
> Do not harm me
> My heart was so unflagging
> And behold it is disheartened by spring
>
> Spring that is beginning in my heart
> Mayst thou be able to burn like a torch
> And may the scorching stone of the summer touch
> And wither the supple grasses
> Breath ablaze I slipped on the stone
> And the seed-germs were burning, kindled by the wind
> Breath frozen on the snow
> I slipped, hard and transparent
> And the world was of marble and I was the wind
> But behold the exile of spring returned.

All these days, I've been working morning and evening at the Hôtel du Soleil, a big, cold café which for some reason or other reminded me of the Jesuit 18th century. But orders have become stricter since the general returned from leave, and this morning a gendarme damn well kicked me out. I went up to the first floor, into a big hall which was used as a cinema in peacetime and which the Salvation Army has converted into a Soldiers' Home. The back wall is still covered by a screen. The long, rather dark hall contains some fifteen tables, crowds of chairs, a ping-pong table and Russian billiards – and it's decked out with pious stylishness. There are chequered cloths on the tables and flowers in vases. At the busiest hours, fifty silent soldiers are playing, reading or writing there: on their faces, they wear the dull resignation of male worshippers at mass. A little old woman, with the cheeks of a *backfisch* but a hard expression, scurries about among the tables.[16] It smacks of an English club, an old people's home, or the municipal library. A radio discreetly transmits great music. I was almost happy to be there. In any case, pleased to have seen that. I'll go back every day for the time being, morning and evening, since I have no other refuge.

I've reread the poem I wrote just now and am overcome with shame, not just because it's bad, but because it's a poem – in other words, for me, an obscenity. To think I addressed the spring as 'thou' – it was grudging, but I still did it. To make the poem bearable, it seems to me one would have to suppress almost the whole thing and write it like this:

> Melted the rustlings of light under the dead trees
> In water the thousand lights of water that hid their name
> Melted the pure salt of winter, my hands wither
> I twist between my hands the greasy wadding o´ the sky
> Melted the needles of white joy in my heart.

That's all. The rest should be thrown in the bin.

Monday, 26 February

Reread with deep admiration the first sixty pages of *La Chartreuse de Parme*. Stendhal's natural style, charm and liveliness of imagination can't be matched. That feeling of admiration is rare indeed with me, yet I've experienced it in full measure. And the artistry of the novel! – the unity in its movement!

Tuesday, 27 February

Return of Paul, in a high state of merriment. I wonder why. I should have thought, rather, that he'd come back from leave in a state bordering on dejection. But he's bright as a button and has a perpetual smile on his lips, which he tries in vain to hold back. To the point where I wonder if he wasn't drinking this morning at Dettwiller. He tells me he has read *L'Enfance d'un chef*, and got two of his colleagues to read it too.[17] 'They told me: "But your friend is anti-semitic!" And, I must say, if I didn't know you . . . '

---

16. *Backfisch*: colloquial German term for a teenage girl.
17. 'The Childhood of a Leader' is included in *The Wall and other Stories*.

Life here is always the same. Without any charm; without any intensity. We drag along. What happens to me comes from back there, from Paris, and I can't speak of it here. But, since yesterday, I've felt the present re-forming like a crust around me. I've made myself a niche, as Mistler says. That means that objects stand out more sharply. I have little expectations, limited to the hours which immediately follow; my life here surrounds me like a thick fog, and prevents me from striving vainly towards worrying absences or distant futures. My life reacquires a dismal sweetness: I pay attention to the taste of my tobacco, the savour of a coffee or the atmosphere of the Home. The whole problem of feelings (grief, happiness, indifference) depends upon the different degrees of *density* of the present. In most cases of affliction, the present has become so thin and transparent that one's gaze pierces right through it; it's no longer anything but the wall of glass separating one from the future, which one cannot break; it's lit by a theoretical light, a studio light, without shadow – and one feels ill at ease there, as in some great, deserted hall.

In every imperialism of feeling like mine, there's some kind of inauthenticity or other. It's an attempt to escape from solitude. But it's necessary to understand what that means. I'm struck this morning by that universal demand: wanting 'to be loved'. It's not so obvious, at first sight, that one must want to be loved when one loves. Especially with the principles of psychology usually adopted. If one accepts these, and if man is an existential plenum, he should want to possess the object he loves: have it wholly at his disposal, day and night; read its total dependence in its servile looks and its smiles. But what need does he have to go further?

Well, dependence of that kind arises more frequently than is thought, and is pretty clearly very far from satisfying. It merely increases the fierceness of the search which goes – beyond absolute submission – towards what escapes from servitude itself: towards that free consciousness whose love one wants. I quite understand that, for the owner, the love of the living being who's his property simplifies things a lot. I can also see, however, that the person who wants absolute power couldn't care less about love: he's content with fear. Absolute monarchs and dictators have only ever sought their subjects' love as a matter of policy; and if they've found a more economic means of enslaving them, they've made use of it at once.

But, on the contrary, what happens is that a total enslavement of the loved one kills love in the person who loves. It's always both comforting and a nuisance to be loved more than one loves. These commonsense truths show pretty clearly that the lover doesn't dream at all of the loved one's total enslavement. He isn't keen to become the object of a boundless mechanical passion. What he wants is a needle-point: an unstable equilibrium between passion and freedom. Above all, he wants freedom to determine itself to become love – and that, not just at the beginning of the adventure, but at every instant. Nothing is more precious to the lover than what I shall call the autonomy of love in the loved one.

For my own part, I've always read that business about the love-potion in Wagner and Bédier with a secret displeasure.[18] If Tristan and Iseult were driven wild by a love-potion, they no longer hold the least interest for me: their love is a mere sickness, a poisoning of the blood. And I recall I used to remain unmoved by the most touching episodes in that story, because I couldn't lose sight of the origin of that love. So far as I'm concerned, if somebody proposed, by a magic spell, to excite the most beautiful woman in the world with passion for me, they might just as well suggest I sleep with a doll of human dimensions. Nothing is dearer to me than the freedom of those I love. That's an odd kind of imperialism, people will say. Yes – but the fact is, this freedom is dear to me provided I don't respect it at all. It's a question not of suppressing it, but of actually violating it. But can a freedom one violates still be freedom? Does a 'seduced' woman remain free? Therein lies the whole question.

It seems to me, however, that in love there's precisely a sure and as if metaphysical knowledge of the reply: freedom can under no circumstances stop being free. I know that a somewhat outdated accessory of love is servitude – symbolized by chains, fetters and all that paraphernalia. But I don't take too seriously people who complain about being captives. But it will be said that one must choose: if freedom by its essence must remain free – if nothing can put it in chains – how in the world could one violate it? There's a contradiction here: how can one wish to put in chains what one wishes to remain free? Yet there's no shadow of a doubt that that's what the desire to be loved means: to hit at the Other in the Other's absolute freedom. Such is the root of sadism, for example, whose ideal is to extract groans. The sadist pushes tortures to the point where the victim can't refrain from asking for mercy. And he enjoys putting this cry down to the victim's freedom: the tortured one *could* have not cried, could have

18. Joseph Bédier (1864–1938), French mediaevalist who revitalized study of the *Chansons de Geste*, and published a modernized version of the story of Tristan and Iseult.

chosen to perish beneath the blows without opening his lips.

So one often finds that the sadist proposes a choice in advance: either you surrender willingly to a practice that repels you – that you condemn – or else you'll suffer in your flesh. The choice is proposed in this way in order to provoke a giddy feeling of freedom in the victim, and to maintain the whole discussion on the terrain of autonomy. The broken victim who yields, the battered Jew who cries out 'Down with the Jews!', is still making a real choice. The instant of orgasm for the sadist is precisely that ambiguous instant in which constraint unleashes freedom: in which freedom adopts as its own the constraints that sadism inflicts. And the sadist knows there will always be a moment when the choice will be made; and that he only has to wait, tightening his constraint from one moment to the next; and that the victim will, nevertheless, remain free at the very moment of yielding. This certainty that freedom is not destroyed might discourage the sadist – or rather, it would discourage anybody other than him. But the sadist is so made that it's this contradiction which excites him: this very impossibility, this marriage of conflicting words. A slave freedom – that's what attracts him. There's always an essential void at the heart of the vice, and the vice-lover's pleasure is bitter.

And I don't say that love is a sadism; but sadism takes its origin from love. The person who wants to be loved is exercising no constraint over free choice. But the gestures and phrases that move him most are those which 'escape' the loved one. In other words, those which show the desire for discretion, restraint or refusal suddenly overcome by a brand new freedom: the freedom that yields, chooses acceptance and decides to let itself go. That kind of freedom is subjegated *by itself*; it turns upon itself – as in madness or as in dream – to will its captivity. A freedom that itself creates its own need to see, touch and caress the loved one – that's what we demand of those we love.

And in order that this freedom may remain freedom – even in this distracted state – we are ready to fear lest it extricate itself and escape: lest it recover and present itself, an instant later, as freedom *against* what it was. But that's precisely the very nature of freedom. Every thought of love and every avowal of love bring us back to the instant – squeeze us against the present – because they're the effect of a freedom which is absolutely free in the future. In vain do they engage the future: the one who loves will not cease trembling before those pledges, since a silent knowledge of freedom is given in love. The proof of this is the fact that we wouldn't be satisfied, in our loved one, with a love which was pure fidelity to the pledge of fidelity we have just torn from her. The woman who gave us the answer: 'I love you, because I once gave you my word and I don't want to go back on it, out of fidelity to myself', would be sure to see us jump out of our skin. We want her to love us, today as yesterday, in a freedom which puts its freedom into escaping itself. Which will not prevent us from demanding, on the spot, a new pledge of love. Thus, what we want from the Other is that freedom, ever tottering and ever renewed, which is addressed to us and takes us indefinitely as its principal motive. What we demand of the loved one is that her freedom should *act out* for us the determinism of passion.

It remains to be understood *why* we want it. For that form of love, which is the commonest and strongest – the love that craves slave-freedom; the love that wants freedom in others only so that it can violate it – that form of love is utterly inauthentic. There are other ways of loving. But that very inauthenticity can serve as a guide, since one can lay down as a fact that every form of inauthentic existence is willed for its inauthenticity. Inauthenticity, as we know, consists in seeking out a foundation in order to 'lift' the absurd irrationality of facticity. The desire to be loved seems to me to have the aim of positing the Other as the foundation of our own existence. The person who loves us – on condition that we love that person – will lift our facticity.

That's what I should like to explain now.

It must be understood that love doesn't create relations with the Other; it appears against the existential background of the *for-the-Other*, which attacks us in our very existence. As I've said, it's in the nature of the for-itself to exist *for the Other*; in other words, to exist as a defenceless outside projected onto the Other's infinite freedom. It's in my nature to be it for-myself, in the midst of the for-itself. My only way of *not-being* the Other *is to be-for* the Other. And insofar as I'm personally my own 'not-being-the-Other', I'm personally my own 'being-for-the-Other'. By nature, I 'lay myself open' to the Other; I'm personally 'in danger' before the Other's infinite freedom. It's impossible for me to not worry about it, claiming the Other has a 'representation' of me that doesn't touch me. That's not at all true. In fact, I'm *engaged* in the Other by my very existence; engaged in the Other's freedom, upon which I absolutely cannot out of principle act. This aims to represent the ordinary relations among consciousnesses, based on the fact that consciousnesses exist plurally in the unification of the for-the-Other. Here, inauthenticity consists in disguising from oneself the existential unity of the for-the-Other, by claiming that the Other 'manufactures an image of me'. But the pre-ontological comprehension given in the for-itself's very irruption into the world renders these attempts to disguise the truth from oneself inoperative – if not always, at least intermittently – so a disclosure takes place. Shyness is one of these disclosures. Wanting to be loved by the Other is wanting to 'recuperate' one's being-for-the-Other by acting in such a way that the Other's freedom subjugates itself before the defenceless nakedness which we are *for* it.

However, one must avoid confusing this will to be loved with, for example, the will to be respected. In the case of the will to be respected, one proposes oneself to the Other as an existent upon which the Other, on the basis of his own principles, has to pass specific judgements. But the Other remains absolutely free: he can use bad faith, for example. In the case of love, on the contrary, we expect the Other to bewitch himself in his own freedom; to set his freedom to denying his freedom in face of us. To that extent, however, we cease to lay ourselves open to his freedom. If freedom puts itself in chains in face of us, we cease to be defenceless in face of it; and, as far as possible, the *outside* that we are in face of it ceases to be an *outside*. With what we are *for it*, we maintain relations which are similar to those of the for-itself with itself. Instead of the for-the-Other being torn from the for-itself, it seems to be the latter's natural prolongation. In the midst of the freedom of the person who loves us, and for as long as we're loved, we're *in safety*. Thus, to make oneself loved by someone is not to try and give him a flattering image of oneself: it's to *exist in safety in the midst of his freedom*.

But that isn't all. I showed the other day how every desire is a *desire to appropriate*. And how every appropriation is appropriation of the world through a particular object. Desire is so made that the desired object always appears to us the condition *sine qua non* that makes our *being-in-the-world* possible. I saw that very clearly five or six years ago, when I made a resolution not to smoke any more. What had previously prevented me from deciding on it wasn't any consideration of the thousand little specific privations that would come to torment me in the course of the day. But it had seemed to me that the 'world without tobacco' would be completely colourless and as good as dead. I could no longer imagine what pleasure I'd have at the cinema, if I couldn't watch the film while smoking my pipe. I no longer expected anything very good from a glass of alcohol, if I couldn't take a puff between swallows. Nor yet from a conversation with friends, if I didn't have my pipe in my hand. To renounce any of the things one loves is to change worlds. And when one sees the object of a desire escaping, it seems the world is slipping through one's fingers. That's probably why an appropriate cure consists in reducing the object to itself. But also, from the moment of this reduction, one stops caring about it. When I took it into my head to reduce tobacco to being only what it was—a certain amusement among others *in* the world—I stopped smoking with no difficulty.

So desire is desire *for the* world, and appropriation means fusion of the in-itself and the for-itself in the ideal unity of the *causa sui*. Now, if someone loves and desires me, not only am I reassured as to that person's freedom, but the 'for-the-Other' which I am for the one who loves me is *the world*. There I am, a real existent (in the mode of the for-the-Other), as the condition *sine qua non* that makes possible the Other's being-in-the-world. And the world that I am is precisely that which is the primary object of my desires – those trees, those streets, that sky, that sea (this is the underlying meaning of Stendhal's crystallization: the loved one metamorphosed into a world) – because we, the Other and I, have only one and the same world. Thus the nihilating and nihilated for-itself, which in its primary structure is desire for the world, exists qua for-the-Other precisely as the desired world. Which means that the unification of the for-itself and the world is tightened one notch, since it now has just the type of unity of the for-itself and the for-the-Other for a single human-reality. This is precisely what's called wanting to make oneself loved: *effecting the unification of the for-itself and the world in accordance with the type of unity of the for-itself and the for-the-Other, while existing in safety in the midst of a freedom which subjugates itself in order to desire you as world.*

It will be said that I'm expressing quite simple things in a very complicated way; and that it's hardly a new discovery that the lover wants 'to be everything in the world' for the loved one. I'm well aware of that, and am not claiming to produce a psychology of love. I want only to signal that, if the relationship of human-realities among themselves is not in the mode of the *for-the-Other*, it's utterly fruitless to try and understand why someone would get the idea into his head, one fine morning, of being 'everything in the world' to a woman. Because he cares for her? But, if he can see her all day long and sleep with her as much as he wants, that's not necessary. Because he wants her to care for him in the same way that he cares for her? But why should he want that? Out of a will to power? But the will to power itself, as I showed the other day, requires an existential explanation. The error of psychology to date has been analogous to the one a physicist would be making, if he reversed a test-tube full of air over a tank of mercury, in order to show how pressure makes the mercury rise up in the tube: the mercury wouldn't rise, *because the tube has to be empty*. And if we're not ourselves an existential vacuum, we shall never understand the strange vanity which, according to Pascal, leads us to commit the direst follies in order to give people flattering 'images' of ourselves.[19]

But let's continue, since it's here that inauthenticity lurks. We want the loved one to love us, in order to be able to overwhelm her by our existence. But this generosity is not disinterested: this existence, which we henceforth feel to be *summoned*, loses its facticity in our eyes; we claim to bring ourselves personally and freely to existence, in order to satisfy the desire of a free consciousness. These loved veins on our hands: it's out of kindness that they exist. How kind we are, to have eyes, hair, eyelashes – and to offer them tirelessly up, in an outpouring of generosity, to that tireless desire of the Other! Before being loved, we were worried about that unjustified protuberance that was our existence, which was spreading in all directions. But, behold, that same existence is now recovered and willed in its infinite details by a freedom analogous to our own: a freedom that we ourselves will with our own. Herein lies the basis of love's joy: feeling oneself justified for existing.

In fact, we're not in the least justified. We've merely lost our solitude. The being who loves us absorbs us into herself, and we hide our head in her bosom as the ostrich hides its in the sand. For our solitude doesn't exist without our having made the assumption of our unjustifiable facticity. No love can justify our existing. To be honest, the people I have mainly to reproach for such inauthenticity are those who get involved in being loved without loving. But, precisely, I have very often been of their number. What drew me most often into an affair was the need to appear to some consciousness as 'necessary' – in the same way as a work of art. Like a manna that came forward itself to satisfy it. But, I must say, as soon as you love in your turn – and whatever love the loved one may feel for you – you emerge into solitude.

It would take too long, however, to speak of this here, since it would then be necessary to say what love is. I have my own ideas about that, but a whole volume would undoubtedly be needed. Especially since love by its nature is *sexual*. I merely wanted to get to the heart of that strange inauthenticity which makes us *depend* on a person, precisely because we're everything for her. It may not seem that way, but I portrayed myself life-size in that metaphysical description. I shall try tomorrow to describe myself more simply in my relations with the Other.

---

19. Perhaps a reference to Pensée 145 in the Pléiade edition of Pascal's *Oeuvres complètes*(B.N.382): 'Nous ne nous contenterons pas de la vie que nous avons en nous et en notre propre être: nous voulons vivre dans l'idée des autres d'une vie imaginaire, et nous nous efforçons pour cela de paraître. Nous travaillons incessamment à embellir et conserver notre être imaginaire, et négligeons le véritable.'

It must also be recorded that I'm in the process of regaining, painfully, the kind of authenticity lost during my trip to Paris. Which means, at bottom, that once again I feel alone. Not alone *beside* the people and things I love (that's the old, absurd, monadic anarchism), but alone *beyond* all those whom I care for and who may care for me. I'm finding 'my' war and my destiny. Especially since things are not going too well at the moment; and since time – as some Italian paper or other said – doesn't at all seem to be working against Germany. The terrorized Scandinavian countries allow Finland to be strangled and promise to behave nicely. Italy seems to be effecting a rapprochement with the Reich. And as for us, we still don't seem to know how to tackle the enemy. Pretty gloomy prospects, which suffice to deflect me from my little private affairs.

Today, at 10.15, first vaccination against typhoid. It's now 19.45, and I've had only a bit of a temperature and a slight pain under the arm. Spent the day at the Home. At present, I like it pretty well there. Letter from Mistler, now transferred to Army HQ, training and operations section, at Wangenbourg: 'My mind still boggles – after ten days – at some of the red tape which gives the war a pretty weird look here. Pity I can't supply material for the Notebooks. What's to be done? . . . . Here, I'm "the fellow who's back from the front". Comical! But what prestige! – among lads who, for six months, have been carrying on a barrack-room existence all the better preserved in that, last September, they were most of them passing out.'

The ultra-swift tempo of the second round of leave is making the men extremely distrustful. They ask: 'What d'you think, are they afraid the real rough stuff's coming in spring?' And add with a sigh: 'Well, at least it's one thing they can't take away from us!' The more optimistic point out that, if the second round is over by 30 April, it will make two leaves in eight months – just the quota – so perhaps the military authorities are hurrying the departures through only in order to comply with their own decisions. People say too, with a sneer: 'They do it to improve morale.' And they all say, with a cunning look: 'Mus' be someth'n' underneath it, 'cos it ain't their way to do anyth'n for noth'n.' There are some of our lot who are refusing to go, because they've just got back from their first leave; and others, who comment with rather bitter irony: 'They'll be thinking they're seeing us all the time, back home!'

Wednesday 28

Good night, but a bit feverish. Bitter taste in my mouth. I learn that, among yesterday's vaccination cases, two strapping fellows 'passed out like a light' in the course of the day. I then recall how I felt a baleful tenderness yesterday, to which I paid hardly any attention. I'd have needed merely to apply my mind for it to have overwhelmed me entirely, and I should certainly have passed out too. Once again, I reflect with a kind of satisfaction on the extent to which fainting, hysterics, sea-sickness, etc. are a matter of consent. Some time, I'll explain here how people can be classified according to the nature of their self-consent: how the Beaver, when we go walking, consents to her fatigue and bathes in it, in such a way that it becomes an agreeable and wished-for state; and how, by contrast, the same fatigue is disagreeable to me – until I feel definitively 'beyond' – because I don't consent to it. There's a way of adhering to oneself that I don't know – which has both advantages and awkward aspects.

But for today I'd like to take up again, from a purely descriptive and historical point of view, that question of my imperialism and my relations with the Other.

As I've said, surprising as it may seem, in my childhood I was pretty. Pretty and pampered: in other words, lavish with my promises. I had 'fiancées' in all the towns I passed through, and their doting families would sponsor these betrothals (I was six or seven years old). I definitely preferred the company of girls to that of boys. Besides, I had neither father nor brother to teach me rough manners, and I lorded it like a little king in a world of women.

Even as early as that, moreover, I was a real play-actor. I sought to please by contrivances of eminently aesthetic design: by inventing games, poetic fictions, speeches, etc. Around my ninth year, my mother had bought me a Punch-and-Judy; and whenever I had a bit of money, I'd purchase a new actor for my theatre. I had: the Jew, the Gendarme, the Old Woman, Punch himself, etc. – and a character who filled me with admiring astonishment, though I wasn't sure quite how to use him: Bi-Ba-Bo, who used to be sold at the Casino de Vichy, and whose distinctive feature was that one could change his costume, since his head was detachable. These characters all disappointed me somewhat, because their heads were made of pasteboard – or (in the case of Bi-Ba-Bo) of celluloid. I should have preferred the heavy, magnificent, wooden heads of the original Lyons puppets. But no matter: like many children, I was sensitive to what is refined, inhuman, artificial and necessary about a play for puppets. It took me a long time to understand that one can find all the same features in the real theatre, if one doesn't let oneself be diverted by a stupid realism.

I used then to read a very old children's book entitled *Monsieur le Vent et Madame la Pluie*, which I thought highly respectable because it smelled of mildew and was torn and stained: it must have delighted my mother's childhood. That used to enrapture me. I still often tell myself today how I should like to find it again. In that book, one of the heroes owned a magic puppet theatre, and at three taps of a wand the puppets moved of their own accord. I can still vaguely remember engravings which used to fill me with religious ecstasy, and which showed soldiers with their little wooden arms raised stiffly by thick strings.

To cut a long story short, I personally conceived and acted countless plays. At first, in the lavatory of our flat (I was then living with my grandparents, on the sixth floor in Rue Le Goff, which leads off Rue Soufflot). Then, little by little, I grew bolder: I'd carry my puppets, with a towel, to the Luxembourg; I'd pick a chair in one of the walks in the 'English Garden'; I'd crouch down behind this, draping my towel round its feet; and I'd then display the puppets, fitted over my raised hands, between the uprights of the chair's back. The chair would thus be transformed into a very acceptable little stage. I used to perform and speak aloud as if for myself alone. But I'd know perfectly well what I was waiting for – and which didn't fail to occur, right from the very first time, within quarter of an hour: the children broke off their games, sat down quietly on chairs, and gave all their attention to that free performance.

I acquired girl-friends by this means: particularly a certain Nicole, who must have been about my age and whose face was dotted with freckles. She was my current 'fiancée', and she was particularly dear to me because I'd obtained her affection by means of my contrivances. As early as that, I was connecting – and it was perhaps the deepest element in my desire to write – art and love in such a way that I felt it was impossible to obtain the affection of those little girls otherwise than by my talents as an actor and story-teller. Not just impossible, but base. I should have hated anyone to love me for my looks or my physical charm; what was necessary was for them to be captivated by the charm of my contrivances, my plays, my speeches and my poems, and to come to love me on that basis. That's why Zamacoïs's *Les Bouffons* enchanted me beyond all measure at the time, because one found there a princess who was captivated by an eloquent personage named Jacasse despite his enormous hump (it was, in fact, false: but the princess didn't know that).[20]

It will be said these were the hopes of an ugly man: to make up for it by fair speech. But I insist on the fact that I wasn't yet ugly. I had fine, fair hair and plump cheeks; my squint wasn't yet very visible. Let us say rather that, even if I wasn't ugly, with sure instinct I was getting ready to be so. If *Les Bouffons* enchanted me, Cyrano shocked and distressed me.[21] How could Roxane love that stupid Christian? How had she failed to single out Cyrano, from the very first day? For me, at that time, Cyrano represented the model of the perfect lover. Underlying all this, more than a presentiment of my future ugliness, there was a certain conception of human greatness – which, although it has lost that naive form, has never left me since. I explained about it in Notebook 2. Greatness, for me, rose above abjection. The mind took responsibility for the body's miseries, dominated them, suppressed them in a sense and, by manifesting itself through the ill-favoured body, shone all the more brightly. I liked the story of Beauty and the Beast, because the Beast first wins Beauty's interest and affection in his guise as Beast. Later on, when I was about sixteen, I even wrote a story on that subject.[22]

Much later, at the École Normale, I again found – in an emotion which passed like a lightning-flash – something of that original feeling. I was reading a book by André Bellessort on Balzac, which gave an account of the first encounter between Balzac and Mme Hanska.[23] They didn't know one another, were to meet on the Promenade, I think, and had agreed on some distinguishing sign or other. Mme Hanska was horrified to see advancing towards her, wearing the agreed sign, a large man dressed with flashy elegance. She was afraid, and on the point of taking to flight. 'But,' according to Bellessort, 'she saw his eyes and she stayed.' That was all it took to stir me deeply for a few moments. It's true that I'd discovered my ugliness by then, and was unhappy about it.

The reading I used to go in for of the romantic writers, when I was about ten, certainly helped to form that idea of greatness: Triboulet

20. Miguel Zamacoïs (1866–1939) wrote his romantic verse drama *Les Bouffons* in 1907.

21. *Cyrano de Bergerac* (1897): poetic cape-and-sword drama set in seventeenth-century Paris, by Edmond Rostand (1868–1918).

22. It has not, apparently, survived.

23. Comtesse Éveline Hanska (1801–82): Balzac's *Étrangère*, whom he married shortly before his death in 1850, after a correspondence lasting eighteen years. See André Bellesort, *Balzac et son oeuvre*, Paris 1924.

and countless others – sublime souls in ill-favoured bodies.[24] But it wasn't really the sublimity of the soul which roused me to envy: it was rather that power to string lines together into wonderful tirades –which must, I thought, leave a woman quite helpless, at the speaker's mercy. It goes without saying that the loves I imagined were chaste. The speaker would take her in his arms and coax her gently: the story would stop at that point. Not only did I not envisage at all the physical pleasures which must result from that poetry recital, I didn't even bother to imagine the sequel of the adventure. Well, they probably loved each other tenderly and were very happy together. But that prospect hardly thrilled me. What most delighted me was the seductive enterprise. Once the woman had been captivated, I used to abandon her to her fate. And I'd already be envisaging new seductive enterprises for the hero.

Quite certainly, it was from the pedagogic climate wherein I dwelt that I drew that idea of the seductive power of *words*. It was another way of acknowledging the superiority of spiritual values, to dream thus of being a scholarly Don Juan, slaying women through the power of his golden tongue. Underlying all this, moreover, was certainly the spiritualist ignorance of what a body was, and the impossibility of conceiving clearly what physical turmoil could be. A very normal impossibility in an eight-year-old child – but one which will seem more monstrous when it's known that I kept it until almost the end of my youth. Not that I was unaware of the thing, at twenty-five; but it struck me as a preposterous scandal.

An audience of willing admirers surrounded me in my childhood, and encouraged my words. I became more and more confident, and was soon quite unbearable – though I was crafty enough not to show it too much. Yet I wasn't really proud – pride came later – I was acting out the part of pride to myself. At the age of ten, at Vic-sur-Cère, where I used to spend my holidays with my grandparents, we used often to go for a walk with a former deputy-headmaster (he and my grandfather had been brought together by their common profession), his wife and a young woman called, I think, Mme Lebrun, whose husband had been called up. This collection of individuals – who were so kind as to look upon me as a child prodigy (such were the rules of the game) – represents pretty well the type of society in which, at the time, I used to display my graces: retired teachers; old men and women who doted on me; and then, from time to time, a young

24. Triboulet (died c. 1536): court jester of Louis XII and François I, celebrated by Rabelais and the central character in Victor Hugo's drama *Le Roi s'amuse*.

woman tagging along.

That young woman, Mme Lebrun – I desired her as much as a child of ten can desire a woman: in other words, I'd have liked to see her bosom and touch her shoulders. I turned on the charm with her; and one day, carried away by my lyricism to the point of forgetting my age, I confided to her that a girl had made me suffer, and that I'd decided in a spirit of vengeance to make all the women I met suffer likewise. This was invented, of course, on the spur of the moment; but I at once felt, with violence and pathos, the imaginary injury which the faithless one had done me. I can't think of that little episode today without gritting my teeth, and conclude from it that I was then entirely rotten. Shortly afterwards, Mme Lebrun declared with a serious air: 'I'd like to know the boy when he's twenty. I'm sure all the women will be crazy about him.' I accepted this forecast without blenching. The fact was, I found it entirely natural. I was a disgusting little monster of conceit.

The only thing I can say to defend myself is that, basically, I wanted to love as in books. Love appeared to me like a courtly adventure – a game with its own rules – basically very like those played in mediaeval love-courts. There was also some sort of idea of chivalry mixed in with it – but on the sly. I often used to picture myself saving some beautiful girl. Sometimes, I liked also to imagine myself misunderstood; wrongfully accused; abandoned by all, even the one I loved – and then having my name cleared, ten years later. To tell the truth, I used to hesitate about my beloved's role. For my misfortune to be complete and my final triumph unalloyed, it was necessary that she at first misjudge me. But I read everywhere – and had easily let myself be persuaded – that love involves a kind of divinatory instinct. So, if that woman truly loved me, she oughtn't to entertain any doubts as to my innocence. I got myself out of this by throwing all kinds of obstacles into the midst of our love.

What I see underlying all those ill-starred, touching adventures is the impossibility I was in of conceiving a happy love *after* the seduction. Once the woman had been conquered, I no longer had any idea what to do with her. And if I nevertheless wanted to continue the story, I had to invent misunderstandings and obstacles so that each reconciliation was a new seduction. To be honest, for a long time –and perhaps to this very day – nothing struck me as more moving than the moment at which the avowal of love is finally wrenched forth. And I think today that what used to captivate me in that avowal, even back in my childhood, was the spellbound freedom from which it emanates.

For the pampered child I was, love was dirt-cheap: it sprang up beneath my feet. Among the old ladies, I found none that was cruel; it was always like that. So I came down with a bump when, at La Rochelle, I found myself ugly and abandoned; when I realized that it was difficult to win a woman's love, and that others managed it better than me. I fell into a deep state of gloom, and experienced the torments of unrequited love. Not for a girl, actually, but for two of my comrades: Pelletier and Boutillier. It wasn't a question at all of homosexual attraction, but of a boundless admiration and affection, which was promptly turned to their advantage by those two fine young fellows. They forced me to dance to their tune; I made myself their lackey. I stole from my mother for them; I fought for them, on countless occasions; and they betrayed me shamefully.

At the same time, to my great misfortune then and to my great future good fortune, I became a whipping-boy for all the kids at the lycée. Is it around that time that the dream was born in me of a select society in which I should be king? I suppose so. Inasmuch as the origin of that dream, for some reason, is connected for me with a play by Verlaine – *Les Uns et les autres*[25] – which I read at about that time, I imagine it was a compensatory dream. So I pictured a whole little phalanstery of handsome young men – elegant, intelligent and strong – and charming girls. I too was there, and I ruled by my strength of mind and my charm. This fiction – a social one, in me who was so unsocial! – was certainly cherished by me out of revenge. For there was, in fact, a group facing me – but I wasn't its king, but its whipping-boy: it was entirely formed against me.

However, I had neither girl-friend nor 'bird' (to use the dreadful term they'd then employ), and spent all my time despairing about it. From that time on, the great thing for me was to love and be loved. Especially to be loved. I couldn't understand how that feeling, which used to seem so very cheap to me in my childhood, had become so rare and precious. I used to repeat gloomily to myself Mme Lebrun's prophecy: 'At the age of twenty, all the women will be crazy about him.' I had some hope that, at twenty, things would change. Meanwhile, however, time was passing and I was becoming more and more deeply imbued with the feeling of my ugliness.

At the same time, the dream of seductive speeches – for which I was anyway never given any opportunity – became clearer and more intense. This would have involved 'presenting' the world to a woman; dissecting for her the most veiled meanings of landscapes or of

25. Paul Verlaine (1844–96) published his one-act comedy, *Les Uns et les autres*, set in a Watteauesque eighteenth-century park, in 1884.

instants; giving her a work already half-done; substituting myself for her – for her thought and her perception – everywhere and always; and presenting her with objects already fashioned and perceived: in short, acting the enchanter, being always the person whose presence causes the trees to be more tree-like, the houses more house-like and the world suddenly to exist more. I was then quite incapable of it. But I note that desire because, yet again, it meant achieving harmony between art and love. To write was to grasp the meaning of things, and to render it as well as possible. And to captivate was the same thing, quite plainly. Furthermore, I'm amazed to see the degree of imperialism involved in this. For, when one really thinks about it, it was a question of actually perceiving in a woman's place; thinking in her place; stealing her thoughts, in order to replace them with my own. My thoughts, experienced by an enchanted consciousness, would thus have become enchantments in my own eyes: would have acquired precisely the necessary relief and distance for me to be charmed by them.

In the meantime, the woman to be captivated still didn't make her appearance. Which didn't prevent me, at about that time, from deciding I preferred the company of women to that of men. I shall return to this. It was at that moment that my stepfather came out with a pronouncement which branded me: 'He's like me,' he said pointing at me, 'he'll never be able to talk to women.' I can see the history of that pronouncement so clearly. I can so well picture how it was said: out of the blue, absent-mindedly and without any malice on the part of my stepfather – who, on the contrary, must have imbued it with respect for the hard-working, solid, uninspired boy he supposed me to be. But in a child's life there are always words of this kind, thrown out absent-mindedly, which are like the absent-minded smoker's match in some forest in the Estérel – and which set the whole lot ablaze. I'm not so sure that this pronouncement wasn't one of the main causes, in later life, of all those conversations I stupidly wasted in spouting sweet nothings – just to prove to myself that in fact I did know how to talk to women. My stepfather, moreover, certainly forgot it years ago. Indeed, he later said to me severely (it was a reproach in his mind, but a balm to my heart – which wiped everything out): 'Pooh! you're a ladies' man.' By that, I think he meant a man capable of doing crazy things for women. I preferred to take it as meaning: a man festooned with women. Undoubtedly, however, those two pronouncements had the greatest influence on me.

So, I had no female conquests in La Rochelle. When I came to Paris, I hardly did any better. Jules Laforgue became my favourite author: he boasted proudly of having a thousand palaces in his heart, which the foolishness of women prevented them from visiting.[26] I turned him to good account. I wept over his verses. Especially one night, when I'd been with my parents to see an operetta called *Madame*, in which I'd seen an ugly but charming woman called Davia sing: 'She isn't as bad as that at all!' She had won my heart. When I got home, I reread some of Laforgue's poems and sobbed – or practically did. Nizan used to suffer from similar melancholy fits, though he had more success than I did.

But what had changed profoundly since my arrival in Paris was the fact that I'd found comrades and a friend. Friendship was the main thing. It's something which appeared in my life with my sixteenth year and Nizan, and which, in different guises, hasn't left it since. I've had three 'bosom friends', each of whom corresponded to a specific period in my life: Nizan – Guille – the Beaver (for the Beaver was *also* my friend, and still is). What friendship brought me – far more than affection (whatever that may have been) – was a federative world, in which my friend and I would pool all our values, all our thoughts and all our tastes. And this world was renewed by ceaseless invention. At the same time, each of us buttressed the other, and the result was a *couple* of considerable strength.

This is perhaps less true of my friendship with Guille, since we never managed to pool our worlds. Although we had for each other the strongest possible attraction and the highest respect, too many things separated us. What is more, our group wasn't formed: there was Maheu; there was above all Mme Morel, whom Guille clearly preferred to me and whom I ended up preferring to him.[27] In the two other cases, however, what counted above all was that powerful couple we formed. For a long time, people at the École Normale said: 'Sartre and Nizan'—and the image was so strong that we'd sometimes be taken for one another. For ages, people went on ascribing *Antoine Bloyé* to me and believing Nizan to be a teacher at Le Havre. As late as last year, Brunschvicg, encountered at the *NRF*, said to me: 'I must tell you, in spite of the attacks you have published against me, that I like your books a great deal.' I stood there flabbergasted, while he went off without leaving me time to reply. For it was Nizan who'd made those attacks on Brunschvicg, in *Les Chiens de garde*. And which

26. See n. 34 on p. 155 above. I do not think that this is a specific reference, although the concept of 'palace' of the heart or soul is a favourite of Laforgue's, e.g. in his *Complaintes*.

27. René Maheu: friend of Sartre from their student days at the École Normale; known as 'le Lama', he appears in De Beauvoir's autobiography as 'Herbaud'.

books did he 'like'? It was hard to decide. *La Conspiration? Les Chiens de garde? La Nausée?*[28] The important thing, in any case, is that we constituted an envied, respected *force*.

What it comes down to is that, since my seventeenth year, I've always lived as part of a couple – and by that I don't at all mean a loving couple. I mean that·I was engaged in a kind of radiant, and somewhat torrid, existence – without any inner life and without any secrets – in which I felt the total pressure of another presence constantly upon me, and in which I hardened myself to endure that presence. Life as part of a couple made me hard and transparent like a diamond; otherwise I shouldn't have endured it. It's one of the main reasons, no doubt, for the 'publicness' of my life. As I've already said, my least feelings and thoughts were public from birth. T. used to be amazed that I could envisage publishing notebooks of total sincerity. But that has become natural to me, and I'm tempted to believe it comes from my friendships. I had the impression, at every instant, that my friends were reading my innermost self; that they could see my thoughts forming, even when they were still only bubbles in the dough; and that what was becoming clear to me was already clear to them. I could feel their gaze to my very entrails: it obliged me to clarify my ideas as quickly as possible and to track down the penumbra in myself; as soon as a thought belonged to me with complete transparency, moreover, at the same stroke it belonged also to them.

From that period on, a pitiless clarity ruled over my mind: it was an operating-room, hygienic, without shadows, without nooks or crannies, without microbes, beneath a cold light. And yet, since intimacy never lets itself be expelled entirely, there was nonetheless – beyond that sincerity of public confession, or rather before reaching it – a kind of bad faith which was really mine, which was me: not so much in the fact of keeping back secrets as, rather, in a certain way of escaping that very sincerity and not giving myself up to it. In one sense, if you like, I was completely up to my neck in it; in another sense, I escaped it by *seeing* myself up to my neck in it – and by desolidarizing myself from that public part of myself, by the very fact of viewing it. As I've already said, the essential form of my pride consists in having no solidarity with myself. Was this constituted as a defence against the stifling translucidity of friendship? Or, on the

28. Paul Nizan (1905–1940), a friend of Sartre since their lycée days, published the novels *Antoine Bloyé* (1933), *La Conspiration* (1938) and the philosophical essay *Les Chiens de Garde* (1932), among other works, before being killed in action in 1940. A prominent member of the Communist Party until his resignation over the Nazi–Soviet pact, he contributed to the character of Brunet in *Les Chemins de la liberté*.

contrary, was it what allowed me to endure that glaring public life? I couldn't say, but the relationship is obvious. Only the firm consciousness of always being beyond what I was, allowed me for years to yield myself up unveiled and in total nakedness to my friends. Only my pride allowed me that total sincerity. Sincerity, moreover, which was total only *in the facts* stated, but which left intact my *attitude towards my sincerity*.

All that I used to say about myself detached itself from me when I said it – became common property, federal moneys: it was *us* much more than myself. But what then was I myself? A mere look – neither sad nor gay; contemplative and reserved – at what I was saying, at what entered my mind or my heart. I was living dissociated from myself, like M. Teste.[29] I didn't have that warm, intimate intercourse with myself which, for so many people, serves as a consolation and cradlesong. All that I felt, I'd at once grasp gingerly and express in words, before even letting it come fully to fruition: I'd force it a bit, then serve it up piping hot to my friend. The latter would at once give me his opinion on the matter, and by so doing help me to construct it fully. No sooner was it born than the movement of humour or tenderness, generosity or egoism, would receive its label, be filed among other similar movements and even be attached to a value: together we would decide that it was worthy of censure or praise, in terms of the moral code we both accepted.

As a result of this, there was something missing in me. What was missing is inexpressible, so much so that I lived for long without realizing it. It was nothing at all, except a certain way of dwelling in oneself: of being an integral part of oneself. T. – alone at Laigle and able to rely only on herself – arrived, on the contrary, at an intimacy with herself which admittedly didn't exclude a certain bad faith, but which was soft as a caress. The feelings within her, unnamed and unnameable, would develop with a kind of nonchalance to the point they wished to reach, but no further – without running the risk of at once being dragged by the hair; exposed to the light, all wriggling; killed with a sharp fist-blow to the nape; and then catalogued, embalmed or stuffed. That's what the Beaver was expressing when she said: 'You aren't psychological': which doesn't so much mean I don't have the same psychological reactions as other people, but rather that, in me, they at once appear like dried plants in a herbarium.

29. M. Teste: character created by Paul Valéry in *La Soirée de Monsieur Teste* (1895)—a 'monster of the intellect'.

That total translucidity, I must say, was more typical of me than of my friends: whence I came to the conclusion it was mainly I who placed friendship on that terrain. Even the Beaver was always able to retain zones of shadow, or modesty, that were a home for the 'psychological': where a thousand tender or bitter viruses developed. Nizan and Guille, of course, maintained their reserve meticulously. And yet, I managed to drag them some way into that effulgence of cold light. The result of that federation of ours – when, with the Beaver, it was carried to its highest state of fulfilment – was an overwhelming happiness similar to summer. The Beaver complained gently about it in her novel.[30] Its heroine, Françoise, sometimes remains speechless before that happiness – which doesn't even leave her the possibility of desiring anything other than it; and which yet, at times, before the obscure charms of countenances sweet that know each other not, may appear intolerably harsh.

I think it's something I haven't stressed enough in these notebooks, even though they're explaining me: until the present war, I *lived publicly*. And these notebooks are basically a way of continuing to live publicly. Often, I force my impressions. Let me be understood: I force them in the good sense – but a cool, dark error might perhaps be preferable to their blinding truth. For this truth no longer has anything historical about it; it no longer concerns the man I was on that day, at that hour. It's an *essential* truth: essentially, a man of a certain kind had to experience such an impression in such circumstances. Circumstances, character, impression – all are meticulously defined: but all that is already no longer me. The truth is, I treat my feelings as ideas: with an idea, one pushes it till it cracks – or finally becomes 'what it really was'. But if the psychologist has a right to proceed in this way with feelings, the *man* calls for mercy: he'd like sometimes to have reactions he couldn't name.

But I'm not 'psychological', precisely because I behave like a psychologist towards myself. And my friendships have certainly helped to give me this attitude. However – while I was yielding to it fully; while I was encroaching on Maheu to the point of wearying him; while I was constructing tireless spotlights with the Beaver – I was dreaming of another man, who'd have been handsome, hesitant, obscure, slow and upright in his thoughts; who'd not have had any acquired grace, but only a silent, spontaneous kind: I saw him, for some reason, as a worker and hobo in the Eastern USA. How I should have liked to feel uncertain ideas slowly, patiently forming within me! How I should

30. *L'Invitée.*

have liked to boil with great, obscure rages; faint from great, motiveless outpourings of tenderness! My American worker (who resembled Gary Cooper) could do and feel all that. I pictured him sitting on a railway embankment, tired and dusty; he'd be waiting for the cattletruck, into which he'd jump unseen – and I should have liked to be *him*. I even invented, together with the Beaver, a charming (to my mind) character called Little Head-high, who thought little, spoke little and always did the right thing.[31] Since, by a singular fatality, everything I imagine always ends up happening to me, I finally encountered Little Head-high: to wit, Little Bost. But I'll come back to that. What's certain is that, in the midst of friendship, I've always envisaged love as an opportunity to lose my head and finally act without knowing what I was doing.

As I've said, the counterpart of that overwhelming transparency was strength, Olympian security and happiness. Those various couples to which I belonged always appeared crushingly powerful to the people round us. And they were. Especially the last – the one I formed with the Beaver. Our bonds were so solid and fascinating for other people, that nobody could love one of us without being gripped by a fierce jealousy – which would end by changing into an irresistible attraction – for the other one, even before meeting them, on the basis of mere accounts. So that, for me, friendship has always been not a vague affective connection, but a milieu, a world and a strength.

Yet I'm not cut out for friendship. I've disappointed all my friends – not by betrayal, neglect or lack of consideration, but by a profound lack of warmth. So far as consideration is concerned, I've always showed it to everyone: I'd never miss an appointment, never be neglectful. But there was something put on about it, which must have shown despite my efforts. Guille used to reproach me with always trying to appear 'perfect'; he claimed that, on leaving Mme Morel's, I must have rubbed my hands and said to the Beaver: 'Well, my dear Beaver, as you saw I was perfect again.' In actual fact, in our friendship Guille was the more neglectful, the more capricious and for long periods the more indifferent. But he usually had a communicative warmth, an almost feminine tenderness, a jealous exclusivity that I was very far from possessing myself.

I never grew angry – yet he sometimes tried me sorely. I'd arrive at Mme Morel's to meet him – he'd have made an appointment with me – and I'd find a note on a table in the sitting-room: 'We've taken the car

31. For the character of *Petit Crâne*, see De Beauvoir's *The Prime of Life*, p. 245. *Crâne* as a noun in French means 'skull', as an adjective 'dauntless'.

to St-Germain. Wait for us.' I'd wait for two or three hours, reading seventeenth-century tales of amorous intrigue discovered in the sitting-room bookcase. Then they'd return and Guille would say: 'That Lady was quite unbearable. She kept saying "Poor Sartre, he's waiting for us" and wanting to come home. But the weather was so lovely . . . .' Yet my train for Le Havre would be leaving at 8 p.m. and I'd just have enough time for quarter of an hour's chat with them. I wouldn't get angry – I'd never get angry – but I'm not sure that my even temper wasn't held against me: it looked like indifference, and in a sense really was. When the Paris train was carrying me towards Guille, I don't recall having had the same movement of joy he certainly used to have, when he was in a good mood and went to wait for me at the station. I wouldn't even be thinking about seeing him. If he left me alone for two hours in Mme Morel's sitting-room, I'd not get bored – busy as I was, reading and enjoying being there (as I've said, I liked other people's interiors and especially that one): I'd find my solitude poetic.

Whenever Guille showed a certain tenderness for me – always very discreet and charming – I used to be as embarrassed as if a homosexual had propositioned me. As soon as relations with a man are no longer just superficially cordial, it embarrasses me. I neither like confiding, nor being confided in by him. Not that I'm discreet – quite the contrary – and I sometimes talk about my life, giving the kind of details one might take to be confidences. But in my eyes they're not: I'm saying only what I'm willing to tell everybody. What I call a confidence is defined more by its form than by its content: by a certain carelessness; a certain moist abandon; a desire to be understood and sustained. If a man confides in me, I become icy.

I had a passion for Pelletier and Boutillier, to be sure – and for Nizan. But that was in the days when my sexuality wasn't yet very well defined, and my feelings certainly contained an element of platonic love. A man's moral or physical nakedness shocks me to the highest degree. Guille could see no harm in appearing naked before me; but for my part, I was shocked to the highest degree and didn't know where to turn my eyes. I wrote in these notebooks that this was perhaps repressed homosexuality; but when the Beaver read that remark, she thought she'd die laughing. And, indeed, I suppose it isn't that. But what is it then? I don't know. Perhaps a certain coarseness in the line of the male body invites me to coarseness myself; what is more, there's a whole part of me which is coarseness and crudity, and which perhaps grasps that opportunity of displaying itself. Or, perhaps, tenderness is so clearly sexual with me – as intimacy is, too – that I can't conceive of being tender with a man without at once feeling something like a brief surge of sexuality, which finds no outlet and at once repels and embarrasses me.

I'm not speaking here of *desire*. Yet I can see, for example, how my purely friendly tenderness for Mme Morel finds sustenance in the delicacy of her features, her skin and her gestures. There's as if a natural kinship there. Besides, I've often noticed in tenderness an odd lack of distinction that's established, between another person's face and my own. The phenomenon, when exaggerated, bears a name in psychiatry: patients have been known to raise a glass to their lips and say to their neighbours: 'Here, want a drink?'; or, conversely, seeing their neighbours taking a gulp, to imagine they were drinking themselves. Yet this is what happens to me, when my tenderness is shared: it's the play of my own features I can read on the other's face; that strikes me as precisely the look I'm wearing. And this, no doubt, comes from the fact that my own expression – as happens in shared loves – moves the other, at once giving birth to the gentle smile I see on her lips. So I have the impression it's my smile which is being born over there, on those beautiful lips. But the fact is there: I always have the impression I'm being tender with the help of the other's body. Yet, I can still feel myself, still control my facial expressions: but I perceive them over there, on that other face. So that, for me, tenderness is not merely a feeling, but rather a situation for two.

And, quite obviously, if the other is a man, the coarseness of his physique is an insuperable obstacle to the establishment of that situation. That's why I've always understood better than others the resistances a young girl has to overcome before she can desire a man properly: resistances which the Beaver and I – taking our cue from a remark by Charles Du Bos, in a bad preface to a bad novel by Hope Mirrlees[32] – used to call the 'nymph-like character' of every young girl. A man's body has always struck me as too highly spiced, too rich, too strong-tasting, to be capable of being desired immediately. Some apprenticeship is certainly required. O. confirmed this for me one day, in the Café Victor at Rouen, when she said that the charm of a woman or young boy is disclosed at once, whereas long familiarity and particular attention are needed before a man's is revealed. I've always thought, when taking delight in kissing fresh, tender lips, of the singular impression my own must be making – all rough and smelling of tobacco. It will be said that the woman desires the man because she's a woman – but, for me, that doesn't mean anything. On the

---

32. Probably *The Counterplot*, translated in 1929 as *Le Choc en retour*.

contrary, I think that, for the woman as much as for the man, it's the woman who's the absolute object of desire. For the man to become desirable in his turn, a 'transfer' must be effected.

But this is not the place to discuss that. I wanted to note only that, for my own part, I can't imagine tenderness in my relations with men. So I've had friendships only with what I shall term women-men: an extremely rare species, standing out from the rest thanks to their physical charm or sometimes beauty, and to a host of inner riches which the common run of men know nothing of. Guille, in his palmy days, could waste hours talking to me about a face; about a fleeting effect of the light or his mood; or about some trivial scene that had just unfolded before us. So I'm a woman-man myself, I think, for all my ugliness – at least in my main preoccupations. But other men are entirely on the outside, as I've said elsewhere: they forget themselves totally – they're calculators.

People like that bore and irritate me: I avoid them, and for long – throughout my youth – used to flatter myself that I was the accomplice of women against them. I remember how, only two years ago, that little Lucile – a depraved, lying actress from the Atelier;[33] a flirt, full of crude feminine wiles, but a woman all the same – had arranged for me to be asked to lunch by her 'fellow': a splendid Egyptian with burning eyes, darkly jealous, who seemed to me to represent the perfect male type – the sort of man to swoon with sensual pleasure on a poor woman's breast; to protect her with a strong arm when she has no need of it; to subside at her knees after great, stormy outbursts; to overwhelm her with clumsy attentions, without understanding anything about her character; to be crazy with anguish when she loves him, and tranquil when she's thinking about another man; to weep, at times, as though his heart were breaking; and to be led a fine song and dance. She loved him, that's for sure – and precisely because of all that. She felt herself alone, beside that great body whose sensual warmth suffused her. She loved him because she could deceive him.

She'd tried to flirt with me, but I hadn't let her – knowing very well that, without letting a finger be laid on herself, she'd lavished the most explicit caresses on every actor in the Atelier, whether he was aged fifteen or sixty. For a day or two we'd tilted at each other with stupid cunning, and I'd carried the day: I really can't think what strange kind of pleasure I took in that game. The fact remains, throughout that lunch she played footsie with me under the table. Her aim in this wasn't at all to show me that she was ready to bestow her favours on me

33. Théatre de l'Atelier, see note 58 on p. 74 above.

– since I knew where I stood, and the matter was settled between us. I imagined that she derived a sly pleasure from deceiving her fellow. I even imagine that – in making that gesture, which had no real consequence either for herself or for me, since it could no longer engage either of us – she was thinking of him, not me. Ridiculing him like that, without any risk – in his presence, and while he was talking to me with great courtesy about his *agrégation* exams in law – was her way of loving him: she must have been all slippery, with a sensuality that was directed in no way at me, but at him.

What amused me, however, was the fact that she'd chosen me as an accomplice *against that male* whom she loved. She couldn't hope to arouse me: I'd made my position clear to her on that score, and she knew very well I was taking her game for what it was worth. But, for that very reason, she drew me into that game with the same lack of modesty towards me as if I'd been a eunuch or a woman. In a way, she knew I was of the same kind as her, and sufficiently feminine for it to be possible to laugh at a man *with me*. (If I'd been liable to let myself be aroused by those pressures, she'd have laughed at her male all alone and against me – but the game would have been more dangerous.) That was my last, fleeting complication of that kind. In the O.Z. affair, it was my own turn to feel male, alas!

What is more, friendship has something austere about it, which bores and oppresses me. Precisely because I don't feel anything very much in myself, it mainly presents itself to me as a duty. I've tried to maintain friendly relations with women to whom I was once united by quite other bonds. But, as soon as I no longer love, I grow bored. I think I have no *need* of friends because, basically, I don't need anybody: I don't need assistance – that austere, constant help which friendship offers. I've never, for example – ever since I set off to war – wanted to meet somebody with my kind of intelligence who'd find interesting the same things that I did. I prefer to derive everything from myself. Per contra, I don't make the most of others. The Beaver has often told me I don't listen to the stories people tell me. That's a bit unjust – but I do listen pretty badly and often wriggle about on my chair, waiting for the tale to come to an end. It's the same with friends as with other people's philosophies, which I have so much trouble assimilating. Since, moreover, I've no desire to talk to them about myself, I soon grow bored. I certainly lack any individual humanism. I'm touched by crowds, by passers-by; but, for individuals, I don't have that spontaneous sympathy upon which a good friendship could be founded. My first movement, on the contrary, is one of mistrust and suspicion. I'm writing this in the Soldiers' Home. There are a hundred fellows in the room. Taken en masse, they move me somewhat; if I consider them one by one, however, there are few who do not shock me by their attitude or speech. There's not a single one of them whose acquaintance I should like to make. I don't like men – I mean the males of the species.

Yet, at the École Normale with Nizan, I discovered camaraderie – and for me that was a good use to make of men. Being one of a set – that was what suddenly entranced me. I think there's a quite special pleasure in feeling oneself stand out against the background formed by a group; in feeling a kind of solidarity round one, which one escapes at the very moment one yields to it. I think what entranced me above all was felt simultaneity. Normally, while I write, my neighbour's leafing through a review and, not far away from me, two fellows are playing chess: that too is a simultaneity. But in a sense it's abstract – scattered in a thousand little local, isolated acts. I only think it, and scarcely feel it. Whereas, because of the solidarity that united us, each of my gestures in the unity of our set would give itself as simultaneous with some other gesture of one of my comrades: that used to confer upon it a kind of necessity. I was horrified, in Berlin, to see how much the Germans enjoyed that kind of simultaneity. At the Neue Welt, an immense hangar where thousands of Germans come to drink beer, they used to present teams of Bavarians on the stage, who could do nothing except sharply indicate that simultaneity: one would throw his hat into the air, while another danced and the third sounded a hunting-horn, etc. The charm of the display was very obviously the '*while*' – which has nothing in common with the multiplicity in unity of a corps de ballet, since it's real diversity in a merely affective unity.

So it was something we used to feel quite strongly, and which delighted me. Moreover, I wanted to be leader – or the 'moving spirit', at least. This was assuredly to get my revenge for the humiliations suffered at La Rochelle, which, as I've said, had marked me deeply. Was I that leader? Moving spirit, perhaps – but though I may have been feared and sometimes admired; though I certainly provided amusement (I used to throw my energies unstintingly into doing take-offs, singing ditties and organizing countless pranks with Nizan): I always saw about me a kind of republican mistrust, when there was any question of choosing me officially as leader in some undertaking. No one, I suppose, would deny my spirit of initiative or my persistence. But I worry people because I lack dignity: there's certainly something of the buffoon about me, and in social groupings my buffoonery wins the upper hand. People view me with a mixture of amusement and consternation: they're on their guard. Besides, almost immediately afterwards I realized the ignominy of being a leader. But my desire to rule was merely transformed. I hadn't lost that dream of ruling, through love, over a gracious, idle community. Little by little, the dream was transformed anew (here again, I must say I've on several occasions had what I wanted) and became a desire for spiritual authority: I should have liked to be the wise man people consult – more precisely, a *starets* like those of Dostoevsky.[34]

I'm not so sure that if I were really to probe myself deeply, I shouldn't find particles of that old desire. I was very disoriented and gloomy when I left that group life, after passing out from the École Normale. No friendship or love could at first replace that distinctive, easy-going density of life. Nowadays, I'd find it unbearable. Years later, whenever I found myself in a male community I conducted myself there as a fierce and lonely critic. The astonishing thing, in view of this, is that I nevertheless inspired affection; Brunschwick and Copeau in Berlin, Pieter here. I swear on my life it was undeserved. If by any chance, out of curiosity, I've allowed some fellow creature to approach me, I have but a single desire: to drop him as soon as circumstances permit. The male relationships one forms at my age – which are neither the camaraderie of a set, nor friendship – are unbearable to me. It has been years now since I *asked* to see any man, or made the slightest effort to meet one. They seek me out and I put up with them. I live surrounded by women who'd all give their right arm to know a Faulkner or Caldwell. For my own part, though I admire the former greatly and have the most sympathetic feelings for the latter, I have no wish whatever to see them. Nor Hemingway, who everyone says is so agreeable. If it were just a matter of crossing the road and climbing to the third floor to see them, I'd probably do it – but I wouldn't go much further. Or rather, I'd give a lot to see them live, while myself remaining invisible: to haunt their house unseen. But what sickens me in advance is any idea of the relationship being mutual – of being seen by them while I see them: the idea that there could be any affective connection between us, be it merely one of cordiality or even politeness.

In short, have I ever really been fond of a man of my own age – except for Nizan in the old days? I don't believe so. Nor ever wanted one to be fond of me.[35] In friendship, the consciousnesses retain a solidity and freedom which used to strike me as very austere: I had no

---

34. *starets* = elder.
35. I have adopted the somewhat ambiguous 'be fond of' because *aimer* means both 'to love' and 'to like' (and is etymologically cognate with *amitié* = friendship).

need to yield myself up to consciousness of that kind (not that I feared the lucidity of their judgement – it was more that they were like beautiful marble women, who failed to arouse my desire). I was drawn only by the distraught swoonings and voluntary enslavement of consciousnesses in love. In short, there's one half of humanity that hardly exists for me. The other half – well, there's no denying it, the other half is my sole and constant concern. I take pleasure only in the company of women; I feel respect, tenderness and friendship only for women. I wouldn't move an inch to see Faulkner, but I'd make a long journey to make the acquaintance of Rosamond Lehmann. To speak like Bost: 'On my knees, I'd go!'

I blush to write all this, because it's a tiny bit reminiscent of that Tino Rossi song *J'aime les femmes à la folie* – but that's the situation. One might have thought, initially, that this more or less indiscriminate passion came, in a very young man, from an adolescent romanticism. But I'm almost thirty-five, I've been surrounded by women for years, and I still want to meet new ones – or, at least, I still wanted to until very recently: now it's over. Though I'm a person who gets horribly bored in the company of men, it's very rare for the company of women not to entertain me. I prefer to talk to a woman about the tiniest things than about philosophy to Aron. It's because those are the tiny things which exist for me; and any woman, even the stupidest, talks about them as I like to talk about them myself: I *get on* with women. I like their way of talking, and of saying or seeing things; I like their way of thinking; I like the subjects they think about.

For a long time, I thought I could best express the esteem in which I held them by declaring them to be the equals of men, and by demanding equality of rights for them. At the same time, I used to refuse to admit there was any radical difference between the sexes, and I used to ascribe the secondary differences to education and to society. But this was to do them a disservice. That they ought to have the same rights as us goes without saying. But it's a fine compliment to make them, I must say, to call them men's 'equals' – and assure them that, were it not for their humble social situation, they'd certainly manage to think as well as we do. The real idiocy, demonstratively committed by Auguste Comte, was generously to allot them sensitivity as their portion. As if that meant anything. As if there could be a human faculty called sensitivity, with which certain representatives of the species were more handsomely endowed than the rest. As if each human-reality did not exist, in totality, in each of its undertakings. The whole question must be looked into further. But it's certainly not by asserting equality of the sexes, like a good Kantian rationalist, that the problem will be solved. That notion of equality means nothing, and I was completely mistaken.

29 February

I'm not so sure I didn't seek out women's company, at one time, in order to get rid of the burden of my ugliness. By looking at them, speaking to them and exerting myself to bring an animated, joyful look to their faces, I'd lose myself in them and forget myself. It must have been something of the kind, since at the same period (roughly between the ages of 20 and 25), no sooner would I find myself paired off with an ugly or ill-favoured woman, than I'd feel – very acutely, and with cynicism – what a pair we made. I didn't redeem her, quite the contrary – and the whole was as ugly as its parts. I hated us then, mercilessly. On the other hand it seemed to me, quite wrongly, that an entourage of beautiful people redeemed me: that in the combination we then formed, the dominant element was beauty.

If I want to express what I then felt, I think I'd say that I wouldn't in the least have wished to change my face; but I'd have liked beauty to extend – like an efficacious grace – over precisely that face. I certainly had an appetite for beauty, which wasn't really sensual, but more magical. I should have liked to eat beauty and incorporate it. I suppose, in a certain way, I used to suffer from an identification complex with respect to all those good-looking people; and that's what explains why I've always chosen handsome men as friends – or ones I judged to be such. Maheu said to the Beaver one day, quite perfidiously: 'What makes Sartre both great and tragic is the fact that, in all things, he has a thoroughly unhappy love for beauty.' He meant by that, not just that I was sad about being ugly and liked beautiful women, but also that I tried to catch a beauty in my literary endeavours for which I wasn't at all cut out. Heavily influenced by Barrès and Gide, he could conceive the beauty of writings only in a certain extremely narrow form. At the same time, I was certainly trying in those days to translate craggy, unpolished thoughts into the style of Anatole France; and that did result in failed works – vain efforts to capture beauty.

But it strikes me today that Maheu's thought was much more correct than he himself thought. I'm only a desire for beauty, and outside of that: void, nothing. And, by beauty, I don't mean just the sensuous charm of the moment, but rather unity and necessity over time. The rhythms and recurrences of periods and refrains bring tears to my eyes; the most elementary forms of periodicity move me. I note that these regulated progressions must be essentially temporal – for spatial symmetry leaves me cold. A good example is the desire I felt in February that my leave should be *precious*: in other words, that I should feel it, right to the end, as a regulated flow towards its term. It goes without saying that music, therefore, is for me the most moving and directly accessible form of the beautiful. Basically, what I've always passionately desired – and what I still desire, although by now there's no hope of it – is to be at the centre of a beautiful *event*. An event: that's to say, a temporal flow that *happened to me* – that wasn't *in front of* me, like a picture or piece of music, but that was made around my life and in my life, with my time. An event in which I was the main actor; which rolled my wishes and desires along with it, but was oriented by my wishes and desires; of which I was the author, as the painter is author of his picture. And that this event should be beautiful: in other words, that it have the splendid, bitter necessity of a tragedy, a melody, a rhythm – of all those temporal forms which advance majestically, through regulated recurrences, towards a term that they bear in their womb.

I've already explained all that in *La Nausée* – it will become clear shortly why I'm returning to it. What I'd like to note for the time being is that I used to ascribe that fierce, vain desire for temporal beauty to *man*. Whereas I now consider it a characteristic of my own. I see that the Beaver is moved, above all, by the presentation outside her of a wholly inhuman aesthetic necessity – let's say, by a Bach fugue or a picture by Braque: she doesn't want her life to form the material of that necessity. O.Z., by contrast, was moved by the sensual content of a beautiful form. I can still see her telling us, with a kind of aggressiveness, in Zuorro's room: 'Composition and melody don't matter much to me; what moves me are the notes.'[36] I'm tempted to believe that a momentary sensuous magnificence would be enough to satisfy her.

In reality, the affair is more complicated, since the movement never suffices; but at least, for her, it's an ideal value – and, after all, that unrealizable dream is not more contradictory than my own, but equally so. I was speaking last week about unrealizables. Let's say that I have my own unrealizable: the beauty of the event. When I say that I have my own unrealizable, I don't mean it's a vague dream which I sometimes entertain. No: I'm thrown into this situation; my being-in-the-world is an unrealizable-being-in-the-world; I'm wholly in this

36. Marc Zuorro was a university colleague of Sartre's in Paris, who appears in Simone De Beauvoir's autobiography as Marco.

event, whose beauty attracts me and escapes me: it's my life. It's what explains those little acts I'm constantly putting on – without really being too much taken in by them – which are like pantomimes to capture the unrealizable: magic dances. It's what also explains those abrupt recurrences of coarseness and cynicism, which have so often put out or shocked the people who surround me. In short, it's my passion – and my passion is myself.

If I insist on this fact, it's because I see in it the major reason for my loves. For a long time, almost up until the present, I had the illusion that the loving event could – and must – be that necessary and indeed beautiful event I was looking for. This was certainly due to the fact that I considered love as a courtly game of seduction. Viewed in this way, it carried its end within it. The end was the avowal. Later, it was the act of love – which Leiris considers to be like the kill in bull-fighting. What was involved was a regulated progression towards a known goal – but known in the manner of the dénouement of Greek tragedies, foreseen yet feared and desired by the Athenians; known in the manner of melodic resolutions, foreseen yet wholly unforeseeable. And I had to bring about that terminal event, by my words and gestures.

It's clear how far away I was from understanding purely sensual turmoil. I wasn't unaware of it, but I didn't feel it. And I was by no means particularly keen for my partner to feel it at first – any more than the torero can want the bull to collapse from the effects of a stroke, after the placing of the banderillos. It had to be *deserved*: in other words, occur at the end of the play, at the very moment when the curtain falls, provoked by the last line. Assuredly, a strong sensual passion – if some woman had conceived one for me – would have totally disconcerted and shocked me.

I thought of women – on the basis of my reading, assuredly – as beings who first say No, then allow themselves gradually to be imposed on, still resisting but each time rather less. So both of us had our roles fixed in advance. The woman would refuse and I would gently, patiently insist, each day winning a little more ground. But I didn't envisage seduction as a Machiavellian game of trickery, in the way the young Stendhal did. I shouldn't at all have liked to obtain a woman by guile. And that even proves pretty conclusively I was less keen on the woman than on the play-acting she gave me an opportunity for – since I'd not have agreed to obtain her by just any old means. Once again, possessing her counted for less than the prospects of possession.

In order to seduce, I counted on my power of speech alone. I can still recall the trouble in which I found myself in Berlin. I'd set off determined to experience the love of German women, but I soon realized I didn't know enough German to converse. Stripped thus of my weapon, I was left feeling quite idiotic and dared attempt nothing – I had to fall back on a French woman. And what sympathy I did feel, for the naive remark a frustrated Hungarian once made to the Beaver: 'If you only knew how witty I am in Hungarian!'

Yet, for me, it wasn't a matter of being witty – still less of dazzling. As I've said, it was a matter of capturing the world in words; capturing it *for* my companion; making it exist more strongly and beautifully; helping it – as Gide says in *Narcisse* – to 'demonstrate'.[37]

What was necessary, moreover, was not just to talk. It was necessary to handle silences adroitly and choose viewpoints. In fact, it was a whole literary labour. And my aim wasn't at all to make myself indispensable as a dragoman – as an intermediary between the world and her – but rather, in her eyes, to merge indissolubly with the world's beauty. Basically, it was a matter of artificially provoking crystallization. Apart from the fact that this little technical feat had its rightful place in the regulated progress of the seduction, it pleased me in its own right – just as a development of the theme can please in the midst of the melody, without one therefore having to detach it from the ensemble. It was even what I cared about most.

In reality, since most of my companions were intelligent and hard to please, I used to have to exert myself – and in the evenings would take away with me the satisfied memory of having 'done a good job'. Today, when I can speak coolly of that bygone era, I think that what I used to say – even to the best women in the world and my equals – was pretty wretched. In order to pass muster, it had to be supported by the place, the atmosphere, the hour, and that sly certainty we both felt about establishing amorous relations. The truth is, it was all easy – much too easy – and, as the Beaver said later, 'it was prompted'. At about the same period, we also used to employ the expression 'putting on a show' to characterize the thing.

Nowadays, I have a horror of those speeches, those silences and those graces. But, when it comes right down to it, did I not already have a horror of them even then – at the very time I was delighting in them? I'd come back from a rendezvous, mouth dry, facial muscles tired from too much smiling, voice still dripping with honey and heart full of a disgust to which I was unwilling to pay any attention, and which was masked by satisfaction at having 'advanced my affairs': at

37. The reference is to *Traité du Narcisse* (1891).

having surprised certain gleams in a look or certain involuntary movements. The comical thing is that, only too conscious of putting on an act myself, I didn't for a second imagine that the woman could be putting on an act for her own part – and that those discreet avowals and confidences let slip were as meticulously controlled as my speeches. Yet I'm sure this is what was happening most of the time – it was, of course, a question of those semi-conscious, and relatively uncynical, acts which are found in most amorous relations – and this, not just thanks to the woman's character, but because, it seems to me, I was inducing those acts by my behaviour. Had I known it, I should have been outraged by it. For me, it wasn't a question of a sketch for two, in which each had their role to play. I can see clearly now that I required a total naivety on the woman's part. In that perishable work of art I was trying to construct, the woman represented the raw material which I had to mould.

NOTEBOOK 14
MARCH 1940
BOUXWILLER/BRUMATH

6 March, '40

Cartoon in today's *Le Petit Parisien*. A tough of Herculean proportions has grabbed a young lady, who's struggling energetically but vainly. Cringing againt the wall in terror, a tiny middle-aged soldier is watching the scene without moving. And the young lady is shouting indignantly: 'Hey, soldier boy, I must say you needn't have told me you were such an ace at commando raids!'[1] This cartoon – after countless others; after the song by Chevalier that I discussed in one of my earlier notebooks[2] – strikes me as significant. It's the destruction of the military idea.

The military idea, born in the epoch of professional armies, a fortiori confers civil courage on the soldier. And the latter, more or less a mercenary, is in fact always a bit of a 'hothead' – like those American sailors made famous by the series of films that began with *A Girl in Every Port*. It has often been his skills as a brawler which have led the recruiting-officer to pick him out, and besides they come in useful in war – where men fight first with swords, then with knives and finally with fists.

But the 'Nation in Arms' has changed all that, since it's no longer the village strongman who becomes a soldier, but the grocer, the baker, the Town Hall secretary – all those puny, peaceable men whom the peacetime papers used gently to scoff at for their petty failings: meanness, cowardice, pernickety attention to detail, etc.[3] It was still

1. 'Commando raids' does not capture the play on words of the French *coup de main*, which in military parlance means a surprise attack, but in everday speech means simply 'a helping hand'.

2. The song in question was *D'excellents Français*, sung by Maurice Chevalier in 1939 and expressing a bluff patriotism.

3. The theory of the 'nation in arms' dates from the catastrophic French defeat of 1871, after which the pressure for conscription became irresistible (though it was only from 1905 onwards that a two-year period of military service for all was instituted).

the case that being a nation in arms, and becoming conscious of oneself as a nation in arms, were two quite separate things. Just as *being* the working class, and becoming conscious of oneself as the proletariat, are two quite separate things. It seems to me that the first reaction to itself of the nation in arms was mythological. In 1914, there was a Golden Book for grocers, another for bakers, etc. Such illustrations as I recall provided the final idealizing touch. One still found those same puny bodies, clumsy gestures and civilian faces. But, by an artistic effect, those pinched features breathed an indomitable energy; they had an ascetic leanness; holy anger was depicted in their eyes; and, in their clumsy attitudes, there was a warlike dynamism. Abel Faivre was a specialist in that golden legend.[4] They returned home, resumed their jobs and old ways – and behold, the second national war arrives!

It seems to me that, this time, the nation in arms has become conscious of itself. This long wait at the beginning of the war has given it leisure to do so. And, this time, everyone knows that those soldiers awaiting the enemy on the Maginot line *are the same as* the radical small traders and minor civil servants of peacetime. Granted, people think – for they still do think it – that they'll be suitable, and even adequate, for military tasks. But a clear disjunction is made between the different forms of courage and action. That soldier who trembles before a hoodlum – he's an ace at commando raids. For commando raids have their own set rules: surprise; encirclement; gunfire, rather than hand-to-hand combat. If there's proper organization, the grocer can get by in a commando raid. But that doesn't make him capable of fighting decently with his fists. He hasn't been filled with any holy fire, nor would one look for any indomitable gleam in his eyes. And if one thinks he's carrying out his 'job as a man' there, one thinks that he's getting the strength to do so from a kind of good-natured humanism: precisely the humanism which helped him to bend his neck and endure the hard blows of peace.

That's what I call anti-heroism. And a democratic nation in arms which becomes conscious of itself as such – I claim it's at the antipodes from heroism. For heroism has always been, and must be, the business of specialists. It must remain wreathed in mystery, impenetrable. But if one discovers that, as Faulkner says, 'every man may stumble into heroism', there are no more heroes. The 'nation in arms' is destructive of the holy privilege of war, since it proceeds to assimi-

---

4. Jean Abel Faivre (1867–1945): painter and cartoonist, creator of patriotic posters in 1914–18.

late the warrior's function to a civic service: to a statutory duty incumbent upon all. This very fact leads to a civilization of war. At the very beginning, people still kept at a respectful distance from those who'd been called up: my pupils Chauffard and Kanapa were still writing to me: 'It's difficult for a person who hasn't been called up to write to one who has.' But nowadays they're treated with easy familiarity, and that's a very good thing.

What all this will lead to, if we end up at the front, I don't know. What I do know is that all the men mutter a bit about the civilians' ironical, protective familiarity towards them. And it's inevitable, since the civilian's working: he's still doing a job of which he's proud, and to which he gives of his best. But if the soldier has stopped being a hero, he's no longer anything but an idler against his will – who's no longer held in check and redeemed by the exigencies of a technical profession: who's fed to do nothing. In short, as that other fellow was so rightly saying, a man out of work. And we should rejoice at that – despite all those grievances accumulating in the soldiers' breasts – because it, too, plays its part in killing war.

When I rejoice at this dissolution of the military spirit, I say what I can see – and no more. I'm not unaware of the fact that, in Germany, the spirit is entirely different. If I don't speak about it, that's because I don't know it personally. But I do know that this change heralded by the French spirit is subordinated to the victory of the democracies. If we were defeated, however, a future, tough-minded historian would see in it a proof of our decadence, and the underlying reason for our defeat. Thus, the underlying meaning of this state of public opinion is ambiguous. If, however, I place my hopes in a final victory of the pluto-democracies, I'm relying not on their heroism, but on their wealth. I'm reckoning on a war without 'greatness' – principally economic. In that case, 'decadence' can remain harmless – indeed become a positive factor.

The whole problem revolves round the following question: Is there an iron law of history which says that peoples who are 'over'-civilized, and 'over'-peaceloving as a result of that civilization, must in the end be devoured? Or does this law apply only to the 'warlike' era – in other words, to the past period in which military and economic problems were relatively separate? If the iron law still exists, we're confronted by the piece of nonsense that a certain quota of absurd brutality, involving the myth of the hero and the military leader's infallibility, is indispensable to a nation's health, even though it's condemned by reason; and we even find that any reasonable condemnation, by weakening the power of that brutality, weakens the nation itself – and thereby peace. So the 'health' of a nation becomes a kind of balance between a certain quota of basic aggressiveness and reason.

But if cynical economic materialism arrives to clip the warrior's wings; if oil is more indispensable to war than courage – then what might have appeared the pernicious, sickly cowardice of *over*-civilized people can become a new spirit. And the inglorious throttling of the warrior by the cowards becomes, in its turn, the new iron law. Then the historian who judges ideology by its success is obliged to see, in that supposedly decadent ideology, an expression of the contradictions of contemporary capitalism – which leads to war but *cannot* wage it. And therefore, precisely, if victory is given to the richest rather than the bravest, that ideology can become a factor of progress. So, for this reason and many others, it remains true that we're at a turning-point – since victory alone will decide as to the value of *our* ideology or the Nazi ideology.

1888 – speech by Bismarck, addressing the Reichstag. In it, he expresses for the last time the conception of the Nation in Arms seen *through* the outworn conception of the professional Army. 'If we in Germany should wish to carry on a war with the full strength of our national forces, it must be . . . a people's war . . . A war which is not initiated by the popular will may be carried on when the leading authorities of the country regard it as necessary and explain why it is needed, but it will not be from the first animated with impetus and fire . . . Of course every soldier believes that he is a better man than the enemy. He would not be a particularly useful soldier unless he wanted war and believed in the coming of victory.'[5]

How surprised he would have been at the spectacle of this war: we don't think we're superior to the German soldiers; we didn't want this war; on the contrary, we rejected it with all our might. Finally, we're *hoping* for victory, and all have the impression that it depends on circumstances quite external to our military worth: on economic circumstances. And yet we make usable soldiers, all the same.

I am certainly the monstrous product of capitalism, of parliamentarism, of centralization and of officialdom. Or if you prefer, those are the primary situations beyond which I have projected myself. To capitalism I owe the fact of being cut off from the labouring classes, without at the same time acceding to the circles which run

5. Emil Ludwig, *Bismarck, the Story of a Fighter*, London 1927, p. 553.

political and economic life. To parliamentarism I owe the idea of civil liberties, which is the source of my obsessive passion for freedom. To centralization I owe the fact that I have never experienced agricultural labour; that I hate the provinces; that I have no regional ties; that I am more sensitive than most people to the myth of 'Paris the great city', as Caillois says.[6] To officialdom I owe my total incompetence in money matters, which is undoubtedly the last avatar of the 'integrity' and 'disinterest' of a family of public officials; to it I owe also the idea of the universality of Reason, since in France the official is the vestal virgin of rationalism.

To all these abstractions taken together I owe the fact of being an abstract, rootless individual. I should perhaps have been saved if nature had endowed me with sensuality, but I am cold. So there I am, 'up in the air', with no ties, having known neither union with the land through work in the fields, nor union with a class through solidarity of interests, nor union with bodies through pleasure. The death of my father, my mother's remarriage and my disagreements with my step-father released me at an early date from any family influence. The hostility of my schoolfellows at La Rochelle taught me to fall back upon my own resources. My healthy, vigorous, docile, discreet body never excites attention – except occasionally by rebelling clamorously in an attack of renal colic. I feel no solidarity with anything, not even with myself: I don't need anybody or anything. Such is the character I have made for myself, in the course of thirty-four years of my life. Truly what the Nazis call 'the abstract man of the plutodemocracies'.

I have no liking for this character, and I want to change. What I have realized is that freedom is not the Stoic detachment from loves and goods at all. On the contrary, it supposes a deep rootedness in the world – and one is free *beyond* that rootedness: it is beyond the crowd, the nation, one's class, one's friends, that one is alone. Whereas I used to assert my solitude and my freedom *against* the crowd, the nation, etc. The Beaver is correct when she writes to me that genuine authenticity does not consist in overflowing one's life in every direction, or in stepping back to judge it, or in perpetually freeing oneself from it, but on the contrary in plunging into it and becoming an integral part of it. But that's easier said than done, when one is thirty-four and cut off from everything – an aerial plant. All I can do for the moment is criticize that freedom in the air which I've so patiently given myself, and uphold the principle that it's necessary to become rooted. By this, I don't mean that it's necessary to prize certain things – since I prize a

6. Roger Caillois, 'Paris, mythe moderne', *NRF*, May 1937.

goodly number of things with all my strength. What I mean is that the personality must have a *content*. It must be made of clay, and I'm made of wind.

Having no great social passion, living outside my class and time, I resemble Claude Bernard's rabbit – isolated and starved for experimental purposes – which would digest itself.[7]

'Freedom, like reason, can only exist and be apparent through constantly rejecting its own creations. It perishes as soon as it begins to admire itself. This is why irony has always been the work of the philosophical and liberal spirit, the seal of human intelligence and the irresistible instrument of progress' (Proudhon, *Confessions of a Revolutionary*).[8]

7 March

With great interest, I'm reading Ludwig's *William II*.[9] Through it, I'm trying to re-examine and rework a problem that has been bothering me for some time – since September '38 to be precise – and that we've often discussed, the Beaver and I. I recognize, with Aron, that in the explanation of the historical event as in its comprehension various layers of signification may be found. And these layers of signification – each at its appropriate level – allow one to describe the evolution of the historical process in an adequate manner. But these significations are parallel, and it's not possible to move from one to the other.

Thus, one may explain the war of '14 by the rivalry between German and English imperialisms: we're on the terrain of Marxist or strictly economic explanation and join Lenin's book on Imperialism and Capitalism. But one may *also* explain the war by placing oneself upon a terrain of more purely historical signification, and show Pan-Germanism as the expression of Germany's tendency to complete its unification, begun by Bismarck. On the same level, and sticking to German responsibilities alone, one may indicate that the hegemony of Prussia is tantamount to domination by a nobility of militarized Junkers. At a 'diplomatic' level of signification, one may show how the rupture of Bismarck's alliances with Russia and Austria – alliances whose aim was to check those two powers, always ready to attack each

7. Claude Bernard (1813–78), French physiologist.
8. See *Selected Writings of Pierre-Joseph Proudhon*, London 1970, p. 263.
9. Emil Ludwig, *Kaiser Wilhelm II*, London 1926.

other over the Balkans – had the effect of throwing Russia into the French alliance, and freeing the Austro-Russian antagonism. Finally, one may come down to Emperor William's court, his government, his counsellors and his personality.

At each level, the description of the process is satisfactory and we can even find causes (if, according to Weber's formula taken over by Aron, a cause is identified if one can establish that, in the absence of a particular phenomenon, it's most likely that the phenomenon in question won't occur). However, those descriptions and those explanations *never* meet. A common error of historians is to put these explanations on the same level, linking them by an 'and' – as if their juxtaposition ought to give rise to an organized totality, with ordered structures, which would be the phenomenon itself enfolding its causes and various processes. In fact, the significations remain separate.

In another order of ideas, you can establish a bond of comprehension between Rousseau's Genevan origin and the *Contrat Social*: in other words, 'produce' the *Contrat Social* out of the ideological currents of Geneva. You can also derive the *Contrat Social* from Rousseau's personality: in other words, start off from Rousseau's personality to show that *if he* wrote a *Contrat Social*, he had to write it *like that.* So we'll follow one of Rousseau's character-traits to the point where it's projected into the *Contrat Social.* We'll thus be able to explain the book by Rousseau's previous works and by itself: in other words, *introduce* the work on the basis of Rousseau's previous ideas, or explain such and such a chapter of the work by the book's internal coherence and the requirements of logic. But in no case can these explanations be simultaneous. For they concern autonomous regions of existence, and in each of them the work is grasped from a different angle.

It's obvious, for example, that when one explains the *Contrat Social* by Geneva, Rousseau's personality fades away and he becomes merely the abstract consciousness – the signifying milieu – in which the connection takes place between Genevan ideology and the *Contrat Social* considered as *one* juridical work, one synthesis among others of those ideological currents. But if, on the contrary, I envisage the *Contrat* on the basis of Rousseau, it becomes a mere extension of his personality; an objectification of his personal tendencies; in short, a strictly individual and incomparable object. In that case, determination of the comprehensive bonds uniting Rousseau with his book becomes a strictly psychological affair. Finally, if we consider the book within Rousseau's oeuvre and in itself, we shall find ourselves confronted by ideas which develop according to their concrete logic and almost autonomously. And, to be sure, the book really is all that – but it isn't all that *simultaneously*. Whence that kind of historical scepticism in Aron.

I was quite convinced of all this in September '38. I can recall the difficulty we encountered, the Beaver and I, when we wished to grasp the causes of the war which loomed. Not that they were lacking – quite the contrary. But according to what principles were we to coordinate and order them? How were we to move from the rivalry between proletarian peoples and plutodemocracies to Hitler's actual personality? It was perhaps all the more disturbing that Hitler and his counsellors, on various occasions, really did have a free choice between war and peace. And that was perhaps still truer in September '39, when it would really have taken only a gesture to safeguard peace. I can see today, moreover, that the discussion about war aims stems from the fact that each individual places himself 'according to his own philosophy' – as Aron would say – at a particular level of signification, in order to view the responsibilities for the war. For by now, if one wants to prevent it, one must strike at its cause.

The person who'd be content to see the collapse of national-socialism places himself at the individual level of signification: those responsible are Hitler and his lieutenants. Eliminate Hitler, and Peace will return. The person, however, who wants a dismemberment of Germany and annexation of the left bank of the Rhine, declaring that 'peoples are responsible for their government', places himself at the level of the historical collectivity. He may do so with greater or lesser success, depending on whether he recycles the fable of the 'evil Boche' and believes in an inherent principle of evil radically vitiating the soul of every German, or whether he bases himself on genuinely historical considerations: origins of German unity; perpetual threat constituted by a central Empire; geographical situation of Germany, laying the basis for it to be perpetually in danger and dangerous; etc. Finally, when Valois asserts that Peace can be obtained only by a veritable economic revolution, and a new type of organization of production and consumption, he's viewing the war as one consequence of the great economic crisis of the twentieth century, and of the struggle of the new, proletarian nations against the vast Anglo-French empire. Here we're back with the 'materialist' explanation.

Moreover, it would doubtless be possible to argue that, if we're victorious, we must *simultaneously* overthrow Hitler, take precautions against the German nation, and effect a better division of wealth. But the fact still remains that logically those ideas are independent. For example, it isn't at all the same thing to consider Hitler as an usurper, who has seized power thanks to the disarray of a conquered population and maintains that power through terror; or as an emanation of the German nation, a perfect and adequate expression of German desires and needs, an 'embodiment' of that people; or again as an instrument – which would have been replaceable – of a great economic evolution. If peace were made bearing in mind the three exigencies I've just mentioned, it would be due to the uncertainty felt by the leaders regarding the war's essential factor.

Well, although all that strikes me as quite accurate, it still doesn't seem entirely satisfactory. For, after all, it would be wrong to forget that those different layers of meaning are *human*, and as such produced by a human reality that historializes itself. For example, Marx writes in *Poverty of Philosophy* that 'poverty may be a revolutionary force'. And Albert Ollivier (*La Commune*) rightly replies that the effect of poverty, on its own, can hardly be other than paralysing.[10] The truth is that for poverty to become a revolutionary force, it must be taken up and adopted by the pauper as *his* poverty. And not only that, but it must be taken up as a situation that *must change*: in other words, must be replaced by the pauper in the midst of a human world in which it would be strictly intolerable. But poverty on its own is never intolerable: it is strictly *nothing*. The workers of 1835 had a standard of living infinitely below that which the worst off today would deem unacceptable. And yet they endured it, since they hadn't grasped it as a contingent situation not inherent to their essence.

Likewise, the person who shows economic forces in struggle or equilibrium mustn't forget that those forces are human. When one speaks of rivalries over markets, or even of a country's geographical situation – when, for example, one shows that the geographical situation of Germany determines its history – it mustn't be forgotten that these rivalries are human; and that there's a 'situation', whether geographical or any other, only for a human reality that pro-jects itself through this situation towards itself. No situation is ever *undergone*. If man were a being 'in the midst of the world', there would never be any situation, there would be only positions. And not only does human-reality 'hatch' the situation by irrupting into the world, it also decides

10. See Albert Ollivier, *La Commune*, Paris 1939, p. 71, n.1. In *The Poverty of Philosophy*, Marx wrote of utopian socialists: 'So long as they look for science and merely make systems, so long as they are at the beginning of the struggle, they see in poverty nothing but poverty, without seeing in it the revolutionary, subversive side, which will overthrow the old society.' Marx/Engels, *Collected Works*, vol. 6, London 1976, pp. 177–78.

alone – and in its primitive pro-ject – on the signification of this situation. Thus there's no mechanical force that can decide on History, and we can repeat (in another sense) Marx's famous formula according to which men are 'both the authors and the actors of their own drama'.[11] But that makes the parallelism between historical significations still more irritating. For, if we find man everywhere as author and actor of his drama; if all significations are human and man is a unitary totality: how are we to take account of that sharp, irreparable separation between the signifying layers?

The problem is all the more complex in that man exists under the sway of the *Mit-sein*[12], which means that each time one wishes to find in an individual the key to a social event, one is thrown back from him to other individuals. Napoleon lost the battle of Waterloo because he'd engaged it prematurely. Yes. But if Grouchy . . . etc., Napoleon, even though he'd engaged the battle wrongly, would perhaps have won it. And would one then say he'd engaged it prematurely?

Furthermore, as Pierrefeu says, if Wellington hadn't been so stupid, he'd very quickly have seen that he was beaten and withdrawn, in accordance with the rules of the game – instead of stupidly persisting on the battlefield, which ended by giving him victory. So one's deflected from consciousness to consciousness, without ever finding the sufficient consciousness – the effective consciousness – and without an aggregation of consciousnesses being able to constitute an organic whole either. There's a second difficulty, moreover: historical relativism of the Simmel type could easily accommodate itself to making the event vanish into *representations* – which would, in effect, give a theoretical basis to the scepticism we were speaking of just now, at the same time as allowing it to remain within human limits. But it's obvious that although the event is *human* – in other words, felt and experienced in the mode of the for-itself – it nevertheless *is*: in other words, it's recaptured from behind by the in-itself. In other words, it cannot be reduced to mutual perceptions of consciousnesses. It escapes – and transcends – consciousnesses, in that it's a sudden reciprocal existence of those consciousnesses. I discussed this in Notebook 12.

In that case, although the event has man as 'author and actor', it escapes and suddenly dominates him. To pursue Marx's comparison, I imagine an actor-author like Shakespeare or Molière – a stage-manager into the bargain – writing, producing and acting a certain

11. Ibid., p. 170.
12. *Mitsein* = Being-with (in Heidegger).

play. Everything's of his own devising. If I wish to dispossess him of anything, I shall at once fall back on the consciousnesses of the other actors, and finally on those of the spectators. Yet something's beyond all that. I won't so much say it's *the* play: granted, the actor-author isn't 'inside', nor are the other players, nor the public; it's before them – if you like, it's between the stage and the footlights. However, albeit an *object*, it's an object *for* consciousnesses: it's the transcendent unity of the consciousnesses which converge *towards* it, and it exists only in relation to consciousnesses. But what's much less human and rational – what recaptures author, spectators and players in the indistinction of an existence *in itself* – is the *fact* that all those consciousnesses have converged towards a single play, on 6 May 1680, at the Hôtel de Bourgogne.

And even if the Hôtel de Bourgogne, or the 6th of May, were relieved of their substantial being – by the remark that there could be a hôtel or a date only for consciousnesses – it remains the case that, in an undated lapse of time, a certain synthetic unity of consciousnessss existed in the mode of the *in-itself*. And that particular unity is opaque and inexhaustible: it's a genuine absolute. I may add that its content is entirely human, but that the unity itself – qua existence *in itself* – is radically inhuman. It's the facticity of the for-others. For man can exist only insofar as he is for-himself or for-others. But he escapes himself by his facticity, which overlays this for-itself with a certain density of in-itself. The same goes for the mutual relations of the for-others. That is the *event*.

Well, it's this event – in its absolute existence – that the historian aims for. You only have to see the way he speaks. Take Ludwig, speaking of the incessant quarrels that used to break out between Holstein and Eulenburg: 'By such convulsive tremors, working in two neurasthenics, was the foreign policy of the German Empire tossed and torn in those distracted years' [p. 17]. In order to speak in that manner, he must obviously be aiming for what neither of those two consciousnesses can grasp; basing himself on a truth that's not guaranteed by the evidence of the for-itself. Similarly, if he writes: 'His mother did nothing to dissuade him', he here has as his guarantee a consciousness that was saying to itself: 'I shall do nothing to dissuade him.' But it can be seen that he rises above that consciousness, to the level at which it has become a *fact* for which the Empress Victoria – inasmuch as it is a fact – is no longer responsible.

The historian is always at the level of facticity. However, the deep ambiguity of historical research is that it will *date* that absolute event – in other words, replace it in human perspectives – whereas it's the inhuman in-itself of human reality: its very facticity or fact that human reality is not its own foundation. And if it proceeds thus, that's because this inhuman fact, at first, has a human content and thereafter will be recovered, assumed and transcended by other conscious-nesses, which pro-ject themselves beyond the facticity of the event and transform it into a *situation*. *That* is really what's inhuman in history – a metaphysical inhumanity – and not the geographical existence of oil-wells in Rumania or in Mexico. For the oil-well is 'already-in-the-world' when the irruption of a human reality 'makes it blossom into itself'. Whereas the historical event is, beyond that, what ensures there is a world.

Consequently, man really reacts in the same way to the fact 'Pierre didn't visit Thérèse yesterday' as to the fact 'there's a ditch on the left'. In both cases, he considers himself as in presence of the in-itself. He proves it by his acts. However, thereby, the inhuman in-itself is humanized, replaced in the world, assumed and transcended: 'Pierre didn't visit Thérèse? – Good, I still have time to telephone, etc.' Thus the *event* is ambiguous: inhuman, inasmuch as it clasps and surpasses all human reality, and inasmuch as the in-itself recaptures the for-itself which escapes it by nihilating itself; human, in that, as soon as it appears, it becomes 'of the world' for other human realities which make it 'blossom into itself' – which transcend it, and for which it becomes a *situation*.

Lived in the nihilating unity of the for-itself; recaptured in the inhuman lime of the in-itself; recovered and surpassed – like the totality of the in-itself besides – by another consciousness: the event is strictly indescribable. And the historian himself moves on three planes: that of the for-itself, where he tries to show how the decision appears to itself in the historical individual; that of the in-itself, where this decision is an absolute fact, temporal but undated; finally, that of the for-others, where the pure event is recaptured, dated and sur-passed as being 'of the world' for other consciousnesses. That's what is clear when, for example, a historian strives to disentangle what the taking of the Bastille *was*, in itself, from what it was *made* into. Otherwise, the debate wouldn't even be engaged; if the historian was a relativist like Simmel, the event wouldn't be distinguished from what's made of it.

But if this essential ambiguity is set aside, isn't it possible to effect a conversion similar to the one which A. Comte was making, when he showed how sociology – latest in date of the sciences and dependent upon all the others – was turning back upon the sciences, to embrace all of them and found them in their individual concretion? Couldn't one try to show *not* the situation acting upon man – which leads to disjunction of the signifying layers – but man throwing himself through situations and living them in the unity of human reality? Wouldn't one thus manage to realize an unexpected and unforeseeable unity of the signifying layers? Don't the signifying layers remain parallel – just as the sciences are at first, in Comte – because they're considered first and in isolation? But what if one considers them on the basis of human reality's project?

For example, for the classical historian, William II's policy towards England on the one hand, and his withered left arm on the other, represent two quite distinct types of psychological motivation. But that's because one begins by positing the withered left arm as a *fact* and the existence of Anglo-German relations as another fact. Let's suppose we began from William II as human reality projecting itself through a series of situations. Who knows if we won't find an inner relation of comprehension between that English policy and that withered arm? Ludwig precisely allows one to ascertain it. However, one mustn't take the viewpoint of psychoanalysis, which is still a determinism and as such – though it boasts of having introduced explanation by history into the individual's life – anti-historical. For History can be understood only by *the recovery and assumption of monuments.* There's history only when there's assumption of the past, and not pure causal action of the latter.

I should like here to try, following Ludwig's interpretations, to draw a portrait of William II as human reality assuming and transcending situations – in order to see whether the different signifying layers (including the geographical and social layer) are not found unified within a single project, and in order to determine to what extent William II is a *cause* of the '14 war. So I shall outline another type of historical description, which reverses the explanation and moves from the man to the situation, rather than from the situation to the man. It matters little whether Ludwig's interpretations are *all* accurate. It's enough to consider them true, as a working hypothesis – since it's a matter of giving an example of method, not of discovering an actual historical truth. To tell the truth, it's even less a matter of establishing procedures that would be of benefit to history, than of instituting a kind of metaphysics of historiality and showing how the historical man freely historializes himself in the context of certain situations. I shall attempt the thing tomorrow, probably.

A slight young man with spectacles and the look of a fool who's got the habit of intelligence sees that I'm reading Ollivier's *La Commune,* buttonholes me cautiously, then reveals to me that he's a socialist and 'actively involved with the working-class movement'. He describes to me at length the disarray of the workers' parties, their pessimism. 'People are so sick of the war that if Daladier brought us peace at present, he'd be a God; he could do whatever he liked; the proletariat would let itself be muzzled.' I say, to test him out: 'Well then, it's lucky he's quite incapable of doing so.' But he doesn't carry his ideas through to the end.

He's just back from leave and has seen a fair number of people working in reserved occupations in the factories of the Paris region. 'There's a reign of terror in the factories,' he tells me. 'As soon as a worker complains publicly, wham!, he's shut up and sent without trial to a concentration camp. The workers are demoralized and alarmed.' The information strikes me as valuable, but the fellow's personality diminishes its significance – for he tells me with a conspiratorial air: 'And . . . your officers . . . do they let you read books like that, here . . . ? Don't you . . . hide your feelings a bit . . . to be on the safe side?' So I imagine if that fellow wasn't subjected to a régime of terror, he'd invent his own little terror for private use. He ends on an optimistic note: 'The workers' movement is tainted to the core by communism; but Russia will be the first to collapse, and I think the workers' movement will recover its purity then.' Very mistrustful when it's a question of government measures, and observing with good sense the partial failure of the blockade, he becomes naive again as soon as it's a question of the proletariat and is still counting on a popular revolution in Germany.

Friday 8 March

Jacques Chardonne, in *Chronique privée*, quotes an unnamed historian: 'Everything has gone very badly, always.'

What the classical historian would be tempted to see, first of all, if he wished to write William II's history, is the *fact* – or rather ensemble of facts – which seems to pre-exist his individuality and influence the development of his own self. Those facts are sufficiently rigid for one to be able to enumerate the most important ones – and they immediately appear as belonging to irreducible layers of signification. I'd say the foremost is the fact of Empire: in other words, that sacred power that awaits him in the future, without his having particularly to deserve it or to conquer it. But it's not a matter, here, of just any empire: this concrete empire is a brand new one, ratified definitively in 1870. And the 'imperial hero' is also leader of a military State: he is King of Prussia. As such, he will be chief of the Army and *Kriegsherr*, like his grandfather. One would have to define very precisely here what powers the German Constitution confers upon him, in order to have a clear idea of that imperial function which Bismarck forged for him, and which awaits him.

The second fact concerns his *family*. One would first have to show him as grandson of William I on the one hand and, through his mother, of Queen Victoria on the other. Nephew of Edward VII. Son of a weak, foolish Prussian and an anglomaniac Englishwoman who'd converted him to liberalism. One would have to stress the very particular character of the father: eternal *Kronprinz*, who languishes in the shadow of the throne. So that William II is not a *king's son*, but a king's grandson. The inheritance leaps a generation. When his father finally reaches the throne, everyone will already know he's dying.

The third fact – connected, moreover, to that absence of a transitional generation – is that the government *personnel* is not in harmony with the future sovereign's age. In most cases they're old men, often in their eighties – as at the time of King Louis XIV's court in 1713. A young emperor quite obviously cannot govern with so old a personnel. It is a future fact, but an entirely foreseeable one, that he'll have to renew it. But since the all-powerful master of Germany is Bismarck, the renewal will have to take the aspect of a palace revolution – since Bismarck, head of that personnel, will allow himself to be evicted only by a revolution.

The fourth fact is that the whole apparatus of government has been forged *by* Bismarck and *for* Bismarck. The weakness of that institution is that it has any meaning only if Bismarck himself controls and directs it. William will find the Reichstag such as the Bismarckian terror has made it for him. The fallen Bismarck recognizes and deplores the fact: 'For years I fought the Reichstag tooth and nail; but I perceive that institution was debilitated in that very battle with William the First and myself . . . We need the fresh air of public criticism' [p. 185]. Thus what awaits William II is not an old royal suit made supple through having been worn by numerous predecessors, but a brand new suit – and one cut to fit someone else.

The following facts can be found described everywhere: geographical, economic, social and cultural situation of Germany in that period – expansion of industry; problem of the birthrate; advance of social-democracy.

Finally, last fact at once inherent in – and external to – the Emperor's *own self*: his congenitally withered left arm.

Such as they are, those facts enumerated without any order (a historian would start off by portraying the state of Germany, and move on from there to the throne, Bismarck's achievements, the governing personnel, the family and lastly the physical disability – after which he'd give some general assessment of the Emperor's character) belong to very disparate signifying layers. Struck by the fact that they are all *independent* of the Emperor William II's action, the historian would present them as motivating his action. He wouldn't exactly present the Emperor's character as virgin wax, but his psychological description would be vague enough for him to be able to present that character as moulded by the action of those various forces.

Let's see how this would work out. I first note that the personality of a hereditary prince is defined, above all, by the future crown; and that it's useless to distinguish his own character from his nature as Crown Prince, as people customarily do. We're not dealing with *a* man, weak and hesitant, who *in addition* – as a contingent fact – finds himself confronted by a dignity and power which will one day cloak him. But each weakness and each hesitation appears against the basic background of the essential, 'a priori' relationship of the man to the crown. What's deceptive here is the fact that all of us, who at a certain age have opted for a line of work, are not so bound to that social function. We may, perhaps, have exercised others – and we can perfectly well imagine ourselves in some other situation. But it must be admitted that kings are another human species. The Crown Prince has a blocked-off, accomplished future as soon as he appears in the world. His being is a 'being-to-reign', just as man's being is a 'being-to-die'. As soon as he's conscious of himself, he finds before him that future in which *to reign* is his most essential and most individual possibility. And if there are even Crown Princes who refuse to reign, they still make their decisions in the face of their essential destiny. They cannot evade their 'being-to-reign': they cannot cause themselves not to have been Crown Princes, in their innermost natures; they cannot cause being-to-reign not to be a *quasi-existential* characteristic for them. Their future doesn't have the contingent character ours has – ours which must be earned, and which even when earned escapes us: which is 'in God's hands'. If theirs is contingent, if it can be deserved, that is beyond the primary existential fact – which is that royalty *awaits them*.

It has often been said that kings are alone. And that's true, but the real reason for it hasn't been given. Alone, because always brought back to the plenitude of their individuality; escaping by nature from the impersonal 'one' of everyday banality; alone, like a man medi- tating his death. The only destiny they can deserve is that of *great* king – a title they'll win after their coronation, and which will reflect back upon that coronation itself, to justify it. A title that will finally give them a society – for one is a great king *among* kings – but without drawing them out of their isolation. Yet that primary situation is not undergone: it's not a passively received quality. On the contrary, it's the primary effort – the original free pro-ject, towards a finite future which one surpasses towards oneself. Royalty, as Heidegger says of the world, is that whereby the future sovereign discloses to himself what he is.

So it seems to me that William II's original freedom is called royalty. Moreover, freedom intervenes again in the *manner* of being- to-reign. I see that William, initially, wants to be a 'great' king. But even that requires a description. One may want to be a great king in order to excuse oneself for being a king. One may want to *use* royalty in order to be great. But William merely considers greatness as the individualization of royalty. He wants to be great in order to be *that particular king*; in order to be more deeply, more individually king; in order to appropriate more firmly to himself the title of king. It's absolutely normal, in these conditions, that a king should freely grasp that original situation in the guise of divine right. Which is the case for William II. He merely gives a mythical expression to the fact that, alone among men, his being is a being-to-reign. He *is* the reign. And this he establishes *in his being*: his pre-ontological self-understanding coincides with the pro-ject of himself towards coronation. For, in the very constitution of his being as a being-to-reign, the Crown Prince remains free to assume his facticity (I am to reign, but my very existence is without justification), or to hide it from himself (the foundation of my existence is the reign – not only I am-to-reign but *I exist* in order to reign). Here, divine right loops the loop, and the future sovereign encloses himself within an inauthentic solitude. Behold how he's wholly and deeply responsible *in his being* for what the historian first gave us as an external and contingent fact. The reign is not an *outside* for William II. Neither is it an inner and privileged representation. The reign *is* him.

But let us here note that the man who's going to reign is disabled. He has a withered arm. I should like to draw attention to the fact that this disability is in no way comparable to other, physiologically similar, disabilities that may occur among subjects or *free citizens*. For the future free citizen, the disability is grasped as an indeterminate impediment, which suppresses a badly inventoried category of possibilities. But, at the same time as it suppresses them, it orients – insofar as it's grasped and transcended – towards other possibilities. My manner of *being my withered arm* is, at one and the same time, to eschew a military career; to renounce and perhaps even despise sports; and to hurl myself beyond that disability toward study, the liberal professions, art, etc. My own manner of being my dead eye is certainly my way of wanting to be loved through intellectual seduction; of refusing an easy abandon that wouldn't become me; and also of regretfully refusing to view films in 3-D or look through stereoscopes. I *am* that man with a blank eye only when I'm it freely. And I am it insofar as I choose myself beyond that blank eye.

But what is the case with a future king, who's *already king* when he assumes himself as disabled? It matters little here that chronologically the latter discovery precedes the former. The essential thing is the hierarchy. The king is to-reign, but he's not to-be-disabled. The disability is discovered against the background of divine right. Let us register that the being-to-reign is very particular here. The dignity of King of Prussia gives this reign a military character. The king is a soldier-king. Thus the disability cannot appear as defining more clearly the contours of a life, by blotting out certain categories of possibilities. It ought no more to prevent from reigning, than it will prevent from dying. So it's grasped by a being who reviews it as *king already*: it's grasped from the vantage-point of royalty. It's the constant impediment, which must be constantly overcome and *never accepted*. For acceptance would be tantamount to the abandonment of certain possibilities, which William has freely constituted as belonging to his own being.

The attitude freely taken here is that of refusal – since disability is royalty's hidden flaw. It represents *scandal*, and – very precisely – the facticity which it's sought to deny. So William can accept only to *mask* it, and to *compensate for* it. These, obviously, are merely magical procedures. But, if we use the term 'inferiority complex' here, one should clearly understand that it's in a special sense. An inferiority complex couldn't be of the same type for a king as for a citizen, since in the king it appears against the background of the being-to-reign – which has already isolated the king, and which wafts him above men's heads. What's involved is a kind of absolute inferiority, which isn't inferiority vis-à-vis anybody, since all comparison is forbidden. (Of course, this needn't exclude certain melancholy regrets in front of some staff-officer's two, solid, agile arms.) Whence the tendency to wish to keep all his essential possibilities, *despite* the physical inferiority. Whence the special cape masking the left arm. Whence an all the more marked taste for military and sporting exercises, and for hunting. Whence a thousand tricks: 'Cleverly did he learn to support his left arm in his belt or pocket, to let the reins slip into his left hand from his normal right one, to handle his horse in every sense without the aid of a groom; but in this way the right arm became so over-developed and heavy that frequently, when riding, it caused him to lose his balance, and slide off on that side' [p.4].

Whence, also, downright lies. Especially the one about hunting. The Emperor couldn't really hunt: 'His loader has to lean his right arm on a long pole, thus serving the Prince as a support for the rifle' [p.27]. And yet, he wants to be the first huntsman in the realm. So he transforms every hunt into a battue: 'An army of foresters attended on bicycles, in carts, on horse and on foot, so that actually every . . . point was under the keenest observation from first to last . . . the shoots were horrible . . . the hapless wild creatures . . . driven into an immense enclosure, in the centre of which the noble sportsmen are posted, pouring their shots upon the panting desperate brutes, as they hurl themselves perpetually against the farthest hedges: and this never stops till all are dead' [p.142]. It's impossible that William doesn't feel the *complicity* of his entourage, in this case as in so many others. Yet he 'could . . . in his forty-third year cause to be inscribed in golden letters on a block of granite: "Here His Majesty William II brought down His Most High's fifty thousandth animal, a white cock-pheasant" ' [p.143].

If there's self-deception, it's a lie carried out with the totality of human reality – a royal lie. For in actual fact divine right, by separating its beneficiary from other men, confers upon him the right to a sacred complicity. Ritual lying forms part of the ceremonies whereby subjects communicate with the taboo object. It's a homage the sovereign *expects* of other men. And the degree of belief that he places in it, without totally preventing clear-sightedness, does dim it. It's a ceremonious belief. All the more ceremonious, in that the sovereign has ceremonious relations with himself. The very tonality of his intra-conscious relations, at the level at which consciousness is self-consciousness, is the sacred. It is the subject's duty to lie, and the sovereign's duty to believe in the lie. For the only human relations which exclude lying are those of equality – and the sovereign is the individual who cannot wish equality.

However, this way of masking his disability is not just a flight: it's a free and energetic effort to surpass it. And Ludwig is right to write: 'The few who then could estimate the significance of this victory of moral force over bodily infirmity, felt justified in their proudest hopes for this royal personage. In reality, the moral victory over his physique was his destruction. If this was the greatest of days for the youthful Prince, riding in glittering uniform upon a galloping horse under the morning sunlight at the head of his regiment before his astonished elders, it was but the prelude to countless parades and processions, resounding orations, and menacing gestures, whereby he endeavoured for a decade to justify himself in his own eyes' [pp.8–9].

And this further text allows us to understand what William's 'infirmity' is: 'Only those who can appreciate this lifelong struggle against the congenital weakness will be fair to him when the future Emperor is seen to strain too far, or lose, his nervous energy. The perpetual struggle with a defect which every newcomer must instantly perceive and he, for that very reason, the more ostentatiously ignore – this hourly, lifelong effort to conceal a congenital, in no way repulsive stigma of Nature, was the decisive factor in the development of his character. Feeling himself a weakling, he sought to emphasize his strength; but instead of doing so in the intellectual realm, as his lively intelligence would have permitted, tradition and vain glory urged him to exhibit it through an heroic, that is to say a soldierly, attitude' [p.27].

Ludwig is wrong to treat William here as just any citizen, otherwise he wouldn't be surprised at his trying to hide 'a defect which every newcomer must perceive'. The sacred complicity, which he regards as his right to demand of anyone, allows William to pose as a principle that all *ceremony*, aimed at masking a defect that otherwise must be perceived, must needs cause the eyes of all to be shrouded magically by a fog. William's sacred bad faith is a claim – founded on divine right – upon the bad faith of his subjects. Furthermore, he's wrong to say, in terms of vulgar causality, that tradition and ambition 'urge him' to compensate for his disability by a heroic, soldierly attitude. For Ludwig views the Emperor's disability in isolation. He doesn't approach it *from the angle of* the Emperor's being-to-reign. Being-to-reign in Prussia, as a soldier-king. The free choice isn't exercised at the level of his attitude to his disability. It's far more total, since it's exercised in relation to being-for-the-throne. William, seeking to succeed 'in the intellectual realm', wouldn't just be another man: he'd be another *king*, choosing another reign and another Prussia – striving to change Prussia. And that change would have been so weighty, that Ludwig can see quite well himself that the whole subsequent course of history would thereby have been modified. It was at the level of the free project of his being-in-the-world that the choice would have been possible; and William, pro-jecting himself as *other* beyond his disability, would forthwith have suffered from an *other* disability.

It remains the case that the choice, which involved the totality of his person, would have been possible. Which allows us to understand that William *chose* his weakness. We mustn't say, like Ludwig: '*Feeling* himself a weakling, he sought to emphasize his strength.' For by making himself master in the intellectual realm, and by cynically displaying his disability, he could have *really been* strong. Instead – understanding himself as a soldier-emperor by divine right, who had to surpass and deny his disability as a scandal through perpetual struggle – he *chose* that his strength should be weakness. He *chose* the hidden flaw. He '*made himself*' a weakling. In other words, he chose himself to be defective.

But the text we've just quoted from Ludwig has the considerable advantage of showing us that William's disability couldn't be quite simply a visible physical defect – a certain withering of one arm. Considered thus, as it would be by a classical historian, it bears no relation at all to William's policy towards England, for example. Yet it's already apparent that it can exist for him only as a signifying situation. Through it, Ludwig already reveals to us 'orations, menacing gestures, parades and processions'. Let us be clear that it isn't the *cause*, or even the *motive*, for these manifestations. But these manifestations, on the other hand, represent the *manner* of apprehending the disability as a situation. From this point of view, we'll grasp William's dispatch to Kruger, for example, as a way of *being-his-own-disability*.[13]

But that wouldn't be sufficient – and we'll thereafter see apparently unassimilable layers of signification become suddenly linked to that congenital disability. For it's certain that, for Wilhelm, disability = England, and conquering England = suppressing his disability. I shall continue tomorrow.

It's the bourgeoisie which prevented war in '38 and decided the capitulation at Munich, from fear of victory even more than of defeat: it was afraid war might benefit communism. In September '39, on the other hand, war was welcomed by the bourgeoisie – because the Russo–German treaty discredited communism; and because everyone now realizes that this war, which is being waged directly or

---

13. The 'Kruger Telegram' sent by William II to the president of the then Transvaal, congratulating him on repulsing the Jameson Raid without outside aid, caused resentment in British ruling-class circles against what was seen as unwarranted meddling in Britain's colonial affairs; it also raised false hopes among the Boers about possible German aid in the event of a conflict with Britain.

indirectly against the Soviets, will necessarily be accompanied by a police operation domestically. The communist party will be dissolved. What ten years of politics haven't been able to achieve, the war will achieve in a month. Such, it seems to me, is the main reason why the bourgeoisie rallied to the war. Beneath its trappings of a national war, it's to a great extent a civil war. While many of us are struggling against the ideology of Hitlerism, behind the scenes they're liquidating what's left of communist ideology. War in '38 could have been the occasion for a revolution – in '40 it's the occasion for a counter-revolution. The war of '38 would have been a 'left' war – that of '39 is a 'right' war. Hitler's blunder was not to see that, in '38, the capitalist democracies were defending themselves on two fronts: threatened in their imperialism by Nazi ambitions, they were threatened in their inner constitution by communist action. They didn't want war, lest they should have to defend themselves on two fronts at once. By making a common front with Stalin, Hitler relieves them by allowing them to expel communism – henceforth viewed as an *external* danger. And doubtless he was indeed hoping to maintain the two fronts – counting on the disintegrating effect of the 'moral Front'. But how did he fail to allow for the swift repression which the bourgeois governments must *have been only too happy* to carry out?

I read the French Yellow Book and note there's nothing in it about the notorious '2 July coup': alleged attempt at a putsch in Danzig, followed by a German climbdown.[14] Yet the rumour of this circulated widely at the time and Tabouis, of course, echoed it.[15] At a meeting of the *NRF* at which I was present – on 1 July I think – there was a lot of talk about it, and Nizan told me: 'We're risking war tomorrow.' The rumour, in my view, had its sources in a report from M. Coulondre, dated 27 June, which alluded to the possibility of an annexation of Danzig from within; a note from Georges Bonnet to the French ambassador in London, inviting him to entreat Lord Halifax to unmask the manoeuvre on the occasion of his 29 June speech; a frontier incident, concealed by both the German and the Polish press

14. Danzig was in the hands of local Nazis after 1933–35, and the putsch rumoured on 2 July would supposedly have proclaimed the formal incorporation of the Free City into the Reich, thus provoking Polish intervention and giving Hitler a *casus belli*. When nothing happened on the date in question, the German press denounced the rumours as officially inspired French and British warmongering. Coulondre was French ambassador in Berlin at the time, Bonnet the French foreign minister, Halifax his British counterpart.

15. Geneviève Tabouis, well-known radio commentator on foreign affairs.

(a Hitler Youth group crossing the frontier in Pomerania); and Bonnet's interview with the German ambassador in Paris.

Saturday, 9 March

I return to William. I want to show that it's not a matter of external facts having *acted* upon his personality, but that he *is* himself a totality in situation: that the situations exist thanks only to his way of projecting himself as a totality through them. I want to show how his disability is not just a physiological defect, but a signifying situation. I've shown that it signified cavalcades and processions and menacing gestures. I want to show its signifying relationship with William's English policy. It's necessary, first, to pass via the *family*. Here again the sovereign is radically different from his subjects. William is grandson to Queen Victoria, and when the latter upbraids him for his attitude to Lord Salisbury, she writes: 'I doubt if one monarch has ever before written in such a tone to another, and this to your grandmother' [p.215].

For the sovereign, State relations are family relations. Yet neither should the concept of family be taken in the sense it is when citizens are in question: there, on the contrary, one might say that family relations are State relations. Victoria's letter is significant. Her first reproach to William is that he has disregarded the ceremonials which are fitting between monarchs. And the fact that one of those reigning personages is grandmother to the other is presented as an *aggravating* circumstance. I could compare the thing only to the respect that our officers demand from us: I have to respect my colonel *because* he's a colonel. And if, into the bargain, he's an old man of sixty-five, this circumstance functions – but into the bargain – as an additional tinge to my respect. It would be quite out of place, for instance, for me to tell him: 'You have a right to my respect as an old man, but not as a colonel.'

So there's a singularity here – which is signalled, for example, in the fact that no sooner does William become emperor than he impresses his dignity upon his Uncle Edward, then merely heir to the throne. 'At his first visit to Vienna, in September 1888, the young Emperor, knowing that Edward had announced himself for the same time, laid down as a condition that he must be received alone, even refusing Edward's offer to be present in Prussian uniform at the Vienna railway-station. He obliged him to leave Vienna for a week and go to Hungary' [p.162–3]. Yet Edward is twenty years older than him. Family relations come to colour relations between monarchs: they come to signal, in concrete fashion, that monarchs are *peers*. That equality doesn't exclude isolation, however, because it's a sacred equality. Furthermore, every family reunion takes on an international and diplomatic dimensions. It signifies 'rapprochement'. For example, in '99 Queen Victoria objects for political reasons to her grandson coming to visit her on her eightieth birthday.

Basically, in the being-to-reign of each there's given the being-to-reign of the Other. And that Other who reigns has the concrete bond with the monarch of being *of the same family*. And as each, in his being-to-reign by divine right, *is* the State over which he reigns, the relations of the monarch with other sovereigns' countries are family relations. William II is English through his mother, we'd say, if we were dealing with a simple citizen. But in relation to a sovereign, in fact, the formula is shocking. He's not English, because he's first an emperor. But qua emperor he belongs to a great family of lone wolves, whereof each member *is* a certain country. And the relations of each sovereign with other sovereigns' countries are defined thereby: they are *concrete*, *individual*, *affective* and, therefore, easily *passionate* and *sacred*. Between the sovereign and other nations there's a *tie of blood*. William II's being-to-reign over Germany implies, for example, from the outset a curious blood-tie, sacred and passionate, with England. There's a familial, sacred geography from the outset in William II – analogous to the renowned 'Swann's Way' and 'Guermantes' Way' of Proust. It's really a sacred, primitive, 'hodological' space – very similar to that of Australian clans.[16] Austria, Russia and England are sacred directions and vectors of homogeneity.

Ludwig has rightly stressed that particular character of the world: 'The Emperor, on the other hand, said to his Generals: "Russia wants to occupy Bulgaria, and is claiming our neutrality. But my word is pledged to the Emperor of Austria, and I have told the Tsar that I cannot leave Austria in the lurch." . . . The friendship with Austria, which was ultimately to be the ruin of Germany, was – in so far as the Emperor was concerned – inspired by the feudal House of Habsburg, and would never have been manifested by him to a confederation such as Switzerland, in which the eight States would have been united not under a monarchy but a republic . . . his friendly feeling for the Habsburg and the Sultan was less a political sentiment than a dynastic emotion, which kept him in permanent alliance with these two Imperial rulers, and with them only. Nothing in William the Second

16. For 'hodological' space, see note 9 on p. 129 above. The Australian clan structures are those studied by Radcliffe-Brown and the Oceania unit in the nineteen-thirties.

was more genuine than this disastrous idea of "fraternal loyalty", but only in so far as it attached the Emperor to a sovereign whom he reckoned as his equal . . . And so, as between Vienna and Petersburg, the Emperor's conscience was never at rest' [pp. 156–7].

The fact is, that 'disastrous idea of fraternal loyalty' isn't an 'emotion': it's a situation originally grasped in the free-project of himself towards the reign. The spatial orientation is given in the being-to-reign as the original being-for-others. Naturally, Republics will – in this geographical and dynastic map – form barred, forbidden zones. We shall see later the familial origin of the fear and hatred the Emperor felt for them. But before all hatred, in the project of himself towards his reign, Republics are given as dead zones, as areas of 'no man's land'.[17] I shall continue after lunch.

I break off to record here the conversation of three chasseurs behind me. First chasseur: 'The Capt'n – 'e sez, with a threat'nin' look: "I'll give you a chance to redeem yourself, don't you worry." Well, me old mate, I tell you straight, if I can find me an 'ole, you jus' watch me go to groun' in it. I ain't got no need to redeem meself.' Another chasseur: 'Christ, to redeem yourself you 'ave to 'ave sold out first: I ain't sold out!'[18]

For once, I approve Montherlant (*NRF* – note on the Olympics): '[Play is] the only defensible form of action; the only one that is worthy of man, because at once intelligent and constructive; and this, moreover, has been said before: "Man is fully a man only when he plays" (Schiller).'

Why does he have to add foolishly that this form of action is 'the only one that can be taken seriously'? How can he fail to see that play, by its nature, excludes the very idea of seriousness? If there's some unity in my life, that's because I've never wanted to live seriously. I've been able to put on a show – to know pathos, and anguish, and joy. But never, never have I known seriousness. My whole life has been just a game: sometimes long and tedious, sometimes in bad taste – but a game. And this war is just a game for me. There's a certain solidity about the real, which makes it into something resembling a pear flan – and which, thank God, I do not know. I've seen people who'd throw themselves upon that semolina pudding, and they've disgusted me. I

17. English in text.
18. The play on *racheter* (literally 'buy back', here 'redeem') and *être vendu* cannot really be reproduced in English.

shall have to explain here (when I've finished with William, who's beginning to bore me) what a game is – the happy metamorphosis of the contingent into the gratuitous – and why the assumption of oneself is itself a game. The other side of the coin is my unspeakable frivolity. Lyrical, painful state at this moment. There's a piano in the Home, hidden behind black curtains; some fellow's playing jazz-tunes – extremely well. It reminds me of the milky light of those summer evenings – the pianists at the College Inn. We'd be sitting at the bar, T. and I. From time to time, the curtain across the entrance would part onto the night – round and blue as a globe – and that was peace.

Received a letter from Adrienne Monnier. She writes: 'Your signature has changed a bit. The J.P. has grown amazing and very . . . aerial – it must come from being in the Met.!' I was weak enough to be moved by this: I saw in it a sign of those changes which I strive to achieve in myself – a sign and a promise.

It makes me furious not to be a poet – to be so ponderously tethered to prose. I'd like to be able to create those sparkling, absurd objects: poems, resembling a ship in a bottle, which are like an instant's eternity. But there's something throttled in me – a secret shame, a cynicism too long learnt – and also a certain misfortune: my feelings haven't found their language. I feel them, I stretch out a shy finger and, as soon as I touch them, I change them into prose. The choice of words undoes me. If I begin, if I find a poetic phrase, some word will have slipped in that rends it: some too pointed, too plain word. The movement of the phrase is rhetorical, it rolls – and if I wish to stop it, behold it weighty and sonorous in the arrogant immobility of a braggart! I don't know what the solution is. Perhaps to rely on regular rhythms. Or rather, I know it only too well: I should shut up. I'm thinking all of that as I read these lines – by someone or other, Aragon perhaps – which I'm going to copy here because they're beautiful and I'd like to write some like that . . . Upon reflection, I'm not going to copy them: they irritate me now, they're not pure. I prefer these two, which apparently come from a song:

'Oh you'll find boulders on every roadway,
On every roadway you'll find some woe . . . '

Sunday, 10 March

Letter from J. Duboin to Bayet on abundance:[19]

'The war does not slow down the rhythm of technological progress: on the contrary, it accelerates it. This is clear from the following observation. In the world, there exist 25 million men under mobilization: from the production point of view, that's zero. There are also 75 million men manufacturing arms and munitions: from the particular point of view which interests us, this necessary production is useless production. In total, 100 million outside useful production, but who live off the labour of others. So these others have recourse to more and more powerful techniques, to make up for their numerical inferiority.'

What interests me in this text: war as a *world phenomenon* – 100 million men outside the circuit of useful labour, including 25 million destroyers. To be related to the following remark by Ramuz (*NRF*): '*Asymmetry*: There is a great disproportion between making and unmaking; constructing and destroying. That is to say, between the time man takes to build anything and the time he takes to eliminate it. The construction of a house requires the work of a whole team of masons for weeks and months: an instant suffices to bring it to the ground. There is an asymmetry, since if nature too knows these ways of proceeding, it makes use of them only exceptionally. It raises a mountain chain gradually, and is no less gradual about wearing it away; it constructs a man gradually, but usually only destroys him little by little.'[20]

We are soon going to be recalled to the rear lines. Captain Munier had written to Colonel Weissenburger, chief of the Air Battalion, to point out that we were auxiliaries, and that he ought therefore to take away our rifles. To which Colonel Weissenburger replied: 'Impossible to take away the rifles, but I shall take away the men.' So they'll give those rifles – old, outdated carbines – men to fit them: young regulars. As for us, where shall we go? If it's to Tours, or some such posting, I'm delighted: I'll go to Paris more often, and I'll be able to arrange for my friends from Paris to visit me.

But I wonder if I'll keep up this notebook. Its principal significance

19. Jacques Duboin, theorist of abundance, author of *La Grande relève de l'homme par la machine* (1932) and *En route vers l'abondance* (1935).

Albert Bayet (1880–1961), sociologist and moral philosopher, president of the underground press association during World War Two.

20. Charles-Ferdinand Ramuz (1878–1947), Swiss novelist.

was to accentuate the isolation I was in, and the rupture between my past and present lives. As long as I was 'on the front line', 10 kilometres from the advance posts, liable to be bombarded, it had its meaning. Perhaps, in the rear, it will be necessary to put a full stop after this 'calling into question', and begin again to construct: finish my novel – write a philosophy of Nothingness. Likewise, I was very directly mixed up in the war here, seeing chasseurs returning every day from the outposts, officers, etc. Shall I be, in the rear? And will it be worth the trouble of recording scraps of trivial gossip on a daily basis? Or, if I go on with this journal, then it will be only by fits and starts. In any case, another two months will be needed for our recall to the interior to be put into effect. I'm happy, but all the same something's ending: my first period of war.

I return to William. I've noted those curious family relations which characterize the sovereign. But what's important in William's case is that England was *in his home*. His mother is English and anglomaniac. And England is first of all his mother. But this mother despises and hates him: first and foremost, because he's disabled. 'The ambitious Victoria, daughter of the powerful Queen of England and her sagacious consort, could not forgive the imperfection of this child, especially as she regarded her husband's blood as less illustrious than her father's . . . she cherished in her heart a secret grudge against her misshapen son, precisely because he was her firstborn, and openly displayed a preference for her healthier children' [p.6]. Childhood humiliations. *English* humiliations: the child is brought up in the English manner and he hates his English education. And yet, he remains dominated by English arrogance: it's towards England that he has his inferiority complex.

But he finds a kind of revenge in the very singularity of his being-to-reign. Frederick-William his father is languishing in the shadow of the throne. He's not a monarch, he perhaps never will be – at any rate not for long: the real crown prince is William. He understands himself as such. And since he's not heir to a reigning *father* – the crown passing from grandfather to grandson – he doesn't grasp himself as receiving his right to reign from his father: there's a kind of spontaneous generation of divine right in him, which is *without roots*. He throws himself towards his reign *against* his parents. It goes without saying that the 'against' is ambiguous: he wants to dominate them and finally compel their admiration. But this is what, from the outset, gives his being-to-reign a strained, uneasy, ill-assured character. That divine right is a revenge. He'll reign against that father and that mother, who'll have proved unable to win the throne or who'll have possessed it only cursorily. His 'reign' lacks tradition; he's a parvenu to the throne, though reigning by divine right. It's in William's being to be-to-reign as a parvenu endowed with divine right.

But, thereby, he-is-to-reign-young. Ludwig writes that it was a great misfortune for him to begin his reign at thirty, before his maturity. But he'd long been preparing to reign young. That premature coronation did not occur out of the blue. It was a situation lived through at length in advance, and constitutive of his very being for William – who discovered it gradually from adolescence on. It was his own possibility, and he'd been living it for fifteen years when he finally realized it. What would have happened if Frederick-William, instead of being killed by an English doctor, had been cured by a German doctor? I've no idea. But in the new attitude of William, long condemned to remain Crown Prince, there'd certainly have entered – as the main element – that concrete possibility of reigning young which, before collapsing, had for many years at least been his *own* possibility.

So there he is now: a man who made himself king by divine right, who made himself a young king well before being one. King against his father, against his mother, against England and – at the same time, by a single act of self-propulsion, before he could even understand them – against the liberal ideas which his mother was seeking to inculcate into his father. 'The more "liberal" his parents would have him, the more unapproachable he became. At Kassel he was soon "quite the future emperor" ' [p.8]. (He was twelve.) That hatred of liberalism – which will be expressed by a 'reigning-against-liberalism' – is, all rolled into one, his hatred for England, his refusal to find a refuge in intellectual life from his disability, and his original determination to reign *in the Prussian manner.*

One can see how the throne and the disability are indissolubly linked in the unity of a single self-projection, which rebounds from the throne to the disability and nuances the being-to-reign in terms of the disability. One can see that neither *throne*, nor *premature coronation*, nor *family*, nor *deformity* are contingent facts – in the sense that they could be other and would act from outside upon William; or that one could imagine William – if other facts had acted upon him – as different, assuredly, but nevertheless basically identical. In fact, it's impossible to imagine an *other* William than the one who has launched himself through that situation: who *is* the free project of himself in that situation. His character is not *one* thing and his being-to-reign another – his temperament one thing and his disability another thing.

There's a free human totality which is nothing *in* itself – in an immanence outlined in advance – but which is wholly in its project.

In that sense, one might say of the 'reign' in being-to-reign that it is – as Heidegger says of the world – neither subjective nor objective. Not subjective: it's not an intrinsic property of William, something resembling a quality in his inner life. Nor objective: it's not an external fact, since being-to-reign is a unity and the 'reign' cannot be extracted from being-to-reign. Put otherwise, William is nothing but the way in which he *historializes himself*. And one can see that, in the unity of that historialization, the most disparate layers of signification are linked: the reign reveals the disability, which in its turn exposes the family, England, the anti-liberalism and the Prussian militarism. It's a question not of one single thing, but of situations that are hierarchized and subordinated according to the unity of a single original project.

It would now be necessary to show how the fall of Bismarck is the culmination of this project. (The renewal of a personnel that is too elderly – since contemporary with the grandfather – must be a revolution. If it were the father who reigned, it would be a slow evolution. And precisely because the prince understands himself as a parvenu endowed with divine right, this revolution is the culmination of his project – whatever may be the variations in his attitude towards Bismarck.) Also, how the prince's attitude towards the proletariat (hatred and fear of social-democracy; attempts to win over the workers) is included in the basic project. In such a way that this project is truly a pro-ject of himself into the world, and the prince's weak, changeable policy towards England, Russia or the proletariat is not an effect of William II's character – it *is* William II himself, historializing himself in the world. But all that goes without saying, if one grants the preceding description.

One would need, of course – and this is a serious lacuna in this essay – to discuss William's homosexual tendencies, to see whether they can be conceptualized within the unity of the primary project and in their hierarchical relationship with the being-to-reign. What is a homosexual king? What is a homosexual king of Prussia? But if I don't discuss them, that's not my fault: it's because Ludwig is extremely vague and discreet on this vital question.

All I've sought to show is that it's the historical method – and the psychological prejudices governing it – rather than the actual structure of things which produce this division of the factors of History into parallel signifying layers. This parallelism disappears if one deals with the historical personage in terms of the unity of his historialization.

But I acknowledge that what I think I've shown is valid only where the historical study is a *monograph*, and shows the individual as shaper of his own destiny. Nonetheless, he acts also *upon others*. In a few days time, if Ludwig's book lends itself to that, I'll try to reflect upon William II's share of 'responsibility' for the '14 war.

Saw C., deputy-director of the Agence Havas.[21] Tall, handsome fellow with white hair – would resemble Gary Cooper, if he weren't a bit stout. Very distant, normally, and ill liked. Makes it insolently clear that he belongs to a different order of being. He deigns to speak to me and shake my hand, even to seek me out – since my inertia and small liking for males mean that I don't even greet him when we encounter each other, but pretend not to see him: he draws up to me then with all the nonchalance of a sailing-boat. For my part, I have a soft spot for him because he's handsome. Ugly, I shouldn't tolerate him. I've already explained the mechanism involved here. He's the one, incidentally, I spoke of in one of my first notebooks, saying that I felt vaguely attracted by him because of his beauty. Always that same taste for enslaving beauty, wherever it may be; and, not being able to possess it upon myself, that desire to possess it 'by proxy'. But when a male is involved, this doesn't go very far.

He seems not to be stupid – at least, he has a veneer. He's proud of his Arts degree. The other day in the Home, he hailed me, in order with feigned carelessness to show me an issue of *Match* which was lying half-torn on a table: 'I'm in it', he told me. I had a look. In a photo which showed the managing director of the Agence Havas and his colleagues, he could be seen – haughty, in black suit and starched collar – leaning towards the director. That naivety pleased me. He'd rediscovered himself as a civilian, and in a dead civilian world where he'd had his place. But he'd not been able to keep his discovery to himself alone – it had to be registered by somebody. Rather as the Beaver says she'd hate to die without anyone being there to register the fact. The resurrection of his past wouldn't have been total if it had not had a witness.

Today, at the Home, I was sitting on a chair near the stove while the duty soldiers busied themselves with blacking out panes and windows in preparation for the film show. It was one o'clock in the afternoon. Sun outside – golden half-light in the great, deserted hall. Pre-performance atmosphere: I enjoyed it, though quite determined to

21. Agence Havas: Large combine (now state-run) specialized in business services, insurance, advertising and travel.

get the hell out before the programme began. I didn't want to see *A Rare Bird* or some documentary on the Maginot Line. But in that sombre, golden mist which filled the hall, something remained like a vague recollection of those spring afternoons (Sunday afternoons, like this one) which we used to spend, the Beaver and I, in the cool, dark Ursulines cinema, very aware of the sunlight that was flooding down outside: as St-John Perse says, the sun was not named, but its presence was among us.[22] I was reading; I was thinking about that notion of 'situation'; I'd found an idea – and then C. made me lose it. I shall find it again. I'm counting on repeating myself. One always thinks by repeating oneself. A forgotten idea is never lost: one doesn't find it when one looks for it, but another one comes to you – a brand new one – and it's the very same.

So C. approaches, I see him, I pretend not to see him, I lower my head – and finally I see his boots standing to attention before me. We greet each other with studied indifference. He yields up to me the secret of his bitter soul:[23] 'So you're leaving, it seems?' – 'Yes.' – 'I prefer to stay here, myself. If one must play the fool, one may as well do it here.' – 'Yes. One's more free. But look at the trouble you had bringing your wife here. If you were in the rear, you could fix things up with your family.' He, drily: 'The family isn't everything.' There's always a kind of secret unconcern at the heart of his tough phrases, as if he were above what he was saying.

The soldiers begin to file into the hall and sit down. Noise of chairs. He goes on, without looking at me – he's side-face on and I can see his firm chin: 'I don't want to do anything, I wash my hands of it. If the military authorities find they need an Arts graduate to light the stoves, let that be their responsibility. I won't budge.' – 'All right,' I say, 'but Havas could have recalled you into some reserved occupation.' (He's the only person here whom I address as *vous* and who does the same for me. In the beginning I used *tu*, but since he persists in calling me *vous* I follow suit.) 'Yes,' he says – then quickly: 'Havas doesn't have a deputy-director any more . . .' He continues flatly: 'It's up to them to decide if they need me. I won't budge . . . go on a training course to become an officer . . . cross over to the other side of the barricade . . . No! So there it is: I remain in the military proletariat where I've been put.' In short, he's sulking; that's the core of the matter: he'd have liked to have been served up a reserved occupation

22. 'Et le soleil n'est point nommé, mais sa puissance est parmi nous', in *Anabase* (1924).

23. I have not been able to identify this allusion.

or lieutenant's rank on a silver platter.

A bit later, Hantziger comes up. His pear-shaped face is all red and glowing, his lashless eyes blinking. 'C.,' says Hantziger, in the wheedling whisper he uses to ask a favour, 'if you visit Havas when you go on leave, please bring me back an English or Canadian paper.' – 'I don't know if I'll visit Havas,' says C. in the same gloomy voice. 'When you've worked in a firm, it's better not to go back there. You're a nuisance. There are lots of newcomers, you get in their way all the time, and they don't know what to say to you.' – 'It's unfortunate,' says Hantziger, 'all those newcomers who've taken our places: when peace comes, however will they be got rid of?' C.'s gloomy, angry look intensifies: 'Don't you worry. We'll make a clean sweep and get rid of the whole lot. The lads coming back from the war won't be in the same stupid state of national euphoria as the '18 ones were. They'll come back determined to defend themselves. People have made asses of us quite long enough – we'll show our teeth. It'll be easy, so long as there's a really strong solidarity among us. Not like war veterans parading under the Arc de Triomphe – another kind: a solidarity in pressing demands. And if a group comes forward to organize that, then we'll see something!'

I take this opportunity of noting a curious, dirty little trick I often play and whose origin I know. It pertains to the schema: greatness misjudged, then restored to favour. I've already mentioned the importance of that schema, which in my childhood used to lead me into seemingly masochistic reveries – but far from masochistic ones at bottom. I used to shed a tear or two over Grisélidis – even today I'm moved by King Lear's daughter Cordelia.[24] So first there's some mistake, judicial or other, and a disaster which the person endures with dignity and in silence. Whereupon the apotheosis supervenes – which derives from his abandoned state itself and from his silence. Thus the most terrible fall bears its recompense within it. The ordeal has nothing Christian about it, since no God comes to tailor the final happiness to the sufferings endured: that comes spontaneously. The recompense is the natural completion of the ordeal. As for my forlornness during the ordeal, that's quite typical – and basically very akin to C.'s sulking, for example. One doesn't defend oneself, but withdraws: exactly that way – already registered here – of putting an absolute distance between other men and myself. The first pretext is enough

24. Grisélidis: the patient Griselda of the last tale in Boccaccio's *Decameron*, translated via Petrarch into two French versions at the end of the fourteenth century (as also into Chaucer's *Clerk's Tale*).

for me to retire from the scene – always my pride. And to complete the picture, I wait for people to come to me.

Throughout my life I've waited for people to come to me: I've never taken the first step – I want to be solicited. At the age of fourteen, I recall passing in front of a group of my closest comrades, pretending not to see them, in order to give them the opportunity to call me over. Unfortunately, I'd chosen my time badly: for them, I was a butt and a nothing; they didn't call me. Whereupon I ran in a long detour to pass before them again – still with an absent-minded air – to give them a new opportunity to hail me. And so on till one of them said to me: 'You stupid imbecile, what's the matter with you, circling round us like that for the past three quarters of an hour?'

In those reveries, moreover, I've no doubt but that people will come to me in the end. That solitude isn't pure: the hero of my dreams leaves, not in order to flee men definitively, but with the certitude that men will one day go down on their knees to him. Pride, false solitude, optimism – how odd that it should all be present already in my first childish dreams. And in the very idea I formed of greatness there was the need for a recompense. I've kept that. I mean, I obviously do know a certain type of dry, intent suffering, which is self-oblivion and is truly unbearable: that's the kind I most esteem. Over certain of my sorrows, however, there's always an angel bending. It seems to me that – thanks to a favour of providence – the most beautiful recompense will be born of that sorrow itself: every sorrow must have its beautiful outcome.

The war very soon appeared to me, basically, through that schema: years of tribulation and greatness, for which I'd be recompensed by a renewal and a fresh youth. I'm not one to believe in the labours of war, the labours of love now lost.[25] Yet, yesterday, that's where I was aiming to end up. Filled with melancholy at not being a poet, I started writing in this notebook about how melancholy I was. And an angel's wing was caressing that melancholy; that melancholy bore within it a carefully concealed hope – namely, that the very passage in which I was writing of my sorrow at not being a poet, through a spontaneous recompense, would beneath my fingers become – without my realizing it – the most beautiful prose; and that a little later, on rereading that thoroughly modest and honest lament, I'd discover in wondering amazement that with my prose I'd precisely created the beautiful object – the ship in the bottle – which I was vainly asking of poetry. I cannot say that this base hope was the *motive* which caused me to

25. *Les Peines d'amour perdues* is the French translation for *Love's Labours Lost*.

write. No, God be praised! But it tinged my writing. I wonder if it will have been noticed. In any case, the schema is clear: cast into the depths of despair because he's not a musician, he simply breathes out his suffering – and *precisely* his suffering becomes music: that rough, innocent lament turns out to be the loveliest harmony.

Monday, 11 March

I meant to copy a passage from Gide's journal on 'diminished reality', and was wrong not to do so.[26] He explains to Roger Martin du Gard that there's a certain sense of the real which he lacks, and that the most important events strike him as masquerades. I'm like that, and it's probably the source of my frivolity. I long remained in doubt as to whether it was a trait specific to certain people, including me; or whether all and sundry weren't basically like that: whether reality wasn't an ideal impossible to feel and placed at infinity. Today, I'm still not too sure. But I observe that both Gide, as a big bourgeois, and I – as a public servant from a family of public servants – were only too ready to take the real for a stage-set. After all, nothing irreparable has ever happened to Gide, any more than to me.

I've had a premonition of the irreparable only on one or two occasions: for example, when I thought I was going mad.[27] At that time I discovered that anything could happen to *me*. It's a precious feeling, entirely necessary to authenticity, which I strive to preserve as much as I can. But it's highly unstable, and, except in great catastrophes, a certain application is needed to maintain it in oneself. Besides – except in that instance of supposed madness, when my supreme consciousness was caught in a stranglehold – I often used to extract myself from those fits of anguish for *my* fate by taking refuge in the bosom of a supreme consciousness, absolute and contemplative, for which my fate and the very collapse of my personality were mere avatars of a privileged object. The object could disappear, my consciousness was still affected: my personality was but a transitory incarnation of that consciousness – or, better still, a certain bond which connected it to the world like a captive balloon.

Whether this contemplative attitude had its origin in my contemplative function as guardian of culture within society, as a Marxist would state without further ado; or whether it represents a primary object of my existence (and one does find in it pride, freedom, the

26. *The Journals of André Gide*, vol. II, p. 363.
27. For an account of Sartre's 'madness', see Simone De Beauvoir, *The Prime of Life*, pp. 208–13.

destabilization of oneself, the contemplative stoicism and the optimism which certainly form part of my primary project) – that's what I do not wish to decide here. It's certain, in any case, that this way of taking refuge at the top of the tower when its base is under attack, and of looking down from above without blenching, albeit with eyes somewhat widened by fear, is the attitude I chose in '38–'39 faced with the threats of war. It's also the one which, a little earlier, inspired my article on the transcendence of the Ego – where I quite simply eject the Self from consciousness, like some nosy visitor. With myself, I didn't have that tender intimacy which causes there to be adhesions (as in medical parlance) between the Self and consciousness – so that if one tried to remove the former, one would be afraid of tearing the latter. It was perfectly all right outside, on the contrary. It remained there, granted; but I watched it through the pane with all the calm and severity in the world.

I long believed, moreover, that the existence of a character couldn't be reconciled with the freedom of consciousness: I thought character was nothing but a bunch of maxims, more moral than psychological, in which our neighbour sums up his experience of us. Consciousness-as-refuge remained, as was proper, colourless, odourless and taste-less. It was only this year, with the advent of war, that I understood the truth: character assuredly must not be confused with all those recipe-maxims of the moralists – 'he's quick-tempered; he's lazy; etc.' – but is the primary, free project of our being in the world. I tried to show this for William II.

In short, the existence of a consciousness-as-refuge allowed me to decide at will on how much seriousness to attribute to the situtation. I was like someone who, amid the direst adventures, scarcely feels the threatening reality of the tortures being reserved for him – because he always carries with him a pellet of deadly poison, which will deliver him before anyone can lay a finger on him. There's a character called Katow in *La Condition humaine* who's like that. So he's great only when he gives his poison to his comrades. It seems to me at that moment he's truly human reality, because nothing holds him outside the world: he's fully inside it, free and without any defence. The passage from absolute freedom to disarmed and human freedom – the rejection of the poison – has taken place this year, and as a direct result I now see my destiny as *finite*. And my new apprenticeship must consist, precisely, in feeling myself 'in on it': without any defence. It's the war and Heidegger which put me on the right path – Heidegger by showing me there was nothing beyond the project whereby human reality realized itself. Does that mean I'm going to allow the Self back in? No, certainly not. But though the ipseity or totality of the for-itself is not the Self, it's nevertheless the *person*. I'm in the course of learning, basically, to be a person.

But that's not the aim of my present remarks. I wished simply to indicate that – not having been directly involved in things; not having felt *responsible*; not having had money worries – I've never taken the world seriously. In other times that could have led me to mysticism, since those whom 'diminished reality' fails to satisfy are only too ready to seek surreality. (And I imagine that fifteen years ago, it was the origin of the surrealist faith for many people – though not all: the influence of the war, which is often mentioned, seems to me far more decisive for the leaders.) But I was an atheist out of pride. Not out of a feeling of pride, but my very existence was pride: I *was* pride. There was no place for God beside me: I was so perpetually the source of myself that I didn't see what part an Almighty could play in it all. Subsequently, the wretched poverty of religious thought reinforced my atheism for good. Faith is stupid or it's bad faith. My mother must have grasped something of that frivolous coldness towards the world, for she's fond of repeating that a few centuries earlier I should have become a monk.

Lacking faith, I confined myself to shedding seriousness. There's seriousness, basically, when one starts off from the *world* or attributes more reality to the world than to oneself. Or, at the very least, when one confers a reality upon oneself insofar as one belongs to the world. It's by no means accidental that materialism is *serious*; nor is it accidental that it is always and everywhere found as the chosen philosophical doctrine of the revolutionary. For revolutionaries are serious: they first know themselves because they're crushed by the world; they know themselves by virtue of that world which crushes them; and they want to change the world. In this, they find themselves in agreement with their old adversaries, the owners of property, who also know and value themselves by virtue of their situation in the world.

I hate seriousness. Through an engineer's serious concern there passes the whole world – with its inertia, its laws, its stubborn opacity. All serious thought is thickened by the world and coagulates: it's a resignation by man in favour of the world. See that man who shakes his head, saying: 'It's bad! It's very bad!', and try to understand what he puts into that head-shaking. It's this: that the world dominates man; that there were laws and rules to observe – all outside us, stratified, petrified – which would have given a favourable outcome; but those rules have been violated, the catastrophe has arrived and behold man without any recourse. For he no longer has any recourse *in himself*: he's 'of the world', the world has installed itself within him, and that violated taboo is violated also *within him*.

One is serious when one doesn't even envisage the possibility of *leaving* the world. When the world – with its alps and its rocks, its crusts and its oozes, its peatbogs and its deserts: all those obstinate immensities – holds one fast on every side. When one gives oneself the same type of existence as the rock: solidity, inertia, opacity. A serious man is a coagulated consciousness. One is serious when one denies mind. Those unbelievers Plato speaks of in the *Sophist*, who believe only in what they touch – they're the ancestors of the spirit of seriousness. It goes without saying that the serious man, being *of* the world, doesn't have the least consciousness of his freedom; or rather, if he does have consciousness of it, in terror he buries it deep within him, like some filth. Like the rock, like the atom or like the star, he's determined. And if the spirit of seriousness is characterized by the application with which it considers the *consequences* of its acts, that's because, for it, all is consequence.

The serious man himself is merely a consequence – an unbearable consequence – never a principle. He's caught for all time in a series of consequences, and sees only consequences without end. That's why money – sign of all the things in the world; consequence and *of* consequence – is the object par excellence of seriousness. In short, Marx posited the first dogma of seriousness when he asserted the priority of the object over the subject. And man is serious when he forgets himself; when he makes the subject into an object; when he takes himself for a radiation derived from the world: engineers, doctors, physicists, biologists are serious.

Well, I was protected against seriousness by what I've said. Too much so, rather than not enough. I wasn't of the world, because I was free and first beginning. It's not possible to grasp oneself as consciousness, without thinking that life is a game.

For what is a game, after all, but an activity of which man is the first origin: whose principles man himself ordains and which can have consequences only according to the principles ordained. But as soon as man grasps himself as free, and wishes to use his freedom, all his activity is a game: he's its first principle; he escapes the world by his nature; he himself ordains the value and rules of his acts, and agrees to pay up only according to the rules he has himself ordained and defined. Whence the diminished reality of the world and the disappearance of seriousness.

I have never wished to be serious – I felt too free. At the time of my love-affair with Toulouse, I wrote a long poem – extremely bad I imagine – entitled *Peter Pan*: song of the little boy who doesn't want to grow up. Always those 'little boys' and those 'little girls' – those clichés of our amorous relations! On the part of a sturdy fellow of twenty and a strapping girl of twenty-three, I find that as incestuous as Rousseau sighing out 'Mother!' all those times to Mme de Warens.[28] But that's not my subject. In any case, that little boy didn't want to grow up for fear of becoming serious. I could have set my mind at rest: I'm fourteen years older today and I've never been serious – except once, within the walls of the cemetery at Tetuán, because the Beaver wanted to make me put my straw hat on and I didn't want to. I've always claimed responsibility for my acts with the feeling of escaping them entirely by some other route. Because of consciousness's tower, into which I could ascend at will.

But the question which interests me today is the following: is authenticity, by walling up the door to the tower for ever more, going to reinstil in me the spirit of seriousness? I think there can be only one reply: No, by no means! For to grasp oneself as a *person* is quite the opposite of grasping oneself in terms of the world. And however authentic one is, one's still free – even freer than in the hypothesis of the tower – since one's condemned to a freedom without shadow and without excuse. And, after all, being-in-the-world isn't being *of* the world. It's even the opposite. Renouncing the ivory tower, I should like the world to appear to me in its full, threatening reality – but I do not, therefore, want my life to stop being a game. That's why I subscribe whole-heartedly to Schiller's phrase: 'Man is fully a man only when he plays.'

Tuesday, 12 March

On Friday or Saturday we are leaving for Brumath again. Probably to leave room here for some division coming from the interior and posted to the front. I'm glad to be seeing Brumath again – I've kept an extremely poetic memory of it. Of Morsbronn, I have a dazzling, icy image: very hard, snow, imbued with poetry but full of wind. Brumath appears to me like a soft, filtered light. I see again those early mornings at the Taverne de la Rose, the long afternoons in the schoolroom. Brumath, for me, is the Beaver's visit and my return in the dark after leaving her near the railway-station. It's also my paroxysm of passion for T. and that new, tragic world wherein I

28. Mme de Warens (1700–62), protectress of Jean-Jacques Rousseau from 1729 to about 1742.

dwelt, guided by St-Exupéry and Koestler. It's there I sensed what authenticity was (in the very last days, at the Taverne du Lion d'Or); it's there I sloughed off my old skin. I'm curious to see the Écrevisse again, the baths too – I wonder what effect it will all have on me.

For my own part, I shall hardly be stopping there: if we arrive on the 17th, I'll be there for barely a week – after which I'm going on leave – and when I get back we'll probably be recalled to the interior. Already I'm detaching myself slowly from the division's destinies, as from an old husk. When anyone speaks to me of its destiny – that it will perhaps go to Bitche; that after this round of leave we shall perhaps wait six months for the next one – all that already strikes me as dusty and wilted: it's no longer me. By contrast, I have some images of a kitchen garden on a hillside – very 'Île de France' – which symbolize my immediate future. That means meteorological station in the rear – because, when I was doing my military service at the St-Symphorien meteorological station above Tours, a civilian meteorologist called M. Ledoux used to cultivate his garden not far from the station. In fact, I do have a vague, stupid expectation *of that station* at Tours. Naturally, my reason tells me I may be sent anywhere but there.

Germany – explanatory study by Edmond Vermeil. His general thesis is the following: 'That which is unhealthy and fanatical, hence dangerous, in German nationalism – with its dizzy dream of a religious, racial community destined to exercise absolute hegemony over this old continent – can be explained by the former territorial parcellization; and by the pluralism of the institutions, tendencies and parties which succeeded it, within the framework of the Bismarckian Empire and the Weimer Constitution. Pan-Germanism, in other terms, is compensation for the Germanies.'[29] Very true, that's obvious – so much so that I'd thought it myself, though I'm none too hot at historical explanations. But now we have a comprehensive connection between two natures, one of which is a *fact* – the de facto existence of a political and administrative parcellization – and the other an ideal: 'community' appears as the specific possibility of the German nation qua ruling community in Europe. All at once, I see the significative connection: the aspiration to unity surpasses simple unification of the Germanies – it aims at unification of the Germanies *as* unifying unification of Europe. The phenomenon of unification appears as unable not to have meaning for the totality of the continent. Unification gives itself an aim which surpasses it, and which merely

29. Edmond Vermeil, *L'Allemagne: essai d'explication*, Paris 1940, p. 328.

increases its urgency: it is unification in order to reign.

All right, but that doesn't satisfy me: I don't see how the parcellization of the Germanies could of itself produce that mythic representation. The intermeshing of parcellization with Pan-Germanism is significant only because it's *human*. It must be conceived as existing through men who historialize themselves. But nor is it admissible that parcellization should act upon minds from outside, to induce them to forge a mythic representation of unity that will suppress it. In itself, parcellization is nothing and doesn't act; all that it can do is be indefinitely parcellized. Nor would it be of any use to show the dream of unity arising from the difficulties which the unitary forces (economic, cultural and religious) encounter as they confront that parcellization – and from the resulting conflict. One factor is missing from that dialectic – always the same: it's necessary that the resistance be felt; it's necessary that the economic forces which throw themselves through the parcellization be human; it's necessary to come back to man. In other words, that intermeshing of natures that presents itself so blatantly to understanding is, by itself, *unselbständig*: it refers back to the human reality *for whom* it exists.[30]

There's only one possible explanation: parcellization is a *situation*, and Pan-Germanism is the possibility towards which human reality throws itself through that situation. Consequently, it's by transcending parcellization towards Pan-Germanism that human reality constitutes it as a situation and grasps it as such. Without that free surpassing, there would be neither situation nor even de facto parcellization. And what if it were grasped as pure parcellization? That's impossible – or at least it's impossible at first. If it were grasped as parcellization, that could be only by a human reality that surpassed it towards something else: for example, towards federalism. But, in order to consider it as *pure* parcellization – as the *fact* of parcellization – the mind must effect a contemplative withdrawal: it must try to *dismember* the situation, extract the given and transform it into a *position*.

So there are no grounds for resorting to those obscure forces which are so often evoked by the wisdom of diplomats – for example, that irresistible attraction which supposedly exists between the fragments of a parcellized country and leads it inevitably to unity. We are at the antipodes of the Marxist theory of myth. Myth, according to Marxist historians, is a product of the action of a state of fact upon consciousnesses. I reverse the terms, and say that the state of fact is itself

30. *unselbständig*: unable to stand by itself; dependent.

constituted only by the project of a human reality through it, towards the myth that constitutes its own possibility. But *what* human reality? There are only individual ones – so there we are, referred back to a historical individualism which doesn't easily tolerate those great collective natures. For it's quite certain that when Vermeil derives Pan-Germanism from the parcellization of the Germanies, he is a long way away from individuals: it's not really a matter of knowing what Peter or Paul may grasp of the situation – we're at the level of the national collective. Yet, I repeat, there are only individuals.

How to get out of the impasse? By the very notion of situation which we initially invoked. If the individual refers back to the situation, and the situation to the individual, that doesn't mean one can get the situation back into the individual by squeezing a bit. Any more than being-in-the-world means that the world can fit into the individual. In reality, there's *a* Pan-Germanism because there are *some* Pan-Germanists – but there's just *one* Pan-Germanism. The *situations* correlative to the project of an individual who throws himself into the world are proposed, by virtue of the *Mit-sein*, as situations *for* others; and one is oneself only by projecting oneself freely through the situations constituted by the Other's project. I explained all about this with respect to the fatherland. Each individual finds himself faced with signposts which will indicate only *through him*, but whose legend has already been constituted by others.

Thus parcellization and Pan-Germanism can blossom into themselves only through individuals; but their nature infinitely overflows each individual – and must not be confused *either* with the simple sum of Pan-Germanists, *or* with some kind of collective consciousness, which would grasp individuals from behind and take shape at their expense. Before the war, every German emerging into the world found himself faced with Pan-Germanism as a situation. He could freely determine to grasp that situation in any way whatsoever (refuse, scorn, combat, adopt, approve, follow the movement benevolently from afar, etc.). But it was impossible for him to prevent Pan-Germanism from being a situation for him; it was impossible for him not to *animate* the 'comprehensible' relationship parcellization/Pan-Germanism. And, by that very assumption of a position – which was himself – he was enriching the situation for the Other: it was presenting itself to the Other as richer, suppler and more urgent.

The historian – by describing the relations of signification between ideas, movements, a political situation and tendencies or demands – is dealing with real objects, but ones which all have the character of *Unselbständigkeit*. And the bonds of concrete logic which he finds between them refer to a human reality which they pass over in silence. That's their right: they even cannot proceed otherwise. But the error they then commit is to show those connections as being independent and *then* acting *upon* men – whereas they don't exist without men, and are only that which men project themselves towards and cause to exist by their very project. In that sense, any description of the concrete development of an ideology, on the basis of political data, should be accompanied by a monograph on one of the important individuals of the epoch – in order to show the ideology as a lived situation, and one constituted as a situation by a human project.

We'd benefit from seeing, instead of the simple abstract comprehensible schema (for example, parcellization/Pan-Germanism), a synthesis of significations belonging to the most diverse layers, of which the abstract schema would be only the axis and central structure. In short, a synthetic corrective to abstract decomposition: something like what the concrete sciences are for Comte – a synthetic recomposition of the real through simultaneous utilization of the various abstract sciences – whereas the abstract sciences merely involve study of the conditions of possibility of a general phenomenon. In that sense, too, one could say that there's neither any great mystery, nor any great difficulty, in that separation of significations into parallel layers. They're parallel only because the historian studies the abstract conditions of possibility of a concrete human phenomenon by setting aside the human on principle. The famine, the defeat of France and Proudhonian federalism are parallel – and will never meet if one first abstracts them as conditions of possibility for the Commune. But, in the total project of himself that a Belleville worker could effect on 18 March, all those factors were united in the unity of a single movement.[31]

At the Home, two MPs are playing ping-pong. The lieutenant from the legal department – a southerner of whom I've already spoken – comes up to them with a friendly air: 'Let's see if you're as good at catching balls as you are at catching offenders.'

Read *Angelica*, by Leo Ferrero.[32] Weak. Absurd plot. It's Orlando's

31. 18 March 1871: date when government troops fraternized with the rebellious *Garde Nationale*, leading to the establishment of the Commune a few days later (26 March). Belleville is a working-class district of Paris to the north of the Père Lachaise cemetery.

32. Leo Ferrero (1903–33), Italian author, refugee from fascism, who mainly published in French. His play *Angelica* appeared in 1929.

fault if he fails in his work of liberation. The first duty of a revolutionary who has made the revolution is to take power – even if that revolution has been made to restore freedom to a people. To free a nation from a tyrant and then – having deprived it of a leader without having taught it to use its freedom – decline the responsibilities of power means delivering it up bound hand and foot to another tyrant. There's no revolution without dictatorship. For want of having *first* been dictators, the leaders of the Commune lost their way.

Wednesday, 13 March

Strange alternation in my mood. Yesterday, at about six, my eyes suddenly flicker and half fail and I have quarter of an hour of empty, nervous anguish – that anguish which in 1935 I used to take for madness. That passes and leaves me fagged out for the evening. Whereupon this morning I wake up happy: with a strange blindfolded happiness – a happiness by default. I, who until yesterday was sensitive and stretched out every which way over my universe like a spider's web – so little in my narrow present, only to feel the time pass by – behold me now: huddled, doltish, thrifty, even miserly, from inability to blow up my worries to the scale of my real life! I no longer concern myself either with Paris, or with my future, or with the future of the collectivity to which I belong. On the back burner – doltish in a shrunken universe – I have a frivolous, surly kind of determination not to let any damn thing bother me. Happy sluggishness, imbecile pleasures: I do the crossword in *Marianne* conscientiously, I find *Le Canard Enchainé* funny. All the objects which surround me fascinate and grip me: I plunge into them. My eyes still very tired.

I go down a little muddy short-cut, between two long walls, to carry my letters to the post. I look at the black earth, littered with scraps of plant debris, and the memories are there. First of all, for some reason, a walk I took with O. – at four in the morning, in June. in the Rue Eau-de-Robec: we didn't go to bed that night.[33] Then a track carpeted with pine-needles at Arcachon, where we're walking – the Beaver and I – surrounded by a consumptive silence: there was a smell of sea, warm sand and resin.[34] I tried to think: 'I've had all that, yes, *me*' – like my Roquentin, who tries to think how he has seen the Ganges and the temple of Angkor[35] – and that produced nothing. What I'd above all

33. In Rouen, in 1936.
34. Arcachon is near Bordeaux, and probably Sartre and De Beauvoir visited it on their way back from a holiday at Bayonne in 1938.
35. *Oeuvres romanesques*, p. 78.

have liked would have been to feel that surly, scabby individual – who was carrying letters to the post, as he did every day – clad in the passion and (why not) the grace which I was able to have on that night in Rouen. That was a moment of my life that had had a *value*.

I recalled everything: we'd been for a stroll in the darkness round the new swimming-pool and the nightwatchman had come out in a rage: 'It's forbidden! If I'd put a bullet up your backsides, you'd only have got what you deserved!' We'd passed the same places a score of times; we'd seen them make their night-time toilet and fall asleep. The Café Victor, which stood facing a big, green advertisement across the Seine with its lights at first all aglow, had shilly-shallied. First it had closed, and the chairs stacked up on its vast terrace had been silhouetted on the window like shadow-play figures against the wan lights of the interior – where the cashier was doing her accounts and the waiters were unknotting and folding their aprons. Then, even those lights had been extinguished and the windows had grown black and dull: the chairs had been recovered by the outside – they belonged to the quays, to the night, like the motionless cranes of the port. They were already rather more like scrap-metal and rather less like chairs.

The Océanic had changed its clientele four or five times. The beautiful whores who worked as hostesses in the city's big dancehall (I've forgotten its name) – and whom we'd seen coming down at eight from the bedrooms of the Océanic to eat a solid meal in the bar: curled, painted for war, polished and powdered in their lamé dresses – we saw again at midnight or one in the morning, sweating, red and dishevelled, taking supper with fellows. Then the Océanic too had closed, but through the gaps in its wooden shutters we'd seen rays of light which had shown us that it remained mysteriously open for initiates – the friends of the boss, a silent brute known as 'the Canadian'.

We'd traversed dark, narrow streets where footsteps echoed, and we'd instinctively lowered our voices in those streets and whispered. Then we'd been to the Nicod Bar, the only brasserie in Rouen which stayed open all night: there was a harsh, pallid atmosphere – a blinding glare of 'sunlight'[36] in a jam-packed room, where the musicians who'd just left the dancehall were rubbing shoulders with Norman peasants waiting for the first morning train. And there she'd been ill and absented herself. I'd asked her 'Are you ill?', and she'd replied: 'I've just been sick; I'm so fond of you this evening I can't hide it from you' – with a comical, charming look which touched my heart.

36. English in text.

And then we'd left – we'd been in Rue Eau-le-Robec. As dawn was breaking, we'd returned to Rue Jeanne-d'Arc and in the first light had looked at the shoes on display in the shoemakers' windows, because she was always saying how ugly mine were. It was strange how those shoes – the evening before still set ablaze by the lamps on the slope – now, under the grey light of early morning, looked drab, unmade-up, dead and yet brazenly new with the black, empty shop behind them. We climbed back up to the station, sat on a bench in the Boulevard de la Marne and played poker-dice.

That particular night is embalmed: I had a value, she too – I'm sure of it. I wasn't very happy, I had no hope, but we were together and I had her to myself for the whole night and the night enclosed us on every side – there was no use seeking to know what would happen in the morning (in the event, that morning was a disaster: hatred, quarrelling and I don't know what else). I truly believe that night was a privileged moment for me. I wonder what memory she has kept of it. Perhaps none; perhaps she had arrière-pensées I didn't suspect; perhaps the next day's hatred masked the abandon of ːhat night from her for ever. What is more, it's no longer the same O. – neither for me, nor for herself. And I myself am no longer the same.

That's what I wanted to record here – and then I let myself be drawn into describing that night. When the memory came, I addressed a kind of appeal to it: I'd have liked it to colour me discreetly, to lift me out of my filthy-dirty soldier's skin. And, in a sense, it responded well: it yielded to me as much as it could; like the Old Woman Who Lived in a Shoe it opened itself up to me and let a whole crowd of other little memories escape. But it didn't do what I was asking of it – it didn't *act* upon me. What I wanted to be, basically, was *the man who lived that night*. I didn't just want it to be *before me*, like a fragment of lost time; I wanted my former passion to be in me like a virtue. I precisely wanted that time – lost, but experienced with so much force – not, precisely, to be time lost.[37] To be frank, I wanted it to 'do me good', as when people say 'Eat up, it can't do you any harm and it'll do you good.' I felt so frail and sickly on that muddy path – so much the 'soldier off to post his letters' and nothing else – that I'd have liked to fatten myself up with all my past loves and woes. But in vain: I felt totally free in the face of those memories. That's the price of freedom – one's always outside.

One is separated from memories, as from motives, by *nothing*.

---

37. *temps perdu*: the Proustian echo should not itself be lost, as a result of the 'Things Past' chosen by Proust's English translator.

There's no period of life one could *catch* onto, as the custard 'catches' on the bottom of the pan. Nothing marks one – one is a perpetual flight. In the face of what one has been, one is always the same thing: *nothing*. I felt myself profoundly *nothing*, in the face of that past night: for me, it was like an other's night. I'd sensed that helpless weakness of the past in *La Nausée*, but I'd drawn the wrong conclusion: I'd said that the past is annihilated [p. 114]. That's not true, it still exists. On the contrary, it exists *in itself*. Only it no more acts upon us than if it didn't exist. It's of no importance to have this or that past. For it to exist, we have to throw ourselves through it towards a certain future: we have to adopt it as our own *for* some future end or other. Each time, it's some act of freedom which decides its efficacy – and even its meaning. But it serves no purpose to have travelled the world or experienced the strongest passions: we shall always, when necessary, be that poor, empty soldier setting off to take his letters to the post-box. All solidarity with our past is ordained in the present by our complaisance.

Five days ago, I received a letter from the *Cahiers de Paris*:
'Sir – your name has been put forward, together with a number of others, for the Prix du Roman Populiste.[38] If you agree to be a candidate, we should be grateful if you would send a copy of your book to the members of the jury, together with a letter of application.'
First of all, satisfaction: I'm a long way away in the Army, so I won't have to get involved in it. Always that pride which makes me not want to ask for anything. Yet I'd be very pleased if I got it – that prize of 2000 francs. Whereupon, I reread the letter and realize – calamity! – that it's necessary to put oneself forward as a candidate. All that insular pride collapses – I can no longer wash my hands of the whole thing. Then I notice that the prize is *populist*. To put myself forward is to range myself under the populist banner – since it's a populist prize I shall receive, and since I'm claiming it – so I decide to refuse. But the deeper reason is that I want the prize just to fall into my lap, without my having to compromise myself. Falsity, and inauthenticity, of that point of view: for if I scorn prizes, then I really should refuse them; and if I want them, I must take it upon myself to bid for them. The trick here was to mask that sudden lash of pride – on the pretext of refusing the title of populist.
Whereupon, I write to the Beaver about the whole matter and ask

---

38. Prize set up as an expression of the Populist movement, which emerged c. 1929 and held that literature should be written for and about ordinary people.

for her opinion. It was, of course, quite normal to consult the Beaver: on any occasion of that kind I should have done so. Yet, by the very fact of asking her for advice, I'm causing the wind to shift – because I know what she'll reply. The Beaver is authentic without trying: by her very nature, I'd say, if authenticity could ever have its source in nature. I knew she'd answer me quite simply: 'What do labels matter – we need money. When it's offered, try to grab it!' In writing to her, therefore, I was more than half convinced by the reply she'd not yet given me. Fresh swinishness here: knowing that the Beaver would pose the question on the terrain of money, I posed it there myself by writing to her – and thereafter kept it there. Whence the possibility of tinging any eventual acceptance with cynicism: whatever I do is for money; it's quite all right to take a somewhat humiliating step for money. It was a further way of wriggling out and soothing my pride: it's a matter not of submitting myself to the judgement of writers older than myself, but of extorting two thousand francs from some suckers. And I winked to myself as I thought: the poor fools! This, moreover, was made easier for me by the impression I've always had that people who take my works seriously are mugs. It obviously comes from my sense of 'diminished reality', and from my inability to take myself seriously.

But is my position, in fact, so plain? What exactly do I think about *prizes*? Well, on the one hand, it makes me really uneasy to imagine all the furore of applause that's unleashed around a Goncourt winner, for example. Furthermore, the idea that one owes one's worth to the *judgement* of certain people is intolerable to me. A photo in *Match* showed the aged Rosny congratulating Troyat, who'd just been awarded the prize.[39] Troyat was bending over respectfully, with an attentive smile – the kind of smile one wears when one's trying to understand the words of some venerable dotard with his mouth full of pap. And the old man was saying: 'Very well done, young man, keep it up!' And I felt nauseated. So the prize, inasmuch as it's *given*, disgusts me. And I certainly don't find one cuts much of a figure when one possesses it – when one becomes 'So-and-so, the Renaudot or Goncourt prizewinner'. It's all a bit too reminiscent of being crowned queen of the May – and for ages one wears the look of a May-queen, till the memory of the prize has faded.[40]

39. Joseph-Henri Rosny (1856–1940), novelist (often in collaboration with his brother Séraphin-Justin, under the collective pseudonym J-H. Rosny).

Henri Troyat (1911–), French novelist of Russian origin, and author of biographies of Russian historical figures such as Gogol, Catherine the Great, etc.

40. A *rosière* is a young girl chosen for her chastity, crowned with roses and given a small dowry, in an annual ceremony that still survives in some French villages.

Yet, I don't know, there's an agency or manner whereby the *prize* appears as a social phenomenon, quite independently of those who give it – rather like the return of some annual sun festival, which arrives to settle capriciously upon a chosen head. And considered in this way – in other words, basically as the beneficiary for one year of an honorific institution – I shouldn't dislike it all that much. My cynicism thus masks a dubious taste for consecration. The fact remained, my poor little pride was still bleeding a little – because I wasn't sure of getting that prize at all! I reluctantly played the comic role of perpetual candidate in '38–'39. The papers were talking about me for the Goncourt. Then Nizan came and as good as offered me the Renaudot: Charensol and Descaves had told him the thing was in the bag.[41] After those two rebuffs, the *NRF* lobbied hard to get me the Prix de la Renaissance: that was a third rebuff. Finally the war came, I forgot that such things as prizes even existed – and then I had the comical surprise of seeing that two obstinate souls had given me their votes, unasked, for the Renaudot '39.

That had all left me quite unmoved, since it had been argued over outside me. But was I now going to get started for the fifth time, only to see some rival come in five lengths ahead of me? It was becoming a case of luckless courage. Yet I had a sort of vague confidence: it really was going to happen this time. Whereupon, my perusal of that article in *Match* – reminding me that Troyat had won the Prix Populiste – supervened to rob me of one excuse: Troyat was in no sense a populist novelist. Furthermore, the members of the jury (Duhamel, Jaloux, Romains) aren't all populists either.[42] In short, I was shaken – and it's here that this little self-portrait I'm attempting in these notebooks was useful to me. I recalled what I'd written about the tricks of my pride and decided – if the Beaver encouraged me to do so – to play the part of applicant bravely, at my own risk. The Beaver's reply arrived today, true to my predictions – so I wrote seventeen letters of application and my hand ached. It was as much as I could do to stop myself choosing the properest turns of phrase – so that I might still represent myself, in my own eyes, as someone who does the strict minimum to obtain what he desires.

Simultaneously, a little comedy was being enacted which, after satisfying my pride, was now fizzling out. *L'Imaginaire* was about to come out and on the 7th Paulhan wrote to me: 'Wahl, in cahoots with Brunschvicg, is thinking of making you a doctor against your will.

41. Georges Charensol (1899–   ), art and film critic. Lucien Descaves (1861–1949), author of naturalist novels.

42. Edmond Jaloux (1878–1949), novelist, critic and historian of literature.

The idea is to transform *L'Imaginaire* into a thesis – you wouldn't have to do a thing about it, except delay its publication a bit.' No doubt about it, that's how I like to be treated. Conferring a dignity upon me *against my will*; almost apologizing for it. I was quite excited about it and – still in order to avoid gratitude – imagined Wahl saying to Brunschvicg, like Favre of Rochefort on 4 September '70: 'Better to have him inside than outside.'[43] I wrote a proper letter of acceptance. But the comical thing is that, in fact, *L'Imaginaire* had in the meantime been published. I suspect Paulhan – for his own Machiavellian political purposes – of having postponed writing to me till he was sure *L'Imaginaire* would be published before he'd received my reply. Two surreptitious kicks to my pride – or rather, since it's not even pride, to my vanity.

1945. I learn by telegraph of the capitulation of Finland. Painful impression.

Thursday, 14 March

We're leaving for Brumath tomorrow afternoon. Apparently they're glad to be seeing us back.

Poupette, who's typing *L'Âge de Raison*, writes to the Beaver: 'Typing Sartre's works always makes me gloomy. Talking to him is a tonic. Reading his works, then thinking about something else – that might still be all right. But living up to one's neck in them is dreadful. I hope that, within himself, he isn't like the people he portrays in his books, for his life would be scarcely endurable.'

That gives me food for thought. Why is it that Antoine Roquentin and Mathieu, who *are me*, are indeed so gloomy – whereas, Heavens!, life for me isn't all that bad? I think it's because they're homunculi. In reality, they are *me, stripped of the living principle*. The essential difference between Antoine Roquentin and me is that, for my part, I write the story of Antoine Roquentin. What happens here is something analogous to that disintegration of the lower functions by which Mourgue seeks to explain hallucinations.[44] In all our thoughts and all

43. Jules Favre (1809–1880), republican politician who, in the revolution of 4 September 1870, proposed the abolition of the Empire and became a leading member of the Government of National Defence.

Henri Rochefort (1830–1913), founding editor of the violently anti-Empire *La Lanterne* in 1868, for which he was exiled to Belgium; after the September revolution he too became a member of the Government of National Defence.

44. See Constantin Monakow and R. Mourgue. *Introduction biologique à l'étude de la neurologie et de la psychopathologie*, Paris 1928. Doubtless Sartre's knowledge of this work dates from the time of his own 'madness', and his experiments with mescaline, in 1935, when he suffered from hallucinations.

our feelings, there's an element of terrible sadness – in its proper place. But when the hierarchical integration is strict and the internal organization ensured by synthetic principles, that sadness is inoffensive: it merges into the ensemble, like the shadow which makes the light stand out more strongly. If, however, one extracts a directing principle from the mixture, the secondary structures previously subordinated to the whole begin to take on a life of their own. 'Cosmic sadness' arises for itself.

That's what I did: I stripped my characters of my obsessive passion for writing, my pride, my faith in my destiny, my metaphysical optimism – and thereby provoked in them a gloomy pullulation. They are myself beheaded. And, since one cannot touch a synthetic whole without causing it to die, those heroes are unviable. I hope they aren't entirely so, as imaginary, fictional creatures; but they can exist only in the artificial milieu I've created round them to sustain them. Apart from the sadness of disintegration which I just mentioned, they have another, still deeper kind: the sadness filled with reproach and bitterness of Homunculus in his jar. They know themselves to be unviable, sustained by artificial feeding – and insofar as the reader constitutes them with his time, he feels pervaded by the metaphysical sadness of prehistoric animals doomed to imminent extinction by the inadequacy of their constitutions.

Fabrice, by contrast, in *La Chartreuse de Parme* – even in his worst despairs – is a perpetual source of joy for his readers because he's *selbständig*. He can stand on his own feet; he's viable; there's no disintegration in him. I say this without either envy or humility: if Stendhal is superior to me, that's for other reasons. The fact is, we don't have the same aim in view. My novels are experiments, and they're possible only through disintegration. It seems to me that the ensemble of my books will be optimistic, because through that ensemble the *whole* will be reconstituted. But each of my characters is a cripple. To tell the truth, Mathieu is to become a totality in my last volume – but he'll die immediately afterwards. That's the reason, I think, why I can write gloomy books without myself being either sad or a charlatan, and believe in what I write.

That word to 'pullulate' – which so often recurs beneath my pen, and which I wrote once again on the preceding page – has retained for me the charm it used to have in my childhood. It's not a learnt, but an encountered word. One fine day, opening a book illustrated by Boutet de Monvel on the history of France (I was six),[45] I saw a big coloured

45. Louis-Maurice Boutet de Monvel (1851–1913), painter and illustrator of children's books, influenced by the English pre-Raphaelites.

plate depicting naked, fair-haired children surrounded by clean little pink pigs. The whole scene was a delectable jumble. The pigs were trampling the children underfoot, the children were tugging at the pigs' tails – all this in a gay, prehistoric landscape: the gaity was represented by beautiful trees and greenery, the prehistory by big, grey rocks riven by deep caverns. The caption underneath read: 'A veritable pullulation of little pigs!'

I didn't know the word – and that sufficed to make me see it with wondering eyes, in its pure individuality. The 'pullu' amused me greatly, and the presence of the two 'l's' after the 'u' made me think of *bulle – bulle de savon* [soap-bubble], for example (the word *bulle* was already exquisitely pleasurable to me, whether to read or speak). And the little pigs and children in the picture had all the lightness and aerial cleanliness of bubbles. Really, even before being understood the word had an affective signification which it has always retained: a pure, multicoloured profusion of those balloons which sellers used in those days to hawk in the Luxembourg, hitched to long poles.

One would like to write with words of that kind only. But it's not certain that they produce the same impression on the reader – and then supports are needed: a connective tissue of words with a purely semantic value. At the same time, that experience, together with a number of similar encounters, profoundly convinced me of the profound cleanliness of pigs – contrary to their common reputation. This belief is not unconnected with my taste for pork. Whereas the calf, pale and sad, even when alive looks as though it has already been chewed.

The indignation provoked in the French press by Swedish 'cowardice' is exactly the same as that which our attitude towards Spain provoked three years ago.

A very revealing letter from William II on the occasion of his last trip to England (1912): 'I found that my parents' old apartments in Windsor Castle, where I often played as a little boy, had been assigned to me . . . Manifold were the memories that filled my heart . . . They awakened the old sense of being at home here, which attaches me so strongly to this place, and which has made the political aspect of things so personally painful to me, especially in recent years. I am proud to call this place my second home, and to be a member of this royal family . . . And they had kept my memory green, as a child who was so much addicted to pudding that he once was violently sick!' [p.376]

Received the *NRF* for March. Reread my article on Giraudoux. I should have stressed the 'rationalism of politeness'. The world of Giraudoux is a world of manufactured objects. Only of a table can it be said that it has four feet because it's a table. To be related to the victory of capitalism, and the appearance of the mass-produced article – which emerges 'endowed with form' without man's labour having been expended *upon it.*

Also received the first 180 pages of my novel, typed out by Poupette. Disappointment: too lyrical; the linking of the chapters isn't clear enough. Hesitations over Mathieu's character and aspirations. One doesn't sense sufficient past behind each character's present. To be gone over again.

Terrible wind this evening; it tangles the electric wires and the whole town is plunged into darkness. I'm writing this by the light of the candle – inconvenient but charming form of illumination.

Friday, 15 March

Departure for Brumath at 14.30 – arrival at 17.00. We return to the school, but our offices are on the first floor. Pieter and Paul have rooms in the town, I'm sleeping in the office.

Saturday, 16 March

Went back to the Rose this morning. In November there was a charming little waitress called Jeannette – red-haired, stupid, always half-asleep. I liked watching her. Now she has fluffed up her hair, paints her face, wears a dress tucked up high and says *'Punaise!'* (a division from the Midi preceded us here).[46] Alice, the fat brunette who used to sleep with all and sundry, makes a noisy entrance at twenty past eight. She's wearing a black fur coat and reeks of perfume. She has married a soldier. Naudin, who has had her, sniggers and says: 'Being a cuckold has its advantages!'

Odd, none too agreeable impression – at once of return to the fold and of strangeness. The soldiers are received here with open arms – every Jack finds his Jill, or the people he's lodging with, who'd be shedding tears of emotion – but the game is played without me: no one recognizes me and I don't rediscover any old acquaintances. Except the fat old lady from the Rose, who clasped my hand warmly.

What I do rediscover are the creakings of the door at night in the

46. *Punaise!*: literally 'bug', but also a mild imprecation.

dark, echoing schoolhouse. They all had a mysterious, familiar meaning, like a promise of remembrance. And there's a bygone atmosphere in this schoolhouse, which I cannot enlarge upon but which is everywhere present. People say we shan't be staying more than a week, and this makes me somewhat concerned about my leave. This morning, for the first time for ages, I find the time dragging.

Albert Ollivier: *La Commune*, p. 221:
   'Liberalism is the right way of ensuring liberty, the Commune had to learn that to its cost . . . Tolerance is often merely an opportunism which is unwilling to speak its name.'

Excellent comment in *L'Oeuvre:*
   'Among the bad slogans spawned by war, one of the most exasperating is the famous catchphrase: "Time is working for us."
   'People say this with a knowing or a smug look, accompanied by a wink. For two pins they'd add: "Time is working: let it alone, we mustn't disturb it!"
   'How do they fail to realize that this is the best way of encouraging indolence, lack of imagination and lack of initiative?
   'Is time really working for us, when Sweden and Norway pass over from the camp of the democracies to that of Hitler?
   'Is time really working for us, when the heroic people of Finland must suffer the Russo–German diktat?'
   And this comment by Déat: 'The nickel and iron have now been secured by Germany; the Scandinavian countries are becoming the clients of Stalin and above all of Hitler. Tomorrow the fjords will doubtless shelter German submarines, until such time as air bases can be established on those tame lands . . . We have just lost the Scandinavian countries. If we go on in this way, we shall finish losing the Balkans likewise. One of two things: either we manoeuvre in military style on the flanks, since a thrust in the centre is wisely ruled out – in which case we make use of the flanks while there's still time. Or else we admit there no longer are any flanks, and that all operations are precluded. In that case, it's a different war that we have to wage. No less arduous; no less dangerous; no less total. But it requires a different diplomacy, a different economic organization, a different morale, a different propaganda and different methods of government.'

Chaumeix (*Paris-Soir*): 'For England and France it's an undeniable reverse.'

Our first defeat. Here, it's met with a kind of indifference. People say: 'Now the war will last ten years.'

Sunday, 17 March

I'm reading A. France's *La Vie littéraire*, volume IV, and perceive with astonishment that he writes in the way Brichot talks in *Sodome et Gomorrhe* – and that he certainly served Proust as a model.[47] Same concern to intersperse literary or philological erudition with the concrete detail that shows him to be a 'connoisseur of modern life' – in order to win on both counts. Same affectation of familiarity with famous men; same way of calling Shakespeare 'the great Will'; same deep, terrible *ugliness* beneath the stylistic artifices. It's *appalling*. The relations between Brichot and Mme Verdurin must, in part, be inspired by those of France with Mme de Caillavet.[48]

Monday, 19 March

Courcy: obliged to make a noise, in order to reassure himself that he exists. He clicks his heels as he walks; he blows noisily as he exhales each puff of his pipe; in the midst of a silence, he cries out: 'What should the poor woman do?', or else 'How now, old pal?', or again ' "Ah!" says he in Japanese'. Each of his gestures, apart from its particular function, has as its secondary purpose to demonstrate to himself that he exists. A perpetual 'I drink, therefore I exist', 'I smoke, therefore I exist', etc. At present, he's walking up and down, he's nibbling peanuts, and he's thinking about how he's nibbling peanuts – it shows. I'm writing, Hantziger's typing, Grener's reading. No one is paying any attention to him. He says in a loud voice, his head utterly empty: 'It's no joke – you feel like going over to Hitler.' Then, reflecting vaguely on what he has just said (for he demonstrates as he speaks, then reacts to his own demonstrations): 'It's true, when you see how things are go-o-oing.' This 'go-o-oing' is ironical – and equally empty. His aim is to fill his mouth with his 'o' – which will allow his palate and tongue to verify their existence – and simultaneously to strip his words of all seriousness: for he'd tremble with fear if anyone were to take him for a subversive spirit, or simply for a person

47. *Sodome et Gomorrhe*: fourth volume of Proust's *A la recherche du temps perdu*; in English, 'Cities of the Plain'.

48. Anatole France (1844–1924), novelist and essayist, frequented the salon of Mme Arman de Caillavet from about 1888 onwards, especially after the end of his first marriage in 1892. *La Vie littéraire* (1888–92) was a collection in four volumes of France's fortnightly literary column in *Le Temps*.

capable of thinking for himself. Out of politeness, and with stupidity, he forces himself to say some sprightly, optimistic word to everyone. This morning, for example, abruptly to me – and without listening to the reply: 'So it's coming soon then, that leave of yours, you lucky dog, you!' From time to time he acts violence and virulence in speech: 'Shit! How bloody boring it all is, old pal!' But with carefully proportioned flabbiness and a certain distraction – as if he were unaware of that loudness in which his mouth alone was involved.

Conclusion of that story I called 'The melancholy of leave': my mother, who knows the clerk of the military tribunal, writes: 'When the soldier who strangled that little girl, being sentenced to death, saw the preparations through a hole in the wall, he began howling like an animal.'

Letter from Bonnafé: 'Wherever do you get the notion that your writings (and your own self) lack that flame of fellow-feeling – which is like an embrace amid sweat and blood with one's gloves still on one's fists, after one has exchanged some good blows? But that's just what you've got most of! M. André Rousseaux doesn't understand anything about it.'[49]
    There's no doubt he sees me like that – and with him I am like that, because I really feel friendship for him. Have I made a mistake? Is it possible – surrounded as I am by fine fellows like Courcy, for whom I *can't* have any liking – that I've exaggerated? There's no doubt that this self-portrait, begun by chance, has become systematic in spite of myself.

I'm hardly writing in this notebook for the time being, because I'm totally absorbed in writing the prologue to *L'Âge de raison*.[50] Absorbed, animated, happy. I wonder if these notes don't all correspond to my moments of low tension, and whether I haven't depicted myself in a state of low tension. That's the defect of diaries in general. I'm delighted to be back at Brumath. Bouxwiller was depressing me.

An English officer says to his Alsatian landlady: 'The war is over, my dear Madam. But the public mustn't know.'

49. Bonnafé, friend of Sartre from the time they taught together at Le Havre in 1934–36, with whom he used to box. André Rousseaux (1896–) was literary editor of *Le Figaro* after 1936.
    50. Sartre wrote a prologue portraying his main characters ten years earlier, but jettisoned it on De Beauvoir's advice.

Wednesday, 20 March

I'm rereading Renard's journal.[51] Strange sort of fellow and strange sort of writer. He suffers from a double contradiction. The first, which is specific to him, is that he was cut out to hold his peace: behind him, he has generations of silence. His mother speaks in peasant phrases, terser and fuller than others; his father is one of those country characters, like my paternal grandfather – who didn't address three words to my grandmother in forty years of married life, and whom she used to call 'my lodger'. He lived all his childhood amid peasants, whose silence and immobility he so well describes; and who all, in one way or another, proclaim the futility of words.

'When he's back home, the peasant is scarcely any more lively than the ai or the tardigrade.[52] He likes the darkness, not just for economy's sake, but from preference. It soothes his smarting eyes.'

Or again, description of Old Bulot. A new servant makes her appearance:

'The first day she asked: "What'm I to cook yer for yer tea, then?" – "Potato soup."

'The next day she asked: "So what'm I to cook yer?" – "I told you, potato soup."

'The third day she asked and he replied in the same way. Then she understood, and henceforward she made him his potato soup each day of her own accord.'

Those full, miserly silences were his childhood landscape. Poil de Carotte was silent, and if Renard was feared and little liked in literary circles, it was because he used to go about representing the rights of silence in the private houses of those talkative folk. He was cut out to be a village 'character': in him, there was a fundamental misanthropy, and something gnarled and solitary which allied him with Old Bulot. That character, however, had a taste for writing. He came to *play the part* of a character in Paris – to assert his solitude in the company he sought. He came to hold his tongue in writing.

Whence – in order to resolve that contradiction – his search for a literary formula that was the equivalent of silence: laconism. The tersest phrase and the fullest: that which contains fewest words and the richest meaning. And at the same time that which as far as possible – like Old Bulot's 'potato soup' – will save going on to utter other

51. Jules Renard (1864–1910), novelist who made his name with the semi-autobiographical *Poil de Carotte* (1894). His *Journal inédit 1887–1910* was published in his *Oeuvres complètes* (1925–27).

52. Types of sloth.

phrases. It must, in itself, realize an *economy* with respect to other possible translations of the idea which at present occurs to you – and also an economy for the future. Whence a great illusion of Renard's regarding style. Style, for him, is the art of rendering terse. The object of his studies will thus be all the various means of ensuring that the maximum of ideas may be held in one sentence: in other words, how to *arrange* the ideas in a sentence. The problem of the basket: how to make the same basket hold most bricks.

Whence this confession: what interests him in novels are 'curiosities of style'. Now, he's clearly stupid to go looking for curiosities of style in novels: in the first place, it's where there are fewest to be found, since in a good novel the style hides behind the story; then, too, that's to spoil the novel and understand nothing about it. Yet it's also clear that he couldn't do otherwise. He claims to have got sick of poetry, because a line was still too long. That goes for the syntax: for the internal organization of the sentence. As for the elements – the *words* – they must be swollen with meaning, absolutely full, without a gap: in other words, not serve simply for the particular signification of the idea, but enrich it with beyond – with harmonics. He invokes Malherbe: 'What a noble role could Malherbe play in this moment! "With well-placed word, instructed power".[53] And throw all other words, which are as flabby as jellyfish, onto the scrapheap.'

The most meaning possible in the words; the most meaning possible in the sentence and its articulations. What occurs here is a signifying over-saturation. Everything crystallizes. Every sentence is a silence closed upon itself and over-saturated. And the oddest thing is that Renard – so intent upon saying most things with fewest words – had absolutely nothing to say. He was not very intelligent, and not profound at all. It's not on the basis of any abundance of ideas that he seeks to economize words: quite the contrary, he seeks economy for economy's sake, impelled by his taste for silence. It's *for the sake of holding his peace* that he seeks the phrase, and it's *for the sake of the phrase* that he seeks the idea. 'How empty an idea is. Without the phrase, I'd go to bed.'

For he has the naive idea that a thought is circumscribed by *one* sentence which expresses it. The sentence, between the two points which limit it, appears to him the natural body of the idea. It doesn't occur to him that an idea may require a chapter or a volume in order to be expressed. Or that it may also be inexpressible – in the sense in

53. François de Malherbe (1555-1628). stylistic purist who defended simple, clear linguistic principles against richness or ornament of language, Latinism, etc. The quotation is from Boileau's *L'Art poétique*, canto 1.

which Brunschvicg speaks of the 'critical idea' – and represent a *method* of envisaging problems. The idea, for him, is an affirmative formula condensing a certain sum of experiences. Idea: condensation of experiences – sentence: condensation of ideas. Example: 'It would give me so much pleasure to be good.'

And such is the primary reason for Renard's pointillism: his laconism imprisons him in the sentence. His style's unit of measurement is the sentence. From one sentence to the next there's neither movement nor transition. There's nothing: the void. By nature he's doomed to the discontinuous. It's also one of the reasons – though not the main one – for his constant search for images. Through the image, one expresses the idea and its harmonic beyond; one gains time – and also words. Example: 'That man of genius is an eagle as stupid as any goose.' One sees all that the relation between eagle and goose signifies – all that it saves us, in the way of approximations. The image, for Renard, is a shortcut in thought. And thereby that scholarly style – that 'calligraphy' of which Arène speaks[54] – meets the peasants' mythic, proverbial speech. Each of his sentences is a little fable.

A salon oyster – brows knit, abrupt air – whose whole person cries out: 'I'm holding my peace! Look how I'm holding my peace!', and whose willed, studied, artistic silence masks the involuntary, defenceless silence of a man who has absolutely nothing to say.

The second contradiction which explains Renard comes from his literary milieu. We arrive at the total disintegration of realism. The naturalism of Flaubert and Zola became the realism of Maupassant, and Maupassant engendered Renard. The aim was to get rid of the romanticism hidden beneath the naturalist label. And, above all, the great frescoes of their predecessors masked all subjects from them. All subjects had been dealt with systematically by Zola, and the newcomers possessed no method that would allow these to be renewed. Renard criticizes Zola, mocking his obsession with documentation. But he acknowledges nonetheless that, like the naturalists, he too is seeking *truth*. Similarly – after the descriptions of Flaubert and the Parnassians which were a vast inventory of the real, a picture in broad strokes (description, for example, of the steam-boat at the beginning of *L'Éducation sentimentale*) – the newcomers felt the need to penetrate further into the *thing*; more closely to grasp the object, the tree or the glass on the table; to penetrate into the *dough* of the real.

But they're restrained by realism itself, since, to achieve that kind of communion with the real, it's absolutely essential to stop being a

54. Paul Arène (1843–96), novelist and poet of Provençal life.

realist. Proust will manage it, precisely because he's not a realist; others too, who'll seek the *substance*. One continually feels that effort in Renard, and how he's blocked, because he can't even conceive of anything but the reality of appearances. Whence the deep meaning of his comparisons: they're made to grasp the real at the level of its emergence – of its substance. But they're at once deflected towards mere parallels because they're pulled back or to one side by a Tainian metaphysics.[55] Behind it all, there's an effort to fashion the tool that will thrust more deeply into matter. As can be seen from these simple notations: 'The strong odour of the dry faggots', 'The palpitation of the water beneath the ice'.

I sympathize fully with these clumsy efforts to make things bleed. Renard is a blocked Proust, a failed Proust, because he remains on the plane of *observation*. He was taught the knack of observation at the same time as that of documentation. It was the wisdom of the epoch – a literary version of empiricism. He got rid of documentation, but he does observe, poor fellow, he observes as much as he can. It's on 17 *January* that he speaks of the palpitation of the water beneath the ice; it's on 13 *May* that he'll speak of lilies of the valley. It wouldn't occur to him to speak of ice, like Proust, on a fine summer's day: he'll never dare *reconstruct*. Likewise, he merely skims over objects. But all the same – in order to skim over them more closely, hugging their curves and movements – he'll utilize the image.

Renard's 'as' is, first of all, a reconstructive approximation: 'A spider slides along an invisible thread as if it were swimming in the air.' Swimming here has the function of rendering the unwonted resistance that the air seems to oppose to the spider – which isn't the same at all as it opposes to the fly, for example – and that one cannot, Renard cannot, grasp other than by a transmutation of elements. However, to take the thing further, one would need to be convinced, like Proust, that there's not even any transmutation; that the notions of air and water are learnt – simply convenient rubrics; and that the 'thing' is beyond all notions – which may be used indifferently, provided they *render* the primary impression.

Renard's realism is that of science and good sense, so his comparisons are relationships with two terms: of which one – the compared term – is delimited, defined, scientifically explained, solidly sited and down-to-earth (a spider slides along an invisible thread: the reason for the impression that follows is *explained*, and even that

55. Hippolyte Taine (1828–93), philosopher, critic and historian, developed a theory of the parallel development of the psychological (or moral) and the physical in man.

thread which cannot be seen is assumed); while the other term is aerial – or rather 'up in the air' – without a basis, utterly fantastic and haunted by the magical. That's the distortion which threatens all Renard's images. He writes: '11 July, '92: replace the existing laws by laws that would not exist.' And his images are made in the same way: on the one hand, the existing law – the object; on the other hand, the law which doesn't exist – the comparison.

And, finally, the image is charged with creating an imaginary world in which spiders swim in the air; in which 'to faint is to drown in the open air', or 'the light is soaked in water', etc. That's Renard's taste for what's 'comical' or 'nice'. He takes it for poetry, and doesn't notice he's going astray. He even finds 'delightful' a remark by St-Pol-Roux: 'The trees exchange birds like words'[56] – and doesn't realize he has neither the necessary power to reconstruct reality (like Proust) by severely filtered comparisons entirely subordinated to the attempted reconstitution, nor the audacity to abandon the material base and solid ground of common sense and, like Rimbaud, create a surreal.

Comparison in Renard is an attempt to straddle two horses. And he ends up writing the following – which is dreadful, and stupid, and above all *means nothing*, because the image develops under its own weight: 'The bushes appeared drunken with sun, tossed about with an indisposed air and vomited white froth from the hawthorn.' In Renard, as Gide says, comparison is 'preferred'. It is hesitation. It would like to grasp tiny fractions of the real – 'scalps of flies' – but the real is no longer to be said, or comes too late, if one doesn't have a totally different metaphysics. And the unreal is dangerous, it inspires fear: Renard doesn't want to lose his way, but one would need to lose one's way to catch it.

Renard: victim of his epoch's impotence. He very well represents the disintegration of naturalism. For, like his contemporaries, he'll pass from the typical to the individual, from the continuous to the discontinuous. Great types – *the* Financier or *the* Woman of the World – that's all over and done with. Zola and the great naturalists exhausted them. What remains is the detail, the *individual*. '17 January: Put at the front of the book "I have not seen types, but individuals". The scientist generalizes, the artist individualizes.' Yet, although those phrases written in 1889 look like a foretaste of the Gidian professions of faith calling for monographs, I see them rather as an admission of impotence. Gide is attracted by what he sees as positive

---

56. 'Saint-Pol-Roux': pseudonym of Paul Roux (1861–1940), Symbolist poet who was hailed as a key precursor by the Surrealists.

in the individual. For Renard and his contemporaries, the individual is *what remains to them*: that which is not the general and typical – material worked by their 'elders'.

The proof is Renard's total uncertainty regarding the nature of that 'individual'. In 1889, he gets annoyed with Dubus because he 'has theories about women. Still? Isn't that over and done with then, having theories about women?[57] Yet this doesn't stop him, in 1894, from advising his son: 'Fantec, author, study but one woman – but search her well and you'll know women.' Properly searched, therefore, the individual fades discreetly away and we rediscover the typical. That tendency towards the individual, moreover, was served by a pluralist, anti-finalist and pessimistic conception of truth, which was born of the difficulties the sciences were beginning to encounter in their respective domains. Renard writes: 'Our "elders" used to see character, the continuous type . . . But we see the discontinuous type, with its periods of calm and its crises, its moments of shame and its moments of spite.' There's no longer *one* truth of man: there are *truths*.

It's odd to notice that France, his contemporary, writes more or less simultaneously in *La Vie littéraire* (in 1891, whereas the Renard passage quoted dates from 1892): ' . . . It has been said that there are brains with watertight compartments. The most subtle of fluids filling one compartment cannot penetrate into the others. And when some ardent rationalist expressed astonishment to M. Théodule Ribot that there should be heads made like that, the master of experimental philosophy answered him with a gentle smile: "Nothing is less worthy of surprise. Is it not, on the contrary, a very spiritualist conception which seeks to establish unity in a human intelligence? Why are you unwilling for a man to be double, triple or quadruple?" '

A page precious despite its stupidity, since it yields us one of the philosophical influences that act, directly or indirectly, upon those men of letters: Ribot. And also since it shows us how that experimental pluralism was expressly directed against rationalism. That whole pessimistic current was to culminate in Metchnikoff's 'Disharmonies of human nature' – and what Renard seeks to undertake is indeed a 'disharmony of nature'.[58] Which will justify his taking only snapshots: 'In fragments,' he exclaims, 'in small fragments – in the

---

57. Édouard Dubus: poet and literary critic, one of the founders of the originally Symbolist *Mercure de France*.

58. Élie Metchnikoff (1845–1916): Russian biologist, colleague of Pasteur, discovered phagocytosis, the process whereby bacteria are ingested by white blood corpuscles.

tiniest fragments!' So here we are, brought back by another route – that which he pompously calls Nihilism – to the phrase, conceived in isolation as the work of art. And indeed, if nature is above all disorder and disharmony, the novel is henceforth impossible. Renard on several occasions writes that the novel has had its day, because it's a continuous development. If man is a broken series, it's better to write short stories. 'Produce a volume with shorter and shorter tales, and call that the *Rolling-mill.*'

But it's always the same: beggars can't be choosers.

Thursday, 21 March

What finished off binding Renard was the idea that he was an 'artist'. That idea of *artist* came from the Goncourts. It bears their stamp of vulgar stupidity. Dialectically, it's what remains of Hugo's poet as *vates*, and the *poète maudit* of the Romantic epoch.[59] A white, bourgeoisified, comfortable malediction: no longer the curse of the solitary caster of spells, but merely that which hangs over an elite – fortunate misfortune, which is reduced to having sensitive nerves and, as Goncourt puts it, particularly delicate 'grey matter'. Gautier and Art for Art's Sake, Flaubert and his false nobility of style – they passed this way. And, indeed, this notion of artist is not merely the survival of a great, quasi-religious myth – the Romantic myth of the poet – it is also the prism through which a little society of well-off, cultivated bourgeois who write see and grasp themselves as an elite. It contains within it the defects and blemishes of that society.

A curious epoch, in which writers mingled only with each other, because they didn't yet want to resign themselves to being just like other men. It doesn't seem to me that people who write frequent each other nowadays; nor, above all, that their common profession strikes them as sufficient reason for intercourse. Formerly, however, they used to feel themselves initiates. It was their duty to talk among themselves. Renard's remark to someone or other 'Won't you stay a moment longer? We could have talked literature.' For one talks 'literature'; sticks together with mutual hatred; feels somewhat despised by other people – those who are alive – but despises them still more. One's not terribly honest about oneself – but oh! so sensitive.

And that's what is surprising today: the writer claiming to be an artist in the same way as the sculptor or musician. It never entered my

59. *Vates* (Lat.) = seer; *poète maudit* = accursed poet: Verlaine published a volume of critical studies (1884) entitled *Les Poètes maudits*, devoted to six poets who, he argued, had not been properly understood or recognized.

head that I was an artist. The word has no meaning for me, in any case. But I see Renard grow irritated because some old violinist claims to experience greater artistic enjoyments than those of a writer: 'Comparison between music and literature. Those folk would like to have us believe their emotions are more complete than ours . . . I find it hard to believe that this little fellow, who's just barely alive, in the enjoyment of art surpasses Victor Hugo or Lamartine, who did not like music.'

Thus the artist is characterized not merely – as one might naively believe – by the fact that he produces works of art, but also by the fact that he enjoys art. Always the elite. And those artistic sensibilities are shared. Whence in Renard – as in so many of his other contemporaries – a quite formal idea of beauty. Matter is snotty and sinister. But those elite sensibilities vibrate to the phrase that expresses these wretched realities with magnificence. The most banal realism is rescued by the splendour of the form. The idea that the *matter* of the work of art should also be beautiful eludes them – or comes to haunt them like a regret. 'Realism! Realism! Give me a beautiful reality – I'll work from that' (30 May 1890). Nothing has ever been more false than this social conception of the writer as member of a college of artists – nor shoddier than this conception of beauty as the seasoning of reality.

Renard: a man bound hand and foot. Bound by his family; by his epoch; by literary fashions; by his marriage; by his laconism. Sterilized by his journal. Has resources only in dream. (Fairly often, the quite banal dream of some poor little adultery he doesn't dare commit.)

Renard's desire for originality at any price: reaction against those importunate precursors, who haven't left him anything to do – and against his too great plasticity, his too imperious tendency to imitate.

Friday, 22 March

Letter from Maurice Saillet: 'I am working away at becoming a true mobilized serviceman – a rarer species, if possible, than the unattached man who derived from the *Nourritures*.'[60]

Saturday, 23 March

Grener, an Alsatian smelter with communist sympathies: 'It isn't going to last a hundred years.'
I: 'No. But it can still go on a long time.'

60. i.e. *Les Nourritures Terrestres*, by Gide. 'Unattached': *disponible*.

He: 'Oh, the lads don't really feel up to that!'

I: 'So what? If any of them complain, they'll be stuck up against a wall, like in '17.'

He: 'I wouldn't say that – not right away. But you'll see! On their side as much as on ours.'

I: 'On their side . . . '

He: 'The only thing is, they're kept more tightly under control than us. But don't you worry! If the shit starts flying on our side, it'll fly on theirs too. This business can't go on.'

Just as many little things are happening to me as in December, and I've got just as many ideas. But I've less stomach for recording them. This notebook will die of lethargy, unless there's some change in my life.

Renard: the event of his life – though he doesn't seem to realize it – is a change of surroundings. He passes from the 'hartistic' milieu of the Goncourts to the milieu of the theatre: Rostand, Capus, T. Bernard, Guitry. He needs Guitry's warmth to live. His whole life is resumed in this passage from Schwob to Guitry. Preferred friendship to love – out of prudence and a relic of the homosexual sentimentalism of his youth.[61]

The terrifying life of J. Renard. His journal is not so much an exercise in lucid severity, as a little corner of shamefaced, tender complicity with himself. It counterbalances the domestic silences of M. Lepic.[62] He's unbuttoned there – but it doesn't seem that way, since his style's in white tie and tails.

The passage from the Goncourts' diary confirming what I was saying about Renard's generation: '27 August '70. Zola came to lunch today. He spoke to me about a series of novels which he wants to write, an epic in ten volumes called *The Natural and Social History of a Family* . . . He said to me: "After the analysis of the smaller subtleties

61. Alfred Capus (1858–1922), author of light-hearted plays and novels of Parisian life.

Tristan Bernard (1866–1947), playwright who wrote farces and good-humoured satires on middle-class life.

Sacha Guitry (1885–1957), another author of light comedies and vaudevilles.

Marcel Schwob (1867–1905), philologist and literary critic influenced by Symbolism; author of mediaeval studies and historical tales.

62. M. Lepic: character in *Poil de Carotte* who reappears in *La Bigote*.

of feeling, such as Flaubert did in *Madame Bovary*, after the analysis of things artistic, plastic and neurotic such as you have done, after these jewelled works, those chiselled volumes, there is no room for the young, nothing for them to do, no characters left for them to conceive and construct. It is only by the bulk of their work, the power of their creation, that they can appeal to the public." '63

All right. But after the ten-volume epics? What's left? It's at this moment that Renard appears: Renard, the tag-end of that literature which goes from Flaubert to Maupassant by way of the Goncourts and Zola. A dying man. He has been dying all his life. And yet, it's he who had most influence on the entire postwar literature.

I swear it's truly staggering – when one's like me and sees all paths free for writing and thinking, all to be started anew, so that each time one chooses one has the impression one's lopping off a thousand virgin possibilities – it's truly astonishing to read that journal by a fellow who, on every page, asserts that all roads are blocked and originality can be achieved only through the sweat of one's brow.

Wednesday, 27 March

All these days, I had no taste for writing in the notebook: I was racing to finish the first chapter of the prologue to *L'Âge de raison*, because I had to go on leave. I'm a bit sick of my novel at present: it strikes me as awkward and empty. After all, it's the work of a débutant: my début in the novel. It must all be gone over again – in its present state, it's rambling and uneven.

I'm delighted to be going on leave, but more simply than last time. I simply want to see people again and Paris again. Everything has become simplified, everything grown relaxed since February. I haven't recovered that tension of the first months. Nowadays, I work, I live from one day to the next and I'm so well adapted to this life that I no longer notice it. For me, the heroic days of this phoney war are over. It's been ages since I worried about authenticity – or Nothingness. I think I'm worth less than I was at Morsbronn, for example. I've grown humdrum.

After Renard's journal, I read a portion of the Goncourts', dealing with the years '70–71. At first I was agreeably surprised to find *full* pages, after those deafening processions of empty pages in Renard. There was the Siege of Paris; there was the Commune. At once Goncourt went up a bit in my estimation. But I didn't take long to

63. *Pages from the Goncourt Journal*, London 1962, p. 167.

grow disillusioned. Ignominy of that egoistic, timorous, peevish, obsessive bachelor – and 'hartistic' to boot. What he recounts, on the other hand – illuminated by the books of Duveau and Ollivier – is riveting.

Begun to reread *La Condition humaine*.[64] Annoyed by a brotherly resemblance between Malraux's literary techniques and my own. 'There was a world of murder which still enveloped him, like the heat.' I could have written that. I've never been influenced by him, but we've undergone common influences – influences that weren't literary. Same way of tripping over concrete details (which Nizan handles so well) and making up for it by the portrayal of atmosphere. Same patient way of choosing some minor detail (Kyo doesn't recognize his voice on a record, because 'we listen to ourselves through the throat') and blowing it up, from page to page, until it's a symbol. Same rather jerky way of switching abruptly to direct speech and out again. Is it because I can see too clearly what makes it tick? None of the effects come off. I *feel* nothing.

Yet, a very fine passage (and this too resembles Mathieu's monologues, for example): ' "We hear other people's voices with our ears, our own through our throat." Yes. The sound of one's life, too, comes to one through the throat; and other people's? . . . The thing that predominated was isolation, securely entrenched as the background to the ephemeral millions who moved in front of it, just as real Night, real primeval Night, loomed behind the covering of darkness which hung low and dense over the watchful waste of city, pregnant with the ferment of unfulfilled hopes. "*To me myself*, what does my life mean to *me*? The cosmos expressing itself in an identity, an idiotic identity: a concentration of forces in the prevailing nebulousness. For others, it's what I've done that counts." Only May judged him other than by his actions: only in him did anything more than the record of her life awaken interest. The fierce embrace with which love seeks to break down isolation brought no comfort to his ordinary self: it was the unbalanced side of him which profited, the unspeakable monstrosity, dear above all else, which self-analysis evokes and which man cherishes in his heart. Since the death of his mother, May was the only person in the world who saw him not as Kyo Gisors but as the partner in a most intimate companionship. "A mutual, triumphant, chosen companionship," he thought . . . "What have other men in common with me? Just so many entities who look at me and criticize. My real

fellow-creatures love me unreflectingly, love me in spite of everything, love me so that no corruption, vileness or betrayal has any
power to alter it: love me for myself and not for what I have done or
will do; whose love for me goes as far as my own – embracing
suicide . . . With her alone do I share a love like that, whatever
batterings it may have undergone, as others share the sickness of their
children, their risk of death . . . ".' [p. 52]

The other day, I could feel how much Schlumberger 'belongs to the
same period' as Gide.[65] But I feel just as strongly how much I belong
to the same period as Malraux (common intellectualism). I have to say
that nothing in him is carried to perfection. The syntax is often loose,
the words ugly and ambiguous. I have the impression of rereading my
own first draft.

Thursday 28

Reynaud Ministry: by the nature of things this isolated rightwinger
reconstitutes a popular-front majority, whereas Daladier – president
of a great party which made the Popular Front – governed with a
national-bloc majority.[66] Skill of the socialists, who allowed the communist party to be persecuted and shattered by a government which
didn't have their votes, and then, once the purge had been carried
through, agreed to join it. Will this government last? I'm not too sure
as yet how it's being taken here. The reactionary officers reproach
Reynaud with being a 'Russophile'. It seems obvious one of the
reasons for the fall of the Daladier cabinet was its temporizing attitude
towards Russia. The recall of Souritz, demanded by the Daladier
ministry, seems intended to give satisfaction to the right.[67]

I'm setting off on leave this afternoon.

The men here are reproaching Reynaud for not having said a word in
his broadcast address about 'the heroism of our valiant soldiers'. 'That
Daladier, he'd never have missed that out!' they complain sadly.

65. Jean Schlumberger (1877–1968), novelist and critic, co-founder of the *NRF*.
66. Édouard Daladier (1884–1970), Radical leader, formed a national-bloc admini-
stration (i.e. centre-plus-right) from April 1938 to March 1940.
Paul Reynaud (1878–1966) formed a cabinet from March to June 1940 with Socialist
participation.
67. Yakov Surits (1882–1952), Soviet ambassador to France 1937–40, sent a telegram
to Stalin on the conclusion of the Soviet-Finnish war in which he referred to France and
England as warmongers, as a consequence of which he was declared persona non grata
by the Paris government.

Long conversation yesterday evening with Grener. With that great, coarse, brutal man – to whom belching and farting come as naturally as breathing – I act the whore because he's a worker. The evening before last, overcome by sleep and alcohol, he was snoring on a bench as I was writing. All of a sudden, he stands up – rosy-eyed, neither asleep nor awake, no idea where he is – turns to face the wall, undoes his fly and pisses. I rush across: 'Stop that, you filthy swine!' 'Leave off,' he growls, carries on pissing while I shake him, then collapses back onto his bench – where he once again starts snoring, moaning and tossing around. In spite of a certain physical repugnance for his smell and his blubber, I want to make him like me – and succeed without any difficulty, moreover, since he's flattered that I talk to him.

Yesterday, he was loquacious. The words flowed from his heavy, impassive face as if drawn by their own weight. Always the same intonation of suppressed vehemence. Short silences, as if to replenish his stock of words – then the flow starts up again. Every so often he drinks some red wine and his vehemence increases. I have no difficulty in listening to him, moreover: he interests me. He hates and despises the secretaries, and explains to me his pride at having secured all that he owns through his own efforts. 'That lot – if they lost their jobs, what on earth could they do? They don't know how to work with their hands – they'd have to beg in the streets. I'm worth as much as them; I know how to do everything. Someone tells me "Use that axe", I use the axe; "Use that saw", I use the saw. For years, I used to do woodcutting on the side, see! That's how I was able to buy myself the house and the two cows. You wouldn't understand that, you wouldn't; but when a person's got two cows, all his problems are over.'

I'm very conscious of his pride at being surrounded by objects which owe their existence to him: which, directly or indirectly, he has produced through the strength of his arms. Also, his sense of security before the prospect of hard blows: he'll always get by, because he can do anything. And his feeling that he's living amid a hostile, catastrophic nature, which he must and can tame. And his scorn for those whippersnappers of secretaries, who can live only on the summit of a well-upholstered, ordered society. At the same time, he grumbles and complains – more in the manner of peasants than workers. He says: 'People laugh at Adolf, but there is some good in what he's done. They laugh at the Soviets, but they've done some good things too.'

Comment by his son, aged twelve, who refuses to do a damn thing at primary school: 'I don't need all that stuff, to be a worker.' The father went to see the teacher and told him: 'Give him a walloping! I was bored stiff when I was a kid, so he can damn well be bored too.'

INDEX

ABOUT THE AUTHOR

JEAN-PAUL SARTRE was born in Paris in 1905. Educated at the Ecole Normale, he then taught philosophy in provincial *lycées,* and in 1938 published his first novel, *Nausea.* During the war, he participated in the Resistance and completed the major work that eventually established his reputation as an existential philosopher—*Being and Nothingness* (1943). After the Liberation, he founded the socialist journal *Les Temps Modernes.* He has been a prolific playwright, producing, among other works, *No Exit* (1947), *The Devil and the Good Lord* (1951), and *The Condemned of Altona* (1959). In 1960, he published his second basic philosophical work, *Critique of Dialectical Reason.* In 1964, his account of his childhood, *Words,* received worldwide acclaim. That same year he was awarded the Nobel Prize for Literature, which he refused. In 1971–1972, the first three volumes of his ambitious study of Flaubert's life and work appeared. He died in 1980.

PANTHEON MODERN WRITERS SERIES

THE SAILOR FROM GIBRALTAR
by Marguerite Duras, translated from the French by Barbara Bray

By the author of *The Lover*, "a haunting tale of strange and random passion."—*The New York Times Book Review*
0-394-74451-9 $8.95

THE RAVISHING OF LOL STEIN
by Marguerite Duras, translated from the French by Richard Seaver

"Brilliant...[Duras] shoots vertical shafts down into the dark morass of human love."—*The New York Times Book Review*

"The drama proceeds savagely, erotically, and...the Duras language and writing shine like crystal."—Janet Flanner, *The New Yorker*
0-394-74304-0 $6.95

THE ASSAULT
by Harry Mulisch, translated from the Dutch by Claire Nicolas White

The story of a Nazi atrocity in Occupied Holland and its impact on the life of one survivor.

"A powerful and beautiful work...among the finest European fiction of our time."—Elizabeth Hardwick

"A cool, brilliant modern horror story."—Mary McCarthy
0-394-74420-9 $6.95

THE WAR DIARIES: NOVEMBER 1939–MARCH 1940
by Jean-Paul Sartre, translated from the French by Quintin Hoare

Sartre's only surviving diaries: an intimate look at his life and thought at the beginning of World War II.

"An extraordinary book."—Alfred Kazin, *The Philadelphia Inquirer*

"These *War Diaries*...breach Sartre's intimacy for the first time."
—*The Washington Post Book World*
0-394-74422-5 $10.95

YOUNG TÖRLESS
*by Robert Musil, translated from the German by Eithne Williams
and Ernst Kaiser*

A classic novel by the author of *The Man Without Qualities*, about four students at an Austrian military academy and their discovery and abuse of power—physical, emotional, and sexual.

"An illumination of the dark places of the heart."—*The Washington Post*

"A chilling foreshadowing of the coming of Nazism."
—*The New York Times Book Review*
0-394-71015-0 $6.95

PANTHEON MODERN WRITERS SERIES

ADIEUX: A FAREWELL TO SARTRE
by Simone de Beauvoir, translated by Patrick O'Brian

Simone de Beauvoir's moving farewell to Jean-Paul Sartre, her lifelong companion, in two parts: an account of his last ten years and an interview with him about his life and work.

"An intimate, personal, and honest portrait of a relationship unlike any other in literary history."—Deirdre Bair
0-394-72898-X $8.95

A VERY EASY DEATH
by Simone de Beauvoir, translated by Patrick O'Brian

The profoundly moving, day-by-day account of the death of the author's mother, at once intimate and universal.

"A beautiful book, sincere and sensitive."—Pierre-Henri Simon
0-394-72899-8 $4.95

WHEN THINGS OF THE SPIRIT COME FIRST:
FIVE EARLY TALES
by Simone de Beauvoir, translated by Patrick O'Brian

The first paperback edition of the marvelous early fiction of Simone de Beauvoir.

"An event for celebration."—*The New York Times Book Review*
0-394-72235-3 $6.95

THE BLOOD OF OTHERS
*by Simone de Beauvoir, translated by Roger Senhouse
and Yvonne Moyse*

A brilliant existentialist novel about the French resistance.

"A novel with a remarkably sustained note of suspense and mounting excitement due to the sheer vitality and force of de Beauvoir's ideas."
—*Saturday Review*
0-394-72411-9 $7.95

NAPLES '44
by Norman Lewis

A young British intelligence officer's powerful journal of his year in Allied-occupied Naples.

"An immensely gripping experience...a marvelous book...his compassion and humor are just plain terrific."—S. J. Perelman
0-394-72300-7 $7.95